Economic Growth and Development in the Tropics

The living standards and scale of development around the world are vastly unequal. One notable observation is that much of the poverty-stricken area is located between the tropics of Cancer and Capricorn. By contrast, affluent nations are situated in more temperate zones. Such a phenomenon gives weight to the geography hypothesis that seeks to explain the occurrence of global economic inequality, by placing an emphasis on the importance of natural elements such as location and climate in determining the economic conditions of a nation. This book concentrates exclusively and in depth on the key economic phenomena and factors which shape tropical economies today.

It examines contemporary economic problems confronting the tropical countries and provides policy recommendations that align with the United Nations' Sustainable Development Goals set in the 2030 Agenda. It contains research works and case studies of tropical economies that are related to the area of development and environment economics. The book's themes range from economic growth, poverty reduction, income inequality, economic globalization, international trade, capital flow, financial development, and institutional development to environmental sustainability within the Tropics. Recognizing the dynamism and diversity of the tropics, the book encompasses empirical and policy analyses that address the key economic issues and challenges in the region so as to provide an important platform from which new policymaking initiatives can flourish.

This book will draw readership primarily from the fields of economics and public policy, particularly under the subject areas of development and environment economics, as well as discussions in the sustainability policy space.

Sook Rei Tan is Lecturer in Economics at James Cook University, Singapore.

Haejin Jang is Learning Advisor at James Cook University, Singapore.

Jacob Wood is Associate Professor of Business at James Cook University (JCU), Singapore.

Routledge Advances in Business, Industry and Trade in the Tropics
Series editors
Jacob Wood, K. Thirumaran and Taha Chaiechi

Situated between the Tropics of Cancer and Capricorn the countries that make up the Tropics are largely developing in nature.

The *Routledge Advances in Business and Industry in the Tropics* series provides a detailed appraisal of the Tropics. With a focus on economic development, business, governance, tourism, and international trade, this series captures the complexities and heterogeneous nature of one of the fastest growing regions in the world. The series uncovers the economies, political institutions, and socio-economic conditions of the region and the growing pains that many countries face.

Each of the books in the series, investigate the ongoing structural changes associated with economic development that takes into account evolving industry compositions and the emergence of new competitive advantages and explore transformative growth and fundamental reorientation of economic resources as part of the solution through a post-Keynesian lens.

The series provides critical, theoretical and practical policy-based content for academics, business leaders, and institutional bodies alike.

Business, Industry and Trade in the Tropics
Edited by Jacob Wood, Taha Chaiechi and K Thirumaran

Economic Growth and Development in the Tropics
Edited by Sook Rei Tan, Haejin Jang and Jacob Wood

For more information in this series, please visit: Routledge Advances in Business, Industry and Trade in the Tropics – Book Series – Routledge & CRC Press

Economic Growth and Development in the Tropics

Edited by Sook Rei Tan, Haejin Jang and Jacob Wood

Routledge
Taylor & Francis Group
LONDON AND NEW YORK

First published 2024
by Routledge
4 Park Square, Milton Park, Abingdon, Oxon OX14 4RN

and by Routledge
605 Third Avenue, New York, NY 10158

Routledge is an imprint of the Taylor & Francis Group, an informa business

British Library Cataloguing-in-Publication Data
A catalogue record for this book is available from the British Library

Library of Congress Cataloging-in-Publication Data
Names: Tan, Sook Rei, editor. | Jang, Haejin, editor. | Wood, Jacob, editor.
Title: Economic growth and development in the tropics / edited by Sook Rei Tan, Haejin Jang, and Jacob Wood.
Description: 1 Edition. | New York, NY : Routledge, 2024. | Series: Routledge advances in business, industry and trade in the tropics | Includes bibliographical references and index.
Identifiers: LCCN 2023041465 (print) | LCCN 2023041466 (ebook) | ISBN 9781032393230 (hardback) | ISBN 9781032393254 (paperback) | ISBN 9781003349204 (ebook)
Subjects: LCSH: Tropics—Economic conditions. | Economic development—Tropics.
Classification: LCC HC695 .E36 2024 (print) | LCC HC695 (ebook) | DDC 330.913—dc23/en/20231106
LC record available at https://lccn.loc.gov/2023041465
LC ebook record available at https://lccn.loc.gov/2023041466

ISBN: 978-1-032-39323-0 (hbk)
ISBN: 978-1-032-39325-4 (pbk)
ISBN: 978-1-003-34920-4 (ebk)

DOI: 10.4324/9781003349204

Typeset in Sabon
by Apex CoVantage, LLC

Contents

Figures

Tables

Contributors

Lakew Alemu Birhane is Assistant Professor at Department of Management, College of Business and Economics, Addis Ababa University, Ethiopia.

Adrian Bradshaw is Lecturer at James Cook University, Singapore.

Lilian Bushiri received an MSc (Applied Economics and Business) graduation from Department of Business Studies, Mzumbe University, Dar Es Salaam Campus College, Tanzania.

Yohannes Workeaferahu Elifneh is Associate Professor at Department of Management, Addis Ababa University, Ethiopia.

Fisayo Fagbemi is a research fellow at Economic Policy Analysis Centre, Ibadan, Nigeria.

Bing Gong is Postdoctoral Research Fellow at University of Chinese Academy of Social Sciences & Tsinghua University, China.

Habtamu Ditta Hirpa is a PhD candidate at Parul University, India.

Joel Yap Qi Hong is a PhD candidate at James Cook University, Singapore.

Haejin Jang is Learning Advisor at James Cook University, Singapore.

Zilmiyah Kamble is Senior Lecturer at James Cook University, Singapore.

Coretha Komba is Senior Lecturer in Economics at Department of Administrative Studies, Mzumbe University, Dar Es Salaam Campus College, Tanzania.

Hooi Hooi Lean is Professor at Economics Program, School of Social Sciences, Universiti Sains Malaysia, Penang, Malaysia.

Changtai Li is Lecturer at University of Science and Technology Beijing, China.

Hong Liang is a PhD candidate at School of Management, Universiti Sains Malaysia.

Joshua Mwakujonga is Lecturer in Business and Entrepreneurship at Department of Business Studies, Mzumbe University, Dar Es Salaam Campus College, Tanzania.

Geraldine Ejiaka Nzeribe is Senior Lecturer at Department of Economics, Nnamdi Azikiwe University, Awka, Nigeria.

Leigh-ann Onnis is Senior Lecturer at College of Business, Law & Governance, James Cook University, Cairns, Australia.

Tolulope Temilola Osinubi is Lecturer at Department of Economics, Obafemi Awolowo University, Ile-Ife, Nigeria.

Usman Sambo is Senior Lecturer at Department of Public Administration, Yobe State University Damaturu, Nigeria.

Ruchi Sharma is Professor at Jagran Lakecity University, India.

Babayo Sule is Senior Lecturer at Department of International Relations, Federal University of Kashere Gombe, Nigeria.

Sook Rei Tan is Lecturer in Economics at James Cook University, Singapore.

Chun Meng Tang is Senior Lecturer at James Cook University, Singapore.

Workneh Kassa Tessema is Associate Professor at Department of Management, College of Business and Economics, Addis Ababa University, Ethiopia.

Thi Thuy Linh Truong is an MBA student at James Cook University, Singapore.

Pengji Wang is Associate Professor at James Cook University, Singapore.

Jacob Wood is Associate Professor at James Cook University, Singapore.

Xiu Wei Yeap is a master's student in Economics Program at the School of Social Sciences, Universiti Sains Malaysia, Penang, Malaysia.

1 Trade and Development in Asia

A Post COVID-19 Economic Assessment

Jacob Wood, Haejin Jang, and Sook Rei Tan

1.1 Introduction

International trade has always been an important driver of economic growth and poverty alleviation in Asia (Heshmati et al., 2019; Kim & Wood, 2020; Wood & Wu, 2020; Du et al., 2021; Wood et al., 2021; Wu et al., 2021a, 2021b, 2022). International trade has also allowed Asian economies to exploit economies of scale by specializing in productive activities in which they have a comparative advantage. Furthermore, trade has also helped boost investment and productivity by allowing for the faster spread of technology, including through links formed when participating in global value chains (GVCs) – trade in intermediate inputs. In addition to this has been a climate in which tariff levels have continued to fall and remain a relatively low barrier overall in the region. However, despite these changes, new measures of nontariff barriers remains relatively high in many Asian emerging markets and developing economies (Wood, 2017; Wood et al., 2017a, 2017b, 2020). Unlike tariffs, these non-tariff measures include policies that introduce new potential barriers such as new health and safety standards or licensing requirements that has restricted not only trade but also payments, or the exchange of foreign currencies.

In addition to these issues has been the profound impact that the COVID-19 pandemic has had on trade and economic development in the region since early 2020 (Atkinson et al., 2022; Wood et al., 2022; Wu & Wood, 2022). Despite the impact, GDP forecasted to fall across the Asia-Pacific region in 2021/22 (see Table 1.1), it remains among the fastest growing areas in the world (IMF, 2021). However, despite its robust performance, concern has been growing divergence between Asian advanced economies and emerging market and developing economies, which can be explained by differences in trade policy provisions and the levels of vaccination coverage that exist.

The service sector has grown significantly in Asia in recent times (Kim & Wood, 2020). However, the COVID-19 pandemic has also significantly affected the level of trade in services across the region. As Figure 1.1 shows, the region experienced a very sharp decline in the second quarter of 2020. At the forefront of this was the overall weakness in tourist arrivals due to border

DOI: 10.4324/9781003349204-1

Table 1.1 GDP constant prices (percentage change 2020–2027)

Country	*2020*	*2021*	*2022**	*2023**	*2024**	*2025**	*2026**	*2027**
Brunei Darussalam	1.113	−0.676	5.83	2.601	2.129	2.08	2.091	2.112
Cambodia	−3.13	2.151	5.098	5.889	6.1	6.346	6.504	6.5
Indonesia	−2.065	3.691	5.409	6.001	5.764	5.41	5.271	5.177
Lao P.D.R.	−0.435	2.061	3.2	3.5	3.75	3.95	4.15	4.3
Malaysia	−5.647	3.133	5.606	5.501	4.886	4.435	4.443	3.943
Myanmar	3.189	−17.938	1.614	3.006	3.051	2.934	2.982	3.298
The Philippines	−9.573	5.598	6.451	6.286	6.544	6.471	6.487	6.503
Thailand	−6.195	1.566	3.334	4.294	3.823	3.349	3.23	3.057
Vietnam	2.944	2.576	6.047	7.246	7.043	6.945	6.836	6.729

Source: International Monetary Fund, World Economic Outlook Database, April 2022

Note: * Forecast data

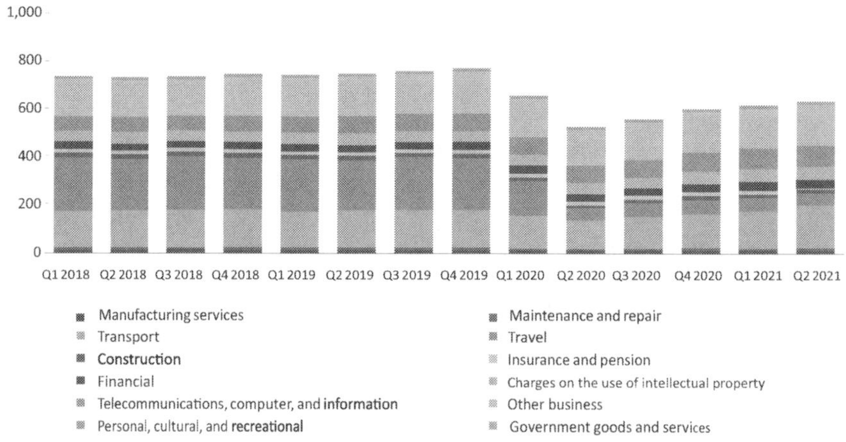

Figure 1.1 Trade in services for selected Asia and Pacific economies (US$ billion)

Source: ADB calculations using data from International Monetary Fund. Balance of Payments and International Investment Position Statistics. https://data.imf.org/BOP

Note: Q = quarter.

Trade in services is computed as trade in services credits plus debits. Asia and Pacific economies include Armenia; Australia, Cambodia; Fiji; Georgia; Hong Kong, China; India; Indonesia; Japan; Kazakhstan; Malaysia; Nepal; New Zealand; Pakistan; the People's Republic of China; the Philippines; the Republic of Korea; Singapore; Taipei, China; and Thailand.

closures and quarantine measures concurs that were implemented, as well as the global decrease in number of flights (see Figure 1.2 [ADB, 2022]). The service sector has become an increasingly important sector for the region, so declines of this magnitude are widely felt across the region.

Interestingly, trade across the region has seen some small positive increases, with Asia's intraregional trade share increasing from 57.5% in 2019 to 58.5%

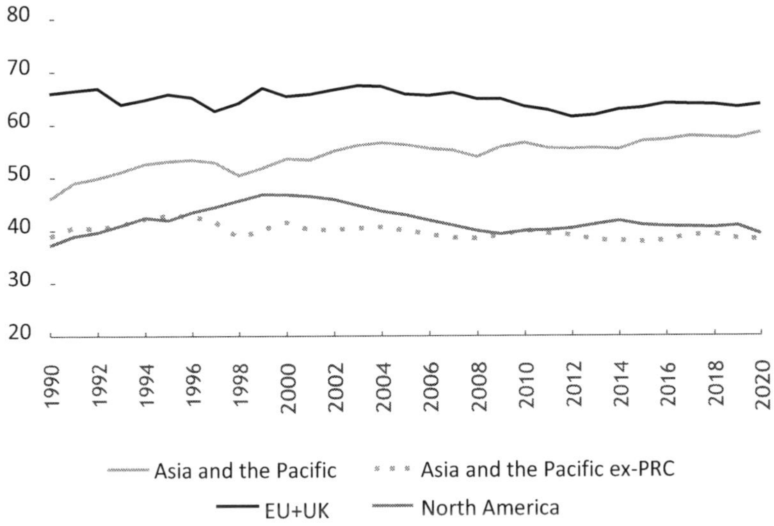

Figure 1.2 Intraregional trade shares by region (percentage)

Source: ADB calculations using data from International Monetary Fund. Direction of Trade Statistics. https://data.imf.org/dot

Note: EU = European Union (27 members), PRC = People's Republic of China, UK = United Kingdom.

Values are expressed as percentage of the region's total merchandise trade (sum of exports and imports). North America covers Canada, Mexico, and the US.

in 2020, the highest result since 1990 (see Figure 1.2). In other results, this figure remains higher than that for North America (39.3%), although still lower than the European Union and the United Kingdom combined (EU + UK) (63.8%) (ADB, 2022). According to the ADB (2022), the respective countries' linkages with China can explain much of the region's increase in intra-regional trade during the COVID-19 pandemic, with China being the first nation to remove many of the restrictions that were implemented in the immediate aftermath of the pandemic first emerging.

Another concern coming off the back of the COVID-19 pandemic, and then more recently with the war in the Ukraine, has been inflation. Over the past couple of years, headline inflation is on the rise across the region, fueled by shifting global demand, rising food and fuel prices, and supply chain disruptions (IMF, 2021). Meanwhile, core inflation has risen, albeit to a lesser extent. The pass-through of prices from producer to consumer prices has been limited, coming in line with general inflationary expectations. Supporting this has been relatively flat growth in export prices, which suggests that profit margins have eroded slightly in tradable sectors, with little clear evidence of Asia exporting inflation elsewhere (see Table 1.2) (IMF, 2021).

With inflationary pressures still very much at the forefront of many Government's minds at present, the future economic outcomes over the next two

Table 1.2 Inflation rate – South East Asia (percentage change)

	2017	*2018*	*2019*	*2020*	*2021*	*2022**	*2023**
Developing Asia	*2.6*	*2.7*	*3.3*	*3.2*	*2.5*	*3.7*	*3.1*
Southeast Asia	*2.9*	*2.8*	*2.6*	*1.5*	*2*	*3.7*	*3.1*
Brunei Darussalam	−1.3	1	−0.4	1.9	1.7	1.6	1
Cambodia	2.9	2.5	1.9	2.9	2.9	4.7	2.2
Indonesia	3.8	3.2	3.8	2	1.6	3.6	3
Lao People's Dem. Rep.	0.8	2	3.3	5.1	3.7	5.8	5
Malaysia	3.8	1	0.7	−1.1	2.5	3	2.5
Myanmar	4	5.9	8.6	5.7	3.6	8	8.5
The Philippines	2.9	5.2	2.4	2.4	3.9	4.2	3.5
Singapore	0.6	0.4	0.6	−0.2	2.3	3	2.3
Thailand	0.7	1.1	0.7	−0.8	1.2	3.3	2.2
Timor-Leste	0.6	2.4	1	0.5	3.8	2.6	2.7
Vietnam	3.5	3.5	2.8	3.2	1.8	3.8	4

Source: Asia Development Bank, April 2022

Note: * Forecast data.

to three years are still very much uncertain. It is therefore imperative that governments understand the economic environments in which they are operating and appreciate the role that international trade can play in driving economic development opportunities. In order to articulate a possible course of action, the rest of this chapter is outlined as follows. First, an assessment of the relevant developmental, economics, and trade literature is conducted to provide some context to the overall current environment in the region. This is followed by some discussion around some of the current policy settings that are in place and offers some insight into what needs to be done in the future. Finally, some concluding remarks are drawn, and some areas of future study are outlined.

1.2 Literature Review

1.2.1 Infrastructure Development

The development of critical infrastructure has played a pivotal role in driving economic growth across the Asian region (Ismail & Mahyideen, 2015). Infrastructure development contributes directly to a nation's growth by creating production facilities, stimulating economic activities, and providing employment opportunities. Meanwhile, it also indirectly impacts the country's economy by reducing trade costs and facilitating trade (Sahoo & Dash, 2012). The trade-facilitating effect of infrastructure is worth emphasizing, given that trade has been a key driving force behind Asia's spectacular economic performance, particularly in East Asia in recent decades (Brooks & Go, 2012). As documented by Brooks (2010), Asia's trade expansion has been spurred by the development of supporting infrastructure, as evidenced by the rapid increase in port capacity and airfreight shipments in the developing Asian region over the past years. As of 2021, nearly two-thirds of container traffic took place at Asian container ports, making the region the global maritime logistics hub (UNCTAD, 2021).

Broadly speaking, trade-related infrastructure can be distinguished between hard and soft infrastructure; each playing its respective role in facilitating trade and promoting economic growth. More specifically, hard infrastructure refers to physical infrastructure, including transport systems like roads, ports, highways, and information and communications technology (ICT). In contrast, soft infrastructure is intangible infrastructure that is related to border and transport efficiency as well as the business and regulatory environment of trade (Portugal-Perez & Wilson, 2012). In the context of Asia, a comprehensive study conducted by Ismail and Mahyideen (2015)[1] found that improvement in hard infrastructure, such as transport and port facilities, telephone lines, and internet security, leads to an increase in trade flows. Furthermore, several indicators of soft infrastructure, such as documents and the number of days needed to complete the import and export procedure, were confirmed to impact trade negatively. Brooks and Stone (2010) found that lowering trade costs by 25% led not only to improvements in transportation capabilities within the Asia-Pacific Economic Cooperation (APEC) region but also increases in welfare and GDP performance. In particular, rises in welfare as proxied by an equivalent variation in income range from US$1.2 billion in the Philippines to US$12.4 billion in China. In terms of percentage gains in GDP, the leading five economies for lowering relevant trade costs are Vietnam, Malaysia, the Philippines, Singapore, and Thailand, with all experiencing more than a 1% estimated increase in GDP. A study with a focus on central Asia by Karymshakov and Sulaimanova (2021) corroborated the positive impact of both the quality and quantity of infrastructure has on trade flows in Kazakhstan, Kyrgyzstan, and Tajikistan. Moreover, research by Rehman et al. (2020), which focused on selected South Asian countries, including Bangladesh, Bhutan, Nepal, India, Pakistan, and Sri Lanka, found that the quality and availability of infrastructure promotes exports and decreases trade deficit in the long run.

Despite rapid infrastructural improvements across the Asia and Pacific regions over time, the current level of infrastructural capability in the transport, power, telecommunications, and water supply and sanitation sectors remains far from adequate (Zhongming et al., 2017). A recent Asia Development Bank (ADB) report estimated that some US$26 trillion in investments is needed across the 2016–2030 period, of which US$14.7 trillion is needed for power, US$8.6 trillion for transport, US$2.3 trillion for telecommunications, and US$800 billion for water and sanitation improvements are required. Developments in these areas will not only help to provide important sources of economic growth but also help to mitigate poverty and tackle climate change. In regard to the infrastructure investment needs lies the challenge of public financing, which requires further reforms for sustainable investment planning (Rillo & Ali, 2017).

1.2.2 Foreign Direct Investment

The remarkable growth of a number of East Asian economies over the past half-century has become known as the East Asian miracle (Wang et al., 2022; Zhang et al., 2022). Such impressive economic achievements are believed to be driven by the national government's pursuit of outward-oriented policies, manifested as the country's embrace of highly open international trade and heavy reliance on foreign investment at the early phase of industrialization (Wood, 2017).

Foreign investment can be broadly categorized as foreign portfolio investment (FPI) and foreign direct investment (FDI) based on the degree of managerial control possessed by the investor over the assets. More specifically, FPI involves foreign purchases of financial assets issued by the companies, while FDI involves the undertaking of a significant stake in fixed productive assets by foreign investors (Ahlquist, 2006). Due to the distinctive differences that exist between FPI and FDI, their economic impacts are also quite different. FPI, sometimes also referred to as "hot money", is deemed more speculative and can be quick to flee the host countries during times of financial uncertainty, thereby exacerbating the currency value and financial risks of the host countries (Tan et al., 2021). In contrast, FDI involves an investor's lasting interest in an enterprise in another country; hence, it is often a type of more stable and long-term investment flow.

The benefits of FDI are well documented in the existing literature. FDI is considered to be a major conduit that facilitates capital formation, technology transfer, and skill and knowledge spillover between developed and developing countries (Ozturk, 2007). Saggi (2002) theorized three potential channels of FDI-led international technology transfer: First, the demonstration effect argument suggests that local firms may adopt more superior technologies following multinational firms through imitation or reverse engineering. Second, the labor turnover argument postulates that workers previously worked in multinational firms may transfer skills and knowledge to local firms by switching employment or starting their own companies. Third, the vertical linkage argument proposes technology spillover to local firms by multinational firms in their upstream supply chain.

Along this line of literature, Lee and Tan (2006) investigated the marginal effect of technology transfer through FDI on the economic growth of selected ASEAN economies (Singapore, Malaysia, Thailand, and Indonesia). Their findings confirmed the positive impact that technology transfers have on output growth and uncovered evidence of positive relationship between FDI inflows and the levels of technology transfers in the region. Petri (2012) discovered that unlike the types of FDI which occurs in other more developed regions, intra-Asian FDI flows were dominated by flows from high-technology economies to medium-technology economies. This dynamic has in turn enabled the less advanced economies to climb up the technology ladder and in doing so contribute to Asia's technological progress and industrial development.

FDI can also spur economic growth through its interplay with exports. Tiwari and Mutascu (2011) examined the impact of FDI and exports on a broader set of Asian economies. Using a panel data of 23 developing Asian countries covering the period of 1986–2008, with the authors finding that both FDI and exports enhance the growth process. However, when they considered nonlinearities associated with exports and FDI in affecting economic growth, there exists a U-shaped relationship between FDI and growth of the studied countries, and therefore their results lend support to the adoption of export-led growth path at the initial stage of development, augmented by FDI-attracting policies in the later period. Likewise, Zhang (2001) found that FDI tends to boost host economic growth focusing on 11 developing economies in East Asia and Latin America covering the period up to 1997, but such growth-enhancing effect of FDI depends on country-specific characteristics. In fact, some FDI-related studies noted that for the host country to effectively reap the benefits of FDI, it should get ready adequate absorptive capacities, through strengthening the macroeconomic and institutional environment within the country (Girma, 2005; Alguacil et al., 2011). This provides plausible explanations for the mixed findings on the FDI-led growth hypothesis across the relevant empirical studies.

1.2.3 Trade Policy and Export Performance

International product fragmentation, the cross-border dispersion of component production/assembly within vertically integrated production processes, has become an important feature of the structural interdependence of the world economy (Athukorala, 2005; Athukorala & Yamashita, 2006; Jongwanich, 2010). An aspect of global trade and business flows is certainly prevalent in Asia. As a result of the rapid advances in production technology and technological innovations that have occurred in the transportation and communication sectors, companies have been able to "unbundle" the stages of production so that different tasks can be performed in different places. Such advances have proved to be a key driver of export performance across the Asian region.

Within the region, East Asia stands out as the top spot of manufacturing outsourcing from developed nations, owing to the region's abundant labor resources, cheap labor costs, improving infrastructure, low transportation costs, and export-oriented development strategies (Athukorala, 2011). The emergence of international production networks in East Asia can be traced back to the signing of the 1985 Plaza Accord, which led to an appreciation in the value of Japanese Yen and a rise in the cost of production in Japan. This consequently drove Japanese multinational enterprises (MNEs) to relocate their production bases to other developing countries within the region, such as Malaysia, Singapore, and Thailand. During the post-Asian financial crisis period, lowering asset prices in East Asia further attracted MNEs from the US and Europe to construct production bases in the region, which then kick started another wave of industrialization in some Asian countries (Cheewatrakoolpong et al., 2013).

Hence, through welcoming FDI and the relocation of supply chains from MNEs operating in industrialized nations, the East Asian region, and particularly China, has gained significant domination in the areas of manufacturing and machinery exports (mostly that of parts and components), earning itself the name "Factory of the World" (Kimura & Obashi, 2016). To date, processing trade remains a pillar of China's export performance. According to the PRC's General Administration of Customs, from January to October 2022, *Processing and Assembling Trade With Foreign-Supplied Materials* (US$69.748 billion) and *Processing Trade With Imported Materials* (US$609.1724 billion) constituted roughly 23% of China's total exports (US$2.992 trillion). Besides China, the ASEAN region has also achieved high levels of export performance by playing a strong role across the global supply chain as a supplier of intermediate products. As pointed out by Chen and Intal (2017), the export value as share of GDP has surpassed 30% by most nations, including Malaysia since the 1970s, Thailand since the early 1990s, and Vietnam and Cambodia since 2000s, with continuous growth anticipated in the future. Moreover, Padilla et al. (2017) found a high participation in product fragmentation by ASEAN members, in which the vertical structure represented 43% of its gross exports. Interestingly, a more recent study of ASEAN's participation in global value chains showed that during the 2000–2017 period, foreign value-added contributions to ASEAN has declined, whereas the portion of foreign value-added contributions from within the ASEAN region and other emerging economies has risen, signifying a localization and regionalization trend among the ASEAN member's production outputs (Zhong & Su, 2021). With the strengthening of regional trade integration, culminating in the formation of the Regional Comprehensive Economic Partnership (RCEP) which includes the ASEAN block and five other Asia Pacific countries (China, Japan, South Korea, Australia and New Zealand), East Asia is likely to maintain, if not strengthen, its role as a global manufacturing and export powerhouse.

1.2.4 COVID-19 Impact on Trade and Economic Development in Asia

The COVID-19 pandemic has caused unprecedented disturbance to the global economy. It poses unique challenges to Asian economies due to the region's critical position within the world trading system and supply chains. Its rich heterogeneity, in terms of developmental stage, poverty level, and political system across the region, has further added to these challenges.

Despite strong GDP growth of 5.2% expected for developing Asia in 2022, the pace of the recovery varies substantially across the region (Asian

Development Outlook, 2022). China, where the COVID-19 cases were first reported, faces a bumpy road ahead as it attempts to kick start its COVID-19 recovery. In early 2020, China was the first country in the world to launch quarantine and lockdown measures in an attempt to contain the spread of COVID-19 disease. Such lockdown measures were then followed by other countries around the world when the COVID-19 became a global pandemic. In China, its efforts to restrict the spread of the virus meant that its production and foreign trade capabilities fell, leading to a 13.5% fall in industrial value-added and a 15.9% fall in exports between January and February 2020 period (Liu & Hu, 2020). However, in the second half of 2020 through to 2021, China's foreign trade experienced a strong rebound with a year-on-year growth rate of exports of 154.7% in February 2021 with respect to its earlier February 2020 figure, and 51.3% when related to its February 2019 levels (Fang et al., 2022). In light of the V-shaped recovery, China was the only major economy to report positive economic growth in 2020, with a 2.3% year-on-year expansion in real GDP. However, in 2022, as most countries began to lift or relax their COVID-19 restrictions, China continued to keep a tight grip on its border controls. The logistical bottlenecks and depressed tourism levels contributed to slower growth in trade in services of the country. Moreover, the deteriorating global environment following Russia's invasion of Ukraine further impeded China's trade performance (China Economic Update, 2022).

Within the Asian region, South Asia was particularly vulnerable to pandemic-induced poverty. In 2020, 21% of the world's poor lived in South Asia, second to that of 64% in sub-Saharan Africa (Kharas & Dooley, 2021). The region has been stricken with poor health infrastructure, uneven socioeconomic conditions, inadequate social safety net, limited access to water and sanitation, and inadequate living space arrangements (Rasul, 2020). The pandemic has exposed the region to the risks of deepening poverty as well as rising unemployment and food insecurity, which may reinforce existing inequalities and social instabilities, thereby creating a significant and long-lasting effect in the region (Rasul et al., 2021). In particular, the collapse of Sri Lankan economy has raised much concern about social and economic frailties in the area. Part of the reasons of the country's crisis was its elevated level of fiscal deficits, unsustainable public debt, and disproportionately high dependence on tourism as its main source of foreign revenue, which was ravaged by the pandemic. As such, the crisis experienced in Sri Lanka has provided many important lessons to its South Asian neighbors and underlines how important it is for a country to have strong political leadership and governance, public financial resilience, inclusive development, and appropriate food security measures.

1.3 Policy Discussion

The ASEAN region, being highly dependent on trade and tourism for increasing its economic growth and development prospects, has been one of the hardest hit regions by the pandemic. By the end of the first semester of 2020, trade and FDI inflows in ASEAN had fallen by 12.4% and 32.9%, respectively, compared to the previous year. The average real GDP of ASEAN 10 recorded a negative growth rate of –3.4% in 2020 (Wood et al., 2020). In response to the pandemic shock, the ASEAN Secretariat (2020) issued a "Comprehensive Recovery Framework" (CRF) that outlines the consolidated recovery strategies embodying five dimensions: enhancing health systems, strengthening human security, maximizing the potential of the intra-ASEAN market and broader economic integration, accelerating inclusive digital transformation, and advancing towards a more sustainable and resilient future. More than two years into the pandemic, ASEAN is showing positive signs of recovery. Output growth in Southeast Asia rose to 2.9% in 2021 and is projected to grow further in 2022, increasing to 4.9% (Asian Development Outlook, 2022). Amid the rising geopolitical upheavals in the post-COVID-19 world, the ASEAN region continues to be outward-looking with an emphasis on intra-regional trade. Furthermore, the region stands as a battleground in the US–China rivalry. The inclusiveness of ASEAN in the China-involving RCEP agreement and the US-led Indo-Pacific Economic Framework (IPEF) initiative is evidence of ASEAN's central role in the US–China rivalry (Kim, 2022). It is anticipated that the region's future trade and economic outlook will be greatly impacted by the opportunities and challenges that has arisen from the US–China geo-economic competition. From a policy perspective, the US–China trade war looms large on the horizon. What can country's in the region do to make the most of this challenging situation? This section outlines some potential areas of policy development and highlights measures that have already been adopted by Governments in the region.

Given the adverse impact of that the COVID-19 pandemic has had on cross-border trade and supply chains (Atkinson et al., 2022), restoring trade connectivity shapes as being a key area of policy development that will help the ASEAN region overcome the impact of the pandemic. At the heart of this are developments in digital connectivity, with cross-border trade being an area where there is a large number and variety of parties involved in an international trade transaction. Moreover, the trade process is highly fragmented, often paper-based, slow, and cumbersome. Therefore, governments in the region need to work together to harmonize and digitize trade documents so that the trade process is able to operate on seamless digital platform that is not only more efficient but also increasingly secure (MAS, 2020). Furthermore, improvements in this area are particularly relevant for Asia where its production networks and trade integration have acted as key catalysts for economic growth and development in the region in recent years. Establishing a stronger digital platform will help to ensure that trade remains a key economic driver in the post COVID-19 era. Furthermore, it is imperative for the ASEAN economy manages the opportunities that a digitalized economy presents along with relevant security and ethical concerns.

Moving forward, a number of key policy priorities are proposed. First, in light of the progress made under the Ha Noi plan, the next critical step is to ensure that the implementation of commitment to ensure supply chain connectivity, particularly of essential goods, is implemented effectively. Second, as the region moves beyond COVID-19, it is important that the trade sector is given its due space within the wider economic development framework. This would allow not only the manufacturing sector of the regional economy to receive the right kind of stimulus so that it can resume normal production after the supply shock but also sellers to have better market access, which would in turn restore business and consumer confidence and grow household purchasing power. In addition to this, ongoing initiatives, such as the general review of the ASEAN Trade in Goods Agreement (ATIGA), provide an opportunity to address existing bottlenecks, such as improving the constraints that exist with some non-tariff measures, while also building on the current level of ambition that exists to drive economic change and new trade policy initiatives. As part of the new trade policy agenda, for the time is also right for Governments in Asia to work together to implement new trade facilitation measures. More focus should also be given to trade in services, which has become an increasingly important component of the regional economy in recent times as well as work with industry to find the right kind of balance that promotes foreign investment opportunities, while also protecting more vulnerable sectors of the economy, which are still weak following the pandemic. Improvements in these areas can also help the region capitalize on the opportunities that may stem from any global supply chain restructuring that takes place. Third, as the region emerges from the COVID-19 pandemic and the depths of the war in Ukraine, there is also a strong need for greater multilateral cooperation, which can lead to reform of the global trading system and the shaping of the global and regional trade agenda. Trade policy in this space must be built upon the premise of transparent, non-discriminatory trade rules that work to protect the most vulnerable in society. It is in the region's interest to play an active role in driving a successful reform agenda through the WTO, so that the institution continues to remain not only relevant but also an important means of resolving trade disputes. Finally, the Asian region must work with the private sector and other stakeholders to ensure that supply chains remain stable and connected, while also providing a platform that allows new business models to flourish. Improvements in these areas will form a critical component of the social and economic developments that take place in the post-pandemic recovery.

1.4 Concluding Remarks

This study has sought to examine the current economic, trade, and geopolitical factors of Asia in an effort to better understand not only the challenges but also the opportunities that exist in the region.

With a war in Ukraine and countries dealing with the aftermath of the COVID-19 pandemic, our study highlights the important role that international trade will play in driving economic and social prosperity in Asia.

Using the relevant extant literature as a guide, we focus on infrastructure development, FDI, trade policy, and the effect of COVID-19 pandemic to understand recent trends in trade and economic development in Asia. We found that both hard and soft infrastructures are crucial to facilitate trade and stimulate growth of Asian countries. Given the current lack of infrastructure in developing Asia, the building and upgrading of infrastructure can be a way to further unleash the growth potential of the region. The positive impact of FDI on growth is less certain and less consistent across studies. However, there is a growing consensus that having sound economic fundamentals and institutions can help the host country to realize the economic gains of FDI. Last but not least, the COVID-19 pandemic has temporarily halted the trend of product fragmentation and caused a breakdown in global supply chains, which has been a key driver underlying the trade performance of Asia. This has exposed the vulnerability of the current global trade and supply chain system. As the region gradually recovers from the COVID-19 shock, governments must take a proactive approach to ensure that they are more resilient in the face of similar events in the future. As such, we highlight a number of key policy initiatives that governments should implement in order for the region to thrive. At the heart of this is digitalization and the way in which technology can stimulate not only strong efficiency gains but also a more robust trade and global supply chain mechanism, something that is very much needed in times of uncertainty and crisis.

Note

1 Based on dataset of PRC; Hong Kong, China; India; Indonesia; Republic of Korea; Malaysia; the Philippines; Singapore; Thailand; and Vietnam from 1971 to 2013.

References

Ahlquist, J. S. (2006). Economic policy, institutions, and capital flows: Portfolio and direct investment flows in developing countries. *International Studies Quarterly*, *50*(3), 681–704.

Alguacil, M., Cuadros, A., & Orts, V. (2011). Inward FDI and growth: The role of macroeconomic and institutional environment. *Journal of Policy Modeling*, *33*(3), 481–496.

ASEAN Secretariat. (2020). *ASEAN comprehensive recovery framework*. The ASEAN Secretariat Community Relations Division (CRD).

Asia Development Bank (ADB). (2022). *Inflation rate in Asia and the Pacific*. Asian Development Outlook (ADO). https://data.adb.org/dataset/inflation-rate-asia-and-pacific-asian-development-outlook

Athukorala, P. C. (2005). Product fragmentation and trade patterns in East Asia. *Asian Economic Papers*, *4*(3), 1–27.

Athukorala, P. C. (2011). Production networks and trade patterns in East Asia: Regionalization or globalization? *Asian Economic Papers*, *10*(1), 65–95.
Athukorala, P. C., & Yamashita, N. (2006). Production fragmentation and trade integration: East Asia in a global context. *The North American Journal of Economics and Finance*, *17*(3), 233–256.
Atkinson, B., Wood, J., & Jang, H. (2022). Does Covid-19 spark the end of globalization? In T. Chaiechi & J. Wood (Eds.), *Community empowerment, sustainable cities, and transformative economies* (pp. 535–550). Springer Publishing.
Brooks, D. H. (2010). Regional cooperation, infrastructure and trade costs in Asia. In *Trade facilitation and regional cooperation in Asia*. Edward Elgar Publishing.
Brooks, D. H., & Go, E. C. (2012). Trade, employment and inclusive growth in Asia. In *Policy priorities for international trade and jobs* (pp. 327–351). OECD.
Brooks, D. H., & Stone, S. F. (2010). Infrastructure and trade facilitation in Asian APEC. *Asian Development Review*, *27*(1), 135.
Cheewatrakoolpong, K., Sabhasri, C., & Bunditwattanawong, N. (2013). *Impact of the ASEAN economic community on ASEAN production networks* (ADBI Working Paper Series No. 409). ADB.
Chen, L., & Intal, P. S. (2017). ASEAN foreign trade, investment, and integration in comparative perspective. In *ASEAN and member states: Transformation and integration* (pp. 13–33). Economic Research Institute for ASEAN and East Asia.
China Economic Update: Between Shocks and Stimulus. (2022). *The World Bank*. www.worldbank.org/en/country/china/publication/china-economic-update-june-2022
Du, Q., Deng, D., & Wood, J. (2021). Differences in distance and spatial effects on cross-border E-commerce and international trade: An empirical analysis of China and one-belt one-road countries. *Journal of Global Information Management*, *30*(2), 1–24.
Fang, J., Ou, J., & Yao, S. (2022). On COVID-19 pandemic and China's foreign trade. *The World Economy*, *45*(11), 3507–3533.
Girma, S. (2005). Absorptive capacity and productivity spillovers from FDI: A threshold regression analysis. *Oxford bulletin of Economics and Statistics*, *67*(3), 281–306.
Heshmati, A., Kim, J., & Wood, J. (2019). A survey of inclusive growth policy. *Economies*, *7*(3), 65. https://doi.org/10.3390/economies7030065
International Monetary Fund (IMF). (2021). Regional economic outlook: Asia-Pacific. *IMF*. www.imf.org/en/Publications/REO/APAC/Issues/2021/10/15/regional-economic-outlook-for-asia-and-pacific-october-2021
Ismail, N. W., & Mahyideen, J. M. (2015). *The impact of infrastructure on trade and economic growth in selected economies in Asia* (Asia Development Bank (ADB) Institute Working Paper Series). www.adb.org/publications/impact-infrastructure-trade-and-economic-growth-selected-economies-asia
Jongwanich, J. (2010). Determinants of export performance in East and Southeast Asia. *World Economy*, *33*(1), 20–41.
Karymshakov, K., & Sulaimanova, B. (2021). The impact of infrastructure on trade in Central Asia. *Asia Europe Journal*, *19*(1), 5–20.
Kharas, H., & Dooley, M. (2021). Extreme poverty in the time of COVID-19. *Brookings*. https://www.brookings.edu/articles/extreme-poverty-in-the-time-of-covid-19/
Kim, J.-S., & Wood, J. (2020). Service sector development in Asia: An important instrument of growth. *Asia-Pacific Economic Literature*, *34*(1), 12–15.

Kim, S. Y. (2022). *Centrality and community: ASEAN in the regional comprehensive economic partnership* (ERIA Discussion Paper Series No. 447). Economic Research Institute for ASEAN and East Asia.

Kimura, F., & Obashi, A. (2016). Production networks in East Asia: What we know so far. In Ganeshan Wignaraja (Ed.), *Production networks and enterprises in East Asia* (pp. 33–64). ADB.

Lee, H., & Tan, H. (2006). Technology transfer, FDI and economic growth in the ASEAN region. *Journal of the Asia Pacific Economy, 11*(4), 394–410.

Liu, Z., & Hu, B. (2020). China's economy under COVID-19: Short-term shocks and long-term changes. *Modern Economy*, *11*(4), 908–919.

Monetary Authority of Singapore (MAS). (2020). *Covid-19: We need more connectivity, not less.* www.mas.gov.sg/news/speeches/2020/covid19-we-need-more-connectivity-not-less

Ozturk, I. (2007). Foreign direct investment-growth nexus: A review of the recent literature. *International Journal of Applied Econometrics and Quantitative Studies*, *4*(2).

Padilla, M. A. E., Sari, D. W., & Handoyo, R. D. (2017). Formation of production networks in ASEAN: Measuring the real value-added and identifying the role of ASEAN countries in the world supply chains. *Business and Economic Horizons*, *13*(2), 237–255.

Petri, P. A. (2012). The determinants of bilateral FDI: Is Asia different? *Journal of Asian Economics*, *23*(3), 201–209.

Portugal-Perez, A., & Wilson, J. S. (2012). Export performance and trade facilitation reform: Hard and soft infrastructure. *World Development*, *40*(7), 1295–1307.

Rasul, G. (2020). A framework for improving policy priorities in managing COVID-19 challenges in developing countries. *Frontiers in Public Health*, *8*, 589681. https://doi.org/10.3389/fpubh.2020.589681

Rasul, G., Nepal, A. K., Hussain, A., Maharjan, A., Joshi, S., Lama, A., Gurung, P., Ahmad, F., Mishra, A., & Sharma, E. (2021). Socio-economic implications of COVID-19 pandemic in South Asia: Emerging risks and growing challenges. *Frontiers in Sociology*, *6*, 629693.

Rehman, F. U., Noman, A. A., & Ding, Y. (2020). Does infrastructure increase exports and reduce trade deficit? Evidence from selected South Asian countries using a new global infrastructure index. *Journal of Economic Structures*, *9*(1), 1–23.

Rillo, A. D., & Ali, Z. (2017). *Public financing of infrastructure in Asia: In search of new solutions*. ADB.

Saggi, K. (2002). Trade, foreign direct investment, and international technology transfer: A survey. *The World Bank Research Observer*, *17*(2), 191–235.

Sahoo, P., & Dash, R. K. (2012). Economic growth in South Asia: Role of infrastructure. *The Journal of International Trade & Economic Development*, *21*(2), 217–252.

Tan, S. R., Wang, W. S., & Chia, W. M. (2021). International capital flows and extreme exchange market pressure: Evidence from emerging market economies. *Open Economies Review*, *32*(3), 479–506.

Tiwari, A. K., & Mutascu, M. (2011). Economic growth and FDI in Asia: A panel-data approach. *Economic Analysis and Policy*, *41*(2), 173–187.

UNCTAD. (2021). *Review of maritime transport.* https://unctad.org/system/files/official-document/rmt2021_en_0.pdf

Wang, P., Zhang, H., & Wood, J. (2022). Achieving sustainable development goals (SDGs): A tropical region perspective. In J. Wood, K. Thirumaran, & T. Chaiechi (Eds.), *Business, industry and trade in the tropics* (pp. 68–96). Routledge.

Wood, J. (2017). An industrial sector analysis of the factors effecting FTA negotiation outcomes. *Global Business Review*, *18*(4), 1–16.

Wood, J., Jang, H., & Atkinson, B. (2022). Covid-19: Its impact on trade and development in the ASEAN region. In J. Wood, K. Thirumaran, & T. Chaiechi (Eds.), *Business, industry and trade in the tropics* (pp. 137–150). Routledge.

Wood, J., Li, Y., & Wu, J. (2021). An analysis of the trends and determinants of intra-industry trade between China and Asia Pacific economic cooperation member countries. *Singapore Economic Review*, *66*(3), 743–766.

Wood, J., & Wu, J. (2020). The sustainability of the WTO dispute settlement system: Does it work for developing countries? *The Journal of World Trade*, *54*(4), 531–566.

Wood, J., Wu, J., Li, Y., & Jang, H. (2017a). The economic impact of SPS measures on agricultural exports to China: An empirical analysis using the PPML method. *Social Sciences*, *6*(51), 1–18.

Wood, J., Wu, J., Li, Y., & Kim, J. (2017b). TBT and SPS impacts on Korean exports to China: Empirical analysis using the PPML method. *Asian-Pacific Economic Literature, 31*(2), 96–114.

Wood, J., Wu, J., & Oh, K. (2020). Do technical barriers to trade restrict exports? Evidence from South Korea. *Korea and the World Economy*, *21*(2), 1–26.

Wu, J., Huh, C.-G., & Wood, J. (2021a). Globally chained economies: Unwitting victims of the US-China trade war. *Asian-Pacific Economic Literature*, *35*(2), 60–76. https://doi.org/10.1111/apel.12334

Wu, J., & Wood, J. (2022). An assessment of trade facilitation impacts on China's outward foreign direct investment to ASEAN countries. In J. Wood, K. Thirumaran, & T. Chaiechi (Eds.), *Business, industry and trade in the tropics* (pp. 97–113). Routledge.

Wu, J., Wood, J., & Huang, X. (2021b). How does GVC reconstruction affect economic growth and employment? Analysis of USA – China decoupling. *Asia Pacific Economic Literature*, *35*(1), 67–81. https://doi.org/10.1111/apel.12319

Wu, J., Wood, J., Oh, K., Li, Y., & Bhuyan, M. I. (2022). The impact of TBT and SPS measures on domestic value-added exports: Evidence from the United States. *Asia-Pacific Journal of Accounting & Economics*. https://doi.org/10.1080/16081625.2022.2077779

Zhang, H., Wang, P., & Wood, J. (2022). Does institutional quality matter for the Nexus between environmental quality and economic growth? A tropics perspective. In J. Wood, K. Thirumaran, & T. Chaiechi (Eds.), *Business, industry and trade in the tropics* (pp. 33–52). Routledge.

Zhang, K. H. (2001). Does foreign direct investment promote economic growth? Evidence from East Asia and Latin America. *Contemporary Economic Policy*, *19*(2), 175–185.

Zhong, S., & Su, B. (2021). Investigating ASEAN's participation in global value chains: Production fragmentation and regional integration. *Asian Development Review*, *38*(2), 159–188.

Zhongming, Z., Linong, L., Xiaona, Y., Wangqiang, Z., & Wei, L. (2017). *Meeting Asia's infrastructure needs*. ADB. http://dx.doi.org/10.22617/FLS168388-2

2 Life Expectancy

Exploring Climate Change-Human Longevity Nexus in Sub-Saharan Africa

Fisayo Fagbemi, Geraldine Ejiaka Nzeribe, and Tolulope Temilola Osinubi

2.1 Introduction

Climate change, which can be regarded as changes in the weather patterns, has been identified as one of the major challenges confronting developing regions, particularly sub-Saharan Africa (SSA). Human and environmental risks associated with climate change are multifaceted (Intergovernmental Panel on Climate Change [IPCC], 2012). Over the past half-century, increasing temperatures and changes in precipitation patterns or extreme weather incidents manifested through the intensification of droughts, floods, storms, and cold and heat waves have amplified the disaster landscape in the 21st century. The alteration of natural ecosystems with increased carbon dioxide emissions and environmental degradation resulting from human activities has made SSA to be more vulnerable to humanitarian crisis (Maino & Emrullahu, 2022). There is no question that a rising threat to human health and safety due to the occurrence of extreme weather is imminent in the developing world. Yet efforts to link environmental degradation to the level of human existence in Africa have been handicapped by the insufficient empirical evidence on the impact of climate change on human longevity. Climate change-human longevity nexus in SSA context is therefore essential to be examined more empirically so as to incorporate it into an overall strategy of sustainable development in the region.

With respect to the view that risks associated with climate change are increasingly becoming more severe, understanding the full dimensions of the problems through the model that links climate change to human longevity is central. This will help mitigate the possible adverse effect of changing climate on human health and safety. Although African countries may be among the lightest polluters, the vulnerability of fragile regions' populations (like SSA) to climate change is much higher (Maino & Emrullahu, 2022). Thus, SSA countries will possibly suffer the most from climate variability in their pursuit of sustainable development. What remains the foundation of resilience building seems to be science-based climate information. While enhancing the state of climate report for Africa can serve as an oasis for sustainable livelihoods and development, concern over the limited study on human longevity impacts of

DOI: 10.4324/9781003349204-2

climate change has strengthened fears that climate-sensitive health risks may escalate. This is because to accurately determine the extent of health threats associated with increasing carbon dioxide emissions as well as the breaching of severe temperature thresholds increasingly depends on the availability of empirical (or scientific) explorations (World Health Organization (WHO), 2021). The paucity of empirical investigations has therefore jeopardized the realization of universal health coverage (UHC) in many ways, especially by compounding the prevailing incidents of climate-sensitive health risks, mostly in low-income and disadvantaged countries/regions.

It is evident that there is rising climate change threats for human health and socio-economic development in Africa (WHO, 2021). Due to this, research study on climate change-human longevity nexus in the context of SSA is needed for sustainable adaptation planning in the region. Although it has been firmly established in the literature that changing climate poses a dire threat to SSA, its human health and ecosystems, few existing studies do not specifically account for the potential impact of climate change on life expectancy in the context of SSA but on other socioeconomic factors such as infant mortality, income per capita growth, and political and security dimensions. Some of these few studies are as follows: Chewe and Hangoma (2020) assessed drivers of health in SSA; Maino and Emrullahu (2022) focused on the effect of climate change in SSA fragile states; Li and Samimi (2022) demonstrated how sustainable development is constrained by international migration under climate change in SSA; and Van der Merwe et al. (2022) analyzed the impact of climate change on children's health outcomes in Nigeria. Given that there could be regional differences in terms of the impact on human longevity, it thus becomes imperative to have a proper view on how human longevity is impacted by climate change in SSA as there is more need for information on the increased climate variability in the region.

The study therefore examines the cost of climate variability on human health and longevity within the context of life expectancy in 32 SSA countries between 2005 and 2020. This is because climate change seems to have undermined many of the social determinants for good health, thereby resulting in human illness and death (WHO, 2021) – especially those with underlying health conditions are disproportionately affected by increasingly frequent extreme weather events. In addition, the significance of this study lies in the fact that negative consequences of climate change are predominant in regions with relatively hot climates, including SSA. For example, in Africa, an estimated 93% of global malaria deaths occurred in 2017 (United Nations, 2020). United Nations had also reported that the occurrence of malaria epidemics is more frequent after periods of unusual heavy rainfall. Thus, with the use of panel fixed effects (FE) and dynamic generalized method of moments (GMM) estimations, the chapter will systematically ascertain whether the incidence of climate change-related excess mortality estimates in SSA is tenable empirically. This will indeed help elucidate the extent to which the climate crisis has further worsened long-term precarious health conditions in the region.

2.2 Literature Review

This section spans over the impact of climate change on human life as well as how human activities can be influenced by climate variability. In this part, discussions on various dimensions through which human health and longevity can be affected by the variability of climatic conditions are specifically covered. In general, the review of the literature helps reveal how the connections between climate change and human life are established.

2.2.1 Climate Change-Human Longevity Nexus: The Common Linkage

The theoretical background for the study rests on the view that extreme weather events or disasters (like flooding or landslides) resulting from heavy rain could directly impact human health in terms of fatalities and injuries (WHO, 2009; McMichael & Lindgren, 2011). Through heat stress, extreme heat events can likewise have direct influences on the state of human life. In addition, too long exposure to high temperatures can result in heat cramps, heat exhaustion, overwhelming stress, fainting and human death (Smith et al., 2014). Furthermore, as established by IPCC (2014), climate change is one of the key drivers of human health. It tends to influence the existing contextual indicators to affect human life in various ways.

2.2.2 Climate Change and Human Life: Empirical Evidence

To understand the human health impact of climate change, economists have sought to measure how the variability of climate conditions impacts human life. With the use of Kompas et al. (2018) modeling data, Okonjo-Iweala (2020) demonstrated that climate change could cause a significant reduction in Africa's GDP through damage to human health, decreased agricultural and labor productivity, and lowered crop yields. However, Okonjo-Iweala's study mainly emphasized on the relationship between climate change and economic growth, not on the direct effect of the former on human health. In Ghana and Kenya, it has been established that high ambient temperatures and increased all-cause mortality are strongly correlated (Azongo et al., 2012; Egondi et al., 2012). Combined with elevated temperatures, heavy rainfall occurrences have been observed to give rise to outbreaks of cholera, which is linked to the contamination of water and poor sanitation (Luque Ferna´ndez et al., 2009; Reyburn et al., 2011). Following severe flooding in Mozambique in 2000 as well as in the province of Cabo Delgado in early 2013, such outbreaks of cholera occurred (UNICEF, 2013). Similarly, Patz et al. (2008) posited that the adverse effect of drought conditions on the availability and quality of water would result in increased cases of diarrhea, conjunctivitis, scabies and trachoma in the affected countries.

Through the impacts of climate change on agriculture, human health could be undermined when the affordability and availability of nutritious food are affected. Although, in SSA, levels of undernutrition are currently high, with warming of 1.2–1.7 °C, projections show that by 2050, the proportion of the population undernourished would rise by 25–90% (Lloyd et al., 2011). Indeed, SSA region is among the regions negatively affected by temperature variations (Sandalli, 2021). In general, Ntinyari and Gweyi-Onyango (2021) revealed that climate change and modeling and projections of greenhouse gases emissions seem to have affected SSA based on review of the literature. However, it has been observed that these studies have not been specifically centered on the direct association between climate change and human longevity. Regarding the projected impact of climate change on European life expectancy, for the average European country, climate change extremes are projected to shrink life expectancy at birth by 0.24 years (Hauer et al., 2021).

Maino and Emrullahu (2022) examined the effect of climate change in SSA fragile states using panel fixed effects model between 1980 and 2019. These authors argued that due to structural weaknesses and governance failure, SSA face huge challenges to address the impacts of climate shocks and rising temperatures, which has added to risks associated with climate variations. While assessing drivers of health in SSA, Chewe and Hangoma (2020) demonstrated that, with the use of GMM estimation over the period 1995–2014, educational attainment, increased health expenditure and health care access quality are drivers of health. These factors (including climate change) are found to have an influence on life expectancy and infant mortality in the region. However, the point of emphasis was on a broader array of determinants not on the impact of a particular factor like climate variability. Li and Samimi (2022) focused on how sustainable development is constrained by international migration under climate change in SSA. Their findings indicate that among other factors, migration and population displacement are affected by environmental stress in SSA. Moreover, throughout both natural and human systems, the repercussions of climate change will be experienced in different ways across SSA countries (Serdeczny et al., 2017). With a focus on 32 SSA countries, Fagbemi et al. (2023) confirmed the negative effect of climate change on food production in the region. In the work of Van der Merwe et al. (2022), the impact of climate change on children's health outcomes was examined mainly in Nigeria's context. The study's outcomes indicated that rising temperature has direct association with higher levels of stunting in the country.

Taylor (2020) argued that the consequences of climate change could be many and serious, which include changes in soil quality and accessible drinking water, rising sea levels, increased climate-sensitive health risks, and an increased risk of the severity of weather like droughts, floods and hurricanes. Other impacts of climate change (particularly global warming) are decreased biodiversity, animal migration and vegetation change resulting from drought and water scarcity, and the negative influence on the ecosystem (Nunez et al., 2019; Upadhyay, 2020). In the history of the planet, Ceballos et al. (2020) maintained that more than half of all living things seem to have been extinct due to the problems caused by climate change. In general, findings of these studies somewhat reflect on the possibility of the direct and indirect effects of the variability of climate conditions on human health.

In summary, it has been firmly established in the literature that changing climate poses a dire threat to SSA and its human health and ecosystems. However, few existing studies in this regard do not specifically account for the possible impact of climate change on life expectancy with respect to SSA but on other socioeconomic factors such as infant mortality, income per capita growth, and political and security dimensions. Thus, since this chapter is concerned with the fact that SSA is among the regions of the world most vulnerable to climate change impacts (IPCC, 2014), the cost of climate variability on human longevity is explored within the context of life expectancy for SSA region.

2.3 Methodology

2.3.1 Conceptual Framework

Based on World Health Organization's overview of climate-sensitive health risks (WHO, 2021), the conceptual framework is constructed. Figure 2.1

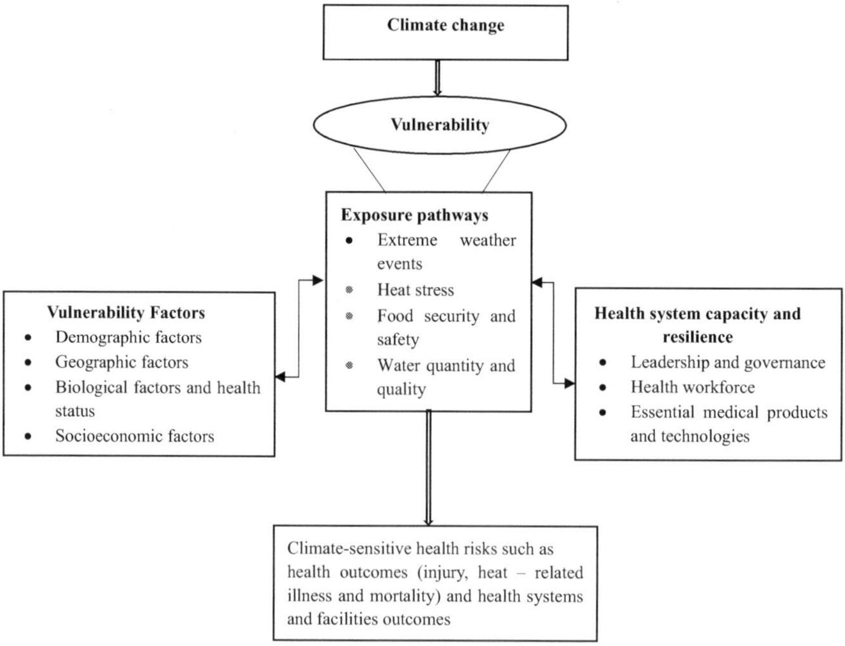

Figure 2.1 An overview of climate-sensitive health risks, their exposure pathways and vulnerability factors

Source: Authors' modification of World Health Organization's overview of climate-sensitive health risks (WHO, 2021)

illustrates how human health is impacted by climate change in various ways. It is demonstrated that an increase in the frequency of extreme weather conditions (such as droughts, storms, heatwaves, floods, food system disruptions, rises in water- and vector-borne diseases, and food insecurity issues) could lead to unusual human illness and death. In addition, by jeopardizing socioeconomic determinants for good health, including access to health care, essential medical products and technologies, and social support structures, climate-sensitive health risks would be disproportionately felt by the most vulnerable individuals (like women and children), especially in fragile economic regions of the world.

Following WHO (2021), since a rise in morbidity and mortality could be attributed to human-induced warming, it is conceptually plausible to assert that human health is susceptible to climate variability. Thus, life expectancy can be undermined by extreme weather events in SSA, as one of the most fragile regions. It is therefore hypothesized that increased carbon dioxide emissions can adversely affect human longevity across SSA countries.

2.3.2 Model Specification and Econometric Techniques

Following the need to examine the impact of climate change on human longevity in SSA, this study specifies the functional relationship between carbon emissions (CO_2 emissions) and life expectancy at birth as follows:

$$\text{LIFE} = f(\text{CO}_2, \text{X}) \tag{1}$$

where LIFE represents life expectancy at birth; CO_2 indicates carbon emissions; and X denotes the set of control variables that could possibly determine human longevity.

Eq. (1) is formed based on Figure 2.1 (conceptual framework), which explains how human longevity can be determined by climate variability. Given that life expectancy at birth seems to be widely recognized and understood by the public (Serdeczny et al., 2017), within the context of life expectancy, the cost of climate variability on human health and longevity is examined. Thus, Eq. (1) is elaborated and specified econometrically as:

$$\text{LIFE}_{\text{it}} = \varphi_0 + \varphi_1 \text{CO}_{2\text{it}} + \varphi_2 \text{COM}_{\text{it}} + \varphi_3 \text{FDI}_{\text{it}} + \mu_{\text{i}} + \vartheta_{\text{t}} + \varepsilon_{\text{it}} \tag{2}$$

where COM = income per capita; FDI = foreign direct investment; φ_0 is the constant; φ_i (where i = 1, . . . , 3) indicate the corresponding intercepts; ϑ_t denotes the time-specific constant; t is the time period; μ_i measures the country-specific effect; and ε indicates the error term.

In order to address the inherent issues associated with data persistence, the incidence of endogeneity and small sample bias which can influence the outcomes of estimations, dynamic panel generalized method of moments

(GMM) in form of two-step system GMM is used to account for the problems of simultaneity and endogeneity. This approach could be more effective in reducing the potential bias and inconsistency associated with one-step system GMM, particularly in case of a small sample and data persistence (Arellano & Bover, 1995; Blundell & Bond, 1998). Eq. (3) is then formed as;

$$\begin{aligned} LIFE_{it} &= \varphi_0 + \varphi_1 LIFE_{it-1} + \varphi_2 CO_{2it} + \varphi_3 COM_{it} \\ &\quad + \varphi_4 FDI_{it} + \mu_i + \vartheta_t + \varepsilon_{it} \end{aligned} \tag{3}$$

Given the need for the elimination of the country-specific effect component, Eq. (4) is therefore presented in the form of first differences as:

$$\Delta LIFE_{it} = \varphi_1 '' LIFE_{it-1} + \varphi_2 \Delta CO_{2it} + \varphi_3 \Delta COM_{it} + \varphi_4 \Delta FDI_{it} + \epsilon_{it} \tag{4}$$

where $\epsilon_{it} = '' \vartheta_t + '' \mu_{it}$.

To ensure that the outcomes of the estimations are robust, panel fixed effects (FEs) and two-step system GMM are employed in this study. Two-step system GMM is specifically applied to address the possibility of biased and inconsistent parameters that could emanate from the estimations of the static model such as FE estimation. In addition, efficiency gains associated with GMM estimation are obtained through Sargan test (for overidentifying restrictions of the model), optimal weighting matrix, and the relaxation of the assumption of independent and identically distributed. The study involves the use of unbalanced panel data. Regarding the nature of the series, all the variables are in logarithm form. As the number of cross-sectional observations is greater than the time period (large "N" > small "T"), the use of System-GMM is appropriate (Arellano & Bover, 1995; Blundell & Bond, 1998).

2.3.3 Data Description and Sources

Life expectancy at birth, which serves as the dependent variable with other three explanatory variables (carbon emissions [CO_2], foreign direct investment and income per capita), are used. The study's scope is between 2005 and 2020, whereas 32 SSA countries are incorporated. Data availability is mainly considered for the choosing of the scope as well as selected countries. The 32 sub-Saharan African countries selected are Equatorial Guinea, Seychelles, Mauritius, Gabon, Botswana, South Africa, Namibia, Eswatini, Cabo Verde, Chad, Republic of Congo, Angola, Nigeria, Ghana, Mauritania, Côte d'Ivoire, Guinea-Bissau, Cameroon, Djibouti, Kenya, Senegal, Central African Republic, Gambia, Lesotho, Mali, Niger, Rwanda, Tanzania, Togo, Uganda, Zimbabwe and Burkina Faso. The description of data and sources of data are presented in Table 2.1.

Table 2.1 Data description and sources

Variable	*Code*	*Description and measurement*	*Source*
Carbon dioxide emissions	CO_2	Carbon dioxide emissions are those stemming from the burning of fossil fuels and the manufacture of cement. They include carbon dioxide produced during consumption of solid, liquid and gas fuels and gas flaring.	World development indicator (World Bank, 2022)
Life expectancy at birth, total (years)	LIFE	It indicates the number of years a newborn infant would live if prevailing patterns of mortality at the time of its birth were to stay the same throughout its life.	World development indicator (World Bank, 2022)
Gross National Income per capita, PPP (constant 2017 international $)	COM	It is gross national income in purchasing power parity (PPP) divided by mid-year population.	World development indicator (World Bank, 2022)
Foreign direct investment, net inflows (% of GDP)	FDI	It represents net inflows – new investment inflows less disinvestment – in the reporting economy from external (foreign) investors (% of GDP).	World development indicator (World Bank, 2022)

2.4 Empirical Results and Discussion

2.4.1 Descriptive Statistics

Features of the variables incorporated by the model are reported in Table 2.2. We conduct the descriptive analysis to be more certain about the particular developmental characteristics of each variable. It has been estimated that the average value of carbon dioxide emissions (CO_2) in the selected countries is 1.37, while the mean value of life expectancy at birth is 59.87. In terms of minimum and maximum values, it is discovered that CO_2 has 0.03 and 11.94, respectively, whereas the respective lowest and highest values of life expectancy are 42.13 and 76.59. This implies that the SSA region is on the path towards experiencing increased climate change given the large gap between the minimum value and maximum value of CO_2, reflecting the intensification of the occurrence of extreme weather events. Based on the standard

Table 2.2 Summary statistics

	Carbon dioxide emissions (CO_2)	*Life expectancy at birth (LIFE)*	*Income per capita (COM)*	*Foreign direct investment (FDI)*
Mean	1.37	59.87	5940.49	4.03
Median	0.49	60.00	3501.69	2.68
Maximum	11.94	76.59	27520.78	57.84
Minimum	0.03	42.13	777.18	-11.20
Std. Dev.	2.21	6.58	5831.62	5.58
Skewness	2.58	0.25	1.63	3.98
Kurtosis	9.46	3.36	4.90	29.78
Jarque-Bera	1281.26	7.25	266.58	14636.32
Probability	0.00	0.03	0.00	0.00
Sum	616.58	26939.38	2673218.00	1812.07
Sum Sq. Dev.	2185.03	19456.39	1.53E+10	13978.95
Observations	460	460	460	460

Table 2.3 Pairwise correlation coefficient

Variable	*Life expectancy at birth (LIFE)*	*Carbon dioxide emissions (CO_2)*	*Income per capita (COM)*	*Foreign direct investment (FDI)*
LIFE	1.00			
CO_2	-0.40*	1.00		
COM	0.46*	-0.51*	1.00	
FDI	0.30*	-0.15*	0.21*	1.00

Note: * represents correlation coefficients significant at the 5% level or better.

deviation of the series, the climate change indicator seems to have exhibited a wide variation in the selected countries.

Regarding correlation matrix presented in Table 2.3, it is indicated that CO_2 and life expectancy are inversely correlated and significant at the 5% level. However, other indicators used as control variables (Income per capita, and Foreign direct investment) are positively associated with life expectancy, indicating a possible direct relationship between the control variables and life expectancy. On the other hand, the association between CO_2 and all the control variables is found to be negative. Overall, this suggests the potential effect of climate change on these variables.

2.4.2 *Panel Unit Root Tests*

Before proceeding with the estimation of the model, knowing whether the variables used are stationary or not is important. Although for dynamic two-step system GMM conducting panel unit root tests may not be necessary, it will help ascertain the specific attributes of the variables. Thus, three panel unit root tests are conducted which include; Im, Pesaran and Shin, Phillips–Perron Fisher

Table 2.4 Panel unit root test

Variable	*Im, Pesaran and Shin (W-stat)*		*ADF Fisher (Choi Z-stat)*		*Phillips–Perron Fisher (Choi Z-stat)*		*Status*
	Level	*First difference*	*Level*	*First difference*	*Level*	*First difference*	
LIFE	-1.22	-6.14***	-1.14	-7.01***	-1.21	-8.11***	I(1)
CO_2	-7.30***	–	-5.64**	–	-7.04**	–	I(0)
COM	-1.11	-5.71**	1.16	-7.12***	1.41	-8.51***	I(1)
FDI	-1.41	-6.31***	-1.23	-5.81**	-0.95	-7.01***	I(1)

Note: ** and *** indicate the level of significance at 5% and 1%, respectively.

and Augmented Dickey Fuller (ADF) Fisher unit root tests, based on the null hypothesis that all the panel series contain a unit root. As reported in Table 2.4, at the selected level, the null hypothesis of the presence of a unit root could not be rejected for the whole variables. In addition, for all the variables, the unit root null hypothesis at the first difference could be outrightly rejected at the 5% level.

2.4.3 *Panel Estimations: Fixed Effects (FEs) and Dynamic Two-Step System GMM*

To have robust estimation outcomes, various diagnostic tests are carried out. For example, through the Hausman test, it is provided that the use of fixed effects (FEs) is consistent and more efficient compared to random effects (REs). Other diagnostic tests (such as Pesaran cross-section dependence (CD) and Heteroscedasticity) conducted also help verify the validity of the estimates of FE, while the following tests give credence to the robustness of dynamic two-step system GMM estimation: Hansen OIR, Sargan test, Arellano–Bond test for the first-order serial correlation (A–Bond AR (1)) and Arellano–Bond test for the second-order serial correlation (A–Bond AR (2)).

Table 2.5 presents the main results. The system-GMM model shows that climate change measured by CO_2 significantly contributes to the reduction in life expectancy. A 1% increase in CO_2 reduces life expectancy by ten percentage points. Similarly, for the FE model, it is observed that a 1% increase in CO_2 leads to a 17 percentage points reduction in life expectancy. This supports the notion that extreme weather events in SSA are a major contributor to fragile human health, leading to reduced human longevity (Serdeczny et al., 2017; Van der Merwe et al., 2022). Given the projection that increased climate change would substantially affect the social and environmental determinants of human health, it could be assumed that every additional tenth of a degree of carbon emissions would take a dire toll on people's lives and existence. While it is empirically plausible to assert that human health is susceptible to climate variability, reducing emissions and avoiding the breaching of severe temperature thresholds will avert destructive health impacts

Table 2.5 OLS fixed effects and dynamic two-step system GMM

Variable	*OLS fixed effects*	*GMM estimation*
LIFE *(lag)*	–	0.21***
		[9.17]
CO_2	-0.18**	-0.11**
	[-3.14]	[-3.01]
COM	0.12***	0.31***
	[4.45]	[4.96]
FDI	0.11**	0.21
	[3.13]	[1.48]
Constant	0.23***	0.25***
	[3.87]	[4.95]
R-square	65	-
Observations	460	415
No. of countries	32	32
No. of instruments	-	25
Diagnostic test		
Hausman test (*P*-value)	0.01	–
Pesaran CD (*P*-value)	0.11	–
Heteroscedasticity (*P*-value)	0.22	–
Hansen OIR (*P*-value)	–	0.13
A–Bond AR (1) (*P*-value)	–	0.02
A–Bond AR (2) (*P*-value)	–	0.12
Sargan test (*P*-value)	–	0.41

Note: ** and *** represent the level of significance at 5% and 1%, respectively.

and prevent many populations from climate change-related deaths. However, when there is no concrete effort taken towards reducing the current rate of climate change, climate-sensitive health risks will further increase, thereby undermining human longevity.

For the FE model, it is also found that income per capita and FDI are significant drivers of increased life expectancy. Positive changes in COM and FDI, by increasing the Health Care Access Quality Index, can bring about greater improvements in human health and substantial increases in years of life expectancy. This substantiates the view that these indicators could be regarded as key drivers of human health in SSA (Chewe & Hangoma, 2020). However, for the system-GMM model, FDI is not significant. This outcome could be attributed to the low level of inward FDI in most SSA countries or the diversion of inward FDI due to pervasive structural weaknesses and governance failure in SSA economies. Thus, promoting increased inflows of FDI together with improved governance will potentially affect the social and environmental factors linked to induced-human health and safety.

2.5 Conclusion

Given that climate change has intensified serious environmental problems that threaten lives and livelihoods in Africa, increasing emissions offer a strong illustration of how SSA can be more vulnerable to climate-sensitive health risks. It is becoming increasingly critical concern that extreme weather events may have profound consequences for human longevity. Due to the possibility of regional differences (i.e., impacts may not be uniform across regions of the world) in terms of the effects of climate change on human longevity, the study mainly demonstrates that climate variability is expected to affect life expectancy at birth in a variety of ways in SSA context.

Estimates indicate that an increase in climate change (CO_2 emissions) is associated with a reduction in life expectancy at birth, suggesting that reducing emissions of greenhouse gases can result in improved human health and longevity. Compared to a scenario without increasing CO_2 emissions and climate variability, SSA already low rates of life expectancy can be expected to aggravate. In addition, the results offer a more informative description of the significant impact of income per capita on life expectancy. However, the insignificance of FDI is somewhat attributed to pervasive poor governance which often results in diversion of public resources.

Overall, findings and conclusions rest on the assumption that climate extremes and little attention to how the impact of climate change could be addressed pose a considerable threat to human longevity. Therefore, in the absence of sustainable adaptation planning, climate change will exacerbate the vulnerability of populations to extreme weather incidents.

Following the devastating impacts of climate change, SSA countries should proactively join the international community and organizations in combating the variability of climate conditions. It is also suggested that the current problem of deforestation resulting from excessive cultivation, wood fuel and construction timber needs to be urgently addressed. Ultimately, promoting improved access to weather and climate services is critical to enhancing human resilience and adaptive capacity to climate change.

References

Arellano, M., & Bover, O. (1995). Another look at the instrumental variable estimation of error-components models. *Journal of Econometrics*, *68*, 29–51.

Azongo, D. K., Awine, T., Wak, G., Binka, F. N., & Oduro, A. R. (2012). A time-series analysis of weather variability and all-cause mortality in the Kasena-Nankana districts of Northern Ghana, 1995–2010. *Glob Health Action*. https://doi.org/10.3402/gha.v5i0.19073

Blundell, R., & Bond, S. (1998). Initial conditions and moment restrictions in dynamic panel data models. *Journal of Econometrics*, *87*(1), 115–143. https://doi.org/10.1016/s0304-4076(98)00009-8

Ceballos, G., Ehrlich, P. R., & Raven, P. H. (2020). Vertebrates on the brink as indicators of biological annihilation and the sixth mass extinction. *Proceedings of the National Academy of Sciences*, *117*(24), 13596–13602. https://doi.org/10.1073/pnas.1922686117

Chewe, M., & Hangoma, P. (2020). Drivers of health in sub-Saharan Africa: A dynamic panel analysis. *Health Policy Open*, *1*, 100013.

Egondi, T., Kyobutangi, C., Kovats, S., Muindi, K., Ettarh, R., & Rocklov, J. (2012). Time-series analysis of weather and mortality patters in Nairobi's informal settlements. *Global Health Action*, *5*(19065), 23–32.

Fagbemi, F., Oke, D. F., & Fajingbesi, A. (2023). Climate-resilient development: An approach to sustainable food production in sub-Saharan Africa. *Future Foods*, *7*, 100216.

Hauer, M. E., Alexis, R., & Santos-Lozada, A. R. (2021). Inaction on climate change projected to reduce European life expectancy. *Population Research and Policy Review*, *40*, 629–638.

IPCC. (2012). *Managing the risks of extreme events and disasters to advance climate change adaptation: Special report of the intergovernmental panel on climate change* (C. Field, V. Barros, T. Stocker, & Q. Dahe, Eds.). Cambridge University Press. https://doi.org/10.1017/CBO9781139177245

IPCC. (2014). *Climate change 2014 – impacts, adaptation and vulnerability: Part A: Global and sectoral aspects: Working group II contribution to the IPCC fifth assessment report*. Cambridge University Press. https://doi.org/10.1017/CBO9781107415379.

Kompas, T., Pham, V. H., & Che, T. N. (2018). The effects of climate change on GDP by country and the global economic gains from complying with the Paris climate accord. *Earth's Future*, *6*(8), 1153–1173. https://doi.org/10.1029/2018ef000922

Li, Q., & Samimi, C. (2022). Sub Saharan Africa's international migration constrains its sustainable development under climate change. *Sustainability Science*, *17*, 1873–1897.

Lloyd, S. J., Kovats, R. S., & Chalabi, Z. (2011). Climate change, crop yields, and undernutrition: Development of a model to quantify the impact of climate scenarios on child undernutrition. *Environmental Health Perspectives*. https://doi.org/10.1289/ehp.1003311

Luque Ferna´ndez, M. A., Bauernfeind, A., Jime´nez, J. D., Gil, C. L., El Omeiri, N., & Guibert, D. H. (2009). Influence of temperature and rainfall on the evolution of cholera epidemics in Lusaka, Zambia, 2003–2006: Analysis of a time series. *Transactions of the Royal Society of Tropical Medicine and Hygiene*, *103*, 137–143.

Maino, R., & Emrullahu, D. (2022, March). *Climate change in sub-Saharan Africa fragile states: Evidence from panel estimations*. WP/22/54. International Monetary Fund (IMF). https://www.imf.org/en/Publications/WP/Issues/2022/03/18/Climate-Change-in-Sub-Saharan-Africa-Fragile-States-Evidence-from-Panel-Estimations-515159

McMichael, A. J., & Lindgren, E. (2011). Climate change: Present and future risks to health, and necessary responses. *Journal of Internal Medicine*, *270*(5), 401–413.

Ntinyari, W., & Gweyi-Onyango, J. P. (2021). Greenhouse gases emissions in agricultural systems and climate change effects in sub-Saharan Africa. In *African handbook of climate change adaptation* (pp. 1081–1105). https://doi.org/10.1007/978-3-030-45106-6_43

Nunez, S., Arets, E., Alkemade, R., Verwer, C., & Leemans, R. (2019). Assessing the impacts of climate change on biodiversity: Is below 2° C enough? *Climate Change*, *154*(3), 351–365. https://doi.org/10.1007/s10584-019-02420-x

Okonjo-Iweala, N. (2020). *Combatting climate change. An urgent call for comprehensive global and local action. Foresight Africa.* Brookings Institute. www.brookings.edu/wp-content/uploads/2020/01/ForesightAfrica2020_Chapter4_20200110.pdf

Patz, J. A., Olson, S. H., Uejo, C. K., & Gibbs, H. K. (2008). Disease emergence from global climate and land use change. *Medical Clinics of North America*, *92*, 1473–1491.

Reyburn, R., Kim, D. R., Emch, M., Khatib, A., von Seidlein, L., & Ali, M. (2011). Climate variability and the outbreaks of cholera in Zanzibar, East Africa: A time series analysis. *American Journal of Tropical Medicine and Hygiene*, *84*(6), 862–869.

Sandalli, A. (2021). The macroeconomic implications of climate change on sub-Saharan Africa: A case for sustainable development. *Review of Business and Economics Studies*, *9*(1), 8–36.

Serdeczny, O., Adams, S., Baarsch, F., Coumou, D., Robinson, A., Hare, W., Schaeffer, M., Perrette, M., & Reinhardt, J. (2017). Climate change impacts in Sub-Saharan Africa: From physical changes to their social repercussions. *Regional Environmental Change*, *17*, 1585–1600. https://doi.org/10.1007/s10113-015-0910-2

Smith, K. R., Woodward, A., Campbell-Lendrum, D., Chadee, D. D., Honda, Y., Liu, Q., Olwoch, J. M., Revich, B., & Sauerborn, R. (2014). Human health: Impacts, adaptation and co-benefits. In *Climate change 2014: Impacts, adaptation and vulnerability. Contribution of working group II to the fifth assessment report of the intergovernmental panel on climate change.* Cambridge University Press.

Taylor, S. (2020). Anxiety disorders, climate change, and the challenges ahead: Introduction to the special issue. *Journal of Anxiety Disorders*, *76*, 102313. https://doi.org/10.1016/j.janxdis.2020.102313

UNICEF Mozambique. (2013, February 1–2). *Flood emergency preparedness and response: Situation report.* United Nations International Children's Emergency Fund (UNICEF). https://docplayer.net/4085074-Situation-report-unicef-mozambique-reporting-period-february-1-2-2013-flood-emergency-preparedness-and-response.html

United Nations. (2020, October 27). *Climate change is an increasing threat to Africa.* United Nations. https://unfccc.int/news/climate-change-is-an-increasing-threat-to-africa

Upadhyay, R. K. (2020). Markers for global climate change and its impact on social, biological and ecological systems: A review. *American Journal of Climate Change*, *9*(3), 159–203. https://doi.org/10.4236/ajcc.2020.93012

Van der Merwe, E., Clance, M., & Yitbarek, E. (2022). Climate change and child malnutrition: A Nigerian perspective. *Food Policy*. https://doi.org/10.1016/j.foodpol.2022.102281

WHO. (2009). *Protecting health from climate change: Connecting science, policy and people* (pp. 1–36). World Health Organization.

WHO. (2021, October 30). *Climate change and health*. World Health Organization. www.who.int/news-room/fact-sheets/detail/climate-change-and-health

World Bank. (2022). *World development indicators*. The World Bank.

3 Fifty Years of Excellence and Beyond

The Electrical and Electronic Industry of Penang, Malaysia

Hong Liang and Hooi Hooi Lean

3.1 Introduction

With its gradual and phenomenal economic growth since the early years of the 1970s, Penang has been successfully transformed into a worldwide international electronics manufacturing center based in Asia (Van der Velden, 2014). According to Amirul (2023), the electrical and electronics (E&E) industry is characterized as an industry that creates electronic gear for enterprises and gadget items for consumers including TVs, handheld gadgets and printed circuit sheets. The Malaysian E&E sector may be separated into four sub-areas: electronic components, consumer electronics, industrial electronics and electrical goods.

As per the information provided by the Performance Management and Delivery Unit of Malaysia (PEMANDU), there are 5,000 E&E corporations which are widely accessible in Malaysia as at 2022. The E&E industry was identified as a key driver of the Penang's industrial economy and has succeeded in attracting large quantum's of foreign investments and also in creating a valued range of job opportunities for the Northern Peninsular Malaysia.

The E&E industry was regarded as the country's largest economic growth node, as it contributed to the highest quantum of imported and exported products. The National Key Economic Areas (NKEA) initiative have set the E&E sector as a strategic objective which will be utilized to outfit the country towards a top-level income economy by focusing on high-worth and high-development-producing activities. E&E sector is also a major contributor to Malaysia's export earnings (Daud et al., 2021). According to the Malaysian Department of Statistics, Malaysia's principal exports include electrical and electronic items (36%), chemicals (7.1%), petroleum products (7.0%), liquefied natural gas (6%) and palm oil (5.1%). Furthermore, Malaysia's overall commerce for January 2022 was RM203 billion, a 24.8% year-on-year (YoY) rise, with exports of RM110.7 billion (+23.5% YoY) and imports of RM92.3 billion (+26.4% YoY) (Azman, 2022).

The National Export Council has identified E&E as the leading industry that promotes the inclusion of domestic organizations in the global supply chain given its importance in the development of new knowledge-based,

DOI: 10.4324/9781003349204-3

high-tech and value-added industries. According to the Economic Report (Ministry of Finance, 2023), manufactured goods accounted for 86.6% of overall exports, while E&E products accounted for 35.7% of total manufactured goods exports. This figure highlights the significance of E&E exports to the economy. This also demonstrates that the economic growth of Malaysia is heavily dependent on the export of E&E goods, which developed an export-centric approach to help promote stable economic growth in Malaysia.

Penang consists of a small island and a larger mainland in northern Malaysia on the west coast of the Peninsular. In the 1970s, the manufacturing sector can be regarded as the starting point of the economic success of the State. It adopted a series of strategies, including the strategy of industrial clusters, multinational cooperative trade and the intensive formation of multinational companies, which enabled Penang to obtain positive economic benefits from its industrial clusters and the positive policies of the government and make its own electronic industry prosperous, thus promoting Malaysia's economic growth. The United Nations has also named Penang as one of the world's top ten "most unique industrial clusters" (EPU, 2018). Therefore, Penang is famous for its powerful industrial development, especially in the E&E industry.

In recent years, industrialization has been identified as an important engine for economic growth in Penang. Penang's economy has grown mostly as a result of the promotional usage of the notion of a free trade zone in order to stimulate and attract foreign investment in export-oriented sectors (Aggarwal, 2022). The support of the Penang State government is also an important reason for Penang's economic growth, such as the promulgation of the Free Zones Act 1990 (Act 438), which allowed the international manufacturing and multinational companies to trade freely in Penang.

In 1972, the first electronic multinational company was established in Penang, which initiated the gradual rise of the electronics industry which also brought considerable economic benefits to Penang's trade. The industrialized economic policy since 1969 has been implemented since then and still prevails until today. It not only encourages foreign direct investment (FDI) but also creates economic prospects in Penang. It gives additional opportunities for local entrepreneurs in terms of the multiplier effects to become the pillar industry of foreign multinational corporations (Alavi, 1996) operating in Penang.

With the support of the government, the emergence of industrial clusters and multinational companies has created an increasingly powerful electronic manufacturing industry, and Penang has been developed into Asia's worldwide electronic manufacturing hub (Van der Velden, 2014) as the "Silicon Valley of the East". As a major export-oriented manufacturing center, Penang has positioned itself as one of the most industrialized states in Malaysia (Ercan et al., 2013). Due to the improvement of global export demand during the US–China trade war, Penang's trade surplus continued to expand, which also provided an opportunity for the export of Penang's electronics industry to benefit from.

Penang promises to make sustainable development one of its top priorities, which means that the electronics industry will become the pillar of Penang's long-term economic growth. Therefore, the attention towards maintaining a good environment, enhanced society building and good governance will attract great attention and become the starting point to achieve sustainability, mainly because these environment-friendly, society-focused and enlightened governance approaches in public administration are consistent with the vision of Penang 2030 "a family centered green smart state to inspire the rest of the country" (Aggarwal, 2022). Many local companies benefited from this dynamic ecosystem in the process of symbiotic co-development with the multinational companies of Bayan Lepas FIZ and the Prai Industrial Estate. In this regard, Penang brings great economic benefits to Malaysia through the electronic industry. Penang has a 30% representation in the Malaysian Electromechanical industry (Ariffin & Figueiredo, 2004). As a result, Penang's economy has undergone a dramatic evolution, from an initial agricultural and trade oriented economy in the late 1960s, while leading Malaysia into becoming an industrialized country with a diversified and extensively sophisticated economic structure.

On the other hand, while Penang developed its favorable competitive advantage and stable economic growth in the 1970s and 1990s, the state must cope with the increasingly fierce competition from the region and other emerging economies (Menon, 2018). This is because Penang is under pressure as a viable investment destination in the face of the rise of China and the positive development of other countries such as Thailand, Vietnam and India (Ansar et al., 2016).

Penang today celebrated its 50th anniversary of industrialization, which means the success and sustainable development of the electronic manufacturing sector in Penang in the present year of 2022. The successful transformation of Penang in the past 50 years shows the unlimited potential for Penang, and the electronic manufacturing industry has laid a solid foundation for Penang's economy. The official slogan chosen for the celebration is "50 years of excellence and beyond", which describes Penang's ambition to use this springboard to cooperate with all stakeholders and take the digitalization, continuous excellence and innovation-driven high-income economy as the strategic driving goals for the state (Ahmad, 2020). Since 1972, Malaysia had established the first free trade zone in Penang, which has attracted important investment from eight multinational companies (known as the eight heroes). Penang had transformed itself from a traditional seaport economy to an "Oriental Silicon Valley". This marks the development of a strong auxiliary industry ecosystem, consolidating Penang's dominant position as a pioneer offshore manufacturing base for multinational companies and improving Penang's importance as a center for sophisticated manufacturing and high-value-added upstream businesses. More importantly, in the past 50 years, Penang has also cultivated many local technology entrepreneurs, company founders and construction companies, who enjoy a high reputation in the world with their own capabilities.

Known as the Oriental Silicon Valley, Penang is the main assembling base of many E&E items in Malaysia and is perhaps one of the world's most powerful focus points for semiconductor and E&E gadget production on the planet, representing an impressive 5% of worldwide semiconductor production and send outs. In 2020, Penang's commodity volume surpassed RM300 billion, 82% of which came from electrical hardware and expert, logical and control instruments (counting in medical and clinical gear). It is a significant fact that Penang produced RM110 billion (US$27 billion) of the exchange surplus in 2020, addressing 60% of Malaysia's aggregate trade (Kementerian Kewangan Malaysia, 2022).

Therefore, this study will provide a valuable and timely perspective to the academics and industry players and enable the policymakers to have a deeper understanding about the development, competitive advantages and challenges of the E&E industry in Penang. This study also helps to fill the literature gap in knowledge on the competitive advantages and challenges faced by the E&E industry in Penang.

3.2 The Development of the E&E Industry in Penang

Penang's economic and social development as an agglomeration can be summarized into five stages – the first stage was in the 1970s, when the export-oriented manufacturing industry was adopted in accordance with the Investment Incentive Act of 1968 (Act 199), and The Free Trade Zone Act 1971 (Act 24). The Penang Development Corporation (PDC) is a Penang state-government linked company (GLC), and a major development organization that operates outside of the formal government framework (Arndt, 1992). PDC is able to perform its duties as the center for the creation, execution and coordination of an industrialization plan that is focused on exports because it is imbued with a well-designed independent organizational structure. In addition, the publicity efforts and financial incentives provided by the government have also helped attract multinational companies to establish manufacturing bases in Penang. This shows that PDC has successfully created an impression of a united and cooperative team in the business community, firmly committed to promoting foreign direct investment (FDI) inflows into Penang State. In addition to giving an appealing venture capital climate through the establishment of the free trade zones (FTZ) (known as free industrial zones) and licensed manufacturing warehouses (LMW), the government also provided investors in the electronics industry with a special ten-year pioneer status incentive (Kofoed & Fonnesbech, 2000). The Penang state government has clearly and forcefully switched its strategy toward export-oriented industrialization, with the electronics sector (inclusive of electronic and electrical products) serving as the primary target of investment promotion. The industrial cluster focus strategy in turn provides a viable environment to promote linkages between transnational companies (TNCs) and small and medium enterprises (SMEs) in export centers and to create a "skills pool", which has proved highly successful, thus being the primary fascination of Penang as an area for TNCs in a large number of businesses with an electronic base. At this stage, the opening of factories in the Penang Free Trade Zone marks a good start for Penang as a foreign trade and economic growth center.

In 1980, the first industrial master plan (IMP) was launched, and the export processing zone was actively promoted from the government usage and consumer electronic parts to full assembly, which can be regarded as the second stage of Penang's development. With the development of precision molds and back-end automation, local small- and medium-sized enterprises are gradually rising. PDC effectively utilized the free trade zones and industrial parks as instruments for key framework improvement in order to accomplish successful worldwide integration of Penang's economy. By the mid-1980s, the number of companies had increased to 52, employing 23,454 workers (Achchuthan & Velnampy, 2013). By carrying out vocational training programs, PDC has played an important role in promoting the absorption of labor by newly established multinational companies. In the late 1980s, when the skills shortage began to hinder the development of the electronics industry, PDC and several multinational companies established the Penang Skills Development Center (PSDC).

From the 1990s to the beginning of the 21st century, the electromechanical manufacturing industry emerged as a place for offshore design and development activities. For example, Intel established a design center in 2001. Electromechanical companies have become the preferred center of excellence and GBS venue for global electromechanical participants. PDC emphasizes the development of domestic supplier networks around the branches of multinational companies. This helped towards expanding the economic impact of TNCs on the domestic economy through the multiplier impact, and it strengthens the anchoring of foreign investors in export centers by fostering closer and more appropriate supplier connections (Garcia Calvo, 2021). Since the early 1990s, the unemployment rate in Penang has stayed unchanged moving between a range from 0.5% to 2.5% every year, which is far lower than the national unemployment average in a range of 1.5%–4.5% (Athukorala, 2014). Accordingly, the manufacturing sector continued expanding with 45.9% of the Penang's GDP in 2010, compared to the 23.4% for Malaysia as a whole (Table 3.1). It shows that the manufacturing of Penang has become the economic pillar of Malaysia.

Figure 3.1 shows that the trade performance of E&E products maintained a strong growth momentum as at April 2021. The value of E&E products was RM387.81 billion, accounting for 69.9% of the total exports. It is an

Table 3.1 Manufacturing output as percentage of GDP

	1970	*1980*	*1990*	*2010*
Penang	12.7	40.0	46.6	45.9
Malaysia	12.2	20.0	27.0	23.4

Source: EPU (1976, 1986, 1991a, 1991b, 2003)

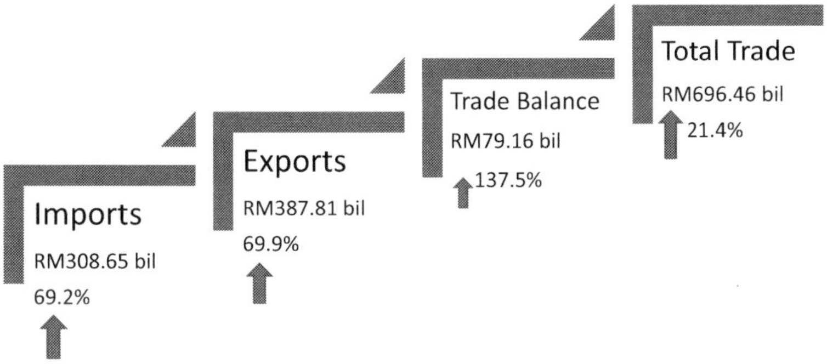

Figure 3.1 Trade Performance (2021)

increase of 42.1% compared to April 2020. The exports growth is due to the increase in global demand for E&E products (mainly semiconductors), the development of digital and 5G technologies, and the increase in demand for rubber products and petroleum products according to the Digital News Asia (2021). The E&E imports increased to approximately RM308.65 billion, accounting for 69.2% of the total imports, a growth of 54.9% compared to April 2020. Therefore, the E&E industry plays a main contributor role in Malaysia's trade performance.

In the 2010s, the E&E manufacturing industry became a leader in producing memory and data storage, and a key manufacturing center for the Outsourced Semiconductor and Test (OSAT) and equipment manufacturing activities. With the rise of the local non-manufacturing enterprises, the industry began providing integrated circuit design, product development and engineering services (Lai, 2005). This then stimulated a new wave of global first-class medical device companies to set up offices in Penang. This is because the E&E plants could operate from either a high production and low-mixing platform or alternatively in a high mixing and low-production platform to maintain competitiveness. In this regard, the E&E sector promotes the value chain to enter the high-tech and high-value range of activities (Panennungi, 2017). The incentive measures taken by the state government includes attempts in trying to encourage more companies to set up operations in Penang. The federal government also encourages enterprise-level skill development by providing extensive tax breaks for multinational firms' contributions to the PSDC program and their own skill development efforts

(Lall, 2000). PDC has established an institutional mechanism to maintain close contact with subsidiaries of multinational companies and local companies operating in Penang. This helps decision makers keep up with the requirements of investors, so as to constantly adapt to the changing investment environment. More significantly, this acceptance technique encourages existing foreign enterprises in Penang to join in investment promotional efforts. PDC frequently uses these firms' reference materials to support the government's commitment to investment promotion.

The E&E industry currently produces 8% of the global back-end semiconductor production (Hutchinson, 2017). Due to the trade war between the US and China, more investment inflows occurred. These companies will benefit from advanced technology achievement themes, such as 5G, sensors, automatic vehicles and the Internet of Things. Penang has experienced 50 years of industrialization (including alternating boom and recessionary times like during the Asian financial crisis and stiff competition from Chinese and other competitor countries) and is recognized as having a strong foundation of electromechanical enterprises (Dogan et al., 2013). The involvement of the government, as well as a variety of policies and institutions, has been cited as being critical to the establishment of the electromechanical agglomeration in Penang (Jing et al., 2021). In 2021, the total export of the E&E industry was RM35.4 billion (5-year CAGR: 13%); The total trade surplus was RM101b (five-year CAGR: 18%).

3.3 Competitive Advantages

Since the 1970s, Penang's economy has seen exponential growth. Penang has evolved into a major worldwide hub for electronic manufacturing in Asia (Van der Velden, 2014). The Malaysian Reserve (2023) reports that the manufacturing output of Malaysia increased by 2.1% in 2020. Manufacturing of E&E goods is a major contributor to this enormous economic growth. Hence, we next discuss the main five competitive advantages that lead to the resounding success of the E&E industry in Penang.

PDC's legal standing as a statutory entity allows it to fulfill national objectives in areas where government agencies would encounter institutional and procedural impediments and restrictions. Its goal is to enhance the attractiveness of the industry through the air transport of materials and products to industries such as semiconductors, clinical hardware and other accuracy-based and machining ventures. PDC has successfully communicated the required talents and flexibility of Penang's skilled workforce to the investing sources worldwide, which may effectively complement and support the advancement of the component assembly technology industry in Penang's high-tech industrial sector (Perbadanan Pembangunan Pulau Pinang, 1990).

At the same time, PDC has the characteristics and legal status as an authorized corporate entity to provide investors in Penang with efficient and fast one-stop investment advisory, approval and convenience services. The stature of PDC as the benchmark of legally authorized institutions in Penang that cater to the needs of investors is well established. To foster and maintain strong investor relationships while also attracting new investments and reinvestment, the chairman of PDC led numerous delegations on frequent visits to the CEOs of potential companies in Penang. These interactions laid the foundation for future win-win cooperation in investment and the development of Penang (Mohan, 2010).

The Penang Export Hub is a novel illustration of the government's collaboration with the industry as part of its development focus. It creates new opportunities for global specialization through the worldwide cycle of creation and sharing. For example, the establishment of business links between MNEs with assembly plants in Penang and local enterprises is an integral part of the national export-oriented development strategy (Kharas, 1954). This policy is primarily concerned about creating a conducive environment to enhance the establishment of domestic supplier networks around the operation of subsidiaries of multinational enterprises operating locally. Many of the local enterprises in Penang that have risen again through product sharing have become global enterprises themselves with their own strengths and their production bases are distributed in many countries.

The Penang state government uses its policies and effective management practices not only to draw more foreign investors into the E&E industry investment project but also to help those investors establish roots in the local economy. Examples of this include the establishment of a free trade zone, the improvement of infrastructure, the development of skills and career opportunities, and the promotion of investments (Lim, 2005). Fostering the supplier network of the local companies around the locally established branches of the MNE is an indispensable piece of the general investment ratio strategy. This novel strategy helps anchor foreign investors in export centers through closer and more appropriate support connections, networking, supply and infrastructure.

Athukorala (2017) stated that the cluster approach in Penang can be considered as a competitive advantage as it provides a desirable environment for enhancing the linkages between transnational corporations (TNCs) and local enterprises in export hubs, such as investment, communication and cooperation. In this sense, the E&E sector of Penang is defined as an international connectivity cluster. The cluster is backed by foreign and domestic multinational firms and is built on policies that encourage innovation at the national and regional levels. Lye King and Mohan (2010) pointed out that Penang's innovation activities mainly include four prediction factors: (1) human resources; (2) cheap fees; (3) entrepreneurial culture; (4) feasible industry methods.

In addition to national organizations, significant players in the Penang regional innovation system include PSDC, universities, training institutes, international corporations and supplier networks. While the enterprise connections within the cluster are weak, the global connections within the enterprise are relatively strong (Rasiah, 2002). This strong orientation guide and connections to the headquarters or R&D centers of multinational companies and the main users in technologically advanced countries have produced a connection mode, in which enterprises can use to "leapfrog" over the enterprises of competitors in neighboring ASEAN countries. The business model encourages the formation of close ties with suppliers inside and outside of Penang. To add advantages on this scenario, the establishment of PSDC provides relevant technical training and skill development for local suppliers to enhance the supply chain. It has a close relationship not only with the Universiti Sains Malaysia (USM) but also with other universities outside of Penang. Cross Organizational Cooperation-centric projects with lecturers and internship students also have a significantly positive effect on supporting innovative activities.

In general, the competitive advantage of Penang can be analyzed and summarized from a wide multi-level spectrum of angles. Penang's advantages are directly tied to its cluster basis and the government's active collaboration – at the national level, the fundamental elements for the successful growth of Penang's economy are related to the government's effective policies and the driving force of free trade (Shafaeddin, 2014). In terms of Penang's policies, the Ministry of International Trade and Industry (MITI) and the Ministry of Science, Technology, and Innovation (MOSTI) are well aware of the progress of Penang's E&E industry, demonstrating that the local government actively supports national industrial development and related innovation policies (Haniff, 1994). In order to actively cooperate with the innovation of industrial activities, the government gives supportive incentives and grants according to R&D activities undertaken. Penang's highly skilled talents and cooperative suppliers have collectively improved Penang's economy and productivity (Henderson & Phillips, 2007). In this regard, Penang's strong industrial base and the active support policies of the national and state governments have played an important role in its establishment, maintenance and settlement in Penang (Mahathir, 2003). For example, the significant quantity of engineering personnel available in the cluster (after decades of internal training) as well as the assistance of national and state governments – incentive support – are essential components in Intel Penang's R&D efforts (via tax rebates, grants and other non-financial support). The key link is the internal connection with various laboratories around the world and the flow of engineers. Intel is a good example. Intel designated the Indian Institute of Technology (IIT-K) in Kanpur, India, as one of the main research sites, with the goal of assisting USM in establishing relationships with IIT-K to strengthen its research capacity (Lim, 1991). This collaboration is significant, since it includes R&D in the fields of engineering and computer science, as well as innovative initiatives to maximize its benefits. It also involves lecturers from the Indian Institute of technology who are to share their professional knowledge in research and development at USM (OECD, 2020). This will provide useful direction and information for USM and their partner organization's own development (Ming, 2021). Therefore, the economic engine that transformed Malaysia from a low-income country into an upper middle-income country relied heavily on these comparative advantages which are based on low labor costs, combined with favorable framework conditions and incentives, and an infrastructure attracting FDI (Wang, 2022).

Bayan Lepas Free Trade Zone is a mature E&E center with over 300 multinational firms, including Intel, Bosch, and AMD, as well as over 3,000 small- and medium-sized industries. The economic restructuring caused by the US–China trade war, as well as the spike in worldwide demand for computer servers, storage media, mobile phones, video games and other auxiliary items as a result of working from home, have boosted Penang's E&E sector. Due to its youthful multilingual talent pool, supply chain ecology and infrastructure, Malaysia enjoys an edge over other Southeast Asian countries in attracting foreign investments (Tan, 2002).

Penang's key advantage over Japan, Singapore, Taiwan, the EU and the US is that it can deliver cheaper talent. The primary problem of China is its unpredictability in financial markets, including weakening global demand, weak currency and trade tensions. Labor prices are growing at an unsustainable rate, making China more costly than Penang. Penang is more advantageous, especially when international corporations strive to develop a long-term strategy, because of its political stability. Another advantage of Penang (particularly for the multinational corporations based in Europe and the US) is that the majority of Malaysians speak English. Penang's living atmosphere is one of the best in the world.

3.4 Challenges

The challenges faced by the E&E industry can be summarized into a few points succinctly: insufficient innovation and human capital formation. The innovation of the E&E industry needs to be improved and indeed constantly and consistently improved to keep ahead of the game. For example, in Malaysia, the E&E product exports' local added value accounts for only 44%, while in China and Indonesia, this item accounts for 70% and 68%, respectively (The Star, 2021).

A consistent area of industry feedback is the shortage of high-end and low-end talents in the E&E industry within Penang. On the contrary, the problem related to talent shortage is the demand for foreign expertise. According to previous research, the challenges faced by employees of Penang in the E&E industry are mainly their lack of technical knowledge, lack of understanding of the use of digital tools, and limited access to technology. Therefore, Penang's demand for foreign labor is expanding. In addition, the shortage of skilled workers in Malaysia has become the biggest E&E industry challenge in Penang due to the strong demand for digital technology trained labor. In addition, there is a shortage of technical and engineering personnel (Akmal, 2021). The state's business network has helped coordinate payroll and employee recruitment, thus reducing the incidences of employee poaching. The nationwide shortage of engineers may hinder the development of the country, especially in the fields of manufacturing and software development (Hutchinson, 2008). Datuk Jimmy Ong, former chairman of the Malaysian Manufacturers' Federation (FMM) in Penang, said that as the country is recovering from the COVID-19 pandemic with many factories increasing their production, the collective sense of being forced to face a talent shortage is now getting much stronger.

There are three reasons for the lack of talent in Penang. First of all, about three years ago, several large-scale FDI were confirmed nationwide. Many large local companies have lost a large number of engineers due to the newly established multinational companies (Jacobsen, 2009). Second, it is due to the COVID-19 epidemic outbreaks. Many factories are unable to operate at full capacity, and production-ready inventory is overstocked. Global demand is now surging upwards, and factories are in urgent need of skilled manpower.

The third reason is the low admission rate of engineering students in colleges and universities. Chief Minister Chow Kon Yeow added:

> [T]he education system needs to be revisited. STEM (Science, Technology, Engineering and Mathematics) subjects are not given enough attention. A factory in Penang needs 200 engineers. I went to a public university in Pahang to attract senior students there, but the enrollment rate for engineering students is very low – perhaps because the epidemic makes them afraid to move to Penang.
>
> (Dewi, 2023)

Besides that, Penang lacks enough innovator individuals, businesses and institutions – to generate the rapid innovation wave needed to move industries and societies towards an age of technology management (TM) 4 and 5 level operations. Penang's high-tech Industrial Cluster in Malaysia is an example of the low innovation ability of enterprises (Musa, 2020). Although Penang's technology and management capabilities are better than the production concentration zones in other regions, the added value of assembly-type operations has been low, partly due to the lack of cultivation by the regional government authorities. Skill formation is the weakness of cluster dynamics which is required for innovation and upgrading, which unavoidably requires the support of enterprises and governments working together in tandem (Jomo & Hui, 2002). Although some companies have been developed to an advanced degree, there are not enough of these types of companies within the cluster or within the state or country. Those companies that are developing these capabilities lack sufficient networks and technical differences to develop these capabilities in the region (Murray, 2021). Therefore, the lack of their skills and information processing abilities is the main disadvantage of achieving a superior innovation culture within the community.

On the other hand, more than 10,000 workers were unemployed in Penang in 2020, accounting for about 10% of the total unemployed in Malaysia (SOCSO, 2020). It is worth noting that according to SOCSO (2020), highly skilled jobs account for 49.2% of total job losses in Penang (Malaysia: 61%). Professionals, managers, technicians and assistant professionals are among those affected. Another 28.2% of layoffs were attributable to factory workers, machine operators and assembler-type job layoffs (semi-skilled workers) (Sucher & Gupta, 2023). As the employment of graduates is still a highly challenging affair, it will further lead to the problem of skills mismatch and underemployment of graduates in the annual process of job hunting. In addition to these considerations, the employment problem in Penang focuses on low-wage jobs (Mok, 2020). According to the report, about 57.7% of Penang's employees were employed with monthly wages below RM1,000, and around 33.5% were between RM1,000 and RM1,499 per month until December 2021 (Surendran, 2021). Only 3.5% of employees' employment placement was found to have offered monthly wages of RM3,000 and above.

On the top of that depressing situation, Penang lacks venture capitalists (the emergence of venture capitalists should ideally be stimulated by the local open system and its strong network relationships), which is an obstacle to creating or attracting new innovative enterprises (Athukorala, 2011). An industrial cluster has emerged in Penang, but the lack of progress after that in new product development capabilities and lack of innovation and open system business models are limiting the growth. Rising production costs and intensifying competition from China and the Philippines have also slowed growth (Weragoda, 2019). Despite encouraging developments, such as the establishment of the Altera Corporation's E&E Design facilities, the first independent design studio, there is still a shortage of skills required for chip design, system integration and application engineering (Kim & Lee, 2022). Improvement of the production and organizational capacity of industrial enterprises is paramount essential, because it is highly relevant to the driving force of a productivity-based developmental strategy of the manufacturing cluster in Penang. Thus, to achieve this and to be ahead of that game, Penang has to put in more efforts and be strategically pro-active to ensure an adequate supply of relevant skills (Leng, 2021).

3.5 Conclusion

Given the contribution of the E&E industry to the expansion of other industries, its impact on the national economy is significantly huge (Productivity Performance, 2017). Therefore, although Malaysia's exports are diversified, with many types of commodities and products, almost all export commodities will be affected when the electromechanical industry slows down. As the electromechanical industry accounts for 30–40% of manufacturing exports, it has had a great impact on the country's economy (PEMANDU, 2011). In other words, any negative occurrence striking the E&E industry's well-being such as a downturn will reduce manufacturing investment, which will then subsequently slow down the country's economic development (Yeoh et al., 2009).

According to the aforementioned discussion, the competitive advantages of the E&E industry in Penang have more than its fair share of challenges. Penang's E&E industry can be summarized into the following information differentials about its characteristics, developed manufacturing base and enterprise network:

1. Penang provides a powerful production platform for multinational companies.
2. Multinational corporations have developed world-class manufacturing capacity in mass production of single products, and there are many examples of multi-product processing operations.
3. Multinational corporations from the US tend to rely on the focused locality for their operations and the online business model, horizontal integration, collective learning and public–private cooperation for skill formation and technology management.
4. An open-system industrial zone is taking shape. In this industrial zone, almost all activities required for rapid development of mass production on the basis of the JIT (Just-In-Time) concept are located in the same place.
5. The electronics sector is driven by global organizations that compete in product development. These forces can be used to strengthen local capabilities.
6. PDC is a typical intermediary and catalyst organization that acts according to collective needs and helps local enterprises seize the development and collaborative opportunities created by transnational corporations operating locally.
7. PSDC is an outstanding example of public–private partnership to meet the internal and external skill needs of the industry.
8. The formation of company skills training has created a powerful "invisible college", which has greatly increased the social, technical and educational capital of the region. Such an example is the so-called "Intel University" and the "Motorola College" which had been formed by their respective MNCs operating in Penang with the purpose of upgrading the skills, expertise and innovative capabilities of their employees.
9. The Penang Industrialized Zones have developed some local capabilities in new product design. According to this strategy, the region can further develop cutting-edge technology services.
10. The Penang Industrialized Zones have also developed a positive interpersonal relationship among stakeholders and industry players. Some cooperation-based capabilities of the Silicon Valley-based companies have been improved under the guidance of PDC.
11. The Penang Industrialized Zones have also a higher-than-average supply and presence of scientists and engineers.

There are very aggressive competitors around every corner along its very rocky path to the future. Fierce competition, like China and Vietnam, has the likely potential to unseat Penang from its lofty premier position in the scheme of things. Thailand, the Philippines, Singapore and Indonesia are the next line of competitors that could threaten the premier position of Penang as the preferred site location for global companies. Besides these fierce competing foreign locations, Penang must also contend with domestic competition from the other states within Malaysia.

Besides the need to keep ahead of the competition, Penang needs to be a "game changer" that will ensure its premier position as a preferred manufacturing base and E&E industrial center. This can be achieved by making strategic efforts and investments to cultivating the higher-value and higher-yield elements, processes, activities and production while maintaining the lower- and mid-range E&E industry value-chain production. Instead of just relying on mere component assembly functions, Penang could perhaps consider to cultivate more investments and efforts into attracting the higher-end chain of R&D. In order to achieve this, a prerequisite requirement is to make greater efforts into education, training and development, skill and expertise building of the workforce and the population.

PSDC, USM, other institutes of higher learning as well as primary and secondary schools need to work together with the industries themselves and the government to create a sufficiently ideal environment that nurtures and develops all these kinds of talents, skills and expertise. There is a very firm need to establish and encourage students towards mastering and excelling in STEM subjects. More of such endeavors are required if Penang is to firmly hold on to its premier global position within the E&E nexus which cannot be underestimated and taken for granted given that the connectivity and symbiotic relationship with many other non-E&E industries and export products are highly dependent on the well-being of the E&E industry (Velnampy, 2013). There is therefore a great need to constantly innovate and be creative as a survival means and industry leadership strategy that must be constantly adopted and practiced.

References

Achchuthan, S., & Velnampy, T. (2013). Export, import and economic growth: Evidence from Sri Lanka. *Journal of Economics and Sustainable Development*, *4*(9), 147–155. https://doi.org/10.7176/jesd

Aggarwal, A. (2022). *Special economic zones in the Indonesia-Malaysia-Thailand growth triangle: Opportunities for collaboration*. Asian Development Bank.

Ahmad, S. (2020). Impact of international trade policies at Indonesia Malaysia Thailand growth triangle. *International Journal of Psychosocial Rehabilitation*, *24*(1), 707–716. https://doi.org/10.37200/ijpr/v24i1/pr200174

Akmal, R. (2021, November 28). Penang ready to celebrate Golden Jubilee of its industrialisation journey next year. *Buletin Mutiara*. Retrieved December 11, 2022, from www.buletinmutiara.com/penang-ready-to-celebrate-golden-jubilee-of-its-in dustrialisation-journey-next-year/

Alavi, R. (1996). *Industrialization in Malaysia import substitution and infant industry performance*. Routledge studies in the growth economies of Asia (Vol. 7, 1st ed.). Routledge.

Amirul. (2023). Outlook for the E&E industry in Malaysia. *MIDA*. Retrieved October 1, 2023, from https://www.mida.gov.my/outlook-for-the-ee-industry-in-malaysia/

Ansar, A., Flyvbjerg, B., Budzier, A., & Lunn, D. (2016). Does infrastructure investment lead to economic growth or economic fragility? Evidence from China. *Oxford Review of Economic Policy*, *32*(3), 360–390. https://doi.org/10.1093/oxrep/grw022

Ariffin, N., & Figueiredo, P. N. (2004). Internationalization of innovative capabilities: Counter-evidence from the electronics industry in Malaysia and Brazil. *Oxford Development Studies*, *32*(4), 559–583. https://doi.org/10.1080/1360081042000293344

Arndt, H. W. (1992). *Growth and structural change in the Malaysian economy*. Jomo Kwame Sundaram. *Economic Development and Cultural Change*, *40*(4), 894–896. https://doi.org/10.1086/451985

Athukorala, P.-C. (2011). *Growing with global production sharing: The tale of Penang export hub* (Departmental Working Papers No. 2011–13). The Australian National University, Arndt-Corden Department of Economics.

Athukorala, P.-C. (2014). Growing with global production sharing: The tale of Penang export hub, Malaysia. *Competition & Change*, *18*(3), 221–245. https://doi.org/10.1179/1024529414z.00000000058

Athukorala, P.-C. (2017). Global Productions sharing and local entrepreneurship in developing countries: Evidence from Penang export hub, Malaysia. *Asia & The Pacific Policy Studies*, *4*(2), 180–194. https://doi.org/10.1002/app5.171

Azman, N. H. (2022). Malaysia's exports grew to RM110.7b in Jan 2022. *The Malaysian Reserve*. Retrieved October 1, 2023, from https://themalaysianreserve.com/2022/02/18/malaysias-exports-grew-to-rm110-7b-in-jan-2022/

Daud, F. E., Ponrahono, Z., Abdul Aziz, F., Rahman, S. A., & Sahrir, S. (2021). A framework of the energy-efficient vehicle initiative and its implementation in a developed country: The case of Malaysia. *Malaysian Journal of Social Sciences and Humanities (MJSSH)*, *6*(3), 297–312. https://doi.org/10.47405/mjssh.v6i3.715

Dewi, K. K. (2023). Stemming students' loss of interest in STEM. *The Star*. Retrieved October 2, 2023, from https://www.thestar.com.my/metro/metro-news/2023/09/02/stemming-students-loss-of-interest-in-stem

Digital News Asia. (2021). *Digital economy*. Retrieved October 1, 2023, from https://www.digitalnewsasia.com/digital-economy

Dogan, E., Wong, K. N., & Yap, M. M. (2013). Turnover, ownership and productivity in Malaysian manufacturing. *Journal of the Asia Pacific Economy*, *18*(1), 26–50. https://doi.org/10.1080/13547860.2012.742714

Economic Planning Unit (EPU). (2018). *Malaysia productivity blueprint*. Prime Minister's Department. www.epu.gov.my/en/content/malaysia-productivity-blueprint

Economic Planning Unit–Malaysia [EPU]. (1976). *Third Malaysia Plan, 1976–1980*. Government Printers.

Economic Planning Unit–Malaysia [EPU]. (1986). *Fifth Malaysia Plan, 1986–1990*. Government Printers.

Economic Planning Unit–Malaysia [EPU]. (1991a). *Sixth Malaysia Plan, 1991–1995*. Government Printers.

Economic Planning Unit–Malaysia [EPU]. (1991b). *The Second Outline Perspective Plan*, 1991–2000. Government Printers.

Economic Planning Unit–Malaysia [EPU]. (2003). *Mid-term Review of the Eighth Malaysia Plan*, 2001–2005. Government Printers.

Ercan, A., Kavvas, M. L., & Abbasov, R. K. (2013). Case study II: Sea level change at peninsular Malaysia and Sabah-Sarawak. In *Long-range dependence and sea level forecasting* (pp. 39–48). Springer. https://doi.org/10.1007/978-3-319-01505-7_5

Garcia Calvo, A. (2021, September 23). Economic development, upgrading, and coordination. In *State-firm coordination and upgrading: Reaching the efficiency frontier in skill-, capital-, and knowledge-intensive industries in Spain and South Korea* (Online ed.). Oxford Academic. Retrieved December 11, 2022, from https://doi.org/10.1093/oso/9780198864561.003.0001

Haniff, N. O. O. R. (1994). The current status and future of electronics manufacturing in Penang. *Journal of Electronics Manufacturing*, *4*(4), 167–175. https://doi.org/10.1142/s0960313194000183

Henderson, J., & Phillips, R. (2007). Unintended consequences: Social policy, state institutions and the 'stalling' of the Malaysian industrialization project. *Economy and Society*, *36*(1), 78–102. https://doi.org/10.1080/03085140601089853

Hutchinson, F. E. (2008). Developmental state and economic growth at the subregional level: The case of Penang. In *Institute of Southeast Asian Studies (ISEAS), Southeast Asian studies 2008* (pp. 223–244). ISEAS.

Hutchinson, F. E. (2017). A look back at how Penang learned to shine through its electrical and electronics sector – articles. *Economic History Malaya*. Retrieved December 11, 2022, from www.ehm.my/publications/articles/a-look-back-at-how-penang-learned-to-shine-through-its-electrical-and-electronics-sector

Jacobsen, M. (2009). *Frozen identities: Inter-ethnic relations and economic development in Penang, Malaysia* (Copenhagen Discussion Papers No. 2009–30). Copenhagen Business School (CBS), Asia Research Centre (ARC). https://hdl.handle.net/10398/7909

Jing, C. K., Seng, A. K., & Teck, T. S. (2021). A study on the factors influencing project success in electrical and electronic manufacturing sector in Penang, Malaysia. *Review of International Geographical Education (RIGEO)*, *11*(8), 1113–1142. https://doi.org/10.48047/rigeo.11.08.95

Jomo, K. S., & Hui, W. C. (2002). *The political economy of Malaysian federalism: Economic development, public policy and conflict containment* (WIDER Discussion Paper No. 2002/113). The United Nations University World Institute for Development Economics Research (UNU-WIDER). ISBN 9291903531.

Kementerian Kewangan Malaysia. (2022, July 7). *Ministry of finance official portal*. Retrieved July 11, 2022, from www.mof.gov.my/portal/en

Kharas, H. (1954). *Cities, people, and the economy: A study on positioning Penang*. World Bank. Retrieved December 11, 2022, from https://documents.worldbank.org/en/publication/documents-reports/documentdetail/802841468331912672/cities-people-and-the-economy-a-study-on-positioning-penang

Kim, D., & Lee, S. Y. (2022). When venture capitalists are attracted by the experienced. *Journal of Innovation and Entrepreneurship*, *11*(1), 1–18. https://doi.org/10.1186/s13731-022-00227-2

Kofoed, M., & Fonnesbech, B. (2000). *Sustainable industrial development in Penang*. Institute of Environment, Technology and Social Studies, Roskilde University.

Lai, P. Y. (2005). Value-added manufacturing: A new paradigm. In Lai, P. Y. (Ed.), *Penang into the 21st century* (pp. 51–63). Kuala Lumpur: Pelanduk Publications.

Lall, S. (2000). The technological structure and performance of developing country manufactured exports, 1985–98. *Oxford Development Studies*, *28*(3), 337–369. https://doi.org/10.1080/713688318

Leng, O. W. (2021, December 3). *Challenges and opportunities for Penang's labour market amid the COVID-19 pandemic*. Penang Institute. Retrieved December 11, 2022, from https://penanginstitute.org/publications/issues/challenges-and-opportunities-for-penangs-labour-market-amid-the-covid-19-pandemic/

Lim, C. E. (2005). *Building on Penang's strengths: Going forward*. Penang Lecture. www.seri.com.my

Lim, P. (1991). *Steel: From ashes rebuilt to manufacturing excellence*. Intel Technology.

Lye King, T., & Mohan, A. V. (2010). *Factors of regional innovation system to help firms move up the value chain – a multi-stakeholder study in Penang cluster* [Paper presentation]. Presented at ASIALICS Conference 2010, Taipei.

Mahathir, B. M. (2003). *The prime minister recollects* (pp. 15–18). Strategy & Success, Penang Development Corporation (PDC).

The Malaysian Reserve. (2023). *Malaysia's economy expected to continue to moderate in the near term – DOSM*. Retrieved October 1, 2023, from https://themalaysianreserve.com/2023/09/27/malaysias-economy-expected-to-continue-to-moderate-in-the-near-term-dosm/

Menon, J. (2018, April 23). *Assessing Asian's economic performance*. Retrieved December 11, 2022, from www.thesundaily.my/

Ming, L. S. (2021, December 3). *Trend of investments in Batu Kawan industrial park*. Penang Institute. Retrieved December 11, 2022, from https://penanginstitute.org/publications/issues/trend-of-investments-in-batu-kawan-industrial-park/

Ministry of Finance. (2023). *Kementerian Kewangan Malaysia*. Retrieved October 1, 2023, from https://www.mof.gov.my/portal/en/

Mohan, A. V. (2010). Linkages for fostering innovation activities – case studies of firms in E & E sector of Penang cluster. In P. Intarakumnerd (Ed.), *Fostering production and science and technology linkages to stimulates innovation in ASEAN*. ERIA research project report 2009-7-4 (pp. 87–144). ERIA.

Mok, O. (2020, December 22). State exco: Hotel occupancy rates in Penang hit 82PC on weekends. *Malay Mail*. Retrieved July 11, 2022, from www.malaymail.com/news/malaysia/2020/12/22/state-excohotel-occupancy-rates-in-penang-hit-82pc-on-weekends/1934095

Murray, B. (2021, January 25). Shipping Container Crunch shows signs of easing, index shows. *Bloomberg.com*. Retrieved December 11, 2022, from www.bloomberg.com/news/articles/2021-01-25/shipping-container-crunch-shows-signs-of-easing-index-shows

Musa, Z. (2020, October 18). Tough times for fresh graduates. *The Star*. Retrieved December 11, 2022, from www.thestar.com.my/metro/metro-news/2020/10/19/tough-times-for-fresh-graduates

OECD. (2020). *Higher education in regional and city development*. Retrieved December 11, 2022, from www.oecd.org/education/imhe/highereducationinregionalandcitydevelopment.htm

Panennungi, M. A. (2017). The SIJORI cross-border region: Transnational politics, economics, and culture. *Bulletin of Indonesian Economic Studies*, *53*(2), 219–220. https://doi.org/10.1080/00074918.2017.1354678

PEMANDU. (2011). *Economic transformation programme*. Retrieved August 8, 2011, from http://etp.pemandu.gov.my/Overview_of_NKEAs_-@-Electronics_and_Electrical.aspx

Perbadanan Pembangunan Pulau Pinang. (1990). *PENANG: Looking back, looking ahead 20 years of progress*. Penang Development Corporation.

Productivity Performance. (2017). Home. *Official website Malaysia Productivity Corporation*. Retrieved October 1, 2023, from https://www.mpc.gov.my/productivity-performance

Rasiah, R. (2002). *Systemic coordination and human capital development: Knowledge flows in Malaysia's MNC-driven electronics clusters*. Research Papers in Economics.

Shafaeddin, S. M. (2014). *Competitiveness and development: Myth and realities* (Vol. 2). Anthem Press.

Social Security Organization (SOCSO). (2020). *Loss of employment*. EIS. Retrieved December 11, 2022, from https://eiscentre.perkeso.gov.my/loss-of-employment/

The Star. (2021, December 1). *Alarm bells over engineer shortage*. Retrieved December 11, 2022, from www.thestar.com.my/news/nation/2021/12/02/alarm-bells-over-engineer-shortage

Sucher, S. J., & Gupta, S. (2023). A better, fairer approach to layoffs. *Harvard Business Review*. Retrieved October 2, 2023, from https://hbr.org/2018/05/layoffs-that-dont-break-your-company

Surendran, S. (2021). The state of the nation: Less than a tenth of Malaysian workers paid below minimum wage. *The Edge Malaysia*. Retrieved October 2, 2023, from https://theedgemalaysia.com/article/state-nation-less-tenth-malaysian-workers-paid-below-minimum-wage

Tan, L. E. (2002, April 18–21). *Conjuncture, confluences, contestations: A perspective on Penang history* [Paper presentation]. Paper presented at the Penang Story – International Conference 2002, Penang, Malaysia.

Trade Performance. (2021). *Malaysia External Trade Development Corporation*. Retrieved October 1, 2023, from https://www.matrade.gov.my/en/faq/187-malaysian-exporters/trade-performance-2021

Van der Velden, D. G. (2014). *Evolution of the electronics and electrical industry in Penang between 1994 and 2013*. [Master thesis, Utrecht University].

Velnampy, T. (2013). Export, import and economic growth: Evidence from Sri Lanka. *Journal of Economics and Sustainable Development*, *4*(9), 147–155. ISSN 2222–1700 (Paper), ISSN 2222–2855 (Online).

Wang, S. R. (2022). *Top investment of Malaysia, Penang's manufacturing stronger next year* {投资冠全国·曹观友信心满满 槟制造业来年更劲}. eNanyang. Retrieved December 12, 2022, from www.enanyang.my/%E8%B4%A2%E7%BB%8F%E6%96%B0%E9%97%BB/%E3%80%90%E7%8B%AC%E5%AE%B6%E3%80%91%E6%8A%95%E8%B5%84%E5%86%A0%E5%85%A8%E5%9B%BD%C2%B7%E6%9B%B9%E8%A7%82%E5%8F%8B%E4%BF%A1%E5%BF%83%E6%BB%A1%E6%BB%A1-%E6%A7%9F%E5%88%B6%E9%80%A0%E4%B8%9A%E6%9D%A5%E5%B9%B4%E6%9B%B4%E5%8A%B2

Weragoda, L. (2019). Athukorala, P. C., Ginting, E., Hill, H, & Kumar, U. (2017). The Sri Lankan economy: Charting a new course. *Sri Lanka Journal of Economic Research*, 6(2), 91. https://doi.org/10.4038/sljer.v6i2.37

Yeoh, S. G. (2009). Review of *Penang and Its Region: The Story of an Asian Entrepôt*, by Y. S. Guan, L. W. Leng, K. S. Nasution, & N. Khor. *Journal of the Malaysian Branch of the Royal Asiatic Society*, *84*(2(301)), 119–121. www.jstor.org/stable/41493805

4 The Effect of Internationalization Decision on Firm Performance of Export Firms Based in a Developing Country

An Insight From Ethiopia

Yohannes Workeaferahu Elifneh and Habtamu Ditta Hirpa

4.1 Introduction

Currently, technology and modern transport infrastructure have become the backbone of globalization process (Goeltz, 2014; Schuckmann et al., 2012). Due to this, the mobility of firms from one country to other countries is fast and comfortable (Caves, 1998; Oettl & Agrawal, 2008; Schulte-Fischedick et al., 2021). Firms from different regions need to expand their size and maximize profit by seeking internationalization process into foreign market (Du & Li, 2020; Paul & Sánchez-Morcilio, 2019). Such operation is not only the interest of particular businesses but also the concern of states/governments as this could have a positive contribution to a country's economy (Rozbicka & Kamiński, 2022).

Internationalization of firms is a dynamic process (Orero-Blat et al., 2021), which involves a process of organizational learning characterized by the increasing degree of involvement of firms in specific foreign markets (Clark et al. (1997). Welch and Luostarinen (1988) described internationalization of firms as a process of increasing involvement in international operation. Johanson and Vahlne (1977) also added that it is a process in which firms, step by step, increase their participation in the international market. And scholars in the field of international business enumerate various forms of international entry modes in a global context, such as exporting, strategic alliances, and joint venture (Kim & Hwang, 1992; Pisani et al., 2017). Nayyar (2008) also elaborated that the internationalization of firms, everywhere, is driven by a wide range of factors such as market access for exports, horizontal or vertical integration, delivery of services, capturing international brand names, access to technology, sourcing raw materials and global leadership aspirations

However, most firms, especially from the developing countries, choose exporting as a major entry mode to foreign markets, and this mode (exporting) is considered as the most frequently used mode of entry into a foreign country even at a global level since the 1960s by countries from the developing

DOI: 10.4324/9781003349204-4

world (Amirahmadi & Wu, 1995; Osland et al., 2001), but despite being the preferred mode of internationalization, it has become increasingly more difficult due to increased global competition and the dynamic nature of the international market arenas (Jones, 2015; Nakos et al., 1998). And worse, many export firms in developing countries are relatively fresh and lack experience (Xiao et al., 2013). Thus, the effect of internationalization decision on firm performance is worth investigating. In addition, there is also dearth of studies from the poorest regions of the developing world regarding the effect of (exporters) internationalization decisions on the performance of the firms. Hence, this study aspires to examine this reality in a developing country context by way of an empirical study involving Ethiopian exporters. Given the dearth of studies on the subject of internationalization decision from this region of the world, this study will contribute to this domain both theoretically and empirically by extending the subject of the study to lesser charted regions of the world.

4.2 Theoretical Review of the Literature

The international business literature offers valuable insights into what enables firms to internationalize (Kafouros et al., 2022). Yet, although theories of the internationalization of firms are broad (Rask et al., 2008), theories of transaction cost analysis, the resource-based view, and institutional theory have been in use for many years and have been involved in a large number of research studies in the area of internationalization of firms (Akter et al., 2019; Andersen, 1997; Brouthers & Hennart, 2007). Thus, this study will draw on these three theories.

4.2.1 Transaction Cost Analysis

Transaction cost analysis (TCA) is one of the most widely used theoretical perspective in the study of internationalization decision and firm performance (Andersen, 1997; Contractor, 2007; Li et al., 2021). This theory has been fruitfully applied to a wide range of organizational phenomena, as reflected in a vast and evolving body of research (Cuypers et al., 2021). According to this perspective, firms choose entry modes that minimize the transaction costs generated by the need to negotiate, monitor, and enforce transactions, thereby maximizing their net benefits, and determining which kinds of assets are difficult to transact is an essential consideration in TCA (Sestu & Majocchi, 2020). Besides, the approach aims to identify environmental factors that, when combined with a set of related human factors, explain how businesses can organize transactions to lower transaction costs; and asset specificity and uncertainty are the most important environmental factors, while bounded rationality and opportunism are the most important human factors (Andersen, 1993). In other words, firms internationalize, according to this theory, because they have a competitive advantage over other firms in the targeted market in terms of access to superior technology or knowledge edge, products, processes, or patents, better access to capital, and superior corporate governance (Danciu, 2012; Deng, 2009; Goedhuys & Sleuwaegen, 2016). And these will help improve firms' business performance in an international market by maintaining a cost advantage and exceeding the target market share (Hill, 1990; Palmatier et al., 2007).

4.2.2 The Resource-Based View

Resource-based view has gained its maturity as a theory, and it has heavily shaped the path of research in the organization and management field (Apriliyanti, 2022). Panda and Reddy (2016) stated that resource-based view energized contemporary researchers to explore firm competency, strategy, sustainability, diversification, and internationalization with respect to firm resources. The resource-based view relying on the notion firms could garner competitive advantage in short run by the virtue of their resources which are rare, valuable, and appropriable; and this short-run competitive advantage leads to long-run competitive advantage when a firm's resources are inimitable, non-substitutable, and mobile (Panda & Reddy, 2016; Wernerfelt, 1984). This view is also instrumental for internationalization decisions as it provides a useful theoretical framework for the internationalization of firms and their specific resources representing competitive advantages, allowing them to develop as well as successfully enter and operate in international markets (Ruzzier et al., 2006; Yehualashet, 2015) Additionally, Brouthers and Hennart (2007) mentioned that the resource-based view (includes knowledge-based and organizational capabilities theories) recommends that firms develop special resources (valuable) that they can exploit in foreign markets or use foreign markets as a source for obtaining or developing new resource based benefits. As such, according to the resource-based viewpoint, valuable firm resources (both tangible and intangible) are typically scarce, imperfectly imitable, and devoid of direct substitutes (Brouthers et al., 2000). Firms gain resource-based benefits by developing or acquiring a set of firm-specific resources and capabilities that are valuable, scarce, and imperfectly imitable, with no readily available substitutes (Luo, 2002). More precisely, the crux of the resource-based view is that a firm's resources (tangible or intangible) are crucial among firms that go for internationalization (Boermans & Roelfsema, 2012; Mariz-Pérez & García-Álvarez, 2009).

4.2.3 Institutional Theory

Institutional theory is an important perspective in international business (IB) field as the firm's strategic choices not only depend on their capabilities and industry conditions but also depend on both formal and informal constraints of their institutional environments (Sahin & Mert, 2022).

Institutional theory of organizations focuses on the central question of why all organizations in the field tend to look and act the same (Miles, 2012); this is because institutional context significantly impacts international behavior of firms by facilitating or restricting internationalization processes (Korsakienė et al., 2015). In other words, institutional theory holds that international firms are impacted by different normative pressures, arising from within the firm as well as external sources such as a given country's institutional environment; and an increasing number of international management scholars are applying institutional theory to the study of internationalization as it provides a rich theoretical foundation for examining a wide range of critical issues and also allows for theorizing at multiple levels of analysis, which is essential for internationalization research (Dacin et al., 2002). Briefly stated, institutions are the rules of the game in a society; which could be either formal constraints (e.g., laws, rules, constitutions) or informal constraints (e.g., norms of behavior, conventions, and self-imposed codes of conduct) (Carney et al., 2009; North, 1994; Korsakienė et al., 2015).

4.2.4 *Internationalization and Firm Performance*

Studies about the relationship between internationalization and firm performance still continues to be intriguing (Cao et al., 2022; Likitwongkajon & Vithessonthi, 2022; Ruigrok & Wagner, 2004). Contractor et al. (2003) suggest that there is a relationship between internationalization decision and firm performance, and this is in line with the international business theory that argues for a positive relationship between the performance of the firm and internationalization. Similarly, Hoskisson et al. (1994) also uphold that internationalization has a positive impact on firm performance. Thus, in view of the theories demonstrated here, Figure 4.1 shows the conceptual framework of this study. As indicated in the conceptual framework, the independent variables are transaction-cost-based induced entry decision; resource-based induced entry decision; and institutional-based induced entry decision; and the dependent variable is perceived international business performance.

4.2.5 *Conceptual Framework*

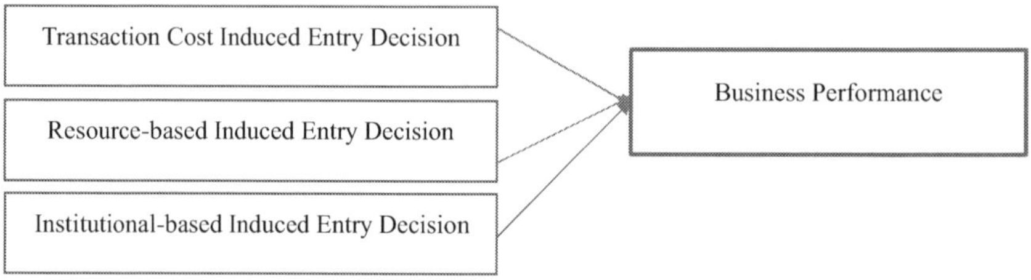

Figure 4.1 Conceptual framework of the study

4.3 Research Hypotheses and Model Specification

The following are the hypotheses of the study based on the conceptual framework presented in Figure 4.1:

Hypothesis 1: Transaction-cost-based induced entry decision has positive relationship with firm performance
Hypothesis 2: Resource-based induced entry decision has positive relationship with firm performance.
Hypothesis 3: Institutional-based induced entry decision has positive relationship with firm performance.

4.3.1 Model Specification

In order to test the three hypotheses, this study investigated the perceived international business performance of exporters in Ethiopia using the following multiple linear regression models:

$$\text{PIBPM} = \beta_0 + \beta_1 \text{TCB} + \beta_2 \text{RB} + \beta_3 \text{IB} + \varepsilon \quad (1)$$

where PIBPM is perceived international business performance measure, TCB is transaction-cost-based induced entry decision, RB is resource-based induced entry decision, and IB is institutional-based induced entry decision.

4.4 Research Methodology

According to Kumar (2011), research design is an approach that researchers use to address the research hypotheses. Accordingly, the research design adopted in this research was explanatory research design. Explanatory research design is suitable for this study because the study aims to examine the effect of internationalization decision on international business performance (firm performance) of exporters.

4.4.1 Sample Design

According to Diamantopoulos (2004), a population is a group of items that a sample will be drawn from. The target population of the study was Ethiopian exporters from Addis Ababa (Capital of Ethiopia), where 90% of the country's exporters reside. The total number of the target population was 1,641. The sampling technique applied for the study was convenient sampling; and based on Yamane's sample determination formula (shown in the following), the sample size was 322. As stated by Yamane, for a 95% confidence level and $p = 0.5$, the size of the sample would be:

$$n = \frac{N}{1 + N(e)^2} = \frac{1{,}641}{1 + 1{,}641(5\%)^2} = 322$$

where N is total population, e denotes precision level, and n is sample size.

4.4.2 Instrument

Data were gathered using a closed-ended, Likert-scale-based standard questionnaire. For the transaction-cost-based induced entry decision, the questionnaire developed by Brouthers and Hennart (2007) was utilized; for the variable-resource-based induced entry decision, a questionnaire constructed by Zhao et al. (2004) and Gomes-Casseres (1989) was used; for the institutional-based induced entry decision, a questionnaire by Brouthers et al. (2003) was employed to collect the needed data. And for perceived international business performance measure, the instrument relied on the works of Deniz et al. (2011); Hult et al. (2008); Katsikeas et al. (2000); and Racela et al. (2007). Besides, in order to enhance the validity of the questionnaire, a pilot study was performed before the actual data collection with 10% of the sample size according to the guideline provided by Connelly (2008).

4.4.3 Data Analysis and Presentation Method

Analyses were conducted through descriptive statistics to describe the phenomenon that exists at the time of the study, and multivariable regression analysis method was used to assess the statistical relationship between variables and testing hypothesis. The Pearson correlation method was used to see the relationship between independent variables and dependent variables. Before the regression results were conducted, the study performed the five key assumption tests for multiple regressions (autocorrelation test, multicollinearity test, linearity test, normality test, and homoscedasticity test), and they are all well met. Moreover, Cronbach's alpha reliability test was applied to measure of internal consistency of the mean of the items at the time of administration of questionnaire. Cronbach's alpha value for international business performance (dependent variable) was 0.760. The coefficient predictors' transaction-cost-based induced entry decision was 0.935, for resource-based induced decision was 0.704, and for institutional-based induced entry decision was 0.781. George and Mallery (2003) stated that a reliability score of greater than 0.9 is excellent, greater than 0.8 is good, greater than 0.7 is acceptable, greater than 0.6 is questionable, greater than 0.5 is poor, and less than 0.5 is unacceptable. In this study, all the Cronbach's alpha values indicated that the reliability of the questionnaire was acceptable.

4.5 Result

4.5.1 Descriptive Results

This section demonstrates the descriptive statistics (mean and standard deviation) of the survey for transaction-cost-based induced entry decision, resource-based induced entry decision, institutional-based induced entry decision, and international business performance measure. A total of 322 questionnaires were administered to the study participants, of which 287 were completed. This suggests a response rate of 89.13%.

Table 4.1 shows the descriptive statistics (mean and standard deviation) of the respondents' level of agreement on transaction-cost-based induced entry decision on international market. The statement 'High market potential influences international presence' had the highest mean and standard deviation of 4.25 and 1.03, respectively, indicating respondents' agreement to the statement.

This is followed by the statement 'The level of technological advancement influences international exposure of my company' with a mean of 4.20 and a standard deviation of 1.01. These figures indicate respondents' agreement to the statement.

The statements 'Our foreign entry decisions are based on making investments that are specific to the buyer', 'Political and economic stability of our target country encourages international operations", and "International investment is influenced if the transactions are recurrent and/or large' with a mean and standard deviation of (3.20, 1.34), (2.94, 1.38), and (2.82, 1.41), respectively, indicate that the respondents are on the fence to decide about the statement.

The statements 'Similarity and familiarity with a country's cultures and environments encourages foreign investments', 'International expansion is encouraged by the perceived simplicity in partner selection and ability to enforce, monitor, and control contractual agreements', and 'Increase in the

Table 4.1 Descriptive statistics on transaction-cost-based induced entry decision

Variables *Transaction cost-based induced entry decision*	*Mean*	*Standard deviation*
Our foreign entry decisions are based on making investments that are specific to the buyer	3.20	1.345
The level of technological advancement influences international exposure of my company	4.20	1.017
Increase in the value and number of employee encourages the decision to expand to other countries	2.29	1.062
Political and economic stability of our target country encourages international operations	2.94	1.383
High market potential influences international presence	4.25	1.038
Similarity and familiarity with a country's cultures and environments encourages foreign investments	2.56	1.435
International expansion is encouraged by the perceived simplicity in partner selection and ability to enforce, monitor, and control contractual agreements	2.56	1.269
International investment is influenced if the transactions are recurrent and/or large	2.82	1.414

value and number of employee encourages the decision to expand to other countries' having mean and standard deviation of (2.56, 1.269), (2.56, 1.435), and (2.29, 1.062), respectively, tell the researcher that the response of the respondents tends to disagreement of the statements mentioned. Overall, transaction-cost-based induced entry decision having eight items used in assessing it has a mean of 3.1032 and a standard deviation of 1.0409.

Table 4.2 displays the descriptive statistics on resource-based induced entry decision. The result indicates that the statement 'increasing length and scope of the company's international experience encourages further international investment' with mean and standard deviation of (3.60, 1.452) leads to respondents' agreement with the statement, followed by the statement 'Possession of a country-specific experience induces setting up international presence in the target country' and 'Possession of unique proprietary technology, tacit know-how, and firm reputation induces our company's propensity to expand to foreign countries' having mean and standard deviation of (3.49, 1.481) and (3.49, 1.519), respectively, which describes an agreement.

On the other hand, respondents with a mean and standard deviation of (3.48, 1.491) agreed with the statement that refers when the company's international experience going advanced, the higher the urge to expand internationally.

Lastly, the statement 'the reputation of our company in the industry encourages international operations' with mean and standard deviation of (3.29, and 1.447) tends to respondents' agreement to the statement. In general, resource-based induced entry decisions assesses using five statements has a mean of 3.4683 and a standard deviation of 1.0006.

Table 4.3 illustrates the descriptive statistics on institutional-based induced entry decision. It shows the statement 'Price stability, controlled inflation and favorable monetary policies in a host nation induce my company's foreign

Table 4.2 Descriptive statistics on resource-based induced entry decision

Variables	*Mean*	*Standard deviation*
Resource-based induced entry decision		
The higher my company's international experience, the higher the urge to expand internationally	3.48	1.491
Increasing length and scope of my company's international experience encourages further international investment	3.60	1.452
Possession of a country-specific experience induces setting up international presence in the target country	3.49	1.481
Possession of unique proprietary technology, tacit know-how, and firm reputation induces our companies propensity to expand to foreign countries	3.49	1.519
The reputation of our company in the industry encourages international operations	3.29	1.447

Table 4.3 Descriptive statistics on institution-based induced entry decision

Variables	*Mean*	*Standard deviation*
Institutional-based induced entry decision		
Acceptability and adaptability of our products in a foreign country/culture encourages international presence in that country	2.84	1.375
Favorable government policy in the host and home countries influences decisions to increase international investments	3.65	1.077
Price stability, controlled inflation, and favorable monetary policies in a host nation induces my company's foreign exposure in the host country	3.69	1.139
Complementary and receptive host nation's organizational structures, processes, and administrative conveniences encourages increased foreign commitment of our company	3.44	1.456
The level, pattern, and government regulation of competition in the host nation influences our company's foreign commitment.	3.55	1.447

exposure in the host country' had the highest mean and standard deviation of 3.69 and 1.139, respectively. The researcher observed from these statistics that the respondents agree with the statement. This is followed by the statement 'Favorable government policy in the host and home countries influences decisions to increase international investments' which has a mean of 3.65 and a standard deviation of 1.077, indicating that the response of the respondents is in agreement of the statement. Following that is the statement 'The level, pattern and government regulation of competition in the host nation influences our company's foreign commitment' with a mean of 3.55 and a standard deviation of 1.447, which indicates agreement with the statement. The next highest statement after that is 'Complementary and receptive host nation's organizational structures, processes and administrative conveniences encourages increased foreign commitment of our company' with a mean of 3.44 and a standard deviation of 1.447, which tells the researcher that the response of respondents tends towards agreement of the statement. And last is the statement 'Acceptability and adaptability of our products in a foreign country/culture encourages international presence in that country' which has a mean of 2.84 and a standard deviation of 1.375, indicating an undecided response from the respondents. Totally, institutional-based induced entry decisions assessed with five items has a mean of 3.4334 and a standard deviation of 0.9555.

Table 4.4 describes the results of the analysis of perceived international business performance measure. The statement 'The foreign sales targets as a percentage of total sales are met by the organization' was rated well above the average with a mean of 4.06 and a standard deviation of 1.213, indicating agreement to the statement. Regarding the company's long-term performance is secured or not, the result shows respondents agreement having a

Table 4.4 Descriptive statistics on perceived international business performance measure

Variables	*Mean*	*Standard deviation*
Perceived international business performance measure		
The foreign sales targets as a percentage of total sales are met by the organization	4.06	1.213
The existing level of international performance is satisfactory to the management	3.53	1.394
The company's long-term international performance is secured	3.77	1.281

mean 3.77 and standard deviation of 1.281. Whether the existing level of international performance was satisfactory to the management or not was rated with a mean of 3.53 and a standard deviation of 1.394. The researcher observed that the respondents' response tends towards agreement to the statement. Overall, perceived international business performance measure having three items used in assessing has a mean of 3.1031 and a standard deviation of 1.0409.

4.5.2 *Inferential Analysis*

The Pearson's correlation statistics indicated in Table 4.5 shows that all independent variables are correlated and statistically significant at a significance level of 0.01, suggesting the strong linear relationship between the independent variables and international business performance.

4.5.3 *Regression Analysis*

The section reports the multiple regression analysis based on Equation (1).

Table 4.6 presents the regression results with model summary. The R value of 0.863 indicated there was a high correlation between independent variables (transaction-cost-based induced entry decision, institutional-based induced entry decisions and resource-based induced entry decisions) and dependent variable (international business performance). The value of adjusted R-squared shows that the independent variables explain 74.5% of the variability of the dependent variable.

Unstandardized coefficients indicate how much the dependent variable varies with an independent variable when all other independent variables are held constant. The coefficient value of transaction-cost-based induced entry decision is positive and significant ($\beta = 0.411$), supporting the hypothesis of a positive relationship between transaction-cost-based induced entry decisions and international business performance. The institutional-based induced entry decision has a statistically significant coefficient value of 0.223, suggesting that institutional-based induced entry decisions have positive relationship with international

Table 4.5 Pearson correlation coefficient

	IBPM	*TCB*	*RB*	*IB*
PIBPM	1			
TCB	0.761**	1		
RB	0.680**	0.441**	1	
IB	0.703**	0.750**	0.431**	1

Note: ** and * denote significant at the 0.01 and 0.05 levels, respectively.

Table 4.6 Regression results with model summary

Model	*(1)* *Unstandardized coefficients*	*(2)* *Standardized coefficients*
Constant	0.339*** (0.130)	
TCB	0.411*** (0.045)	0.425
IB	0.233*** (0.049)	0.211
RB	0.404*** (0.034)	0.402
Model Summary		
R	*0.863*	
R-squared	*0.745*	
Adjusted R-squared	*0.742*	

Note: Standard errors are reported in parentheses. ** denotes significant at the 0.01 level.

business performance. Moreover, we also find a statistically significant and positive coefficient value of 0.404 for resource-based induced entry decision, indicating its positive relationship with international business performance.

The standardized coefficients are also reported in Table 4.6. Transaction-cost-based induced entry decision has a high impact (42.5%) than other predictors mentioned. The following variable having secondary effect on international business performance was resource-based induced entry decision with value of 40.2%. Besides, the institutional-based induced entry level is found to have a 21.1% marginal effect on performance of international business.

4.6 Discussions and Conclusion

The main objective of the research was to examine the effect of successful internationalization decisions of export firms in a developing country context with a perceived international business performance measure. Based on the findings of this study, it is concluded that transaction-cost-based induced entry decision, institutional-based induced entry decisions, and resource-based induced entry decisions have statistically strong positive and significant effects on international business performance.

Generally, to enhance their competitive position in the global market place, Ethiopian export firms should prioritize their efforts to expand internationally; and their decision to expand to foreign markets might need to take into account the political and economic stability of the host countries. Besides, the export firms need to concentrate on host countries that have similar and familiar culture and environment while expanding presence on international activity. Moreover, possession of unique proprietary technology, tacit know-how, and firm reputation shall be increased to influence international exposure of the firms. Furthermore, the export firms shall focus on foreign countries where their products are accepted and adapted to promote international presence and enhance their international business performance. More so, the export firms should focus on host countries that have complementary and receptive organizational structures, processes, and administrative conveniences to positively influence their international exposure.

References

Akter, M., Rahman, M., & Radicic, D. (2019). Women entrepreneurship in international trade: Bridging the gap by bringing feminist theories into entrepreneurship and internationalization theories, *Sustainability*, *11*(22), 6230.

Amirahmadi, H., & Wu, W. (1995). Export processing zones in Asia. *Asian Survey*, *35*(9), 828–849.

Andersen, O. (1993). On the internationalization process of firms: A critical analysis. *Journal of International Business Studies*, *24*(2), 209–231.

Andersen, O. (1997). Internationalization and market entry mode: A review of theories and conceptual frameworks. *Management International Review*, *37*, 27–42.

Apriliyanti, I. D. (2022). A problem waits: Is it true that resource-based theory (RBT) is an empty tautology? *Policy & Governance Review*, *6*(2), 107–122.

Boermans, M. A., & Roelfsema, H. (2012). A resource-based view of internationalization in emerging economies. In *Impacts of emerging economies and firms on international business* (pp. 13–31). Palgrave Macmillan.

Brouthers, K. D., Brouthers, L. E., & Werner, S. (2000). Influences on strategic decision making in the Dutch financial services industry. *Journal of Management*, *26*, 863–883.

Brouthers, K. D., Brouthers, L. E., & Werner, S. (2003). Transaction cost-enhanced entry mode choices and firm performance. *Strategic Management Journal*, *24*(12), 1239–1248.

Brouthers, K. D., & Hennart, J.-F. (2007). Boundaries of the firm: Insights from International entry mode research. *Journal of Management*, *33*(3), 395–425.

Cao, X., Li, P., Huang, X., & Fan, L. (2022). The dual mechanism of social networks on the relationship between internationalization and firm performance: Empirical evidence from China. *PLoS One*, *17*(2), e0263674.

Carney, M., Gedajlovic, E., & Yang, X. (2009). Varieties of Asian capitalism: Toward an institutional theory of Asian enterprise. *Asia Pacific Journal of Management*, *26*(3), 361–380.

Caves, R. E. (1998). Industrial organization and new findings on the turnover and mobility of firms. *Journal of economic literature*, *36*(4), 1947–1982.

Clark, T., Pugh, D. S., & Mallory, G. (1997). The process of internationalization in the operating firm. *International Business Review*, *6*(6), 605–623.

Connelly, L. M. (2008). Pilot studies. *Medsurg Nursing*, *17*(6), 411–412.

Contractor, F. J. (2007). Is international business good for companies? The evolutionary or multi-stage theory of internationalization vs. the transaction cost perspective. *Management International Review*, *47*(3), 453–475.

Contractor, F. J., Kundu, S. K., & Hsu, C. C. (2003). A three-stage theory of international expansion: The link between multinationality and performance in the service sector. *Journal of International Business Studies*, *34*(1), 5–18.

Cuypers, I. R., Hennart, J. F., Silverman, B. S., & Ertug, G. (2021). Transaction cost theory: Past progress, current challenges, and suggestions for the future. *Academy of Management Annals*, *15*(1), 111–150.

Dacin, M., Goodstein, J., & Richard Scott, W. (2002). Institutional theory and institutional change: Introduction to the special research forum. *Academy of Management Journal*, *45*(1), 45–56.

Danciu, V. (2012). Models for the internationalization of the business: A diversity based approach. *Management & Marketing*, *7*(1).

Deng, P. (2009). Why do Chinese firms tend to acquire strategic assets in international expansion? *Journal of World Business*, *44*(1), 74–84.

Deniz, N., Boz, İ. T., & Ertosun, Ö. G. (2011). The relationship between entrepreneur's level of perceived business-related fear and business performance. *Procedia-Social and Behavioral Sciences*, *24*, 579–600.

Diamantopoulos, A. (2004). International abstracts of research in marketing. *International Journal of Research in Marketing*, *21*(1), 89–99.

Du, W., & Li, M. (2020). Influence of environmental regulation on promoting the low-carbon transformation of China's foreign trade: Based on the dual margin of export enterprise. *Journal of Cleaner Production*, *244*, 118687.

George, D., & Mallery. (2003). *SPSS for Windows step by step: A simple guide and reference, 11.0 update* (4th ed.). Allyn & Bacon.

Goedhuys, M., & Sleuwaegen, L. (2016). International standards certification, institutional voids and exports from developing country firms. *International Business Review*, *25*(6), 1344–1355.

Goeltz, D. R. (2014). Globalization and hypercompetition: Drivers, linkages, and industry differences. *Journal of International Business and Cultural Studies*, *8*, 1.

Gomes-Casseres, B. (1989). Ownership structures of foreign subsidiaries. *Journal of Economic Behavior & Organization*, *11*(1), 1–25.

Hill, C. W. (1990). Cooperation, opportunism, and the invisible hand: Implications for transaction cost theory. *Academy of Management Review*, *15*(3), 500–513.

Hoskisson, R. E., Hitt, M. A., & Ireland, R. D. (1994). A mid-range theory of the interactive effects of international and product diversification on innovation and performance. *Journal of Management*, *20*(2), 297–326.

Hult, G. T. M., Ketchen, D. J., Griffith, D. A., Chabowski, B. R., Hamman, M. K., Dykes, B. J., Pollitte, W. A., & Cavusgil, S. T. (2008). An assessment of the measurement of performance in international business research. *Journal of International Business Studies*, *39*(6), 1064–1080.

Johanson, J., & Vahlne, J.-E. (1977). The internationalization process of the firm – a model of knowledge development and increasing foreign market commitments. *Journal of International Business Studies*, *8*(1), 23–32.

Jones, M. T. (2015). Exporting requires us to see things differently. *The Business & Management Review*, *7*(1), 94.
Kafouros, M., Cavusgil, S. T., Devinney, T. M., Ganotakis, P., & Fainshmidt, S. (2022). Cycles of de-internationalization and re-internationalization: Towards an integrative framework. *Journal of World Business*, *57*(1), 101257.
Katsikeas, C. S., Leonidou, L. C., & Morgan, N. A. (2000). Firm-level export performance assessment: Review, evaluation, and development. *Journal of the Academy of Marketing Science*, *28*(4), 493–511.
Kim, W. C., & Hwang, P. (1992). Global strategy and multinationals' entry mode choice. *Journal of International Business Studies*, *23*(1), 29–53.
Korsakienė, R., Diskienė, D., & Smaliukienė, R. (2015). Institutional theory perspective and internationalization of firms. How institutional context influences internationalization of SMEs? *Entrepreneurship and Sustainability Issues*, *2*(3), 142–153.
Kumar, R. (2011). *Research methodology* (11th ed.). SAGE Publications Ltd.
Li, M., Qin, F., & Zhang, Z. (2021). Short-term capital flows, exchange rate expectation and currency internationalization: Evidence from China. *Journal of Risk and Financial Management*, *14*(5), 223.
Likitwongkajon, N., & Vithessonthi, C. (2022). Internationalization and firm performance. *Global Finance Journal*, 100753. https://doi.org/10.1016/j.gfj.2022.100753
Luo, Y. (2002). Capability exploitation and building in a foreign market: Implications for multinational enterprises. *Organization Science*, *13*(1), 48–63.
Mariz-Pérez, R., & García-Álvarez, T. (2009). The Internationalization strategy of Spanish indigenous franchised chains: A resource-based view. *Journal of Small Business Management*, *47*(4), 514–530.
Miles, J. A. (2012). *Management and organisation theory*. John Wiley & Sons Inc.
Nakos, G., Keith, D., & Lance, E. (1998). The impact of firm and managerial characteristics on small and medium-sized Greek firms' export performance. *Journal of Global Marketing*, *11*(4), 23–47.
Nayyar, D. (2008). The internationalization of firms from India: Investment, mergers and acquisitions. *Oxford Development Studies*, *36*(1), 111–131.
North, D. C. (1994). Economic performance through time. *American Economic Review*, *84*(3), 359–368.
Oettl, A., & Agrawal, A. (2008). International labor mobility and knowledge flow externalities. *Journal of International Business Studies*, *39*(8), 1242–1260.
Orero-Blat, M., Palacios-Marqués, D., & Garzón, D. (2021). Knowledge assets for internationalization strategy proposal. *Journal of Innovation & Knowledge*, *6*(4), 214–221.
Osland, G. E., Taylor, C. R., & Zou, S. (2001). Selecting international modes of entry and expansion. *Marketing Intelligence & Planning*, *19*(3), 153–161.
Palmatier, R. W., Dant, R. P., & Grewal, D. (2007). A comparative longitudinal analysis of theoretical perspectives of interorganizational relationship performance. *Journal of Marketing*, *71*(4), 172–194.
Panda, D., & Reddy, S. (2016). Resource based view of internationalization: Evidence from Indian commercial banks. *Journal of Asia Business Studies*, *10*(1), 41–60. https://doi.org/10.1108/JABS-10-2014-0082
Paul, J., & Sánchez-Morcilio, R. (2019). Toward a new model for firm internationalization: Conservative, predictable, and pacemaker companies and markets. *Canadian Journal of Administrative Sciences/Revue Canadienne des Sciences de l'Administration*, *36*(3), 336–349.

Pisani, N., Caldart, A., & Hopma, J. (2017). SMEs' formation of minority international joint ventures and level of internationalization: The moderating role of a global versus regional focus. *European Management Journal*, *35*(3), 414–424.
Racela, O. C., Chaikittisilpa, C., & Thoumrungroje, A. (2007). Market orientation, international business relationships and perceived export performance. *International Marketing Review*, *24*(2), 144–163.
Rask, M., Strandskov, J., & Håkonsson, D. D. (2008). Theoretical perspectives on the internationalization of firms. *Journal of Teaching in International Business*, *19*(4), 320–345.
Rozbicka, P., & Kamiński, P. (2022). Have they already emerged? Mapping the population of national interest organisations in post-communist Poland. *Europe-Asia Studies*, *74*(5), 789–808.
Ruigrok, W., & Wagner, H. (2004, July). *Internationalization and firm performance: Meta-analytic review and future research directions* [Paper presentation]. In annual meeting of the Academy of International Business, Stockholm, Sweden.
Ruzzier, M., Hisrich, R. D., & Antoncic, B. (2006). SME internationalization research: Past, present, and future. *Journal of Small Business and Enterprise Development*, *13*(4), 476–497.
Sahin, K., & Mert, K. (2022). Institutional theory in international business studies: The period of 1990–2018. *International Journal of Organizational Analysis*, Vol. ahead-of-print No. ahead-of-print. https://doi.org/10.1108/IJOA-09-2021-2945
Schuckmann, S. W., Gnatzy, T., Darkow, I. L., & von der Gracht, H. A. (2012). Analysis of factors influencing the development of transport infrastructure until the year 2030—A Delphi based scenario study. *Technological Forecasting and Social Change*, *79*(8), 1373–1387.
Schulte-Fischedick, M., Shan, Y., & Hubacek, K. (2021). Implications of COVID-19 lockdowns on surface passenger mobility and related CO_2 emission changes in Europe. *Applied Energy*, *300*, 117396.
Sestu, M. C., & Majocchi, A. (2020). Family firms and the choice between wholly owned subsidiaries and joint ventures: A transaction costs perspective. *Entrepreneurship Theory and Practice*, *44*(2), 211–232.
Welch, L. S., & Luostarinen, R. (1988). Internationalization: Evolution of a concept. *Journal of General Management*, *14*(2), 34–55.
Wernerfelt, B. (1984). A resource-based view of the firm. *Strategic Management Journal*, *5*(2), 171–180.
Xiao, S. S., Jeong, I., Moon, J. J., Chung, C. C., & Chung, J. (2013). Internationalization and performance of firms in China: Moderating effects of governance structure and the degree of centralized control. *Journal of International Management*, *19*(2), 118–137.
Yehualashet, D. L. (2015). *Determinants and impediments in the internationalization process of small and medium-sized manufacturing enterprises in Ethiopia*. [Doctoral dissertation, University of South Africa, UNISA].
Zhao, H., Luo, Y., & Suh, T. (2004). Transaction cost determinants and ownership-based entry mode choice: A meta-analytical review. *Journal of International Business Studies*, *35*(6), 524–544.

5 The Relationship of Entrepreneurial Orientation and Firm Performance in the Developing Country Context

The Case of Firms in Ethiopia

Workneh Kassa Tessema and Lakew Alemu Birhane

5.1 Introduction

Entrepreneurial orientation (EO) is becoming increasingly important for all types of firms, regardless of size, age, or industry sector (Kraus, 2011). In this regard, prior research suggests that adopting EO (Rauch et al., 2009), chasing innovation and risk-taking market strategies (Miller & Friesen, 1982), and aggressively introducing new products and services (Ireland et al., 2003) enhance firm performance. EO thus has received considerable attention in organization and management research in general and marketing, economics, and entrepreneurship research in particular (e.g., Rauch et al., 2009; Wales et al., 2011b; Covin et al., 2006).

Several research endeavors have examined EO–firm performance relationships and found out EO as important determinant of firm performance (Miller & Miller, 2011). Most of these studies emphasized firms with strong EO likely to engage in introducing new, innovative, and diversified products to enter to new market environments (Brouthers et al., 2015; Dimitratos et al., 2004). Despite burgeoning scholarly interest, the development of body of knowledge in the area of EO is limited due to inconsistent results (Rhodes et al., 2018; Hughes & Morgan, 2007) and lack of integration of the efforts to build up each other's results (Davidsson & Wiklund, 2001; Miller, 2011; Hughes & Morgan, 2007). While some evidence (e.g., Hult et al., 2004; Lee et al., 2001; Wiklund & Shepherd, 2003) have demonstrated positive and significant relationship, other studies fail to find even significant relationships (e.g., Covin et al., 1994; George et al., 2001) between EO and firm performance.

In the literature, EO has been largely conceptualized with its three most common features: *risk-taking, innovativeness, and pro-activeness* (Miller, 1983). However, Lumpkin and Dess (1996) have extended EO conceptualization into five by including *competitiveness and autonomy*. Still there are no consistent positive relationships with all the five dimensions of EO to firm performance. The studies conducted so far have focused on the medium- and

DOI: 10.4324/9781003349204-5

large-sized firms which are located in developed world, with different institutional contexts from developing countries such as Ethiopia. In this respect, previous studies have focused on medium- and large-scale companies, ignoring the small and micro enterprises while analyzing the relationship of EO to performance. But EO is still important for success of all firms, regardless of size, age, or industry sector (Kraus, 2011). In reality, small and micro-enterprises actually represent over 90% of private business in most African countries and contribute to more than 50% share of employment (UNIDO, 1999); and they form the basis of the economy in developing countries for mobilizing entrepreneurial initiative at individual levels to enhance performance (Amoah & Amoah, 2018). Thus, escaping the small and micro-enterprises in EO-performance relationship testing is tantamount to serve injustices for the wider generalizability of EO theory building. Furthermore, evidence has shown that the relationship between EO and firm performance vary across studies, suggesting that the presumed relationship is not yet prudently established, seeking additional research effort (Covin & Slevin, 1991; Miller, 2011). Likewise, regardless of the empirical efforts demonstrated, as to researchers' knowledge, no conscious effort has been made to investigate innovativeness, pro-activeness, risk-taking propensity, autonomy, and competitive aggressiveness and firm performance in the context of the collectivist culture (Hofstede, 2011) such as Ethiopia.

The objective of this study is therefore to analyze the EO-performance relationship among the large, medium, and small enterprises in Ethiopia. The study also examined whether the firm size and networks differently influence performance among firms in Ethiopia. This study is believed to have theoretical, empirical, and practical significance. First, the findings of the study can extend theoretical generalizability of EO firm performance relationship which has been widely tested in developed world for big companies to the context of firms (operating from large to small level) in developing countries. Thus, the study is expected to fill some empirical void by testing the impact of EO dimensions on firm performance relationship in the context of the collectivist culture. Second, the findings of the study can inform how EO dimensions (risk-taking, innovativeness, pro-activeness, competitiveness, and autonomy) are related to performance across different sizes of firms in a developing country context. Third, based on expected findings, policymakers can devise strategies that enhance the role of EO on the firms' performance for economic development.

The next section presents the literature review on the theoretical and empirical aspects of EO and firm performance. Then, the conceptual framework of the relationships and the hypotheses are presented in Section 5.3. Section 5.4 presents the methodology of the study, followed by the presentation of the findings in Section 5.5. Discussion and recommendations are presented in the final section.

5.2 Literature Review

In this section, we briefly present the literature on EO, its dimensions, and their relationships with firm performance based on the extant literature.

5.2.1 Theory on EO

An early work by Miller (1983) and Covin and Slevin (1989) has laid the foundation for the conceptualization of entrepreneurial approach for strategy that suggested firms with strong EO should pursue innovation, and aggressively enter to new markets. EO is described as the processes, practices, and decision-making activities that lead to a higher firm performance (Lumpkin & Dess, 1996, p. 136). In more related way, Rauch et al. (2009) viewed EO as the entrepreneurial strategy-making processes that key decision makers use to enact their firm's organizational purpose, sustain its vision, and create competitive advantages. According to Hart (1992), organizational strategy-making process incorporates planning, analysis, decision-making, and many aspects of an organization's culture, value system, and mission. As Miller (1983, p. 771) states "An entrepreneurial firm is one that engages in product-market innovation, undertakes somewhat risky ventures, and is first to come up with 'proactive' innovations, beating competitors to the punch." Such firm characteristics are not only important attributes in today's business environments where product life cycles are shortened but they are also largely associated with improved firm performance (Hamel, 2000).

In line with Miller's (1983) conceptualization, most prior research viewed EO in terms of the firm's simultaneous exhibition of innovativeness, risk-taking, and proactiveness within its strategic actions and behavior (Covin & Wales, 2012; Miller, 1983). The three-dimensional conceptualization of EO has been extended to five dimensions by Lumpkin and Dess (1996) by including autonomy and competitive aggressiveness in the EO dimensions.

5.2.1.1 Dimensionality of EO

Based on the works of Lumpkin and Dess (1996), EO has five dimensions. While conceptualizing the EO into five dimensions, Lumpkin and Dess (1996) considered autonomy and competitive aggressiveness as additional salient dimensions. In their Meta analytic works, Rauch et al. (2009) have also described the five-dimensional conceptualization of EO. The five dimensions of EO are risk-taking, innovativeness, pro-activeness, competitive aggressiveness, and autonomy (also see Rauch et al., 2009; Lumpkin & Dess, 1996).

Risk-taking: According to Lumpkin and Dess (1996), risk-taking represents a willingness to commit resources to implement projects, activities, and solutions that contain inherently a high level of uncertainty. A tolerance of risk-taking orients the firm toward action and induces it to embrace uncertainty (Hughes & Morgan, 2007). Timely risk-taking has been linked with strategic decision speed and both have subsequently been linked to improved firm performance (Eisenhardt, 1989). According to Lumpkin and Dess (1996) risk-oriented firms' integrated opportunity-seeking behavior with constructive risk-taking enhances their tendency for all the possibilities in exploration and exploitation. Risk-taking involves taking bold actions by venturing into the unknown, borrowing heavily, and/or committing significant resources in uncertain environments (Rauch et al., 2009). Without a certain degree of risk-taking, firms refrain from introducing innovations, from undertaking exploitative activities to react to changing market conditions (Hughes & Morgan, 2007). This in turn leads to a weaker performance as the firm would do little to seize customer and market opportunities from the environment (Hughes & Morgan, 2007).

Innovativeness: Innovativeness is the predisposition to engage in creativity and experimentation through the introduction of new products/services as well as technological leadership through research and development in new processes (Rauch et al., 2009). A strong emphasis on innovativeness mobilizes entry into new arenas, renews the firm's presence in existing ones and embodies a capability to explore new possibilities (e.g., Hult & Ketchen, 2001). Innovativeness changes how a firm applies market information (e.g., Slater & Narver, 1995) and together informs the generation of intelligent solutions. As such, innovativeness is a chief means to create differentiation and develop solutions that undermine those of competitors (Hughes & Morgan, 2007). Firm innovativeness has a positive impact on performance and contributes to competitive advantage by facilitating creative thinking within a firm's learning activities (e.g., Calantone et al., 2002).

Proactiveness: Proactiveness is an opportunity-seeking, forward-looking perspective characterized by the introduction of new products and services ahead of the competition (Rauch et al., 2009). Studies have reported high-performance returns to proactive firms because of their responsiveness to market signals (e.g., Day & Wensley, 1988; Wright et al., 1995). Proactiveness represents a forward-looking perspective where firms actively seek to anticipate opportunities to develop and introduce new or improved products and instigate changes to current strategies and tactics (Lumpkin & Dess, 1996; Slater & Narver, 1995). The proactive firm adopts continuous environmental scanning and acts in advance of change to better serve customers and markets rather than allow its destiny to be guided by external forces (Hughes & Morgan, 2007). By actively anticipating and preparing for change, proactive firms are in a better position to seize market share and customers quickly when change occurs by mobilizing resources far in advance of rivals. In doing so, the proactive firm remains a step ahead of less responsive competitors (Hughes & Morgan, 2007).

Competitive aggressiveness: Aggressiveness is the intensity of a firm's effort to outperform rivals and is characterized by a strong offensive posture or aggressive responses to competitive threats (Rauch et al., 2009). According to Lumpkin and Dess (2001), competitive aggressiveness encapsulates the intensity of a firm's efforts to outperform and undermine its industry rivals. The aggressive firm sees value as accruing from leveraging adaptive capabilities to consistently undermine competitors' efforts in the market as opposed to adopting a passive stance to competition (Hughes & Morgan, 2007). Aggressiveness can improve performance because firm's emphasis on maneuvering competitors strengthens its competitiveness at the expense of the rivals (Lumpkin & Dess, 1996).

Autonomy: Autonomy refers to independent action undertaken by entrepreneurial leaders directed at bringing about a new venture and seeing it to fruition (Rauch et al., 2009). Autonomy conveys the freedom to employees to encourage them to be self-directed, to exercise creativity, pursue opportunities, and champion new ideas which are essential for effective entrepreneurial activity to occur (Lumpkin & Dess, 1996).

Nevertheless, there has been much debate in theory and evidence in regard to the dimensionality of EO construct. While some scholastic works (e.g., Covin & Slevin, 1989) have argued that EO is best viewed as a unidimensional concept, others scholars (e.g., Covin et al., 2006; Lumpkin & Dess, 2001) suggest the multidimensional approach as the best that each dimension representing a different and independent aspect of EO. In relation to this, scholars theorized that the multidimensional EO construct is acceptable as it has been empirically linked to a wide variety of organizational, environmental, strategic, and managerial phenomena (Wales et al., 2011a) and best understood when assessed from multiple perspectives and with different types of indicators (Lyon et al., 2000). Accordingly, we anticipate that each of the dimensions of the EO construct have a relationship with firm performance (Stetz et al., 2000).

5.2.2 Empirical Review on EO–Firm Performance

Several research endeavors have examined EO–firm performance relationships and found out EO as important determinant of firm performance (Miller & Miller, 2011). Most of these studies emphasized firms with strong EO likely to engage in introducing new, innovative, and diversified products to enter to new market environments (Brouthers et al., 2015; Dimitratos et al., 2004). While some evidence (e.g., Hult et al., 2004; Lee et al., 2001; Wiklund & Shepherd, 2003) have demonstrated positive and significant relationship, other studies fail to find even significant relationships (e.g., Covin et al., 1994; George et al., 2001; Hughes & Morgan, 2007) between EO and firm performance. The influence of EO dimensions on performance varies from country to country (Filser & Eggers, 2014). A cross-country study, based on a three-dimensional conceptualization of EO by Filser and Eggers (2014), shows that innovativeness is significant in all the three countries (Austria, Liechtenstein, and Switzerland) considered in their sample. Risk-taking however is significant in Austria and Liechtenstein, but not in Switzerland. Proactivness is found not to have a significant influence on firm performance across all the three countries. Findings by Fadda (2018) show that with the exception of risk-taking, all the dimensions of EO are positively and significantly related to firm performance when profit is taken as the dependent variable.

5.2.3 *Firm Performance*

In the existing EO literature, firm performance has been addressed extensively (Gupta & Wales, 2017). This is by and large because firm performance is an outcome that all entrepreneurial firms must primarily focus (Poon et al., 2006). In addition, EO is considered as one of the important elements for the success of a firm (Wang, 2008). The performance measurements have been largely based on multi-item subjective measurements (e.g., Hughes & Morgan, 2007). Hughes and Morgan (2007) measured firm performance in terms of product performance using two items and customer performance with three items. Much of the research has investigated the direct relationships between EO and firm performance. However, most of the evidence has shown inconsistent results. Lumpkin and Dess (1996) and Miller (2011) argued that the relationships between EO and firm performance is complex and recommended further empirical effort considering contextual factors that influence the presumed relationships.

5.2.4 *Control Variables*

The study controls firm size (as expressed in terms number of active employees) and network relations of the firm with firm performance while testing the EO performance relationships.

Firm size: Studies have been strongly suggesting the need to consider contextual factors that may influence the performances of firms (e.g., Covin & Covin, 1990; Miller, 2011). In many of the previous studies, size of the firm has been recommended as a good context variable that influences the firm performance. Rauch et al. (2009) assumed that flexibility of smaller firms allows quickly change their strategies and enable them to tap new market opportunities, accordingly the effect of EO on performance will be greater for smaller firms than larger ones. Large firms would likely to be attracted to lucrative benefits that might be obtained from their resource base to acquire and get access to additional financial sources to present themselves in a wide range of market opportunities. Conversely, smaller firms will have limited access to additional financial sources that in turn limit their leverage and flexibility to pursue aggressive strategies and will preferably follow more conservative and risk adverse strategies.

Existing network: According to Pratono (2018), social networks with trust allow firms to gain a pricing capability and a selling capability, which brings a positive influence on their performance. A business network allows a firm to concentrate on its competencies and to outsource other non-core activities to its business partners (Papastamatelou et al., 2016). Business alliances that are characterized by collectivism increasingly share information, trust each other, and are able to increase firm performance (Papastamatelou et al., 2016).

5.3 Conceptual Framework

In this section, we present the conceptual framework on the relationship of the variables and the expected hypotheses. Figure 5.1 shows the conceptual framework of the study relating the independent variables (EO dimensions), control variables with the dependent variable (firm performance).

Based on the theoretical and empirical underpinnings in Section 5.2, and the conceptual framework shown in Figure 5.1, we formulate the following hypotheses to test our data on the relationship of the EO dimensions and firm performance.

Hypothesis 1. A higher risk-taking positively and significantly influences performance among enterprises in Ethiopia.
Hypothesis 2. A higher pro-activeness positively and significantly influences performance among enterprises in Ethiopia.
Hypothesis 3. A higher innovativeness positively and significantly influences performance among enterprises in Ethiopia.
Hypothesis 4. A higher aggressiveness positively and significantly influences performance among enterprises in Ethiopia.
Hypothesis 5. A higher autonomy positively and significantly influences performance among enterprises in Ethiopia.

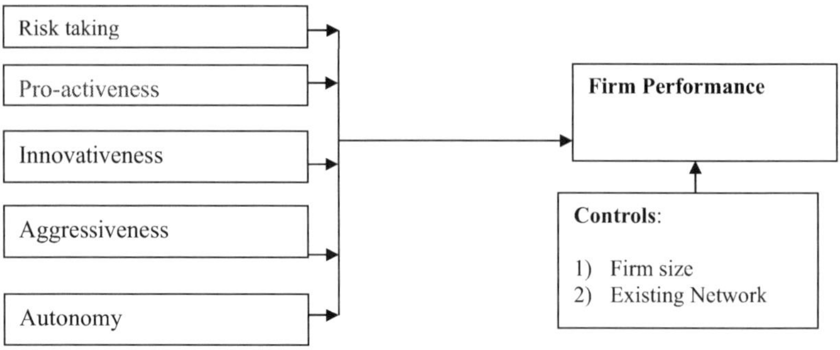

Figure 5.1 Conceptual framework

Source: Own construction based on a review

5.4 Methodology of the Study

5.4.1 Methodology Description of the Study Area

This study is carried out in Addis Ababa, which has ten sub-cities,[1] Ethiopia. Addis Ababa is chosen for this study because being the capital city of Ethiopia, Addis Ababa better gives the context to get all types of firms; large, medium, small, and micro-enterprises. From the ten sub-cities, Bole sub-city, which is the largest with the comparable mix of both manufacturing and service industry, is selected for this study because it is believed to better represent all types of the firms/enterprises considered in this study.

5.4.2 Research Design and Sampling

The research design of this study is survey type which applies structured questionnaire. The structured survey instrument is adopted based on previous established theories on EO among firms. As the context of firms varies based on their institutional and cultural settings where in they operate, the tested instruments might need to be modified to reflect the context of firms/enterprise in Ethiopia. The population used in this study represents all the large-scale, medium-scale, and small-scale enterprises operating in Bole sub-city, Addis Ababa, Ethiopia. The three types of firms[2] are used as sample frame following their registration list by the trade bureau of Bole Sub-city. Simple random sampling technique is used to select the representative samples from 2,442 firms within the three categories in Bole Sub-City.

According to Kothari (2004), simple random sampling applies to sampling without replacement, that is, once an item is selected for the sample, it cannot appear in the sample again and normally one should resort to simple random sampling because under it bias is generally eliminated and the sampling error can be estimated. To capture a suitable sample, this study carefully stratified the business industry into two broader categories as manufacturing and service offerings. Using the registry list of businesses from trade bureau of Bole sub-city, the two industry categories (manufacturing and services) are classified further into strata based on firm size. A proportionate sample size is taken from each stratum. The sample size is determined based on the formula developed by Yamane (1967). To select the sample size, in this study, the population of interest for the total number of firms (large, medium, small, and micro) operating in Bole sub-city is 2,442 based on AACMSEDA (2015) andCSA (2005). We excluded micro-enterprises from the population frame.[3] Further refining on the population frame, because of accessibility and data collection cost issues, resulted to 240 firms/enterprises (categorized under the large, medium, and small) in total.

$$n = N/(1+N\,(e)^{2})$$

where n is the sample size; N is the population size, and e is the acceptable sample error = (5%)

$$=240/(1+240(0.05)^2)$$
$$=147.$$

The sample size 147 is based on the firm classification as shown in Table 5.1.

5.4.3 Data Collection Procedure

This study employed the primary data source using structured questionnaire. As such the data is collected using the questionnaire from the managers of the enterprises and firms. Survey questionnaire was designed in English which we then discussed with experts working in large, medium, and small enterprises to ensure that the instrument contains pertinent variables and for other necessary feedbacks. We used the services of two trained enumerators in the Bole sub-city to pretest and collect the data. Thus, a team of two research assistants and two of the authors were engaged in collecting the data from the target respondents in the specified time. Moreover, two days of training was given for each research assistant to ensure accuracy in data collection. We pre-tested the instrument with six firm managers (one from each category). Any misinterpretations in the contents of the survey instrument noticed during the pre-test were modified accordingly.

5.4.4 Operationalization and Measurement of Variables

The survey instrument among others included questions related to background of the firm such as its size, age, its industry type, education level of the respondents, number of current employees, amount of capital during the start-up of the business, and firm's current capital. The five-dimensional model of Hughes and Morgan (2007) is chosen in this study partly because of the fact that reflective measurements helps to avoid the limitations associated with formative measures and an independent examination of EO's dimensions may be particularly useful for the purpose of assessing variations in

Table 5.1 Classification on firms

Enterprise level	*Hired labor*
Large	50 or more employees
Medium	Between 31 and 50
Small	6–30 employees
Micro	≤5 employees

Source: Ministry of Trade and Industry (1997)

the stability of the dimensions of EO and the outcome variable, firm performance (Covin & Wales, 2011). Hence, multi-item-based predictor variables of EO; risk-taking, pro-activeness, innovativeness, competitive aggressiveness, and autonomy were captured using Hughes and Morgan (2007) scale. Thus, respondents subjected to answer using the five-point Likert type scale (1 = strongly disagree and 5 = strongly agree). The Hughes and Morgan (2007) measurement scale consists of 18 indicators (observable variables) in total. Innovativeness was taped by three indicators (e.g., we actively introduce improvements and innovations in our business), proactiveness was measured using three items (e.g., we excel at identifying opportunities), risk-taking propensity was measured using three items (e.g., the term "risk taker" is considered a positive attribute for people in our business), autonomy was measured using six indicators (e.g., employees are permitted to act and think without interference), and competitive aggressiveness was taped using three items (e.g., our business is intensely competitive). We used two control variables: firm size (represented by the number of active employees), and the current network of the enterprise (social and business networks).

Firm performance was measured using five subjective indicators that tap the perception of the manager's satisfaction with total sales, cash flow, and return on investment, sales growth, and the ability to fund growth from profits. Respondents rated the scale with a seven-point, Likert-type ranging from "Much worse" (=1) to "Much better" (=7) corresponding to their firm performance. For more details, see Table 5.2. To validate the multi-item measures, conventional methods, including the exploratory factor analysis and Cronbach's alpha (Churchill, 1979) were used.

5.4.5 Data Analysis and Model Specification

We used a multiple linear regression model to express the relationships of the dependent and independent variables.

$$Y = \beta_0 + \beta_1 X_1 + \beta_2 X_2 + \beta_3 X_3 + \beta_4 X_4 + \beta_5 X_5 + \beta_6 X_6 + \beta_7 X_7 + \varepsilon,$$

where Y is the firm performance (dependent variable); βs are the parameter estimates; X_1–X_7 denote risk-taking, pro-activeness, innovativeness, aggressiveness, autonomy, firm size, and existing network, respectively.

5.4.6 Reliability and Validity Tests

We used Cronbach's alpha (Churchill, 1979) to evaluate the reliability (see Table 5.3) of the data. All the multiple items have minimum 0.7 alpha values except the risk-taking (which is about 0.7). To check the content validity, the questionnaire instrument was first carefully crafted by the researchers, and then it was pretested with limited respondents to check whether the content accurately assesses all fundamental aspects of the topic under consideration.

Table 5.2 Definition of variables and measurement

Variable	*Representative reference*	*Brief definition of the variable*	*Measurement*	*Expected effect on performance (+/–)*
Risk-taking	Lumpkin and Dess (1996)	It represents a willingness to commit resources to implement projects and activities	Five-point Likert (1 = Strongly disagree, 5 = strongly agree)	+
Pro-activeness	Rauch et al. (2009)	The predisposition to engage in creativity and experimentation	Five-point Likert (1 = Strongly disagree, 5 = strongly agree)	+
Innovativeness	Hughes and Morgan (2007); Rauch et al. (2009)	It signals an opportunity-seeking, forward-looking perspective characterized by the introduction of new products and services	Five-point Likert (1 = Strongly disagree, 5 = strongly agree)	+
Competitive aggressiveness	Hughes and Morgan (2007)	Adaptive capabilities to consistently undermine competitors' efforts in the market as opposed to adopting a passive stance to competition	Five-point Likert (1 = Strongly disagree, 5 = strongly agree)	+
Autonomy	Lumpkin and Dess (1996)	The freedom to employees to encourage them to be self-directed, to exercise creativity, pursue opportunities	Five-point Likert (1 = Strongly disagree, 5 = strongly agree)	+
Firm size	Peng and Luo (2000)	The size of the firm measured in terms of the number of employees (expressed in natural log)	Discrete number	+
Existing network	Pratono (2018)	Existing networks that gives rise to social capital in providing information, influence, and solidarity.	Five-point Likert (1 = Strongly disagree, 5 = strongly agree)	+

Table 5.3 Reliability test of the multiple item variables

No.	*Variable*	*Cronbach's alpha*
1	Risk-taking	0.674
2	Innovativeness	0.819
3	Pro-activeness	0.811
4	Competitive aggressiveness	0.799
5	Autonomy	0.874
6	Existing network	0.723
7	Performance	0.787

Table 5.4 Characteristics of sampled firms

Characteristic	*N*	*Minimum*	*Maximum*	*Mean*	*Standard deviation*
Number of years firms are in business (age)	85	2	70	15.25	9.473
Gender of managers in the firms	83	Male (60)	Female (23)	...	...
Manager's educational level	85	Diploma	Masters	...	...
Number of employees in firms	85	20	16000	3147.81	3743.061
Product types handled by firms	85	1	52	12.12	13.636

5.5 Results

This section presents the results of the study.

5.5.1 Sampled Firm Characteristics

Out of the 147 samples used in the survey, 112 questionnaires were filled and returned. Further checking of each questionnaire resulted in 85 properly filled questionnaires.

As Table 5.4 shows the age of the sampled firms varies from 2 to 70 years. This means that there are firms which have been in operation for the last 70 years in the Ethiopian market. With respect to educational level of the managers of the sampled firms, the results showed that the minimum educational level is diploma and the highest is masters. There is variation among sampled firms in terms of the number of employees (from minimum 20 to maximum 16,000). This means that the firm sizes greatly vary among firms in terms of their employee size. There is also variation among sampled firms in terms of product assortments (types of products) produced and marketed by the firms. To this respect, products (and services) served in market vary from 1 to 52 among the sampled firms. In terms of gender composition of the managers in the sampled firms, 60 are males and 23 are females; out of the 83 respondents who indicated their gender. This may mean that many of the managerial positions are held by men as compared to women.

5.5.2 Descriptive Statistics of Sampled Firms on Dependent and Independent Variables

Table 5.5 shows that the mean values of all the dependent and independent variables are greater than 3 based on the five-point Likert scale.

From the Pearson correlation output (Table 5.6), the firm performance is positively and significantly associated with risk-taking (r = 0.284**), innovativeness (r = 0.363**), pro-activeness (r = 0.306**), competitive aggressiveness (0.384**), and autonomy (r = 0.388**). This shows that there is a positive and significant association between firm performance and the five EO dimensions in the context of firms and enterprises operating in Ethiopia. The direction of relationship between the firm performance and all the independent variables of EO dimensions is positive. While running the correlation of variables, we also tested for any multi-collinearity problem in our

Table 5.5 Descriptive statistics on the variables for sampled firms

No.	*Variable*	*Mean*	*Standard deviation*	*N*
1	Firm Performance	3.506	.725	85
2	Risk-taking	3.192	.861	85
3	Innovativeness	3.318	.847	85
4	Pro-activeness	3.365	.794	85
5	Competitive aggressiveness	3.594	.847	85
6	Autonomy	3.046	.788	85
7	Firm size	6.91	1.89	85
8	Networks	3.702	.561	85

Table 5.6 Correlation coefficients of performance and EO dimensions

Variable	*1*	*2*	*3*	*4*	*5*	*6*	*7*	*8*
1. Firm size	1							
2. Network	.224*	1						
3. Risk-taking	.035	.260*	1					
4. Autonomy	−.031	.411**	.581**	1				
5. Aggressiveness	−.069	.209	.294**	.137	1			
6. Proactiveness	−.208	.115	.182	.307**	.360**	1		
7. Innovativeness	.067	.209	.321**	.286**	.430**	.447**	1	
8. Performance	.071	.135	.284**	.388**	.384**	.306**	.363**	1

** *Correlation is significant at the 0.01 level (two-tailed).*
* *Correlation is significant at the 0.05 level (two-tailed).*

data. Accordingly, our test shows that variance inflation factor (VIF) figures (Kim, 2019) are less than the limited value (10), and hence, there is no multicollinearity problem in our data. The highest VIF figure in our data (1.731) is for autonomy dimension of the EO.

5.5.3 Regression Results

The study proposed that the dimensions of EO (risk-taking propensity, innovativeness, proactive personality, competitive aggressiveness, and autonomy) are independently related to firm performance. Accounting for the impact of the control variables, namely existing networks and firm size, the data indicates that risk-taking propensity is not found to have a significant relationship with firm performance ($\beta = -.045$, $p > 0.05$). Risk-taking involves the willingness to commit significant resources to opportunities with a reasonable chance of costly failure as well as success, and this may mean that given the socio-economic contexts in Ethiopia, the more they commit resources on risky ventures; they might be experiencing no significant change in their performance. As expected in the study, competitive aggressiveness and autonomy found to have a significant and positive influence on firm performance ($\beta = .303$, $p < 0.05$) and ($\beta = .374$, $p < .05$), respectively. However, contrary to what had been proposed by the study, both innovativeness and proactive personality have shown insignificant relationship with firm performance. For more details, see Table 5.7.

We expected that there is a significant and positive relationship between performance and the control variables firm size and existing networks. This is because as the firm size and networks increase, there is a higher propensity for a higher firm performance. To this respect, higher firm size and its existing networks are also expected to be associated with large and experienced firms which might be more related to a higher performance. We found that firm size has a significant influence on firm performance ($\beta = .073, p < 0.1$, one

Table 5.7 Results of regression analyses for firm performance

Dependent variable	*Firm performance*
Risk-taking	–.045
Innovativeness	.123
Proactiveness	.082
Competitive aggressiveness	.303**
Autonomy	.374**
Firm size	.073*
Networks	–.138
F	4.937**
R^2	0.310
Adj R^2	0.247

** $p < 0.05$; * $p < 0.10$.

tailed). However, no support is found for a significant relationship between firm's networks ($\beta = -.138$, $p > 0.05$) and performance in our study.

As depicted in Table 5.7, except for risk-taking, the direction of relationship between EO dimensions and firm performance is positive. In general, out of our five hypotheses, we found support only for two dimensions of EO: competitive aggressiveness (Hypothesis 4) and autonomy (Hypothesis 5). Thus, Hypotheses 1–3 did not support the significant relationship between EO dimensions of risk-taking, innovativeness, and pro-activeness in our study.

5.6 Discussion and Recommendations

This study included the three contexts of firms (large, medium, and small) into its sample and analysis to test the broader generalizability of the EO–firm performance relationship. The descriptive results show that firm sizes greatly vary among sampled firms (minimum 20 to maximum 16,000). The firm size can serve as one of the organizational inputs when emphasis is focused on resource deployment for increased productivity. There is also variation among sampled firms in terms of product assortments (types of products) produced and marketed by the firms (1–52). This may indicate that the strategies of firms are still limited to operate in the market by broadening their product assortments as a means to win competition.

The results of the study show the presence of positive and significant influence of competitive aggressiveness and autonomy dimensions of EO on firm performance. Our study has confirmed the finding of Miller and Miller (2011) with respect to the positive and significant influence of the two dimensions of EO (competitive aggressiveness and autonomy) on firm performance. However, contrary to what had been maintained in the literature (e.g., Hughes & Morgan, 2007; Fadda, 2018), both innovativeness and proactiveness have shown in our data insignificant relationship with firm performance. This may mean that the level of innovativeness and proactive personality of managers among Ethiopian firms is limited in applying as components of strategic marketing to win competition. This could be also related to the fact that firms operating in Ethiopian markets predominantly focus on competitive aggressiveness and autonomy dimensions of EO and hence give limited attention to innovativeness and pro-activeness. Risk-taking dimension of EO is also found to be insignificant in our study. The study thus has shown a mixed relationship between the dimension of EO and firm performance, where two of the dimensions are found to be important to explain the variance of the firm performance whereas the rest are not.

Contrary to the findings by Covin and Slevin (1989) that established the uni-dimensional nature of EO, the study confirmed the multidimensionality of the EO construct and the independent relationship of its dimensions with firm performance. Our findings are in line with what Hughes and Morgan (2007) stated regarding absence of support for all dimensions of EO on their universal benefits in enhancing firm performance. Therefore, improvements in firm performance might be the product of only one or two of its five dimensions (Hughes & Morgan, 2007) and hence expecting the significant relationship of all EO dimensions with performance might not be always a case.

Based on the findings of this study, the following recommendations pertaining to practice and research are forwarded. First, firms operating in the Ethiopian market context need to emphasize on competitive aggressiveness and autonomy components of EO. This is because these two components are found to influence positively and significantly the performance of firms. Firms might need to invest on these two components across their functional units to tap their positive influence on performance. Second, this study is based on one-time cross-sectional data, and hence, it might be limited to make generalizability across broader contexts for the relationship of EO and firm performance. To overcome this shortcoming, further study need to be conducted based on multi-time panel data from different country contexts.

Notes

1 During this data collection, Addis Ababa had ten sub-cities.
2 The micro-enterprises were not included in this study as locating their premises was difficult during our data collection.
3 The number of small and micro-enterprises in Bole sub-city has been reported to be 1,650 (Seyoum et al., 2016), of which we excluded 50% as micro-enterprises.

References

AACMSEDA. (2015). *Inception report on micro and small enterprise development in Addis Ababa.* Unpublished Report. Addis Ababa City Administration Micro and Small Enterprise Development Agency.

Amoah, S. K., & Amoah, A. K. (2018). The role of Small and Medium Enterprises (SMEs) to employment in Ghana. *International Journal of Business and Economics Research*, *7*(5), 151–157.

Brouthers, K. D., Nakos, G., & Dimitratos, P. (2015). SME entrepreneurial orientation, international performance, and the moderating role of strategic alliances. *Entrepreneurship Theory and Practice*, *39*(5), 1161–1187. https://doi.org/10.1111/etap.12101

Calantone, R. J., Cavusgil, S. T., & Zhao, Y. (2002). Learning orientation, firm innovation capability, and firm performance. *Industrial Marketing Management*, *31*, 515–524.

Central Statistical Authority. (2005). *Report on large and medium scale manufacturing and electricity industries survey* (Vol. 321). Ethiopian Central Statistical Authority.

Churchill, G. A. (1979). A paradigm for developing better measures of marketing constructs. *Journal of Marketing Research*, *16*, 64–73.

Covin, J. G., & Covin, T. J. (1990). Competitive aggressiveness, environmental context, and small firm performance. *Entrepreneurship Theory and Practice*, 35–50.

Covin, J. G., Green, K. M., & Slevin, D. P. (2006). Strategic process effects on the entrepreneurial orientation – sales growth rate relationship. *Entrepreneurship Theory and Practice*, *30*(1), 57–81.

Covin, J. G., & Slevin, D. (1989). Strategic management of small firms in hostile and benign environments. *Strategic Management Journal*, *10*(1), 75–88.

Covin, J. G., & Slevin, D. P. (1991). A conceptual model of entrepreneurship as firm behavior. *Entrepreneurship: Theory & Practice*, *16*(1), 7–25.

Covin, J. G., Slevin, D. P., & Schultz, R. L. (1994). Implementing strategic missions: Effective strategic, structural and tactical choices. *Journal of Management Studies*, *31*, 481–505.

Covin, J. G., & Wales, W. J. (2011). The measurement of entrepreneurial orientation. *Entrepreneurship Theory and Practice*. https://doi.org/10.1111/j.1540-6520.2010.00432.x

Covin, J. G., & Wales, W. J. (2012). The measurement of entrepreneurial orientation. *Entrepreneurship: Theory & Practice*, *36*(4), 677–702.

Davidsson, P., & Wiklund, J. (2001). Levels of analysis in entrepreneurship research: Current research practice and suggestions for the future. *Entrepreneurship Theory and Practice*, *25*(4), 81–100. https://doi.org/10.1177/104225870102500406

Day, G. S., & Wensley, R. (1988). Assessing advantage: A framework for diagnosing competitive superiority. *Journal of Marketing*, *52*(4), 1–20.

Dimitratos, P., Lioukas, S., & Carter, S. (2004). The relationship between entrepreneurship and international performance: The importance of domestic environment. *International Business Review*, *13*(1), 19–41.

Eisenhardt, K. M. (1989). Making fast strategic decisions in high-velocity environments. *Academy of Management Journal*, *32*, 543–576.

Fadda, N. (2018). The effects of entrepreneurial orientation dimensions on performance in the tourism sector. *New England Journal of Entrepreneurship*, *21*(1), 22–44, 2574–8904. https://doi.org/10.1108/NEJE-03–2018–0004

Filser, M., & Eggers, F. (2014). Entrepreneurial orientation and firm performance: A comparative study of Austria, Liechtenstein and Switzerland. *South African Journal of Business Management*, *45*(1), 55–65. https://doi.org/10.4102/sajbm.v45i1.117

George, G., Wood, D. R., & Khan, R. (2001). Networking strategy of boards: Implications for small and medium-sized enterprises. *Entrepreneurship & Regional Development*, *13*(3), 269–285. https://doi.org/10.1080/08985620110058115

Gupta, V. K., & Wales, W. (2017). Assessing organizational performance within entrepreneurial orientation research: Where have we been and where can we go from here? *Journal of Entrepreneurship*, *26*(1), 51–76.

Hamel, G. (2000). *Leading the revolution*. Harvard Business School Press.

Hart, S. (1992). An integrative framework for strategy-making processes. *Academy of Management Review*, *17*(2), 327–351.

Hofstede, G. (2011). Dimensionalizing cultures: The Hofstede model in context. *Online Readings in Psychology and Culture*, *2*(1). https://doi.org/10.9707/2307-0919.1014

Hughes, M., & Morgan, R. E. (2007). Deconstructing the relationship between entrepreneurial orientation and business performance at the embryonic stage of firm growth. *Industrial Marketing Management*, *36*(5), 651–661.

Hult, G. T., Hurley, R. F., & Gary, A. K. (2004). Innovativeness: Its antecedents and impact on business performance. *Singapore Management Review*, *30*(1), 429–438. https://doi.org/10.1016/j.indmarman.2003.08.015

Hult, G. T., & Ketchen, D. (2001). Does market orientation matter?: A test of the relationship between positional advantage and performance. *Strategic Management Journal*, *22*(9), 899–906.

Ireland, R. D., Hitt, M. A., & Sirmon, D. G. (2003). A model of strategic enterpreneurship: The construct and its dimensions'. *Journal of Management*, *29*(6), 963–989.
Kim, J. H. (2019). Multicollinearity and misleading statistical results. *Korean Journal of Anesthesiology*, *72*(6), 558–569. https://doi.org/10.4097/kja.19087.
Kothari, C. R. (2004). *Research methodology*. New Age International Limited.
Kraus, S. (2011). The role of entrepreneurial orientation in service firms: Empirical evidence from Austria. *The Service Industries Journal*, 1–18. iFirst Article.
Lee, C., Lee, K., & Pennings, J. M. (2001). Internal capabilities, external networks, and performance: A study on technology-based ventures. *Strategic Management Journal*, *22*(6/7), 615–640.
Lumpkin, G. T., & Dess, G. (2001). Linking two dimensions of entrepreneurial orientation to firm performance: The moderating role of environment and industry life cycle. *Journal of Business Venturing*, *16*(5), 429–451.
Lumpkin, G. T., & Dess, G. G. (1996). Clarifying the entrepreneurial orientation construct and linking it to performance. *Academy of Management Review*, *21*(1), 135–172.
Lyon, D. W., Lumpkin, G. T., & Dess, G. G. (2000). Enhancing entrepreneurial orientation research: Operationalizing and measuring a key strategic decision making process. *Journal of Management*, *26*, 1055–1085.
Miller, D. (1983). The correlates of entrepreneurship in three types of firms. *Management Science*, *29*(7), 770–791.
Miller, D. (2011). Miller (1983) Revisited: A reflection on EO research and some suggestions for the future. *Entrepreneurship Theory and Practice*, *35*(5), 873–894. https://doi.org/10.1111/j.1540-6520.2011.00457.x.
Miller, D., & Friesen, P. H. (1982). Innovation in conservative and entrepreneurial firms: Two models of strategic momentum. *Strategic Management Journal*, *3*, 1–25. https://doi.org/10.1002/smj.4250030102.
Miller, D., & Miller, L. B. (2011). Governance, social identity, and entrepreneurial orientation in closely held public companies. *Entrepreneurship Theory and Practice*, *35*(5), 1051–1076. https://doi.org/10.1111/j.1540–6520.2011.00447.
Ministry of Trade and Industry. (1997). *Micro and small enterprises development strategy of Ethiopia*. Addis Ababa.
Papastamatelou, J., Busch, R., Ötken, B., Okan, E., & Gassemi, K. (2016). Effects of network capabilities on firm performance across cultures. *International Journal of Management and Economics*, 49, 79–105. https://doi.org/10.1515/ijme-2016–0005
Peng, M., & Luo, Y. (2000). Managerial ties and firm performance in a transition economy: The nature of a micro-macro link. *The Academy of Management Journal*, *43*(3), 486–501.
Poon, J. M., Ainuddin, R. A., & Junit, S. O. H. (2006). Effects of self concept traits and entrepreneurial orientation on firm performance. *International Small Business Journal*, *24*(1), 61–82. https://doi.org/10.1177/0266242606059779
Pratono, A. H. (2018). From social network to firm performance: The mediating effect of trust, selling capability and pricing capability. *Management Research Review*, *41*(6), 680–700.
Rauch, A., Wiklund, J., Lumpkin, G. T., & Frese, M. (2009). Entrepreneurial orientation and business performance: Cumulative empirical evidence. *Entrepreneurship Theory and Practice*, *33*(3), 761–787. https://doi.org/10.1111/j.1540-6520.2009.00308.x
Rhodes, J., Cheng, V., Sadeghinejad, Z., & Lok, P. (2018). The relationship between management team (TMT) metacognition, entrepreneurial orientations and small

and medium enterprises (SMEs) firm performance. *International Journal of Management Practice*, *11*, 111–140.

Seyoum, A., Aragie, M., & Tadesse, D. (2016). Growth of micro and small enterprises in Addis Ababa city administration: A study on selected micro and small enterprise in Bole Sub city. *International Journal of Scientific and Research Publications*, *6*(1), 581–592.

Slater, S. F., & Narver, J. C. (1995). Market orientation and the learning organization. *Journal of Marketing*, *59*(3), 63–74. https://doi.org/10.1177/002224299505900306

Stetz, P. E., Howell, R., Stewart, A., Blair, J. D., & Fottler, M. D. (2000). Multidimensionality of entrepreneurial firm-level processes: Do the dimensions covary? In R. D. Reynolds, E. Autio, C. G. Brush, W. D. Bygrave, S. Manigart, H. J. Sapienza, & D. L. Sexton (Eds.), *Frontiers of entrepreneurship research* (pp. 459–469). Babson College.

UNIDO. (1999). *Tanzania women entrepreneurs*. United Nations Industrial Development Organization.

Wales, W. J., Gupta, V. K., & Mousa, F. (2011a). Empirical research on entrepreneurial orientation: An assessment and suggestions for future research. *International Small Business Journal: Researching Entrepreneurship*, *31*(4), 357–383. https://doi.org/10.1177/0266242611418261

Wales, W. J., Monsen, E., & McKelvie, A. (2011b). The organizational pervasiveness of entrepreneurial orientation. *Entrepreneurship Theory and Practice*, *35*(5), 895–923.

Wang, C. L. (2008). Entrepreneurial orientation, learning orientation, and firm performance. *Entrepreneurship Theory and Practice*, *32*, 635–657. https://doi.org/10.1111/j.1540-6520.2008.00246.x

Wiklund, J., & Shepherd, D. (2003). Knowledge-based resources, entrepreneurial orientation, and the performance of small and medium-sized businesses. *Strategic Management Journal*, *24*(13), 1307–1314.

Wright, P., Kroll, M., Pray, B., & Lado, A. (1995). Strategic orientations, competitive advantage, and business performance. *Journal of Business Research*, *33*, 143–151.

Yamane, T. (1967). *Statistics, an introductory analysis* (2nd ed.). Harper and Row.

6 Integrating Corporate Social Responsibility and the Sustainable Development Goals

A Tropics Perspective

Leigh-ann Onnis

6.1 Introduction

The inter-connectivity of business activities and their economic, social and environmental impacts have been highlighted recently through extreme events, such as flooding, wildfires and the COVID-19 pandemic. During such events, the influence of economic and social power differences in outcomes for populations world-wide was apparent. People experienced these events in varied ways depending on where they lived, the industry in which they worked, their socio-economic status, and their ability to access education and health services. For many, the ethical practices of businesses emphasised the role of corporate social responsibility (CSR) during periods of crisis and disruption (Bove & Benoit, 2020; Fallah Shayan et al., 2022). It also highlighted the influence of CSR as a business strategy for economic success, and in progress towards the sustainable development goals (SDGs). Hence, the reciprocal arrangement whereby investment by businesses in communities and the environment for the good of *society*, creates the healthy, educated society that provide the labour and cliental for continued business prosperity.

This study focuses on the tropics, a region spanning from the Tropic of Cancer in the Northern hemisphere to the Tropic of Capricorn in the Southern hemisphere (State of the Tropics, 2022). The tropics is home to approximately 42% of the global population, who are living mainly in parts of Asia, North and South America, Africa, and northern Australia (State of the Tropics, 2022; Wang et al., 2022). The tropics is generally home to some of the poorest and most vulnerable populations in the world (State of the Tropics, 2020, 2022), as well as some of the most vibrant cities. Therefore, understanding how responsible business practices influence sustainable development in the tropics is important in meeting the sustainable development goals. To better understand how businesses are contributing to sustainable development, we must first examine how businesses in the tropics report the responsible business practices and activities they are undertaking to the public, and the positive impact they report arising from these business practices. Hence, the aim for this study was to examine if, and how, businesses

DOI: 10.4324/9781003349204-6

operating in Tropical North Queensland (Australia) were publicly promoting CSR activities and reporting contributions towards the SDGs.

6.1.1 Literature Review

A scan of the literature was conducted to identify what was known about the benefits and challenges with CSR and the SDGs for businesses, including non-financial reporting, and to investigate aspects of sustainable development reporting that could inform the study design.

6.1.1.1 Corporate Social Responsibility (CSR)

CSR generally captures the sentiment surrounding the responsibility of private business to stakeholders, the environment and broader society (Blowfield, 2005; Fordham & Robinson, 2018). First coined in the 1950s, CSR is a contested concept (Carroll, 2016; Fordham & Robinson, 2018). Initially viewed as a business philosophy for *doing good*, CSR originally comprised aspects of philanthropy. In the 1960s, expectations expanded for CSR to encompass wider social concerns (e.g. human rights), but it was not fully adopted as a strategic business practice until the 1990s/2000s. According to Fordham and Robinson (2018, p. 2), "In the 2000's, CSR was viewed as the critical linkage between business strategy and sustainable development" which resulted in companies using CSR to align their business to global standards to gain reputational benefit (Fallah Shayan et al., 2022). Increasingly, expectations to support local issues, and contributing to solutions at a global level (e.g. climate change), have created further complexity around how CSR is viewed. However, growing public expectations for corporations to act for the greater societal good continue to influence CSR activity.

6.1.1.2 The Sustainable Development Goals (SDGs)

The SDGs are ambitious goals seeking to stimulate action "in areas of critical importance for humanity and the planet" (United Nations, 2015, p. 3). Released in 2015, the SDGs comprise 17 overarching goals and 169 targets that balance the three dimensions of sustainable development: environmental, social and economic (United Nations, 2015; Wang et al., 2022) (see Figure 6.2 for a full list of SDGs). CSR and sustainability overlap, particularly where business decisions impact progress towards achieving the United Nation's 17 Sustainable Development Goals. For businesses, CSR practices supporting sustainable development can mitigate reputational damage, provide competitive advantage, and lead to financial gains (Fallah Shayan et al., 2022; Fordham & Robinson, 2018; Pizzi et al., 2021). Hence, where CSR aligns with the SDGs, business performance along with positive societal and environment outcomes improve (Jimenez et al., 2021).

6.1.1.3 Reporting

The frameworks and systems for financial reporting are well established. Business use financial frameworks and economic forecasting to guide the long-term direction for the company. In addition, economic metrics are used to monitor progress towards meeting financial objectives which are reported to shareholders and governments using pre-determined and clearly defined criteria. Yet, despite CSR being a legitimate businesses practice since last century, the criteria for collecting, reporting and analysing the impact of CSR lacks similar systematic design and reporting rigour (Fallah Shayan et al., 2022; Hahn et al., 2023).

The voluntary nature of CSR means that activities are generally aligned with the business' desired external image, often driven by reputation management, or as an attempt to separate the individual business from an industry with a poor reputation (Fallah Shayan et al., 2022; Fordham & Robinson, 2018; Pizzi et al., 2021). The drivers of CSR are typically described as internal (e.g., boards, managers, employees) and external (e.g. competitors, customers); however, some argue that CSR and sustainability reporting are largely motivated by external drivers (Fallah Shayan et al., 2022; Wachira et al., 2020). Generally, external entities appear to be the target audience for voluntary non-financial reporting.

Integrated reporting has emerged in the last decade as a way for businesses to produce one report which, according to the International Integrated Reporting Committee (IIRC) (2011, p. 2), provides a comprehensive outline of business performance in a way that:

> "reflects the commercial, social and environmental context within which it operates" providing "a clear and concise representation of how an organization demonstrates stewardship and how it creates and sustains value".

Integrated reporting was heralded as a way forward for non-financial and financial disclosures to be reported; however, the uptake has varied, and some researchers question whether integrated reporting can deliver as promised if reporting remains voluntary and unregulated (Flower, 2015; Sofian & Dumitru, 2017). Furthermore, Flower (2015) and Wachira et al. (2020) argue that integrated reporting focuses on value for investors rather than value for society. Moreover, there is no requirement to disclose harm (e.g. environmental damage) which means that with voluntary disclosures, it is more likely that businesses will only disclose activities that demonstrate the positive aspects of the business (Flower, 2015). Similarly, Sofian and Dumitru (2017) question the adequacy of integrated reporting given that businesses choose what they disclose, arguing that it is difficult to measure and compare just how integrated a report is when published.

Where sustainability reporting is more commonplace, some studies propose that CSR as a business strategy marginalises smaller actors, creates power imbalances, and allows for private agencies to usurp government standards/regulations for their own profit and/or power (Paoli et al., 2010; Smallwood et al., 2022). According to Hsiao et al. (2022, p. 787), reporting does not have a distinct influence on sustainability activity, saying that the literature "provides evidence suggesting IR [Integrated Reporting] is an incremental innovation for sustainability" that it "builds on established sustainability management and reporting practices and does not lead to transformative changes in organisational practices." In other words, those businesses already voluntarily reporting sustainable development were adopting integrated reporting, but it was not an incentive for those not voluntarily reporting sustainability practices to start doing so or to adopt sustainable development practices (de Villiers et al., 2017; Hsiao et al., 2022). Moreover, Pizzi et al. (2021) propose that the absence of standard reporting frameworks and the varying motivations for reporting non-financial data may lead to under- or over-estimation of business performance towards the SDGs. Studies investigating how businesses are reporting performance aligned to the SDGs found that they lacked consistency across methods (Fisher & Fukuda-Parr, 2019; Hahn et al., 2023).

Given the aforementioned challenges and the voluntary nature of CSR and sustainability reporting, it is not surprising that there are calls for changes to non-financial reporting practices. Adding to the growing narrative about thinking globally, Fallah Shayan et al. (2022) suggest that businesses should not think of CSR solely from a local context because businesses operate in an interconnected world citing the COVID-19 pandemic to demonstrate just how connected the world is both socially and economically. In contrast, Wachira et al. (2020) argue that while the focus on the macro-level is warranted, businesses also need to demonstrate legitimacy in the communities in which they operate. This is increasingly more important given the increase in business activities in emerging economies, some of which are being established in sensitive social and environmental settings, such as the tropics.

The literature scan revealed that sustainability reports contain a plethora of voluntarily reported non-financial performance indicators that are usually disconnected from each other, thus limiting their usefulness as indicators of societal impact (Flower, 2015; Hsiao et al., 2022; Wachira et al., 2020). Add to this, varied opinions about whether integrated reporting and sustainability reports are useful and consensus on the argument that initiatives like integrated reporting were introduced as a mechanism through which to create sustainability transformation (de Villiers et al., 2017; Flower, 2015; Wachira et al., 2020). It appears that the anticipated outcomes for an increase in sustainable development activities, brought on by more widespread practice of sustainability reporting, have not been attained. Yet many still see the benefits of a framework that could provide an integrated approach to sustainability to better track progress towards the SDGs. One promising framework is that of Fallah Shayan et al. (2022).

In many businesses, CSR and SDGs are implemented as separate activities, with little evidence capturing the benefit of an integrated approach to sustainability (Fallah Shayan et al., 2022). In response, Fallah Shayan et al. (2022) proposed a framework for integrating activities to achieve sustainable development. The theoretical framework shows promise; however, Fallah Shayan et al. (2022) note that it lacks the empirical research required to advance the framework for informing macro-level policies and shaping micro-level business strategies (van Zanten & van Tulder, 2021). This study contributes to this absence of empirical knowledge through using Fallah Shayan et al.'s (2022) framework to consider CSR from the perspective of businesses operating on or near areas of world heritage environmental significance, tropical areas where the impact of businesses operating in ways that support sustainable development will be felt at the local level in years to come, if not already.

Furthermore, the need for more consistent reporting on non-financial sustainable development activities are recognised as lacking, and where reported it is difficult to substantiate, and may differ by industry and location. One of the contributions that this study makes is to capture the type of non-financial data that is publicly reported at the micro level and to identify commonalities for reporting across one particular region to inform macro-level policy decisions. More specifically, this study contributes to the scarcity of empirical research about the impact of integrated voluntary CSR and SDG reporting, providing insights from the tropics, a region experiencing great environmental, social and economic disadvantage (State of the Tropics, 2020, 2022).

6.2 Methods

This study analysed data collected through a review of website content for businesses operating in Tropical North Queensland (Australia) to identify espoused actions towards sustainable development. A list of 424 members was compiled from the public websites of Chamber of Commerce groups operating in the North Queensland region. The list was screened, and 50 members excluded for not meeting the inclusion criteria:

1) being "in business" in north Queensland (i.e. selling products or services);
2) having a business website in English.

Next, 374 websites were reviewed to identify the presence of CSR/SDG content. A further 287 members were excluded. Then, a structuring content analysis was conducted on 87 websites containing CSR/SDG content to determine if the selected businesses were promoting themselves as being socially, economically and environmentally responsible, and whether it was relevant to the Tropics. There were 31 websites with content specific to the Tropics on which an inductive thematic analysis was conducted to illicit

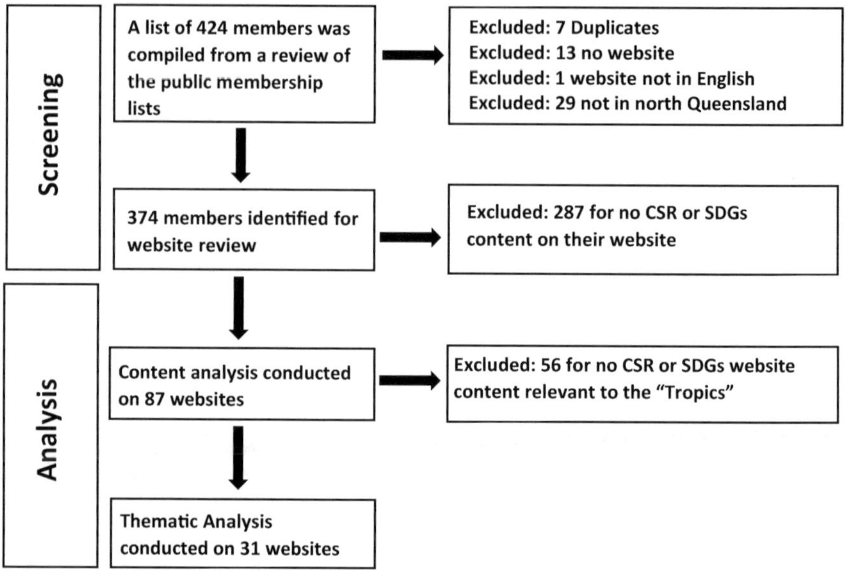

Figure 6.1 Website selection process

a deeper understanding of the sustainable development activities, and the reported impact they had on the local and/or global economy (Figure 6.1).

6.2.1 Content Analysis

Website content was analysed and coded to show whether the business espoused content specific to the Tropics and the potential for value creation in tropical regions (Figure 6.2). The content analysis was conducted in June 2022. In September 2022, 25% of the sample was randomly selected and re-reviewed to check for consistency in coding. The re-reviewed sample comprised almost one-third (32%) of businesses with CSR/SDG content and 20% of businesses without CSR/SDG content on their website. While the review identified new information added after June 2022, the review did not find any differences that would impact the coding for the original content analysis.

6.2.2 Thematic Analysis

A thematic analysis was conducted using NVivo20 to identify the key themes using an *a priori* coding structure based on Fallah Shayan et al.'s (2022) model. The subcategories of "Tropics" and "Other" were used during analysis to further exclude content not specific to the Tropics (Figure 6.3).

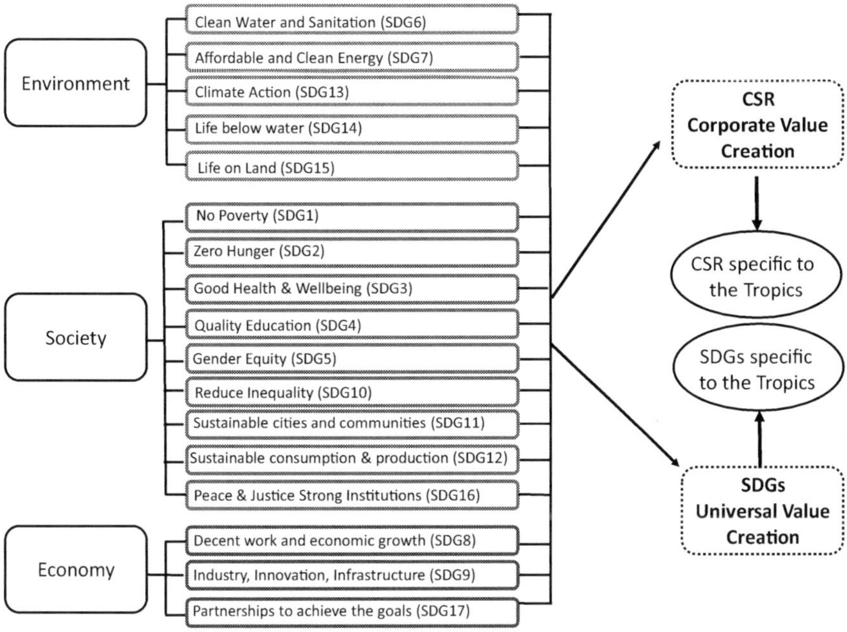

Figure 6.2 Research framework for content analysis
Source: Adapted from *Fallah Shayan et al. (2022)*

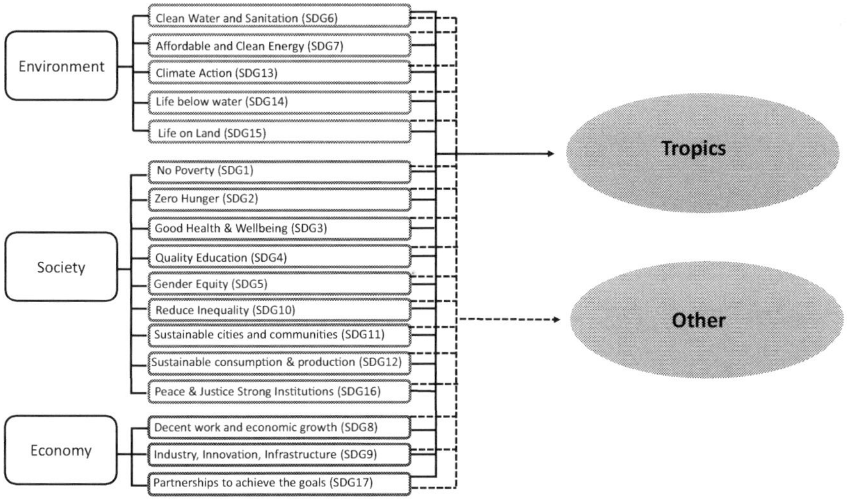

Figure 6.3 Coding framework for thematic analysis
Source: Adapted from Fallah Shayan et al. (2022)

6.3 Results

This section commences with the findings from the content analysis conducted on the websites of 87 businesses of varying sizes, from a range of industries (Table 6.1). More than half (52%) of the businesses were large (>250 employees), 31% were medium-sized businesses (50–249 employees) and the remainder (17%) were small businesses (10–49 employees).

The content analysis sought to identify the extent to which the selected businesses operating in Tropical North Queensland promoted themselves as being socially and environmentally responsible using the following categories:

a) *CSR internal value creation* – aspects of business operations promoted as contributing to sustainable development (adapted from Fallah Shayan et al., 2022).
b) *CSR internal value creation specific to the tropics* is a subset of (a)
c) *SDG universal value creation* – activities that contribute to sustainable development beyond their own business operations that contribute to meeting the SDGs (adapted from Fallah Shayan et al., 2022).
d) *SDG universal value creation specific to the tropics* is a subset of (c)

Table 6.1 Description of businesses by industry* and business size

Industry	*Business size*		*Industry*	*Business size*	
Accommodation and Food Services	Large	5	Agriculture, Forestry and Fishing	Large	-
	Medium	1		Medium	3
	Small	-		Small	-
Arts and Recreation Services	Large	1	Construction	Large	1
	Medium	4		Medium	1
	Small	3		Small	1
Education and Training	Large	4	Electricity, Gas, Water and Waste	Large	1
	Medium	-		Medium	-
	Small	1		Small	2
Financial and Insurance Services	Large	10	Health Care and Social Assistance	Large	1
	Medium	1		Medium	-
	Small	1		Small	-
Information Media and Communications	Large	2	Mining	Large	1
	Medium	4		Medium	-
	Small	-		Small	-
Professional, Scientific and Technical Services	Large	9	Rental, Hiring and Real Estate Services	Large	3
	Medium	4		Medium	-
	Small	2		Small	2
Retail	Large	2	Transport, Postal and Warehousing	Large	5
	Medium	3		Medium	5
	Small	4		Small	-

Source: ABS (2013)

* *Industry classified using Australia and New Zealand Standard Industrial Classifications.*

Table 6.2 CSR business activities promoted by selected businesses

Business ID	*CSR internal value creation*	*CSR specific to the tropics*	*SDG universal value creation*	*SDG specific to the tropics*
BUS3, BUS4, BUS8, BUS18, BUS19, BUS20, BUS23, BUS30, BUS31, BUS33, BUS40, BUS42, BUS43, BUS51, BUS53, BUS56, BUS65, BUS67, BUS69, BUS73, BUS75, BUS82, BUS83, BUS84, BUS86	✓	✓	✓	✓
BUS5, BUS13, BUS72	✓	☒	✓	✓
BUS21	✓	✓	✓	☒
BUS25, BUS27	✓	✓	☒	☒

For each of the four categories, the business websites were reviewed for evidence (✓) or absence of evidence (☒) (Table 6.2). The analysis found that 31 businesses (36%) provided information on their websites about CSR business activities (Table 6.2).

Next, the findings from the thematic analysis are discussed, integrating the espoused CSR activities with the SDGs categorised by environment, society and the economy.

6.3.1 Environment

The theme environment comprises the ways that the selected businesses promoted how they contributed to the sustainability of the planet, for example:

> *We are proud of what we do to protect and showcase the oldest tropical rainforest on Earth and welcome hundreds and thousands of visitors without impacting our environment.*
>
> (BUS84)

6.3.1.1 Clean Water and Sanitation (SDG6)

For SDG6, businesses described water conversation initiatives and water management systems, for example, "we are focused on driving holistic water stewardship" (BUS54). There was one specific innovation discussed that was tailored to the needs of the tropics: "Cairns Convention Centre's double layer pleated plate roof is designed to capture the seasonal tropical downpours, and channel rainwater directly into storage tanks" (BUS20). One tourism business discussed their waste-management system which not only managed waste but also led to water conservation and an innovative approach to recycling and regeneration of the environment, for example, "The waste from the public toilets and restaurant is treated onsite, which is re-used for irrigation or supplementing water features" (BUS51).

6.3.1.2 Affordable and Clean Energy (SDG7)

For SDG7, businesses most frequently discussed ways in which they were conserving energy, for example, "All our hotels use various forms of energy-efficient lighting" (BUS74) or their strategies for more sustainable sources of energy for the community, for example, BUS83 had "Electric vehicle charge stations" so "that guests can charge their electric vehicles while they explore the rainforest"; and BUS84 had solar powered phone charging "made from recycled batteries and solar panels." More specifically related to the tropics, businesses discussed building design aimed at conserving energy with BUS51, saying that "Exaggerated eaves reduce exposure to walls and windows from sunlight," and BUS83 discussing how the "open plan design of our buildings, operates an energy management system controlling use of lighting and air conditioning."

6.3.1.3 Climate Action (SDG13)

For SDG 13, most business provided a statement on their commitment to meeting targets, reducing emissions and improving sustainability for the benefit of the planet, for example, "We're committed to playing our part in limiting climate change to well below two degrees in line with the Paris Agreement" (BUS29). BUS43 educated guests "about the importance of rainforest ecosystems and their vulnerability from the impacts of changing climates," while BUS65 was concerned "about the impact of climate change on our precious reef into the future" so they "implemented strategies to reduce our carbon emissions." Businesses based in the topics often promoted their commitment to *Life Below Water* and *Life on Land* with statements such as "We love this beautiful environment that we live in so we support causes for the local environment, especially the Reef & the Rainforest" (BUS53).

Several businesses reported targets, for example, "Reducing Emission by 30% by 2025" (BUS8) and implementing ethical policies, for example, "no lending directly to fossil fuel or native forest logging projects" (BUS16). Others chose certification to communicate their commitment to climate action, "we've been Certified Climate Neutral since 2019" (BUS14).

6.3.1.4 Life Below Water (SDG 14)

For SDG14, businesses described pragmatic proactive measures, for example, "provide Marine Friendly SPF50+ Broad Spectrum sunscreen for all our guests" (BUS30), education, for example, "our onboard education program and involvement in coral species collection" (BUS30) and consultation, for example, "consult with traditional owners and marine experts to ensure best practices" (BUS69). With the Great Barrier Reef just offshore, most of the businesses who operate in, or by, the coast, or in the industries that depend on the tourism generated by the Great Barrier Reef (GBR) mentioned aspects of what their business was doing to support the sustainability of life below water in the tropics, for example, "work with coastal industries and communities to develop practical and sustainable solutions for our unique coastal and marine environments" (BUS31).

Generally, businesses espoused a commitment to the sustainability of the ocean, and estuaries of the region with some making specific reference to species, for example, one tour operator provided "photos of minke whales and assist[ed] with identification of individuals seen during minke season" (BUS65). Another said, "We feel privileged to be able to nurture and care for our site through monitoring, research, advocacy and removal of predatory crown of thorns starfish" (BUS87).

6.3.1.5 Life on Land (SDG15)

For SDG15, the themes were associated with conservation, for example, "mechanism for visitors to make an active contribution to the conservation of native species and local habitats" (BUS51), education, for example, "support tropical rainforest research and education projects" (BUS83) and innovation, for example, "After a decade plus of farming the "old school way," we have decided to take those practices and innovate!" (BUS1). Several businesses recognised the traditional owners and described working partnerships that were:

> *protecting and preserving the areas in which [the business] operates to ensure not only its own viability but also the viability of the communities which benefit directly from tourism generated by these areas, and with respect to heritage values and the culture of Traditional Owner groups.*
>
> (BUS23)

Several businesses discussed how they sourced local resources (food and labour) which had economic and social benefits, for example, "We hire and buy local wherever we can, which shows our ongoing support for the local communities" (BUS88) as well as environmental benefits due to reduced transportation distances.

6.3.2 Society

The theme society comprises the ways that the selected businesses promoted how they contributed to sustainable communities, for example:

> *[T]he firm, as a mature and responsible business, has a social responsibility to give both our time and resources for the benefit of the community.*
>
> (BUS3)

6.3.2.1 No Poverty (SDG1), Zero Hunger (SDG2)

Few businesses described activities that contributed to SDG1 or SDG2, and none were specific to the tropics; however, it is possible business activities may indirectly benefit tropical populations. For example, for SDG1, BUS26 provided support for "building houses for homeless youth in Australia," and for SDG2, BUS30 donated "excess food" as part of their "food waste reduction programme" and BUS7 had OzHarvest as a charity partner.

6.3.2.2 Good Health and Well-Being (SDG3)

Several businesses reported that for SDG3, their business had a "commitment to good health and well-being" (BUS31). Some businesses supported partners who provided support to populations in the tropics to improve their health and well-being outcomes, for example, BUS5, supported charity activities, including "Donating surplus medical supplies through Medical Aid Abroad" to Africa and Timor Leste, and supported "the Solomon Islands through donation of medical supplies." BUS52 supported a Businesses for Health initiative in Papua New Guinea.

6.3.2.3 Quality Education (SDG4)

Where businesses were education providers, they described the role of Educators in achieving the SDGs, for example, "We will produce graduates who have the knowledge, skills and drive to apply global and sustainable thinking to address complex social, economic and environmental challenges" (BUS31). Other businesses provided their expertise to existing programmes, with BUS51 being "a strong supporter of community focused programs that promote education."

6.3.2.4 Gender Equality (SDG5)

For SDG5, the businesses did not describe anything specific to the Tropics. Many described a commitment to promoting gender equity, for example, "We're committed to promoting gender equality in the workplace and helping our women thrive at work" (BUS66), and challenging stereotypes, for example, "We are committed to challenging long-held systemic gender inequities" (BUS62). Other emergent themes of relevance were "gender pay gap" (BUS66), women in senior roles, for example, "49% of directors on our Group subsidiary boards are women" (BUS62) and developing "pathways to build, and increase, female participation" in employment (BUS52).

6.3.2.5 Reduce Inequality (SDG10)

For SDG10, several businesses emphasised the role of business in reducing inequality, for example, "Immense value is placed on our corporate social responsibility and we're able to assist many local organisations to meet their needs" (BUS3). Most business engaged in philanthropy, for example, BUS76 had "a long history of carrying out business in an ethical and responsible manner – this includes positively contributing to local communities and charities." Some businesses reduced inequality through employment practices, for example, "Achieved 1% Aboriginal and Torres Strait Islander employee representation in our business" (BUS62), and through innovation, for example, "create a positive impact for vulnerable youth and our broader community" (BUS72).

6.3.2.6 *Sustainable Cities and Communities (SDG11)*

For SDG11, BUS4 highlighted the importance of thriving communities, for example, "if we all play our part then economically, our community will thrive." Several businesses described supporting communities as a corporate responsibility, with BUS29 saying, "We're focused on transparent, balanced and sustainable practices, policies and decisions that support positive social, economic and environmental outcomes." BUS18 espoused advancing and sharing "knowledge and best practice tropical expertise in our built environment."

6.3.2.7 *Sustainable Consumption and Production (SDG12)*

For SDG12, most businesses discussed actions to reduce consumption, for example, "Net zero waste" (BUS5), "Plastic knives and forks have been replaced with bamboo cutlery" (BUS40) and "bedspreads and pillowcases made from recycled bottles" (BUS77). A few mentioned changes to production. One mentioned sustainable supply chains, saying, "Our commitment to responsibly-sourced product extends to working closely with our suppliers on the environmental and social aspects of our supply chain" (BUS72).

6.3.2.8 *Peace and Justice, Strong Institutions (SDG16)*

A few businesses mentioned peace and justice. There were a few who acknowledged the role of businesses as institutions for change, for example, BUS16 said "business has a responsibility and a unique opportunity to be a powerful lever of change in the world."

6.3.3 *Economy*

The theme economy comprises the ways that the selected businesses promoted how they aligned to their business' philosophy to sustainability, for example:

> *It's about taking actions today to ensure we can succeed and grow in the future: building value for our shareholders; creating great jobs for our people; providing exceptional service for our customers; and making a positive impact on the environment and community.*
>
> (BUS52)

6.3.3.1 Decent Work and Economic Growth (SDG8)

For SDG8, businesses described how their vision was linked to strategy for improving sustainability of not only the business but also society and the environment, for example, "Our Vision is to embed sustainability in our culture, values, decision-making, operations, products and services to create a sustainable business" (BUS72). Strategy statements were common, for example, "The objective of our business strategy is to deliver balanced and sustainable outcomes for our customers, community, people and shareholders" (BUS29) and so were commitment statements, for example, "We are committed to leading the evolution of our industry to be truly sustainable – environmentally, socially and economically" (BUS59). Several businesses emphasised reputation, for example, "We will sustain our reputation through our commitment to financial, social, environmental and cultural sustainability" (BUS31) and ethical business practices, "responsibility to respect and uphold human rights" (BUS49).

6.3.3.2 Industry, Innovation and Infrastructure (SDG9)

For SDG9, businesses responded to both internal and external pressures for innovation, for example, "Enabling a sustainable future means working together with our people, our partners and our industry to explore innovative ways to tackle our most pressing challenges" (BUS67). Some wanted to driving change, for example, "global leaders who deliver innovative, solutions-focused outcomes and drive change to address real-world challenges" (BUS31).

6.3.3.3 Partnerships to Achieve the Goals (SDG 17)

For SDG17, companies discussed partnerships with peak bodies, for example, "a commitment to sustainable practices by partnering with leading climate bodies and councils" (BUS26), communities and other businesses. Most partnerships aimed to improve sustainability or create impact, for example, "We encourage and support that relationship through sponsorship activities, volunteering activities and pro bono legal support" (BUS82).

6.3.4 CSR, SDGs and the Tropics

Where businesses had ties to the environment in which they operated, initiatives were more likely to be directly related to improving SDG performance in the Tropics. For example, BUS40 is a business located on an island in north Queensland, so when they implement an initiative to "to combat the fight against single-use plastic" by only using paper straws, they are impacting the tropical environment in which they are situated. Likewise, businesses that depend on the tropical environment for their business success described strategies to support partners striving to maintain the environment, for example,

BUS69, supported turtle rehabilitation and the minke whale tagging programme by working "closely with universities by supplying both vessels and crew for scientific research," and BUS75 reported that their Sustainability strategy provides "environmental stewardship, community partnerships and economic prosperity throughout Far North Queensland." Significant environmental habitats appeared to also motivate businesses to focus on local provenance and support for local initiatives with BUS53 "donating a 50% profit share from the sale of every can of our Gold Medal winning" tropical ale. The strategy for this business ties their tropical brand with the tropical environment. Therefore, the data suggests that where the continued operation of the business is closely aligned to the tropical community, and/or environment, it is likely that they will espouse how the business supports the tropical community, environment or local economy.

6.4.5 Impact in the Tropics

The analysis found evidence of activities in the tropics, most commonly donating, fundraising, sponsoring and providing in-kind support to community groups who were protecting the environment and providing services that support the social good in the tropics (see Table 6.3). As evidence of how well they met their objectives, businesses listed awards and accolades received in recognition of their efforts, for example, BUS31 "ranked 29th for SDG 14: Life Below Water." However, the impact of the activities was rarely reported. One exception is BUS40 who estimated that they prevent "70,000 single-use plastic straws per year" from going to landfill.

Table 6.3 Integrating CSR and SDGs

Theme	*Example*
Donations SDG3, SDG4, SDG5, SDG14, SDG15	"more than $63,000 in in-kind gifts and cash donations to local charities" (BUS4)
Fundraising SDG3, SDG10	"raised $10,411 for the Cancer Council Queensland" (BUS3)
In-kind gifts SDG4, SDG5, SDG8, SDG14	BUS64 "Trained 800 disadvantaged people"
Sponsorship SDG3, SDG5, SDG8, SDG10, SDG17	BUS23 "is a proud sponsor of Cairns Taipans, Tourism Port Douglas Business Awards, Northern Pride"
Supporting community SDG3, SDG4, SDG14, SDG15, SDG17	BUS31 has "scholarships available for students with disabilities and/or students from underrepresented groups"
Awards SDG5, SDG7, SDG9, SDG10, SDG11	"Australian Social Enterprise Awards for Social Investment" (BUS64)

In addition, several large organisations reported impacts at the overall business level, some of which may benefit the Tropics, for example, BUS54 reported "43% reduction in water intensity," "62% reduction in landfilled waste" and the establishment of a "global food waste reduction program" across all their hotels.

6.4 Discussion

This study set out to examine if, and how, businesses operating in Tropical North Queensland were promoting and reporting sustainable development activities, by using the theoretical framework proposed by Fallah Shayan et al. (2022). The analysis found that Fallah Shayan et al.'s (2022) framework was suitable for analysing data to inform macro-level policies, and shape micro-level business strategies. It also highlighted many known issues with the quality and inconsistency of reported non-financial information, but was useful, nevertheless. Moreover, the challenges in distinguishing between sustainability-related outputs and outcomes reported at the business level and sustainability-related outputs and outcomes that actually lead to sustainable impact at the societal level in the tropics was typical of other research in this area (Hahn et al., 2023). The extent to which impact is visible at the societal level remains difficult to ascertain despite increases in non-financial reporting and more frequent communication about sustainable development initiatives at the business level. Contemporary research continues to highlight that "research has primarily focused on the various outputs of nonfinancial reporting" with the "more important aspect of the outcomes (or even the impact) of nonfinancial reporting" inadequately scrutinised (Garcia-Torea et al., 2023; Hahn et al., 2023). This study found that some businesses were reporting outcomes that had direct benefits to the tropical economy; there were few studies that attempted to measure impact at the societal level. The findings do, however, offer insights into factors that appear to be associated with the businesses that were more likely to describe business activities that contributed to sustainable development beyond aspirational statements and outputs: business size, industry and the location of the business' central office in proximity to the tropics.

6.4.1 Business Size

The findings revealed that while large businesses operating in the tropics espoused commitment to sustainable development, a few reported impacts specific to the tropics. Of note, small businesses more frequently reported sustainable development activities benefitting tropical environments and societies, and were more likely to give examples of what they were doing in contrast to the more aspirational statements made by larger businesses. Still, there was an absence of reporting impact, and providing evidence of impact using transparent measures so that their impact towards achieving the SDGs was apparent (Hahn et al., 2023).

Generally, the businesses in this study supported the community in which their business operated, with smaller businesses, appearing to have closer ties with the local community. According to Fordham and Robinson (2018, p. 11) where businesses "support philanthropic aspects at a local level," their CSR approach involves "becoming an integral part of the community" and "closely connected to community issues." This was evident in the CSR activities which often involved donations, fundraising and in-kind support for community groups and causes (Fordham & Robinson, 2018). While philanthropic activities create benefits for the local community, they can also be "strategies that generate broader benefits to the region" including the environment (Fordham & Robinson, 2018) and add value to the business (Fallah Shayan et al., 2022). That is, philanthropy can improve business opportunities. Moreover, improved local economies and economic growth have been found to do "more good than harm to the environment in tropical countries" (Wang et al., 2022, p. 88), which further supports the benefit of integrated CSR and SDG reporting.

6.4.2 *Industry*

The argument that industry and location influence CSR and sustainable development activities (Isahak et al., 2013) was supported by this study. This was evident in the eco-tourism industry where businesses were supporting research and rehabilitation work in conjunction with their daily business activities. Similarly, the farming industry was implementing sustainable farming practices as their core business as well as socially responsible behaviours supporting local employment and suppliers. The banking industry, which is compelled to report annually on certain matters, commonly disclosed practices restricting loans to commercial customers for activities detrimental to achievement of the SDGs (e.g. modern slavery, deforestation) (Paoli et al., 2010; Smallwood et al., 2022). In industries where national standards or industry policies existed, more detailed reporting was anticipated. These industries included mining (Fordham & Robinson, 2018; Isahak et al., 2013), banking (Paoli et al., 2010); agriculture and sustainable food systems (Fallah Shayan et al., 2022; Paoli et al., 2010; Smallwood et al., 2022); and healthcare (Fallah Shayan et al., 2022), noting the omission of tropical diseases (Fisher & Fukuda-Parr, 2019). However, a lack of legislative consistency across jurisdictions and challenges in adequately resourcing policy (e.g. monitoring, enforcement) influences the impact of policies on society and the environment (Fisher & Fukuda-Parr, 2019; Isahak et al., 2013; Paoli et al., 2010). Inconsistent reporting across industries was evident in this study, particularly the absence of a common language for describing sustainable development targets and measures of success (Hahn et al., 2023).

6.4.3 Location

Most businesses espoused content that suggested an understanding that the success of their business is tied to the health and wealth of the communities in which they are located. Therefore, CSR statements about respecting and valuing their customers, vision statements about sustainable environmental business practices, and acknowledgement of social issues were present in the content on selected business websites. However, many businesses were excluded from the study due to an absence of content about their CSR or SDG activities on their websites suggesting that the practice is not widespread in the region. As discussed previously, the evidence of businesses converting statements and targets to measures of success and impacts remains scarce (Garcia-Torea et al., 2023; Hahn et al., 2023). Several studies have concluded that there is a need for a framework or a universal measurement system for quality information across a range of consistent measures to be included in non-financial reporting (Fisher & Fukuda-Parr, 2019; Hahn et al., 2023; Pizzi et al., 2021; Smallwood et al., 2022; Tsalis et al., 2020). Hence, agreement is needed across industries and jurisdictions. This study found that many small businesses were demonstrating CSR in daily activities linked to sustainable development. For these small businesses, the burden of frameworks and KPIs may be unfairly weighted with the work they are doing. Yet, if they are excluded due to their size, much of their direct impact in local communities may not be captured when considering progress towards the SDGs.

6.4.4 Future Directions

Commonly, the drivers of CSR activity are described as being motivated by the expectations of stakeholders, shareholders, customers, managers, employees and the media – a group with varying interests in CSR activity outcomes. Furthermore, there is still a lot of scepticism around the motives of business who promote CSR activities and produce non-financial reports, particularly given the scarcity of outcomes and impact reporting (Fallah Shayan et al., 2022; Fordham & Robinson, 2018; Smallwood et al., 2022). Despite the motivation for CSR activities and non-financial reporting towards achieving the SDGs being questioned by some, Pizzi et al. (2021) propose that for early adopters of non-financial reporting, information is disclosed for reasons more aligned to CSR, than it is when businesses have directives for non-financial reporting (e.g. industry requirements). Hence, motivation and commitment may be more readily seen where the business and the environment and the community are heavily dependent on each other for continuance and prosperity. Future research exploring the influence of drivers of CSR activity on aspects of non-financial reporting behaviours and transparency in measures and indicators is needed to progress sustainable development (Hahn et al., 2023; Pizzi et al., 2021).

In addition, there is a need for more transparently reporting across the entire business for larger businesses, particularly multi-nationals. Fordham and Robinson (2018) suggest that having more robust policies can minimise situations where corporate CSR statements, reflective of sustainable development practices in the main office, or company headquarters, are not translated to the site-level, such as regional or international offices. However, policy alone is not sufficient as power imbalances will continue to inhibit progress if not addressed (Fisher & Fukuda-Parr, 2019; Paoli et al., 2010). Similarly, Smallwood et al. (2022, p. 9) warn of "token" polices, decoupling and deceptive interlinkages, by using policy focused on deforestation and ethical supply chains to highlight the influence of "unequal distribution of wealth and resources, food waste and mass consumption." Hence, as Fordham and Robinson (2018, p. 6) recommended, businesses need "robust CSR policies in place to guide company practice and enable transparency."

Overall, minor behavioural changes, donations, building modifications and adapting to the natural environment were the most commonly reported actions in this study. This may be due to the ease in which fitting (or retro-fitting) offices and donating time and/or money to charitable causes can be quantified. The findings are consistent with other studies who have found it difficult to assess contributions where measures are varied (Fisher & Fukuda-Parr, 2019; Pizzi et al., 2021; Tsalis et al., 2020). Regardless of whether reporting is mandatory or not, according to Pizzi et al. (2021, p. 405), there are differences in the measures being disclosed to quantify contribution toward the SDGs. Moreover, the reported information is not necessarily a measure of quality (Fisher & Fukuda-Parr, 2019; Pizzi et al., 2021; Smallwood et al., 2022), and the impact of these contributions is difficult to measure and seldom reported. While increased reporting is desired, transparency and consistency in data are important. As Pizzi et al. (2021, p. 413) explained "a high degree of SDG reporting orientation is not necessarily a signal of a real contribution to sustainable development, given possible greenwashing and impression management behaviors."

6.5 Limitations

It is acknowledged that the small dataset of businesses, all of whom were Chamber of Commerce members may have resulted in a sample that is not representative of all Tropical North Queensland businesses. It was, however, an independent sample of businesses that were unknown to the author at the time of selection and were diverse in characteristics. Also, the availability of information was limited to the content available from each business website, which varied. Therefore, the quantity of data available was not consistent. As quantity does not equal quality, the data collected was deemed suitable for this study. Finally, steps were taken to reduce rater bias; however, it is acknowledged as a limitation.

6.6 Conclusion

While the motives and quality of the reported non-financials, including the methods in which businesses capture, measure, track and report their sustainable development activities, may be contested, one thing remains clear – the role of business as an actor in the environmental, social and economic sustainability of this planet is key. Educational institutions will play a pivotal role in "shaping ethical principles and societal values as well as creating an appropriate system of values for tomorrow's business leaders" (Tsalis et al., 2020, p. 1620). Business leaders need to develop systems for the disclosure of non-financial information, thus demonstrating transparency and corporate stewardship.

The policy implications are broad. There is a need at the macro-level for a universal framework for CSR and SDG reporting that improves the quality of reported non-financial information. However, it must not increase the burden (or exclude) small business where activities at the micro-level appear more likely to have a direct impact on the local environment, businesses and society. For regions like the tropics, the impact of sustainable development activities by small, locally based businesses may more readily be captured at the micro-level. Despite promising signs, until large national and international businesses are compelled to improve the quality of the information disclosed, the impact of reusing towels in a multinational hotel chain on life below water in the Great Barrier Reef marine park will remain unknown. To improve progress towards the SDGs, strategies not only improve the links between the narrative and CSR activities but also show that the impact and benefits at a societal level are vital.

References

Australian Bureau of Statistics (ABS). (2013). *Australian and New Zealand standard industrial classification (ANZSIC) 2006 (cat. no. 1292.0)*. ABS.

Blowfield, M. (2005). Corporate social responsibility-the failing discipline and why it matters for international relations. *International Relations*, *19*(2), 173–191.

Bove, L. L., & Benoit, S. (2020). Restrict, clean and protect: Signaling consumer safety during the pandemic and beyond. *Journal of Service Management*, *31*(6), 1185–1202.

Carroll, A. B. (2016). Carroll's pyramid of CSR: Taking another look. *International Journal of Corporate Social Responsibility*, *1*(3), 1–8.

de Villiers, C., Venter, E. R., & Hsiao, P. C. K. (2017). Integrated reporting: Background, measurement issues, approaches and an agenda for future research. *Accounting and Finance*, *57*(4), 937–959.

Fallah Shayan, N., Mohabbati-Kalejahi, N., Alavi, S., & Zahed, M. A. (2022). Sustainable development goals (SDGs) as a framework for corporate social responsibility (CSR). *Sustainability*, *14*(3), 1222, 1–27.

Fisher, A., & Fukuda-Parr, S. (2019). Introduction – data, knowledge, politics and localizing the SDGs. *Journal of Human Development and Capabilities*, *20*(4), 375–385.

Flower, J. (2015). The international integrated reporting council: A story of failure. *Critical Perspectives on Accounting*, *27*, 1–17.

Fordham, A. E., & Robinson, G. M. (2018). Mapping meanings of corporate social responsibility – an Australian case study. *International Journal of Corporate Social Responsibility*, *3*(1), 1–20.

Garcia-Torea, N., Larrinaga, C., & Luque-Vílchez, M. (2023). Bridging the understanding of sustainability accounting and organizational change. *Organization & Environment*, *36*(1), 17–38.

Hahn, R., Reimsbach, D., & Wickert, C. (2023). Nonfinancial reporting and real sustainable change – relationship status: It's complicated. *Organization & Environment*, *36*(1), 3–16.

Hsiao, P. C. K., de Villiers, C., & Scott, T. (2022). Is voluntary international integrated reporting framework adoption a step on the sustainability road and does adoption matter to capital markets? *Meditari Accountancy Research*, *30*(3), 786–818.

International Integrated Reporting Committee (IIRC). (2011). *Towards integrated reporting, communicating value in the 21st century*. www.integratedreporting.org/wp-content/uploads/2011/09/IR-Discussion-Paper-2011_spreads.pdf

Isahak, A., Surif, S., Sahani, M., Gill, A., & Phang, J. (2013). Environmental stewardship for gold mining in tropical regions. *Journal of Degraded and Mining Lands Management*, *1*(1), 37–42.

Jimenez, D., Franco, I. B., & Smith, T. (2021). A review of corporate purpose: An approach to actioning the sustainable development goals (SDGs). *Sustainability*, *13*, 1–21, 3899.

Paoli, G. D., Yaap, B., Wells, P. L., & Sileuw, A. (2010). CSR, oil palm and the RSPO: Translating boardroom philosophy into conservation action on the ground. *Tropical Conservation Science*, *3*(4), 438–446.

Pizzi, S., Rosati, F., & Venturelli, A. (2021). The determinants of business contribution to the 2030 agenda: Introducing the SDG reporting score. *Business Strategy and the Environment*, *30*(1), 404–421.

Smallwood, J., Delabre, I., Pinheiro Vergara, S., & Rowhani, P. (2022). The governmentality of tropical forests and sustainable food systems, and possibilities for post-2020 sustainability governance. *Journal of Environmental Policy & Planning*, *25*(1), 103–117.

Sofian, I., & Dumitru, M. (2017). The compliance of the integrated reports issued by European financial companies with the international integrated reporting framework. *Sustainability*, *9*(8), 1319.

State of the Tropics. (2020). *State of the tropics 2020 report*. James Cook University. www.jcu.edu.au/state-of-the-tropics/publications/state-of-the-tropics-2020-report

State of the Tropics. (2022). *COVID-19 in the tropics, state of the tropics 2022 report*. James Cook University. www.jcu.edu.au/state-of-the-tropics/publications/2022-state-of-the-tropics-report

Tsalis, T. A., Malamateniou, K. E., Koulouriotis, D., & Nikolaou, I. E. (2020). New challenges for corporate sustainability reporting: United Nations' 2030 Agenda for sustainable development and the sustainable development goals. *Corporate Social Responsibility and Environmental Management*, *27*(4), 1617–1629.

United Nations. (2015). *Transforming our world: The 2030 Agenda for sustainable development*. https://sdgs.un.org/2030agenda

van Zanten, J. A., & van Tulder, R. (2021). Analyzing companies' interactions with the sustainable development goals through network analysis: Four corporate sustainability imperatives. *Business Strategy and the Environment*, *30*(5), 2396–2420.

Wachira, M. M., Berndt, T., & Romero, C. M. (2020). The adoption of international sustainability and integrated reporting guidelines within a mandatory reporting framework: Lessons from South Africa. *Social Responsibility Journal*, *16*(5), 613–629.

Wang, P., Zhang, H., & Wood, J. (2022). Achieving the sustainable development goals (SDGs): A tropical region perspective. In J. Wood, T. Chaiechi, & K. Thirumaran (Eds.), *Business, industry, and trade in the tropics* (pp. 68–96). Routledge. https://doi.org/10.4324/9781003153580

7 The Influence of Interest and Exchange Rates on the Growth of Private Investment in the Tropics

The Case of Tanzania

Lilian Bushiri, Coretha Komba, and Joshua Mwakujonga

7.1 Introduction

The growth and sustainability of a country's economy are associated with its relative level of private and public investment. Investment is crucial in enabling the adoption of new technologies and production techniques that enhance productivity (Agidew, 2014). In developing countries, private sector investment is significant in addressing various economic problems, such as unemployment and poverty (Nyoni & Bonga, 2017). In the long run, if the rate of accumulation of capital stock increases rapidly, investment enhances capital accumulation (Majeed & Khan, 2008). According to Kaputo (2011), public investments in infrastructure (e.g., energy, roads, telecommunication) and non-infrastructure projects (e.g., education, health, security) is crucial in supporting the overall growth of a country's economy.

The low economic growth in most developing countries has been ascribed to poor levels of investment and inadequate savings (Nwachukwu, 2011; Epaphra, 2014). The United Nations Conference on Trade and Development (UNCTAD) (2014) suggests that Africa needs to maintain a minimum of about 7% average growth to address its economic travails, including poverty. This will require a minimum of 25% of GDP in investment. Compared to its regional peers, Tanzania fared relatively well between 2010 and 2020, but its economic growth slowed significantly. The country's annual real GDP growth rate fell from 5.8% in 2019 to 2% in 2020, with negative per capita growth recorded for the first time in almost a quarter of a century (World Bank, 2021). According to the World Bank, the real GDP growth rate peaked in 2011 at 7.7%. Its drastic decline in 2020 resulted from the global COVID-19 pandemic that affected the global economy and heightened the financial sector's challenges (World Bank, 2021).

For more than two decades, low levels of domestic private investment have raised concern among scholars and practitioners. First, this increases economic instability, and second, domestic private investment is significant for job creation and a country's economic growth. The marginal benefit of investment by the private sector plays an important role in a country's economic growth

DOI: 10.4324/9781003349204-7

and development (Agidew, 2014). Even if total investment as a percentage of a country's GDP remains unchanged, increasing public investment at the expense of private investment may cause a decline in the private sector and ultimately decrease economic growth (Majeed & Khan, 2008). The private sector's contribution to economic growth is more meaningful than that of the public sector (Ayeni, 2014) because of apparent low levels of corruption and misuse of funds in the former (Seruvatu & Jayaraman, 2001). Therefore, the private sector should provide a significant share of additional investment and savings for an economy to achieve sustainable growth. Nonetheless, according to Majeed and Khan (2008), some aspects of public investment tend to complement private investment and promote growth, while others may substitute private investment and hence negatively impact growth.

Since the Economic Recovery Program of 1986, there have been substantial improvements in Tanzania's investment sector. Its investment policy reform in 1997 aimed to provide a conducive investment climate for foreign and domestic private investors, which was a turning point in increasing private investment. The reform led to the establishment of the Tanzania Investment Centre (TIC), which assists investors in obtaining registration, authorization, consent, and the necessary permits and addresses all the matters associated with investing in Tanzania. As such, private investment in the country has risen steadily over time compared to the period before economic liberalization. Most private investment has focused on natural resources, notably forest products and minerals. This recent scenario differs from the pre-economic liberalization period when the public investment was disproportionately high due to the government's large size, sidelining the private sector and favoring public resources (URT, 2018). Capital formation in the public sector increased by 17.2% from TZS 13,021.85 billion in 2017 to TZS 15,265.61 billion in 2018 at current prices (URT, 2018). In contrast, the private sector grew by 20.4% from TZS 29,120.07 billion in 2017 to TZS 35,050.63 billion in 2018 (URT, 2018).

To increase employment levels and government revenue, it is suggested that African countries increase their domestic investment to a minimum of 35% of GDP, with 23% coming from private investment (AfDB, 2013). However, Tanzania encounters various challenges in improving private investment. The World Bank report on ease of doing business ranked the country 116th in 2016 and 141st in 2020 out of 190 world economies. In addition, Tanzania's overall investment trend as a percentage of GDP has shown dramatic downward movement despite steady economic growth. During 2015–2019, its average investment reached 25.1% of GDP, peaking at 33.2% in 2016 (URT, 2018). Its investment performance has thus been below expectations considering its natural resources endowments.

As noted earlier, private investment is substantially more efficient than public investment. As a result, there is an emerging consensus that private sector-led growth has a more significant positive influence on the economy than public investment (Frimpong & Marbuah, 2010; Pesaran et al., 2001).

This has resulted in scholarly debates on the determinants of private investment (Nyoni & Bonga, 2017), including macroeconomic factors. The stability of macroeconomic variables, such as the exchange rate, interest rate, inflation, and GDP growth, can improve or reduce private investment. It is thus essential to analyze their effect on private investment.

Against this background, the objectives of this chapter were to:

i. describe the trend of interest rates, exchange rates, and private investment in Tanzania.
ii. assess the macroeconomic factors that affect the growth of private investment in Tanzania.
iii. estimate the short- and long-run influence of exchange and interest rates on the growth of private investment in Tanzania.

7.2 Literature Review

This section begins by critically reviewing previous empirical studies on macroeconomic variables' influence on private investment. This enables the identification of the research gap.

7.2.1 Empirical Review

Numerous scholars have analyzed the macroeconomic variables determining private investment growth in the tropics. However, these studies produced mixed findings. The literature reveals that macroeconomic variables such as GDP growth, capacity use, interest rates, internal funds, market value ratio to its replacement stock (Q ratio), exchange rates, public investment, and the user cost of capital are among the main determinants of private investment. For example, Nyoni & Bonga's (2017) empirical analysis of the effects of budget deficits on private investment in the East African Community (EAC) revealed a significant association between real GDP and private investment in the region. Batu's (2016) examination of private investment in nine sub-Saharan African countries found that exchange rates and national income significantly affect private investment.

Ngoma et al. (2019) analyzed the macroeconomic determinants of private investment in 35 sub-Saharan African countries. Among other things, they found that the inflation rate significantly influences private investment in this region. Similarly, Ekpo (2016) concluded that private investment in Nigeria is significantly affected by the inflation rate, fiscal deficit, interest rates, poor infrastructure, political and economic stability, and the investment climate. Molapo and Damane (2015) revealed that an increase in price levels negatively influences private investment in Lesotho, while Adugna (2013) found that inflation significantly and negatively affects Ethiopia's private investment in the short run. Adugna (2013) also observed that external debt and real GDP significantly influenced private investment in the long run. In contrast, the investment climate significantly negatively affected private investment in the long run. In the short run, it was revealed that external debt and real GDP per capita significantly and positively impacted private investment. At the same time, the inflation rate showed a significant negative effect. A study by Kaputo (2011) revealed that the exchange rate is one of the key determinants of private investments in the long run in Zambia. In line with this finding, Maganga and Edriss (2012) found that the exchange rate significantly impacts private investments in the long run in Malawi. Ajide and Lawanson (2012) reported the same finding in Nigeria.

Studies in different African countries have thus produced mixed results on how these macroeconomic variables determine private investment in the short and long run. For instance, Kaputo (2011) pointed out that public investment had a greater effect on domestic private investment in the short run, while the inflation rate, real exchange rate, real GDP growth, and real interest rates had a greater impact in the long run. These results contradict Maganga and Edriss (2012), who found that the real interest rate determines private investment in the short run while real exchange rates and GDP growth highly influence it in the long run.

Ekpo (2016) asserted that the interest rate is one of the determinants of private investment in Nigeria. Ajide & Lawanson, 2012) revealed the negative influence of interest rates on private investment in the long run. Batu's (2016) study involving nine sub-Saharan African countries found that interest rates significantly and negatively affect private investments. Naa-Idar et al. (2012) revealed that in both the long and short run, GDP growth significantly and positively influences private investments in Ghana. Similar results were produced by Kilindo (2017) in Tanzania, Maganga and Edriss (2012) in Malawi and Mose et al. (2020). However, some studies have reported contradictory results regarding the effect of some macroeconomic variables (i.e., interest and exchange rates) on private investment. For example, Hailu and Debele (2015) found that real interest rates had an insignificant and negative effect on private investment in the short run, which fits with macroeconomic theory. Moreover, these authors concluded that real interest rates have a positive and insignificant effect on private investments in the long run.

Various scholars have pointed to the lack of adequate evidence on the effect of macroeconomic variables (interest rate, inflation rate, and exchange rate) on private investment. For instance, Michael and Aikaeli (2014) noted insufficient evidence to associate interest and exchange rates with private investments in Tanzania, while Dang et al. (2020) reached the same conclusion regarding exchange rates' influence on private investments in Vietnam. In addition, Dang et al. (2020) concluded that interest rates significantly and positively affect private investment. Based on the empirical literature review, we present the research gap that emerges from current scholarly works on this topic.

7.2.2 Research Gap

As noted previously, extensive scholarly debate has been on the macroeconomic determinants of private investment in different countries in the tropics. Several empirical studies support existing investment theories (Ekpo, 2016; Kaputo, 2011; Maganga & Edriss, 2012). However, some empirical studies in different economies have produced contradictory results on how the macroeconomic variables of interest influence private investment (see Hailu & Debele, 2015; Dang et al., 2020; Michael & Aikaeli, 2014; Bosco & Emerence, 2016). In addition, some scholars, including Michael and Aikaeli (2014) and Epaphra and Mwakalasya (2017), based their analysis on the Error Correlational Model, which we regard as a weak analytical method to estimate the short- and long-run effects of macroeconomic variables on private investment. These mixed results and the weak analytical methods employed by previous studies made this research relevant. Using a different analytical approach (the Autoregressive-Distributed Lag bounds (ARDL) model), the primary objective was to confirm whether the effects of interest and exchange rates and other macroeconomic variables on investment are similar to the results found in the literature.

7.3 Methodology

This section provides information regarding data and research methods used to achieve each research objective. The study used various data and analytical methods in response to each objective.

7.3.1 Data

Given the study's nature and objectives, the researchers used time-series secondary data to describe the trend of interest rates, exchange rates, and private investment in Tanzania, examine the influence of macroeconomic variables on private investment, and estimate the long- and short-run influence of exchange and interest rates on private investment. We sourced data from the National Bureau of Statistics (NBS) in Tanzania, the Bank of Tanzania (BOT), TIC, and the World Bank's Global Development Network Database. The data for all variables of interest are in monthly frequency from 2002 to 2020.

For the purposes of this study, the variable *private investment* is defined as investment activities by the private sector, and the values are expressed in millions of Tanzanian Shillings (TZS). The variable *exchange rate* indicates economic competitiveness in terms of imports and exports, where depreciation increases the cost of imported products while appreciation does the reverse. At the same time, appreciation reduces the economy's level of production. The exchange rate here refers to the value of TZS against the US Dollar. The *interest rate* was measured as a percentage of the user cost of capital goods (when it rises, the cost of capital goods rises and investment falls, as the Keynesian theory states). The variable *inflation rate* is measured as a percentage of the Consumer Price Index (CPI) and described as a factor used to detect macroeconomic uncertainty and the information content in the pricing mechanism. Finally, this study defined the variable *GDP growth* as an indicator of a country's real output growth rates measured in percentages.

7.3.2 Analysis

Depending on the specific objective, the study used various methods to analyze the data. The following parts provide details on each objective and corresponding analytical methods.

Descriptive analysis was used to address the first research objective, where we describe the trend of the variables of interest (interest rate, exchange rate, and private investment). We considered descriptive analysis a suitable approach because it provides a clear picture of the trend of the variables under consideration for the entire period covered in this study.

Concerning the second research objective, where we examine the macroeconomic factors affecting private investment in Tanzania, the study adopted econometric analysis (a multiple linear regression model) following the ordinary least squares (OLS) assumptions to establish a causal relationship among selected variables. Gujarati and Porter (2008) note that the multiple linear regression model is an econometric model based on estimating the change in linearity between variables and a specific event. It tends to evaluate changes in the outcome variable (dependent variable) as the independent (affecting) variable varies by a particular number of units of measurement. In this regard, regressed variables of interest, that is, the exchange rate, interest rate, inflation, and GDP growth, were used to establish their influence on private investment. This model was preferred because the study has a single dependent continuous variable (private investment) and multiple independent variables. Building on this, we used the following model specification for this analysis:

$$Y = \beta 0 + \beta 1 \ln \chi 1 + \beta 2 \ln \chi 2 + \beta 3 \ln \chi 3 + \beta 4 \ln \chi 4 + \varepsilon$$

where Y is private investment; $\chi 1$ is the interest rate; $\chi 2$ is the exchange rate; $\chi 3$ is GDP growth; $\chi 4$ is the inflation rate; β_i (for all $i = 0, 1, 2, 3, 4$) is a parameter estimate; and ε is an error term.

For the third research objective, we employed the ARDL testing approach proposed by Pesaran et al. (2001) to estimate the long- and short-run influence of exchange and interest rates on private investment. According to Shrestha and Bhatta (2018), ARDL is a model based on OLS that can be used to model mixed order of integration and non-stationary time series data. This model was suitable because the bounds test can be performed whether the series is strictly I(1), purely I(0), or fractionally integrated. There is no need to pre-test them to determine their order of integration. Furthermore, the model avoids the endogeneity problems associated with other models like the Engle and Granger's (1987) two-step procedure. According to Pesaran et al. (1999), modeling the ARDL with the necessary lags will account for endogeneity and serial correlation problems. If the approximated ARDL model is free from serial correlation, endogeneity is of less concern (Jalil et al., 2008).

Therefore, we used this model to simultaneously calculate both the short- and long-run effects of the exchange rate, interest rate, GDP growth, and inflation on private investment. The following model was employed:

$$\Delta \text{lnPRIN} = \phi 0 + \sum^{k}_{i=1}\phi_1 \Delta \text{lnintr}_{t-i} + \sum^{k}_{i=0}\phi_2 \Delta \text{ln}excr_{t-i} + \sum^{k}_{i=0}\phi_3 \Delta \text{lninfl}_{t-i} + \sum^{k}_{i=0}\phi_4 \Delta \text{lnrGDPg}_{t-i} + \sum^{k}_{i=0}\phi_5 \Delta \text{lngdp}_{t-i} + \beta_1 \text{ln}intr_{t-1} + \beta_2 \text{ln}excr_{t-1} + \beta_3 \text{lninfl}_{t-1} + \beta_4 \text{lnrGDPg}_{t-1} + \beta_5 \text{lngdp}_{t-1} + \mu_t$$

where ϕ_1–ϕ_5 are the short-run coefficients and β_1–β_5 are the long-run coefficients, while the rest of the variables are defined as **PRIN** – private investment; **intr** – interest rates; ***excr*** – exchange rates; **infl** – inflation rates; **rGDPg** – real GDP growth; and **GDP** – Gross Domestic Product.

7.3.3 Diagnostic Tests

We conducted various diagnostic tests before we employed multiple regression analysis (OLS) and ARDL. The following sub-sections present the tests that were conducted.

7.3.3.1 Unit (Stationarity) Test

To avoid spurious results, we performed unit root tests to determine the stationarity of the time series data. The Augmented Dickey-Fuller (ADF) test was employed to determine the stationarity of the variables of interest. The test showed that all variables of interest, except exchange rates, are stationary. Thus, the results indicated an absence of unit roots for all variables except exchange rates. Table 7.1 presents the results of the ADF test.

Table 7.1 Unit (stationarity) test results

Variable	*Test statistics*	*Order of integration*
Private investment	-13.617^{***}	I(0)
Interest rate	-3.492^{***}	I(0)
Exchange rate	-2.910^{**}	I(1)
Inflation	-3.38^{**}	I(0)
GDP growth	-5.877^{***}	I(0)

Note: *, **, and *** denote 10%, 5%, and 1% significance levels, respectively. Critical values are 1% (−3.468), 5% (−2.882), and 10% (−2.572).

7.3.3.2 Cointegration Test

This study used Johansen's maximum likelihood framework to test for the cointegration of the variables of interest. The test's flaw is that it relies on asymptotic qualities, making it vulnerable to specification errors in small samples. However, the new econometric approaches integrated into STATA, which was employed in this research, and can present small sample statistics, mitigated this limitation. The test results show no cointegration among the variables of interest because the trace statistics of equations are greater than the 5% significance level. Table 7.2 summarizes the cointegration test results.

7.3.3.3 Heteroscedasticity Test

We used the Breusch-Pagan/Cook-Weisberg statistical test to test for heteroscedasticity in our data. Table 7.3 shows that the probability value is less than 0.05, indicating the presence of heteroscedasticity for the regressed model.

7.3.3.4 Multicollinearity Test

To determine if there is a multicollinearity problem among the independent variables, we employed a variance inflation factor (VIF) statistical test based on the condition that independent variables with a VIF greater than 10 may provide wrong results if we included them in the model. Table 7.4 indicates that the VIF test results for the independent variables of interest are less than

Table 7.2 Cointegration test results

Maximum rank	*Trace statistics*	*5% critical value*
0	224.834	68.52
1	152.595	47.21
2	82.737	29.68
3	31.213	15.41
4	10.154	3.76
0	224.834	68.52
1	152.595	47.21
2	82.737	29.68
3	31.213	15.41
4	10.154	3.76

Table 7.3 Heteroscedasticity test results

Ho: Constant variance	
	Variables: fitted values $\chi^2(1) = 21.51$ Prob > $\chi^2 = 0.0000$

Table 7.4 VIF test results

Variable	*VIF*	*1/VIF*
lnint	2	0.501
lnexc	1.99	0.502
lngdp	1.22	0.820
lninf	1.21	0.828
Mean VIF	1.6	

Table 7.5 Model specification test

Ho: model has no omitted variables	
F (3, 220)	1.77
Prob > F	0.1548

the threshold of 10. The results imply no multicollinearity problem among all the study's independent variables.

7.3.4 Model Specification Test

To check for model specification, we employed the Ramsey RESET, which tests whether or not the independent variables are optimal for deciding the response variable (i.e., private investment). The results from the test indicate an insignificant p-value of 0.1548. As such, we failed to reject the null hypothesis. These results imply the absence of misspecification of the model and that the independent variables of interest are sufficient in explaining the response variable. Table 7.5 provides detailed results from the model specification test.

7.4 Results and Discussion

This section presents and discusses the study's findings. The presentation of the findings focuses on the results of the data analysis. At the same time, the discussion compares our results with the current literature on the influence of the selected macroeconomic variables on the growth of private investment. We start by presenting the trend of the macroeconomic variables of interest, followed by their effect on private investment. Lastly, we present the long- and short-run impact of exchange and interest rates on private investment.

7.4.1 The Trend of Private Investment, Interest Rates and Exchange Rates

To describe the trend of interest rates, exchange rates, and private investment in Tanzania, we described the characteristics of these macroeconomic variables over time from 2002 to 2020. Figure 7.1 presents some stylized

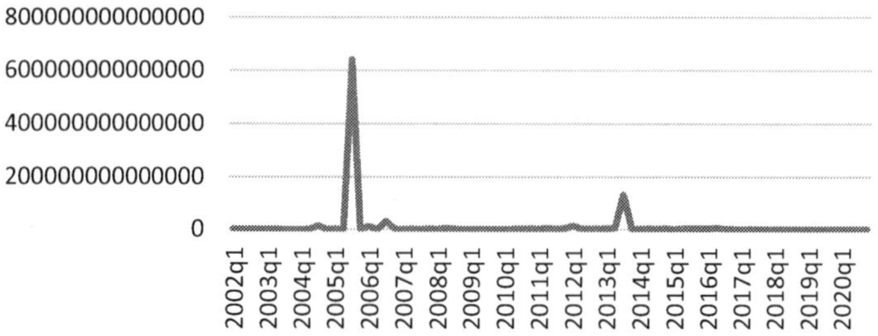

Figure 7.1 Trend of private investment between 2002 and 2020

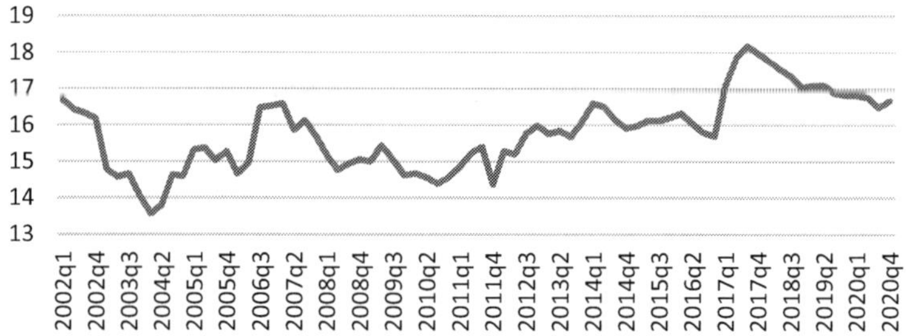

Figure 7.2 Trend of interest rates between 2002 and 2020

facts regarding private investment. It shows that private investment was flat between 2002 and 2004. It increased sharply thereafter and reached its highest level in the third quarter of 2005, followed by a large decrease in 2006. Private investment fluctuated between 2006 and 2012, followed by a significant increase in 2013. In 2014, it dropped significantly, followed by fluctuations between 2015 and 2020.

Figure 7.2 presents the trend of interest rates measured in percentages from 2002 to 2020. The descriptive analysis shows that interest rates recorded a sharp decrease and reached their lowest in 2004, with a slight increase in 2005, followed by a sharp increase in 2017. They continued to drop between 2018 and 2020.

In addition, we describe the trend of the exchange rate measured in TZS per US Dollar between 2002 and 2020. Figure 7.3 shows that the value of the TZS against the US dollar fluctuated significantly during the study period. While there are some pockets of appreciation and stability of the TZS against the US Dollar, the figure shows that, on average, the TZS took a downward trend (depreciation) against the US Dollar. As expected, the highest value of the TZS was recorded at the beginning of the study period in 2002, while its lowest value was recorded at the end of the study period in 2020.

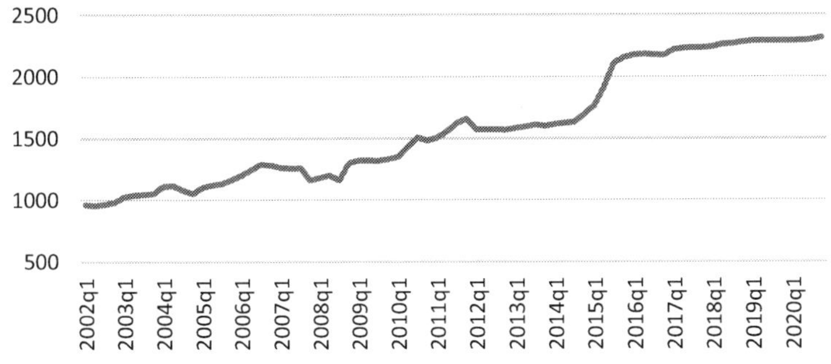

Figure 7.3 Trend of exchange rates between 2002 and 2020

Table 7.6 Effects of macroeconomic variables on private investment

Explanatory variables	*Coefficients*	*Heteroskedasticity-robust standard errors*
Exchange rate	1.046***	.334
Interest rate	2.275	2.015
Inflation rate	.760***	.208
GDP growth	1.002***	.180
Constant	10.997**	5.275
Number of obs = 228		
F (4, 223) = 7.13		
Prob > F = 0.0000***		
R-squared = 0.1133		
Adj R-squared = 0.0974		
Root MSE = 1.3299		

Note: Dependent variable is private investment. *, **, and *** denote 10%, 5%, and 1% significance levels, respectively.

7.4.2 Macroeconomic Factors Affecting the Growth of Private Investment

Table 7.6 presents the findings from the multiple regression model regarding the factors affecting private investment.

Table 7.6 shows that, except for interest rates, all the explanatory variables significantly affect private investment according to the preceding regression results. The variable interest rate, which represents the cost of borrowing, was observed to have a positive and insignificant effect on private investment. This implies that interest rates do not affect private investors' investment decisions.

The results further reveal that GDP growth has a positive and statistically significant effect on private investment. This implies that private investment is boosted by output recovery. The results also show that economic growth boosts people's income and GDP per capita. Increased individual or household income improves disposable income and ultimately increases demand for goods and services. This encourages private investment in an economy as investors are motivated to spend and reinvest more to meet the high demand for goods and services. The results of this study confirm the empirical results of previous scholarly works in this field as well as investment theories. Other scholars have found that GDP growth strongly influences private investment (see Molapo & Damane, 2015; Jalloh, 2002; Mbaye, 2014; Ouattara, 2005; Kaputo, 2011).

The exchange rate depicts a positive and significant effect on private investment. This implies that depreciation of the TZS against the US dollar tends to increase marginal profit from investing an additional unit of capital in Tanzania. These results are supported by several previous studies (see Assa & Abdi, 2012; Mbaye, 2014). This means that investors can obtain higher returns from domestic sales and exports. Depreciation of the TZS attracts private investment because it raises the profitability of tradable commodities (Workie, 1997). Depreciation of the TZS against the US dollar is thus a motivating factor for private investors.

The results for the variable inflation are unconventional as they reveal that an increase in the inflation rate increases private investment. These results are consistent with some previous studies (see Frimpong & Marbuah, 2010; Acosta & Loza, 2005), but inconsistent with the orthodox literature and other studies (see Were, 2001; Serven, 1997; Molapo & Damane, 2015; Adugna, 2013). The positive impact of inflation implies that as the prices of goods and services increase, profit-maximizing private businesses seize the opportunity to make abnormal profit levels. It also suggests that there is an influx of new private investment in lucrative industries when the price for commodities is relatively high. Therefore, from these results, an increase in inflation is considered a catalyst rather than a hindrance to private investment in Tanzania.

Finally, in relation to the second research objective, it was found that interest rates are insignificant in influencing private investment. These results run contrary to the Keynesian theory of investment, which posits that there is a negative relationship between interest rates and the level of investment. In addition, our findings contradict previous studies' findings (Kaputo, 2011; Ekpo, 2016; Agu, 2015), suggesting that the interest rate significantly influences private investment. A possible explanation for these results is that the problem facing investors in Tanzania is not the interest rate but rather the availability of funds.

7.4.3 Short- and Long-Run Effects of Interest and Exchange Rates on Private Investment

This sub-section presents the findings from the ARDL model regarding the short- and long-run effects of interest and exchange rates on private investment.

7.4.4 Short-Run Effects of Interest and Exchange Rates

The results presented in Table 7.7 indicate that, in the short run, interest rates are negative and significant in influencing private investment. These

Table 7.7 Short-run effects of interest and exchange rates on private investment

Variables	*Coefficients*	*Standard errors*
Private investment	.299***	0.066
Interest rate	−7.677**	2.994
Exchange rate	−.101	0.853
Constant	18.039***	4.307
Log likelihood = −359.8518		
Number of obs = 224		
F (9, 214) = 8.29		
Prob > F = 0.0000***		
R-squared = 0.2585		
Adj R-squared = 0.2273		
Root MSE = 1.2341		

Note: *, **, and *** denote 10%, 5%, and 1% significance levels, respectively.

Table 7.8 Long-run effects of interest and exchange rates on private investment

Variables	*Coefficients*	*Standard errors*
Private investment	−.433***	0.105
Interest rate	−7.758	5.275
Exchange rate	1.070	1.027
Constant	18.039***	4.307
Number of obs = 224		
Log likelihood = −359.8518		
R-squared = 0.5899		
Adj R-squared = 0.5727		
Root MSE = 1.2341		

findings are consistent with some previous studies (see Batu, 2016; Kaputo, 2011; Ajide & Lawanson, 2012) but contradict others (see Asante, 2000; Agu, 2015; McKinnon, 1973). The results imply that in the short run, an increase in the cost of capital causes a decline in investment.

Furthermore, the results reveal that, in the short run, the exchange rate has an insignificant and negative effect on private investment. Our results correspond with Ajide and Lawanson (2012). They imply that a short-term depreciation of the TZS against the US dollar would not increase private investment in the economy.

7.4.5 Long-Run Effects of Interest and Exchange Rates

Table 7.8 indicates that interest and exchange rates are statistically insignificant. The results imply that interest and exchange rates do not affect private investment in the long run. Our results are consistent with those of Hailu and Debele (2015).

7.5 Conclusion, Policy Implications and Recommendations

This study confirms the presence of short-run relationships between interest rate, exchange rate, and private investment. However, we could not establish evidence associating interest and exchange rates with private investment in the long run. This implies that these variables, in the short run, influence private investors' decisions to invest in the economy. Similarly, other macroeconomic factors, that is, GDP growth and the inflation rate, positively influence the level of private investment in Tanzania.

These results have various implications for policymakers. One is that the monetary authorities should control inflation and reduce interest rates through appropriate monetary policy tools to stimulate private investment in the country. Regarding economic growth, the study concludes that increased domestic absorption capacity, which is proportional to output growth, is necessary to boost private investment. Increasing income attracts investors in the short run and indicates the potential for firms to expand due to the consumption multiplier.

In relation to public policy, the study's findings suggest that the national budget should be restructured to increase allocations to capital expenditure as one of the approaches to fuel private investment. Reducing some non-essential recurrent expenditures and increasing development funds are integral to growing private investment in Tanzania.

Over the past few years, there have been significant improvements in the development of Tanzania's infrastructure, including social amenities, railways, roads, harbors, and airports, all of which will continue to increase private investment in the country. Thus, the government should allocate a sufficient budget to improve such infrastructure nationwide. The government will develop and sustain a conducive environment for foreign and domestic private investments by doing so. Strategies are also required to boost the drivers of economic growth, which will further increase private investments. This is so because increased income and private investment are interconnected.

Finally, given that many policymakers regard the private sector as a central driver of economic growth, it is recommended that the government, through the Central Bank (BOT), offers incentives for financial institutions to increase loans and credit to the private sector. Appropriate policies should be reviewed to ensure that entrepreneurs can access sufficient and reliable financing.

References

Acosta, P., & Loza, A. (2005). Short and long-run determinants of private investment in Argentina. *Journal of Applied Economics*, *VIII*(2), 389–406.

Adugna, H. (2013). Determinants of private investment in Ethiopia. *Journal of Economics and Sustainable Development*, 4(20), 186–194.

AfDB. (2013). *Report of the international conference on private investment in Africa*. Addis Ababa, Ethiopia.

Agidew, E. T. (2014). *An investigation of macroeconomic determinants of domestic private investment evidence from East Africa.* [Master's thesis, International Institute of Social Studies].

Agu, O. C. (2015). Determinants of private investment in Nigeria an econometric analysis. *International Journal of Economics, Commerce and Management United Kingdom*, *III*(4), 1–14.

Ajide, K. B., & Lawanson, O. (2012). Modeling the long-run determinants of domestic private investment in Nigeria. *Canadian Center of Science and Education*, *8*(13), 139–152.

Asante, Y. (2000). *Determinants of private investment behavior* (AERC Research Paper No. 100). AERC.

Assa, M., & Abdi, E. K. (2012). *Selected macroeconomic variables affecting private investment in Malawi* (MPRA Paper No. 40698), Universitätsbibliothek, Ludwig-Maximilians-Universität München.

Ayeni, R. K. (2014). Macroeconomic determinants of private sector investment: An ARDL approach-evidence from Nigeria. *Global Advanced Research Journal of Management and Business Studies*, *3*(2), 82–89.

Batu, M. M. (2016). Determinants of private investment: A systematic review. *International Journal of Economics, Finance and Management Sciences*, *4*(2), 52–56.

Bosco, N. J., & Emerence, U. (2016). Effect of GDP, interest rate, and inflation on private investment in Rwanda. *International Academic Journal of Economics*, *3*(1), 19–35.

Dang, T. T., Pham, A. D., & Tran, D. N. (2020). Impact of monetary policy on private investment: Evidence from Vietnam's provincial data. *Economies*, *8*(3), 1–15.

Ekpo, U. N. (2016). Determinants of private investment in Nigeria: An empirical exploration. *Journal of Economics and Sustainable Development*, *7*(11), 80–92.

Engle, R., & Granger, C. (1987). Co-integration and error correction representation: Estimation and testing. *Econometrica*, *55*(2), 251–276.

Epaphra, M. (2014). Empirical investigation of the determinants of Tanzania's national savings. *Journal of Economics and Development Studies*, *2*(4), 223–241.

Epaphra, M., & Mwakalasya, A. (2017). Analysis of foreign direct investment, agricultural sector and economic growth in Tanzania. *Journal of Modern Economy*, *17*(8), 111–140.

Frimpong, J. M., & Marbuah, G. (2010). The determinants of private sector investment in Ghana: An ARDL approach. *European Journal of Social Sciences*, *15*(2), 473–491.

Gujarati, D., & Porter, D. (2008). *Basic econometrics* (5th ed.). McGraw-Hill, Irwin.

Hailu, D. B., & Debele, F. (2015). The effect of monetary policy on the private sector investment in Ethiopia: ARDL co-integration approach. *Economics*, *4*(2), 22–33.

Jalil, A., Ma, Y., & Naveed, A. (2008). The finance-fluctuation nexus: Further evidence from Pakistan and China. *International Research Journal of Finance and Economics*, *1*, 67–85.

Jalloh, M. (2002). *An analysis of the macroeconomic determinants of private investment in Sierra Leone.* [Master's thesis, Addis Ababa University].

Kaputo, C. C. (2011). *Macroeconomic policy and domestic private investment: The case of Zambia.* [Master's dissertation, University of Zambia].

Kilindo, A. (2017). Determinants of private investment in Tanzania: 1970–2015. *Tanzania Economic Review*, *5*(1–2), 22–35.

Maganga, A. M., & Edriss, A. (2012, August 16). *Selected macroeconomic variables affecting private investment in Malawi* (MPRA Paper No. 40698), 12: 28. University of Munich, Germany.

Majeed, M. T., & Khan, S. (2008). The determinants of private investment and the relationship between public and private investment in Pakistan. *Journal of Business and Economics*, *1*(1), 41–48.

Mbaye, E. Z. (2014). *Determinants of domestic private investments in Kenya*. [Master's thesis, University of Nairobi].

McKinnon, R. I. (1973). *Money and capital in economic development*. The Brookings Institution.

Michael, I. M., & Aikaeli, J. (2014). Determinants of private investment in Tanzania. *African Journal of Economic Review*, *II*(2), 241–256.

Molapo, S., & Damane, M. (2015). Determinants of private investment in Lesotho, 1982–2013. *European Scientific Journal*, *11*(34), 473–491.

Mose, N., Jepchumba, I., & Ouru, L. (2020). Macroeconomic determinants of domestic private investment behavior. *African Journal of Economics and Sustainable Development*, *3*(2), 30–37.

Naa-Idar, F., Ayentimi, D. T., & Frimpong, J. M. (2012). Time series analysis of determinants of private investment in Ghana (1960–2010). *Journal of Economics and Sustainable Development*, *3*(13), 23–33.

Ngoma, G., Bonga, G. W., & Nyoni, T. (2019). Macroeconomic determinants of private investment in sub-Saharan Africa. *DRJ – Journal of Economics and Finance*, *4*(3), 1–8.

Nwachukwu, T. E., & Odigie, P. (2011). *What drives a private savings in Nigeria?* [Paper presentation]. Paper presented at Workshop Organised by the African Economic Research Consortium (AERC), Nairobi Kenya.

Nyoni, T., & Bonga, W. G. (2017). An empirical analysis of the determinants of private investment in Zimbabwe. *DRJ – Journal of Economics and Finance*, *2*(4), 38–54.

Ouattara, B. (2005). *Modeling the long-run determinants of private investment in Senegal* (CREDIT Research Paper No. 04). Centre for Research in Economic Development and International Trade, University of Nottingham.

Pesaran, H. M., Shin, Y., & Smith, R. (1999). *Bounds testing approaches to the analysis of long-run relationship*. Department of Applied Economics, University of Cambridge.

Pesaran, H. M., Shin, Y., & Smith, R. (2001). Bounds testing approaches to the analysis of level relationships. *Journal of Applied Econometrics*, *16*, 289–326.

Seruvatu, E., & Jayaraman, T. K. (2001). *Determinants of private investment in Fiji* (Working Paper No. 2001/02). Economics Department, Reserve Bank of Fiji, Fiji.

Serven, L. (1997). Irreversibility, uncertainty and private investment: Analytical issues and some lessons for Africa. *Journal of African Economies*, *6*(3), 229–268.

Shrestha, M. B., & Bhatta, G. R. (2018). Selecting appropriate methodological framework for time series data analysis. *The Journal of Finance and Data Science*, *4*, 71–89.

UNCTAD. (2014). *World investment report*. https://unctad.org/system/files/official-document/wir2014_en.pdf

United Republic of Tanzania. (2018). *The economic survey 2018*. Ministry of Finance and Planning.

Were, M. (2001). *The impact of external debt on economic growth and private investment in Kenya: 1970–1996: An assessment* (UNU/WIDER Discussion Paper No. DP2001–120). Kenya Institute for Public Policy Research and Analysis, Nairobi, Kenya.

Workie, M. (1997). *Determinants and constraints of private investment in Ethiopia.* [MSc thesis, Department of Economics, Addis Ababa University].

World Bank. (2021). *Tanzania economic update, February 2021: Raising the bar – achieving Tanzania's development vision.* World Bank.

8 The Impact of Trade Conflict on Economic Development in Asia

A Policy Discussion

Sook Rei Tan, Jacob Wood, and Haejin Jang

8.1 Introduction

The United States (US)–China economic relationship is intricately linked (Archana, 2020), with the level of trade between the two nations growing significantly in recent times (Wu et al., 2021c, 2021a, 2021b). In 1990, exports from China to US totaled US$15.24 billion; however, since its inclusion in the World Trade Organization (WTO), as the institutions 143rd member in 2001, this figure has grown exponentially with Chinese exports to the US totaling US$506.40 billion in 2021. At the same time, US exports to China also grew, increasing from US$4.06 billion in 1990 to US$151.10 billion in 2021 (see Table 8.1). While both nations have undoubtedly benefitted from just a deepening trade relationship, the US also continues to run a burgeoning trade deficit with China (see Table 8.1). Moreover, significant job losses in US manufacturing has also been a significant concern, with more five-million jobs lost across the 2000–2018 period (Guiltford, 2018). In addition to this, there has been a growing protectionist trade policy agenda that has sought to mitigate the negative impact that such job losses may bring to the local economy.

Another major concern for the US has been the theft of intellectual property and the forced US technology transfers to China (Archana, 2020; Wood et al., 2020; Wu et al., 2022). In the case of intellectual property, much was made by the Trump Administration around the cost that infringements in this area had on US businesses (Wood et al., 2020). Moreover, the US has also accused China of turning a blind eye and making little attempt to meet its obligations under the Trade Related Aspects of Intellectual Property Rights (TRIPS) Agreement that exists within the World Trade Organization (WTO) (Brander et al., 2017). However, America is not alone in this regard; many other countries and companies, as well as producers or owners of intellectual property, have also expressed concern (Brander et al., 2017).

In response to these areas of concern, the US Government, under the then leadership of President Trump, set out to establish a new policy initiative, which was highly nationalistic and increasingly protectionist in its trade policy agenda. In the aftermath of this policy change, came a tit-for-tat trade battle that has since become known as the US–China trade war (Wood

DOI: 10.4324/9781003349204-8

Table 8.1 Exports and imports of goods, and trade deficit of the US with China from 1990 to 2021 (US$ billion)

Year	*Exports*	*Imports*	*Trade deficit*
1990	4.09	15.24	-11.15
1995	11.75	45.54	-33.79
2000	16.19	100.02	-83.83
2005	41.19	243.47	-202.28
2010	91.91	364.95	-273.04
2015	115.67	483.20	-367.53
2016	115.59	462.42	-346.83
2017	129.89	505.47	-375.58
2018	120.34	539.50	-419.16
2019	106.62	452.24	-345.62
2020	124.49	434.75	-310.26
2021	151.10	506.40	-355.3

Source: United States Census Bureau, Foreign Trade, US International Trade Data (2022)

et al., 2020). However, the true cause behind the decision to enter into such a conflict started well before President Trump assumed office at the beginning of 2017. In order to fully appreciate the complex dynamics of the US–China trade battle, one must acknowledge that the trade conflict represents a broader set of popular beliefs against globalization, the likes of which have a history that started several decades ago.

Since the end of the World War II, the West, under the leadership of the US, has set about populating a globalist agenda, which has lead not only strong economic growth but also a contradictory set of outcomes that has seen globalization create clear winners and losers (Lund & Tyson, 2018). Of those that did well, the vast majority of the wealth was transferred to the so-called top 1%, while the middle classes in places such as the American mid-west suffered greatly, with significant job losses experienced in these areas. As Autor et al. (2013) note, an increasingly global agenda combined with higher levels of trade with China over the 1990–2007 period led to an estimated 250,000–500,000 job losses in the US. Moreover, these job losses also coincided with the significant widening in the income and wealth gap between the American middle-class and those at the top, with wage growth remaining relatively stagnant in recent decades as well (Sukar & Ahmed, 2019). A liberalized trade platform has increased income inequality by raising the wage levels of the most skilled, highly educated professionals, while also putting pressure of low-income earners, who have seen their pay packets either squeezed or their jobs shipped abroad (Helpman, 2016). These developments have led to fierce anti-globalization protests in many countries around the world, including the US and as part of this gave rise to growing areas of resentment in areas such as the mid-western states of the US, which in turn represented a key area of support for President Trump's election campaign, with many towns in the region seeing their jobs shipped off shore to places like China where businesses could capitalize on the cheaper labor costs that were available.

Given the perceived impact that China's economic development and policy agenda has had on the US, and the measures that have been taken to combat these problems, our research examines the nature of the US–China relationship, the emergence and impact of the trade conflict that exists between the two countries, and its economic effect on trading partners in the region. As the region emerges from the significant challenges presented by the COVID-19 pandemic, our study also provides an examination of the types of policies that could be implemented to drive a positive growth agenda moving forward. Our work builds on previous studies by Atkinson et al., 2022; Wu et al. (2021a); Wu et al. (2021b); and Wood et al. (2022), by examining the impact of not only the US–China trade war on trading partners in the Asian region but also the policy initiatives that can be developed to drive economic development in the post-COVID-19 era.

The remainder of this chapter is as follows. Section 8.2 outlines the background of the US–China trade conflict and the different areas of dispute that have taken place over the last five years. Section 8.3 provides an assessment of the literature around the impact that the trade war has had on the Asian region, while Section 8.4 addresses some of the policies that could be implemented to manage these impacts. Finally, Section 8.5 draws a range of relevant conclusions and highlights areas of future research.

8.2 The US–China Trade Conflict

While the background for a potential trade conflict started some time ago, the current US–China war began during former President Trump's election campaign in 2015, when he was running as a candidate for the Republican Party. It was during this time that his campaign fiercely criticized the Chinese Government for their role in pushing unfair trade practices, currency manipulation, and intellectual property theft (Rusche, 2019). However, it is important to also note that Trump was also quick to part blame of earlier US Governments for their weak leadership and an inability to resolve the problems earlier. Following his successful Presidential Election campaign, the Trump Administration immediately called for tighter tariff enforcement in anti-subsidy and anti-dumping cases and a review of US trade deficits. This was then followed by a plan to significantly reduce the US trade deficit with China within 100 days, which by mid-July 2017 had ultimately failed.

In the aftermath of these unsuccessful talks, President Trump launched a Section 301 investigation into alleged Chinese intellectual property theft. Following the investigation, which found clear evidence of property theft, a so-called "tariff war" was initiated against China. In the five years that have followed both countries have been embroiled in an ongoing battle to undermine each other's economic agenda in which both sides have increased and then removed tariffs on a whole range of products. At the center of US efforts has also been an intense desire to stop China from achieving the key objectives of the "Made in China 2025" campaign which aims to build up and strengthen China's capacity as a global trade power.

Over the last five years, the US–China trade war has experienced many key moments. Since January 2018, the Trump administration had announced tariffs on an array of Chinese products, such as solar panels, washing machines, steel, and aluminum, citing national security concerns (Renee Mayes et al., 2018). In response, China declared imposition of tariffs on several types of US commodities, primarily soybeans and automobiles. In subsequent months, several rounds of announcements on additional tariffs on Chinese imports were made by the US, followed by counteractions of China. July 2018 marked the actual start of the trade war, in which US tariffs on US$34 billion worth of Chinese goods had taken effect (Mullen, 2022). This was succeeded by the publication of a finalized list of 279 Chinese products, worth US$16 billion, to be subject to a 25% tariff from 23 August. On 14 August, China filed a complaint with the WTO against the US tariffs on foreign solar panels. On 30 November, the trade dispute culminated when President Trump endorsed the revised US–Mexico–Canada Agreement (UMCA), which included "rules of origin" provision for automobile. This provision was considered by the Trump administration as a way to prevent Chinese imports and promote manufacturing and investment within North America and the US (Cyrill, 2018).

In May 2019, Trump signed executive order 13873, adding Huawei to the Department of Commerce's Entity List. This designation prohibited Huawei from procuring vital parts and components from American companies without obtaining special permission, and also restricted the use of Huawei's equipment in American telecom networks due to national security concerns (Mullen, 2022). China retaliated by raising tariffs on US$60 billion worth of US goods in June. In August 2019, the US labeled China a currency manipulator after China allowed its currency to fall to its lowest level in over a decade (Borak, 2019). On 1 September, new tariffs went into effect between the US and China, where China imposed 5–10% tariffs on one-third of US imports and the US imposed 15% tariffs on US$112 billion of Chinese imports, affecting more than two-thirds of consumer goods. On 7 October, the US Department of Commerce added 20 Chinese public security bureaus and eight high tech companies to the Export Administration Regulations Entity List, requiring them to seek US government approval to buy components from US companies due to human rights concerns. On 11 October, after a period of trade tension, Trump declared that the US and China had come to a preliminary agreement for the first phase of a trade deal, in which China would purchase up to US$50 billion of American agricultural products and allow for more American financial services in their market, and the US would postpone new tariffs set for 15 October (Swanson, 2019).

In January 2020, the US and China signed a phase-one trade deal, which included commitments from China to purchase more US goods and address intellectual property concerns. In May 2020, the US threatened to cut ties with China over its handling of the COVID-19 pandemic. In July 2020, the US ordered the closure of China's consulate in Houston, citing espionage concerns, and China responded by ordering the closure of the US consulate in Chengdu (Law, 2020). On 26 September, The US Commerce Department imposed limitations on Semiconductor Manufacturing International Corporation (SMIC), China's biggest chip maker due to concerns that the supplied equipment could be used for military purposes. Under such restrictions, the suppliers were required to obtain a license to export the chip (Swanson & Zhong, 2021). In November 2020, President Trump signed an executive order prohibiting Americans from investing in shares of companies with links to the Chinese military.

On 6 January 2021, the New York Stock Exchange announced the delisting of stocks related to China Mobile, China Telecom, and China Unicom (Pound, 2021). On 13 January 2021, the Trump administration banned cotton and tomato products from Xinjiang over forced labor allegations. On 20 January 2021, Joe Biden was inaugurated as the president of the US and said he did not have immediate plans to remove the tariffs but planned to review the phase one trade deal. The US–China trade conflict has since softened with multiple high-level talks took place between the US and Chinese government officials. In 2022, despite the continuing political tension between the US and China, the trading relationship between the two countries has reached record highs (Martin & Monteiro, 2023).

Looking ahead to 2023, the development of US–China trade relationship remains unclear. At the time of writing, several positive trends emerged, with both US and China agreed on tariff exemptions on certain goods. For instance, in February 2023, the Office of the U.S. Trade Representative announced that the tariffs on 124 goods, which were imposed as a countermeasure to the US Section 301 tariffs on Chinese goods, will be suspended until 15 September 2023. However, the US–China tech war appears to heat up, as US issued export bans of design software, semiconductor manufacturing equipment and advanced chips from US companies to Chinese companies in April 2023. In the same month, legislators in the US State of Montana passed a bill that will ban a video-sharing app TikTok, owned by China's ByteDance, from operating within the state (China Briefing News, 2018). This seems to foreshadow a negative outlook for the future of US–China relations.

From a regional perspective, the impact of the US–China trade war has been keenly felt in other areas across the world as well. In today's global value chain environment, intermediate products cross borders many times. Consequently, tariff costs accumulate and are passed on to downstream industries, affecting the cost and price of final products (Wu et al., 2021c). In an attempt to quantify this impact, many studies have examined the US–China trade conflict, and in particular its impact on third party countries as well. In this instance, Wu et al. (2021c) found that not only did the trade war between China and the US significantly increase the cumulative cost of input tariffs for each country, but it also adversely affected the productivity growth of third countries – because higher input tariffs lead to less variety and lower quality imported intermediate inputs.

The trade conflict between the US and China resulted in not only economic losses for the two nations (Sabala & Devadoss, 2019), but it also had a significant impact on other countries' economies, both directly and indirectly (Wu et al., 2023a, 2023b). The direct effect of the trade war has caused a decrease in global trade activities (Bollen & Rojas-Romagosa, 2018), which are crucial for promoting prosperity and can also lead to unemployment (Jiming & Posen, 2018). Additionally, the indirect impact of the trade war has weakened economic performance in Canada (Charbonneau, 2019), decreased commodity exports in South Africa (Lemmer, 2019), and reduced the exports of solar energy in Malaysia (Yean et al., 2019). Moreover, it has adversely affected car and spare parts sales in Japan and the European Union (Abiad et al., 2018).

8.3 Policy Discussion

The US–China trade tension has impacted the global economy significantly, and it is essential for Asian countries to take appropriate policy measures to minimize the negative impacts and drive economic growth. In this section, we will explore several policies that could be implemented by Asian countries to maintain economic resilience in the midst of US–China trade tension.

While the US–China trade war has evidently caused economic costs on third countries as discussed earlier, it also opens up opportunities for developing Asian countries, as global manufacturers are exploring options to relocate their production facilities outside of China to avoid potential tariff increases in the future (Jong, 2022). In particular, ASEAN nations have reportedly been the largest beneficiary from the shift of investments from China towards other economies in the region during the trade war (Hutton, 2021). Research by Kathuria and Srinivasan (2022) showed that during the 2017–19 period, India and Bangladesh only gained US$1.2 billion and US$390 million, respectively, from the trade diversion effects in the manufacturing sector. Pakistan's gains were even lower, at only US$80 million. In contrast, Vietnam had a much more significant gain of US$8.5 billion. Therefore, it is crucial that policymakers from developing Asia, especially South Asia, strategize swiftly to seize any opportunities that arise from global supply chain relocations. In fact, governments across ASEAN had unveiled a series of incentive packages to attract foreign investors affected by the trade war. For example, Thailand, the Philippines, Malaysia, and Indonesia have implemented a range of economic measures such as new tax breaks and other initiatives that seek to provide other efficiency gains which enhance business operations, while Vietnam, Singapore, and Cambodia have been pushing for business reforms such as the signing free-trade agreements (FTAs) and double taxation agreements (Malvenda, 2019).

Moreover, in recent decades, the world has switched from multilateralism to a regionalism-based approach of international trade, a process that has further intensified due to the continued decoupling of the US–China economies. The US and China have been trying to expand and strengthen their dominance in Asia through the development of mega regional trade deals and strategies (Ji, 2021). Such initiatives have given rise to multiple mega-FTAs like the US-led Comprehensive and Progressive Agreement for Trans-Pacific Partnership (CPTPP) and Free and Open Indo-Pacific (FOIP) strategy, and the China-backed Regional Comprehensive Economic Partnership (RCEP) and the Belt and Road Initiative (BRI). Under such a geopolitical climate, the political leaders from developing Asia have gone to considerable lengths to carefully navigate the US–China rivalry and continue to leverage international trade and foreign direct investment (FDI) to drive its economic growth. As a salient example, Vietnam, being one of the largest winners of the US–China rivalry, has proactively embraced the economic components of the FOIP strategy (Tung, 2022) and participated in RCEP. Moreover, Vietnam has emerged as an FDI hotspot due to its conducive investment environment and commitment to global integration through the framework of economic cooperation (Fatharani, 2022).

Developing Asian countries should also prioritize strengthening regional cooperation and integration to maximize economic benefits. As a result of regional integration, small and remote countries can access a broader market for goods and services, increase economies of scale, and increase their competitiveness (Deichmann & Gill, 2008). One way to achieve this is through regional trade agreements (RTAs) such as the ASEAN Free Trade Area (AFTA) and the South Asian Free Trade Area (SAFTA). These agreements can reduce trade barriers and increase trade flows among member countries. Moreover, developing Asian countries can also collaborate on cross-country infrastructure projects to ease goods, services, and people flow across borders. For instance, the Johor Bahru-Singapore Rapid Transit System (RTS) link connecting Southern Malaysia and Singapore is expected to be completed by the end of 2026. The RTS link will be able to serve about 10,000 passengers per hour each way to help ease border congestion, while also bringing an array of significant economic benefits to both countries (Yusof, 2023). By working together, developing Asian countries can achieve greater economic integration and promote shared prosperity, which can in turn reduce their vulnerability to external shocks.

Another policy that developing Asian nations can adopt is to focus on diversifying their export markets. While the US and China are major trading partners for many Asian countries, there are other emerging markets that can offer new opportunities for trade and investment. For instance, the African Continental Free Trade Area (AfCFTA) is a promising platform for Asian nations to expand their trade and investment links with African countries.

The AfCFTA creates a single market for goods and services among 55 African countries, providing a market of 1.3 billion people with a combined GDP of US$3.4 trillion (World Bank Group, 2020). The increasing affluence of the middle class in Asia and its stronger demand present an opportunity for Africa to expand trade with the region (World Bank Group, 2022). Meanwhile, Asian countries can leverage this opportunity by investing in sectors such as infrastructure, agriculture, energy, and technology, which are critical to Africa's development. By diversifying their export markets, developing Asian countries can reduce their dependence on any single market and alleviate the impact caused by the US–China trade war.

Apart from maintaining an open economy, developing Asian nations should also focus on enhancing their domestic infrastructure and progressing towards more sustainable forms of economic development in the long term. COVID-19 has raised awareness of the importance of sustainable growth, social security, and shed light on the role of the digital economy in enhancing resilience. In fact, the digital economy played a significant role in stabilizing the economy during the pandemic (Lestari, 2020). Development Asia must therefore continue its digital transformation by promoting policies that encourage investment in digital facilities and provide skill development programs to equip its workers with higher levels of digital skill capabilities. Furthermore, by integrating digitization into relevant sectors, countries can move towards sustainable development, such as applying digital technologies to agricultural practices, water management, modeling electricity usage and enhancing energy efficiency (Mondejar et al., 2021).

In addition, extensive research has shown that infrastructure plays an essential role in promoting trade and economic growth. Improving hard infrastructure, such as roads, bridges, and ports, as well as soft infrastructure, such as a good business and regulatory environment, transparency, and customs management, can help facilitate trade and achieve higher and stable economic growth (Ismail & Mahyideen, 2015). These policies will position Asian countries for long-term prosperity and success, while ensuring that growth is both sustainable and inclusive. In conclusion, by adopting a proactive and adaptive approach to economic policymaking, developing Asian countries can adopt various policy measures as mentioned earlier to mitigate the negative impacts of the US–China trade tension and maximize the opportunities for economic growth and prosperity.

8.4 Conclusion

Trade conflicts, and in particular the US–China trade war, have had a significant impact on not only the countries involved but also the wider regional economy in Asia. In this study, we examine the nature of the US–China economic relationship and some of the issues that have complicated the ways in which the two nations trade with each other, such as the growing trade deficient, intellectual property infringements, potential currency manipulations and the impact that China has had on the US manufacturing base and the jobs losses that have occurred in recent years because of this relationship. Our research also looked at the trade war itself; the tariff measures that have been implemented by both sides and the economic implications of the protectionist policies have been adopted. From a policy perspective, we discuss the ways in which tariff costs accumulate and are passed on to downstream industries, affecting the cost and price of final products. We also note that while the US–China trade war has caused economic costs for third-party countries, the dispute has also provided opportunities for developing Asian countries, as global manufacturer hubs explore new prospects of potentially relocating their production facilities outside of China to avoid any further tariff increases that may occur in the future. Finally, we also note that in addition to maintaining an open economy, developing Asian nations must also look to further develop their domestic infrastructure capabilities and in doing so explore more sustainable forms of economic development over the medium to long term.

References

Abiad, A., Baris, K., Bernabe, J. A., Bertulfo, D. J., Romance, S. C., Feliciano, P. N., Mariasingham, M. J., & Blackman, V. M. (2018). *The impact of trade conflict on developing Asia* (ADB Economics Working Paper Series No. 556). ADB.

Archana, V. (2020). Who will win from the trade war? Analysis of the US–China trade war from a micro perspective. *China Economic Journal*, *13*(3), 376–393. https://doi.org/10.1080/17538963.2020.1785073

Atkinson, B., Wood, J., & Jang, H. (2022). Does Covid-19 spark the end of globalization? In T. Chaiechi & J. Wood (Eds.), *Community empowerment, sustainable cities, and transformative economies* (pp. 535–550). Springer Publishing.

Autor, D. H., Dorn, D., & Hanson, G. H. (2013). The China syndrome: Local labor market effects of import competition in the United States. *American Economic Review*, *103*(6), 2121–2168.

Bollen, J., & Rojas-Romagosa, H. (2018). *Trade wars: Economic impacts of US tariff increases and retaliations: An international perspective* (CPB Background Document). CPB Bureau of Economic Policy Analysis.

Borak, D. (2019, August 5). Trump administration labels China a currency manipulator. *CNN*. https://edition.cnn.com/2019/08/05/business/china-currency-manipulator-donald-trump/index.html

Brander, J. A., Cui, V., & Vertinsky, I. (2017). China and intellectual property rights: A challenge to the rule of law. *Journal of International Business Studies*, *48*, 908–921. https://doi.org/10.1057/s41267-017-0087-7

Charbonneau, K. B. (2019). *The impact of a trade war: Assessment of the current tariffs and alternative scenarios*. Bank of Canada.

China Briefing News. (2018, October 16). *USMCA trade pact: What it means for China, key stakeholders*. www.china-briefing.com/news/usmca-trade-pact-impact-china-key-stakeholders/

Cyrill, M. (2018, October 16). USMCA trade pact: What it means for China, key stakeholders. *China Briefing News*. www.china-briefing.com/news/usmca-trade-pact-impact-china-key-stakeholders/

Deichmann, U., & Gill, I. (2008). The economic geography of regional integration. *Finance and Development*, *45*(4). www.imf.org/external/pubs/ft/fandd/2008/12/deichmann.htm.

Fatharani, F. (2022, December). Analysis of Vietnam's response to the US-China trade war in times of pandemic. In *International conference on sustainable innovation on humanities, education, and social sciences (ICOSI-HESS 2022)* (pp. 720–730). Atlantis Press.

Guiltford, G. (2018, May 3). The epic mistake about manufacturing that has cost Americans millions of jobs. *Quartz*. https://qz.com/1269172/the-epic-mistake-about-manufacturing-thats-cost-americans-millions-of-jobs/

Helpman, E. (2016). *Globalization and wage inequality* (NBER Working Paper No. 22944). National Bureau of Economic Research INC.

Hutton, J. (2021, May 3). South-east Asian economy gets lift from US-China tensions. *The Straits Times*. www.straitstimes.com/asia/se-asia/south-east-asian-economy-gets-lift-from-us-china-tensions

Ismail, N. W., & Mahyideen, J. M. (2015). *The Impact of infrastructure on trade and economic growth in selected economies in Asia* (ADBI Working Paper Series, No. 553). ADB.

Ji, X. (2021). *Mega-regionalism and great power geo-economic competition*. Routledge.

Jiming, H., & Posen, A. S. (2018). *US-China economic relations: From conflict to solutions—Part I*. PIIE Briefings: Peterson Institute of International Economics, 18–1.

Jong, H. Y. (2022). The art of trade war: Spurring investments in Indonesia amidst the US–China trade war. *Global Journal of Emerging Market Economies*, *14*(2), 204–221. https://doi.org/10.1177/09749101211034110

Kathuria, S., & Srinivasan, T. G. (2022). How India and its South Asian neighbours fared during the US-China trade war. *The Wire*. https://thewire.in/trade/how-india-and-its-south-asian-neighbours-fared-during-the-us-china-trade-war

Law, E. (2020, July 25). China orders closure of US consulate in Chengdu in tit-for-tat move. *The Straits Times*. www.straitstimes.com/asia/east-asia/china-orders-closure-of-us-consulate-in-chengdu

Lemmer, W. (2019). SA feeling the impact of US-China trade war-commodity corner. *Farmer's Weekly*, *2019*(19032), 25–25.

Lestari, D. (2020). International trade in the Covid-19 outbreak: Is the digital economy working? *International Journal of Business & Management*, *8*(2), 86–92.

Lund, S., & Tyson, L. (2018, May–June). Globalization is not in retreat – digital technology and the future of trade. *Foreign Affairs*, 130–140.

Malvenda, M. (2019). Trade war incentive schemes in ASEAN. *ASEAN Business News*. www.aseanbriefing.com/news/trade-war-incentive-schemes-in-asean/

Martin, E., & Monteiro, A. (2023, February 8). US-China goods trade hits record even as political split widens. *Bloomberg.com*. www.bloomberg.com/news/articles/2023-02-07/us-china-trade-climbs-to-record-in-2022-despite-efforts-to-split#xj4y7vzkg

Mondejar, M. E., Avtar, R., Diaz, H. L. B., Dubey, R. K., Esteban, J., Gómez-Morales, A., Hallam, B., Mbungu, N. T., Okolo, C. C., Prasad, K. A., & She, Q., & Garcia-Segura, S. (2021). Digitalization to achieve sustainable development goals: Steps towards a smart green planet. *Science of The Total Environment*, *794*, 148539.

Mullen, A. (2022). US-China trade war timeline: Key dates and events since July 2018. *South China Morning Post*. www.scmp.com/economy/china-economy/article/3146489/us-china-trade-war-timeline-key-dates-and-events-july-2018

Pound, J. (2021, January 6). NYSE will delist three big China telecoms, reversing decision once again. *CNBC*. www.cnbc.com/2021/01/06/nyse-will-delist-three-big-china-telecoms-reversing-decision-once-again.html

Renee Mayes, B., Mellnik, T., Rabinowitz, K., & Tan, S. (2018, July 5). Trump's trade war has started. Who's been helped and who's been hurt? *Washington Post*. www.washingtonpost.com/graphics/2018/business/trump-tariff-trade-war/

Rusche, D. (2019, August 23). Here are the reasons for Trump's economic war with China. *The Guardian*. www.theguardian.com/us-news/2019/aug/23/trump-china-economic-war-why-reasons

Sabala, E., & Devadoss, S. (2019). Impacts of Chinese tariff on world soybean markets. *Journal of Agricultural and Resource Economics*, *44*(2), 287975.

Sukar, A., & Ahmed, S. (2019). Rise of trade protectionism: The case of US-Sino trade war. *Transnational Corporations Review*, *11*(4), 279–289.

Swanson, A. (2019, December 13). Trump reaches 'phase 1' deal with China and delays planned tariffs. *The New York Times*. www.nytimes.com/2019/10/11/business/economy/us-china-trade-deal.html

Swanson, A., & Zhong, R. (2021, July 19). U.S. places restrictions on China's leading chip maker. *The New York Times*. www.nytimes.com/2020/09/26/technology/trump-china-smic-blacklist.html

Tung, N. C. (2022). Uneasy embrace: Vietnam's responses to the US free and open Indo-Pacific strategy amid US–China rivalry. *The Pacific Review*, *35*(5), 884–914.

United States Census Bureau. (2022). US international trade data. *Foreign Trade*. https://www.census.gov/foreign-trade/index.html

Wood, J., Jang, H., & Atkinson, B. (2022). Covid-19: Its impact on trade and development in the ASEAN region. In J. Wood, K. Thirumaran, & T. Chaiechi (Eds.), *Business, industry and trade in the tropics* (pp. 137–150). Routledge.

Wood, J., Jang, H., & Oh, K. (2020). The U.S.–China trade war: Is it more pain than gain? *Journal of China Studies*, *23*, 61–85.

World Bank Group. (2020). *The African continental free trade area*. World Bank. www.worldbank.org/en/topic/trade/publication/the-african-continental-free-trade-area

World Bank Group. (2022). *Expanding African trade to boost growth and reduce poverty*. World Bank. www.worldbank.org/en/news/feature/2022/02/10/expanding-african-trade-to-boost-growth-and-reduce-poverty

Wu, J., Huh, C.-G., & Wood, J. (2021a). Globally chained economies: Unwitting victims of the US-China trade war. *Asia-Pacific Economic Literature*, *35*(2), 60–76. https://doi.org/10.1111/apel.12334

Wu, J., Luo, Z., & Wood, J. (2023a). How do digital trade rules affect GVC trade in services? Analysis of preferential trade agreements. *World Economy*. https://doi.org/10.1111/twec.13412

Wu, J., Wood, J., & Huang, X. (2021b). How does GVC reconstruction affect economic growth and employment? Analysis of USA – China decoupling. *Asia Pacific Economic Literature*, *35*(1), 67–81. https://doi.org/10.1111/apel.12319

Wu, J., Wood, J., & Jang, H. (2022). An assessment of trade facilitation impacts on China's outward foreign direct investment to ASEAN countries. In J. Wood, K. Thirumaran, & T. Chaiechi (Eds.), *Business, industry and trade in the tropics* (pp. 97–113). Routledge.

Wu, J., Wood, J., Luo, Z., & Chen, S. (2023b). How does the WTO dispute settlement mechanism work for WTO members? A comparative analysis of developed and developing countries. *Singapore Economic Review*. https://doi.org/10.1142/S0217590823500066

Wu, J., Wood, J., Oh, K., & Jang, H. (2021c). Evaluating the cumulative impact of the US– China trade war along global value chains. *World Economy*, *44*(12), 3516–3533. https://doi.org/10.1111/twec.13125

Yean, T. S., Yi, A. K. J., & Ann, T. B. (2019). *US-China trade war: Potential trade and investment spill-over into Malaysia* (Economics Working Paper No. 2019-03). Iseas Yusof Ishak Institute.

Yusof, A. (2023). JB-Singapore RTS Link project on track to start operations by end-2026. *CNA*. www.channelnewsasia.com/asia/jb-singapore-rts-link-project-track-start-operations-end-2026-3209646

9 Community-Based Tourism

Addressing Social Needs in Tropical Regions

Ruchi Sharma, Zilmiyah Kamble, and Joel Yap Qi Hong

9.1 Introduction

One of the biggest and most modern industrial sectors in the world is the travel and tourism sector (WTTC, 2021). It is continuously changing due to various factors such as the visitors' need for new experiences, the quick pace of technology change in the world, climate change, pandemic, and other factors (OECD, 2022). During 2019, the tourism sector was one of the world's largest and fastest-growing sectors, contributing US$8 trillion to the global economy (WTTC, 2021), but due to the COVID-19 pandemic, there was a 78% decrease in the global tourists' arrival rate leading to a loss of US$1.2 trillion in export revenues (UNWTO, 2020). The sector has been facing significant challenges and unsettling developments because of the COVID-19 pandemic. Despite being severely affected by COVID-19, there is hope for the future as several countries removed restrictions and opened their borders with visitors resuming travel plans since the lockdown regulations were lifted up. Coping with the challenges of COVID-19, the world officially started to open up for travel in 2022. Tropical regions have been popular tourist destinations due to their natural beauty and unique cultural attractions.

The term 'tropical regions' refers to regions that are found in the tropics, the belt-shaped area of the planet closest to the equator that is bounded horizontally by the Tropics of Cancer and Capricorn. Around 40% of the world's population live in the tropics, which also make up about 40% of the planet's surface area (World Population Review, 2023). It is predicted that the percentage of the world's population living in the tropics would reach 50% sometime in the late 2030s or 2040s due to sub-Saharan Africa's faster-than-average population increase (World Population Review, 2023). Compared to countries in the Polar Regions and middle latitudes/temperate areas, tropical countries climate is hotter, wetter, and more humid. The adverse impacts of hot and humid climate are evident in the tropical regions and the development of these regions is affected due to environmental vulnerability. People residing in tropical regions face variety of challenges which are unique to these regions. On the socio-economic front, it is necessary to recognize

DOI: 10.4324/9781003349204-9

and address developmental challenges faced by the people residing in tropical countries (State of the Tropics, 2014). They are vulnerable to the impacts of climate change (Corlett, 2012) like frequent hurricanes, flooding, droughts, rising sea levels. According to Nurse et al. (2014), Maldives and Tuvalu are at risk of being completely submerged. The extreme climatic conditions cause damage to homes, agriculture, and many times death and displacement.

The prevalence of infectious diseases (malaria, dengue, and zika virus) are difficult to control due to limited access to health care, poor sanitation, and poverty, resulting in significant impact on the health of local people (Silva et al., 2020). The lack of access to necessities leads to malnutrition and ill health. The ill health of people has significant impact on the economy due to increased health care costs and decreased productivity. The lack of educational opportunities leads to illiterate and unskilled workforce leading to increase in poverty and inequality as in sub-Saharan Africa, where more than 40% of the population lives in extreme poverty (Schoch & Lakner, 2020). The tropical regions rely on primary sectors (agriculture, forestry, fishing, and tourism) for their economy. Excessive deforestation results in loss of habitat for wildlife, soil erosion, and poor water quality as in Brazil, where significant deforestation resulted into such problems (World Wide Fund, 2021). Access to clean water is also scarce which resulting in waterborne disease and other related health problems. These primary industries are vulnerable to disruptive climatic conditions and COVID-19 making the tourism-based economy of these regions adversely affected, for instance, the Caribbean region economy which is highly dependent on tourism had to counter climatic conditions and COVID-19 (Srinivasan et al., 2020).

Tourism is considered as the fastest-growing sector, so the relation between tourism and the sustainable socio-economic development is significant in the tropical countries (Lee & Jan, 2019). This indicates that a transformative change is required to overcome the environment induced challenges and this change should equip the local inhabitants to strengthen the social development through community-based tourism. It will attract the tourists who demand authentic local cultural experiences and unique local products, which can be seen as the solution to the problem of underdevelopment of tropical regions (Menon, 1993). Tropical economies rely heavily on the rise of tourism, but managing it requires making trade-offs between ecosystem services and socio-cultural identities. COVID-19 has resulted in new consumer behaviour trends, which influences the tourism sector of tropics (Toubes et al., 2021). The revival from pandemic phase requires coordinated efforts to address emerging issues; at the same time, one need to be cautious as the tropical regions' physical environment, society, and economy could be vulnerable to the changes brought about by tourism and other outside forces (Conlin & Baum, 1995; Briguglio et al., 1996; Lockhart & Drakakis-Smith, 1997).

The involvement of local community promotes tourism sustainability (Hardy et al., 2002) and also creates better opportunities for local community

(Woodley et al., 1993). Community-based tourism (CBT) provides community with a better quality of life and also protects the environment (Roseland, 2012). The local community knowledge and cultural resources ensure unforgettable experiences that tourists cherished and share with others. CBT has its own challenges as well as opportunities. With the objective of investigating the role of CBT in promoting sustainable tourism, the sections in the following are organized as follows. Section 9.2 highlights the tourism destinations in tropical regions and reviews the four dimensions of sustainable development. Subsequently. the concept of community-based tourism is introduced. Section 9.3 presents the process to identify the relevant literature sources. Section 9.4 introduces the framework 'ADAPTATION' for addressing the social needs of local community by promoting community-based tourism. Section 9.5 provides the concise synthesis of the study, and section 'Suggestions for future studies' proposes the future areas of research.

9.2 Literature Review

9.2.1 Tourism and Destinations in the Tropical Regions

The tourism sector varies from countries to regions in the tropics, wherein, gradually, few regions are developing into preferred destinations due to the warm climate, natural beauty, diverse wildlife, and cultural attractions tropical regions. According to the World Tourism Organization (UNWTO), some of the top tropical destinations in the world include the Caribbean, Southeast Asia, and South America. Tourists visit tropical regions due to the presence of popular beaches such as Bali in Indonesia, Phuket in Thailand, Maldives in the Indian Ocean, and Cancun in Mexico, National Parks, and nature reserves (Corcovado National Park in Costa Rica, Tanjung Putting National Park in Indonesia). Tropical regions are also famous for cultural heritage sites (Angor Wat complex in Cambodia, a UNESCO world heritage site and ancient city of Machu Pichhu in Peru). Adventure sports like hiking, surfing, and scuba diving are also popular among tourists (Hawaii is famous for its excellent surfing; similarly, Costa Rica is a popular destination for zip-lining, whitewater rafting, and jungle hikes). The food and beverage (F&B) industry in many tropical regions also attracts tourists (Thailand is famous for its spicy curries and fresh sea food, and Caribbean region for rum-based cocktails and jerk chicken). The UNWTO's latest report shows that the American regions (which includes many tropical destinations such as the Caribbean and Central and South America) received 16% of the world's international tourists in 2019. Southeast Asia, which is another popular tropical region, received 10% of the world's international tourists in the same year (UNWTO, 2021a).

Tropical regions need to have a differential tourism plan focusing on harnessing the local people skills and integration of community-based tourism for sustainable development due to limited resources. Community-based tourism (CBT) needs to be promoted in tropical regions in the post-pandemic phase. 'Community' is a group of social beings living a common life in a geographically defined area (Ginsberg, 1961) having strong social and psychological bonding. According to Cater (1993) community participation in tourism gained its popularity (Beeton, 2006) in literature in 1970s after being recognized by World Bank, United Nations and other international organizations. The importance of community role was mentioned by researchers Cohen (1988) and Graburn (1976). The concept of CBT was first analysed by Murphy in 1985. The sustainable development focused on improving local community as the key strategy gradually started getting attention from various researchers (Tosun, 2000; Ruiz-Ballesteros, 2011).

9.2.2 Sustainable Development

The concept of sustainable development from 1980 to present times has initially evolved into the three pillars of sustainability: social, economic, and environmental (United Nations World Summit, 2005) – later the fourth pillar was added as institutional dimension (Spangenberg & Bonniot, 1998). All these pillars are interconnected and interdependent, and there exists strong relationship between geographical factors and socio-economic development. Sustainable development can foster long-term prosperity and well-being for both the present and future generations. A framework comprehending and advancing sustainable development is provided by the four pillars of sustainability, also referred to as the 'four dimensions or four components of sustainability.'

Environmental sustainability (United Nations World Summit, 2005) emphasizes minimizing the detrimental effects of human activity on the environment while safeguarding and maintaining natural resources and ecosystems. This covers initiatives like lowering greenhouse gas emissions, protecting biodiversity, and supporting renewable energy sources. *Economic sustainability* (United Nations World Summit, 2005) fosters economic progress and development in an equitable and sustainable manner. This includes activities like encouraging fair trade, minimizing poverty and inequality, and making investments in environmentally friendly infrastructure. Hence, tourism is important for tropical regions; for instance, in Thailand, it is the greatest source of income for the nation. *Social sustainability* (United Nations World Summit, 2005) is concerned with advancing social justice and equity as well as making sure that everyone in society has access to opportunities and fundamental rights. It includes activities like advancing gender equality, ensuring access to healthcare and education, and assisting vulnerable and marginalized groups. *Institutional dimension* (Spangenberg 2007) acknowledges the crucial role that institution, including businesses, non-governmental organizations, and government agencies play in promoting and implementing sustainable development. It includes aspects of governance for creating accountable and effective policies, laws, and regulations, capacity building, and engaging a diverse range of stakeholders in transparent decision-making processes.

9.3 Methodology

In order to investigate how community-based tourism (CBT) focuses on meeting social needs of local community in tropical regions, the study adopts a qualitative methodology, using a critical interpretive lens in reviewing the pertinent literary sources. It is developed after reviews of empirical studies, official data, research reports, and case studies, to look at the status of sustainable community-based tourism in the context of tropical regions. Literature pertinent to tropical regions were included in the study. The successful stories/case studies related to inclusive growth in strengthening the social pillar are examined. Based on the theoretical presentations, review articles, and empirical research articles, the authors synthesize and disseminate the findings by proposing a Framework.

9.4 Discussion

9.4.1 CBT: A Strategic Tool for Sustainable Tourism Development

This study proposes community-based tourism (CBT) as a strategy for sustainable tourism development for countries situated in tropical environment. It throws light on the role of community-based tourism as the answer to the pertinent challenges of tropical regions in the post-pandemic phase. Sustainable community-based tourism increases local support for sustainable development by giving local communities the ability to manage tourism (Scheyvens & van der Watt, 2021). In order to develop strategies to promote community-based tourism and to lessen the effects of environmental problems, this research provides an understanding of the relationships between community-based tourism and sustainable socioeconomic development.

The needs of the present generation should be met without compromising the ability of future generations to meet their own needs (Carley & Christie, 2017). To achieve long-term sustainability, local community involvement is essential, as economic, social, and environmental systems are interrelated and interdependent (Li & Li, 2021). The main aim is to create a process where economic development and local community involvement can work together in a way that benefits the tourism sector, local economy, and community. The policies need to be created and the institutions need to be encouraged to promote community-based tourism-like environmental regulations, use of sustainable local resources, planning and promoting local culture and traditions. The well-being of community depends on meeting the needs and empowering them by finding ways to promote tourism sustainably within the limits of the natural world (Scheyvens & van der Watt, 2021). To empower the local community, this chapter emphasizes community-based tourism to address the social needs. The successful stories/case studies related to inclusive growth in strengthening the social pillar are discussed. A framework (*ADAPTATION*) is suggested as a solution to address underdevelopment problems and to suggest ways to accelerate development in tropical regions to accomplish the United Nations Sustainable Development Goals (SDGs) – in particular, target SDG 1 (end poverty in all its forms everywhere), SDG 3 (ensure healthy lives and promote well-being for all ages), SDG 4 (ensure inclusive and equitable quality education and promote lifelong learning opportunities for all), SDG 5 (achieve gender equality and empower all women and girls), SDG 10 (reduce inequality within and among countries), and SDG 16 (promote peaceful and inclusive societies for sustainable development, provide access to justice for all and build effective, accountable, and inclusive institutions at all levels). The proposed '*ADAPTATION*' framework (refer to Figure 9.1) highlights the positive effects of destination image through the promotion of in-depth local culture and traditional art, culture, food, and medicines, which enhances the tourist experience with local community, thus contributing to the sustainable socio-economic development of tropical regions.

9.4.2 Curating 'ADAPTATION' in Strategies for Developing Community-Based Sustainable Tourism

The proposed framework '*ADAPTATION*' highlights the need for constructive contributions from all stakeholders to attain prosperity in the tropical regions. The concept of adaptation refers to the process of adjusting to changing circumstances; this chapter refers to the context of a post COVID-19 scenario in promoting sustainable tourism, focusing on tropical regions. The impact of tourism on communities needs to be acknowledged to make them ready to cope with the impacts and also to maintain their well-being.

A = Approach focusing on inclusiveness
D= Developing sense of ownership
A= Ability enhancement
P= Practices promoting sustainable tourism
T= Teamwork and collaboration
A= Advertising and promotions
T= Taking stock of available resources
I= Innovation
O= Opportunities
N= Need driven

Figure 9.1 Proposed *ADAPTATION* framework

Source: Authors

The proposed framework highlights the actions and strategies to empower local community to be an integral part of tourism initiatives. It also lays emphasis on adapting to changing market conditions or technologies as to be skilled to avail job opportunities.

The proposed '*ADAPTATION*' based on the aforementioned discussions' refers to:

*A – **Approach:*** To accomplish sustainability goals and enhance the welfare of the local community, active local community participation in tourism growth is crucial (Ertuna & Kirbas, 2012). CBT is community-managed tourism, which consists of several locally owned enterprises with the aim of benefiting the community and frequently with the intention of promoting conservation (Tolkach & King, 2015). The community-based tourism approach emphasizes on the inclusiveness, that is, engagement of local communities in the planning, development, implementation, and management of tourism activities to ensure that they benefit economically, socially, and culturally. The involvement of local communities in the planning, management, and implementation of tourism activities promotes the engagement of tourists with the local culture and it also takes care of the employment needs of the local community boosting the economy of the region (Bello et al., 2018). It is promoted as a tool to enhance livelihoods and create opportunities for community development. Local community involvement can take many forms, including work in the tourism industry, local business leasing out land for tourism, and involvement in planning and decision-making for tourism, wildlife, parks, and land uses (Ashley & Roe, 1998). Local community participation in decision-making is very important to improve plans and service delivery as it also fosters a sense of community involvement among those who share similar objectives (Muganda et al., 2013).

Identifying key stakeholders in the community is crucial as they will be affected by tourism development. Engaging them in the planning process by seeking their input and feedback on tourism development plans is crucial; the involvement of local people, community leaders, and other stakeholders in identifying tourism opportunities and setting priorities for development will be beneficial. The assessment of community needs should be done to identify the tourism-related needs and priorities of the local community (Gutierrez et al., 2005). The community meetings and workshops should be facilitated to discuss tourism development and to identify key priorities. This inclusive approach will successfully adapt them to any change initiated by external agency in their community as they will also consider it their responsibility to make the tourism plan successful.

The role of government is critical; with its support, the policy can be drafted and implemented to promote community-based tourism, as evident from Thailand which has developed and implemented national policies to promote community-based tourism (Uddin, 2022). The Ban Rai Kong King community in the Chiang Mai province is involved in community-based tourism by offering homestays, workshops on traditional handicraft, and guided tours for tourists (Cullen, 2023). This has helped the local community in generating income and employment. The promotion of conservation of the area's natural and cultural heritage is also done by adapting community-based tourism (Thananusak & Suriyankietkaew, 2023).

Monitoring and evaluating tourism growth are important to determine how it will affect the environment and the surrounding community (Wu et al., 2021). This can entail regularly evaluating the effects of tourism growth on the economy, society, and environment and modifying tourism initiatives as necessary. Overall, local communities and stakeholders should be involved in the planning process to ensure that tourism efforts are sustainable, responsible, and advantageous to the local community. Inspiring local community involvement serves as a foundation for the sustainability of the tourism destination and industry (Muganda et al., 2013). The following strategies can be adapted for gaining acceptance within local communities:

a. Involvement: The local community needs to be involved in the planning and decision-making process. This will give them a sense of ownership and control over the tourism development process (Giampiccoli & Saayman, 2018).
b. Communication: Effective communication is important in gaining community acceptance. The community needs to be informed and updated on the progress of the tourism development project (Bello et al., 2018).
c. Benefits: The benefits of tourism development should be clearly communicated to the community (Nagarjuna, 2015). This can include economic benefits, such as job creation and increased income, as well as social and cultural benefits.
d. Mitigation: Any concerns or negative impacts that community may have regarding tourism development should be immediately addressed (Wu, 2021). The adequate strategies need to be developed to mitigate these impacts and should be communicated to stakeholders.
e. Consultation: Consultation should be done with the communities on a regular basis to ensure that their needs and concerns are being addressed (Dangi & Jamal, 2016). This can help to build trust and support for tourism development.

Community-based tourism focuses on promoting and preserving cultural diversity and heritage and recognizing the importance of cultural values and traditions. This includes supporting local cultural events and festivals, protecting cultural sites and artefacts, and promoting cultural exchange and dialogue. Regular updates to the community and soliciting their comments and input leads to transparency and accountability in the process of developing the tourism industry (Wei, 2014). Setting up a community advisory committee or another system for community feedback and control can help with this.

D – Developing sense of ownership: According to Armstrong (2012), CBT is tourism owned and/or managed by communities with the goal of delivering greater community benefits. Local community should be given rights to economic resources as well as access to ownership and control over land and natural resources and participation in decision-making. The focus should be on developing community-based tourism initiatives that provide economic opportunities for local residents and promote sustainable tourism practices. This can include homestays, community-based tour guides and other initiatives that allow tourists to engage directly with local communities and promote responsible tourism behaviours. Tourism benefits to the community can be ensured by engaging local community in tourism development thus helping to promote economic growth and cultural preservation. CBT provides control to the local community over tourism management, and they should include in tourism promotion (Simpson, 2008). Promotion of inclusive approach is aligned to needs and values of local community and their participation from planning to implementation and management at every stage, will lead to developing sense of ownership. This was evident from the community of Nanmatta in India who were involved in community-based tourism, offering homestays, guided farm tours and sharing cultural experiences with tourists (Kukreti, 2021).

Community-based tourism is characterized by being located in, owned by, and managed by the community, which consequently receives a sizable portion of the benefits (Tolkach & King, 2015). Engaging locals and stakeholders in the implementation of tourism projects will promote community ownership, like creating locally focused tourism-related goods and services as well as giving local business owners or trip operators opportunities for training and capacity building (Bello et al., 2018). CBT is viewed as a scenario where locals own, have access to, or are allowed to use tourism resources and activities for their own benefit or the equitable benefit of the community through stewardship (Masud et al., 2017). For example, in the Amazon rainforest, the Huaorani people have developed community-based tourism, which includes guided tours through the rainforest, cultural performances, and homestays (Wierucka, 2018). CBT is distinguished by the fact that the community itself manages the tourism and receives a sizeable part of the benefits brought about by such activity (López-Guzmán et al., 2011).

A – Ability enhancement: Community-based tourism prioritizes the involvement of local communities in tourism development and decision-making. The training and capacity-building opportunities should be provided to the local community to ensure inclusive and equitable quality training and

> promote lifelong learning opportunities to continuously develop their skills, abilities, skills, and competencies to enhance their knowledge and empower them to participate in tourism development (Sharma & Kamble, 2021). According to the United Nations Development Program (UNDP), capacity building entails the development of an enabling environment with suitable policies and legal frameworks, institutional growth, and community involvement. Capacity building is a long-term, ongoing process in which all stakeholders are involved. Homestays, locally led tours, and regionally sponsored cultural festivals and events are a few examples of community-based capacity-building tourism efforts (Sharma & Kamble, 2021).

Community members can be trained as guides or hosts, promoting local handicrafts and products, and providing opportunities for local people to share their culture and traditions with visitors. By eliminating gender disparities in education and ensuring equal access to vocational training, the local community will lead fulfilling lives (UNWTO, 2022). Training in communication, hospitality, customer service, marketing, and business management-relevant skills can be provided. Enhancing skills will result in fiscal gains for the local communities through involvement of supporting regional businesses as well as giving local residents chances for employment. For instance, in Cambodia, the community of Banteay Chhmar received training and support to offer tourists homestays and guided tours of temple sites (Aneksuk, 2013). A range of educational activities including cooking classes and bird-watching tours are offered by the Sarapiqui Conservation Learning Centre of Coasta Rica which is run by local community (Sarapiqui Conservation Learning Centre, 2017). The community-based tourism institute in Thailand, for instance, has created a participatory planning methodology that involves involving local communities in the development of community-based tourism projects (Uddin, 2022). Through these training, the local community is skilled in hospitality, food preparation, and tourism marketing to promote homestay initiatives. The department of tourism has created a training programme on sustainable tourist practices for local communities in the Philippines (Marites & Glenne, 2023). To assist local communities in creating and managing sustainable tourism initiatives, this programme offers training in environmental protection, community involvement, and sustainable tourism growth. The Fiji Museum has created a training and capacity-building programme for regional groups engaged in cultural tourism projects (Nemani, 2018). To assist local communities in creating and promoting their cultural tourism projects, this programme offers training in cultural heritage, story-telling, and tourism marketing. It is clear that the local communities' ability to create and manage initiatives for sustainable tourism can be boosted by the capacity development and training programme (OECD, 2020). These can assist in ensuring that tourism efforts in tropical regions are responsible, sustainable, and advantageous to the local community by offering training on environmental preservation, community involvement, and sustainable tourism development.

P – ***Practices promoting sustainable tourism:*** Sustainable development goals emphasize both environmental preservation and inclusive development (Gupta & Vegelin, 2016). Since the 1990s, there has been significant research on the relationship between development and the environment, revealing an inverted U-shaped relationship between per capita income and environmental degradation indicators (Leal & Marques, 2022). Community-based tourism initiatives should be developed using sustainable tourism practices minimizing the impact on the environment and ensuring healthy lives and promoting well-being. The CBT efforts of the local community also support in conservation of surrounding natural resources by being actively involved in reforestation and wildlife monitoring (Charles, 2021). Practices like responsible waste management, promotion of local healthy food and products, minimizing carbon emissions, and protecting natural resources need to be given importance and local community should be made aware about it. For instance, in Thailand, the ecotourism initiative undertaken by the community of Ban Rai Kong Khing involves learning about sustainable agriculture practices and local culture (Cullen, 2023). The objectives of CBT are to encourage sustainable practices and lessen the detrimental effects of tourism on the environment and society. This can involve choosing eco-friendly lodging and transit, cutting back on waste and energy use, and aiding neighbourhood conservation initiatives. The Costa Rican Tourism Board has created a participatory planning process that involves involving neighbourhood groups in the development of sustainable tourism initiatives (Koens et al., 2009). In this process, the social, economic, and environmental effects of tourism growth are identified, and responsible, sustainable, and community-friendly tourism initiatives are created in collaboration with local communities. The tourism ministry of Ecuador has created a participatory planning methodology that includes involving community groups in the creation of ecotourism projects (Maldonado-Erazo et al., 2020). This strategy entails locating local natural resources and assets, creating tourist products and services that encourage the preservation of the environment, and assisting local business owners and tour operators with support and training. Communities may engage in environmental conservation initiatives like clean-ups of beaches, reforestation, or the maintenance of wildlife habitats. For instance, the Eco Baja Tours, run by a local community in Mexico's Baja California Sur, provides eco-friendly tours with an emphasis on whale watching, excursion to islands, and wildlife conservation (Baja Ecotours, 2023).

Communities can also start sustainable tourism practices like waste reduction, energy conservation, and the use of materials that are produced locally in construction. By utilizing renewable energy sources and sustainable construction materials, communities can create eco-friendly accommodations like lodges and homestays. The community run El Remanso lodge on the Osa Peninsula of Costa Rica, which is situated in the middle of a protected rainforest, functions entirely on solar power and only utilizes biodegradable products for cleaning (El Remanso Lodge, 2023). To safeguard the environment and wildlife habitats, communities in tropical areas can engage in conservation efforts. The Santa Cruz community in the Galapagos Islands has implemented measures to safeguard the threatened Giant Tortoise and other endemic species, by creating the breeding centre for tortoises and ecotourism projects (Benitez-Capistros et al., 2018). To lessen the negative effects of tourism on the ecosystem, communities can implement responsible waste-management techniques like recycling, composting, and limiting single-use plastics. The Palau Pledge programme, in Palau, includes a required orientation programme for all visitors and urges tourists to sign a pledge to honour and preserve the island nation's culture and environment (Palau Pledge, n.d.). The Green Fins programme in Southeast Asia promotes sustainable scuba-diving practices, such as reducing anchor damage to coral reefs, avoiding contact with marine life, and minimizing waste (Hunt et al., 2013).

*T – **Teamwork and collaboration:*** Partnerships and collaborations are essential to promoting sustainable tourism in tropical regions, as they can bring together different stakeholders, including local communities, tourism operators, government agencies, and NGOs, to work towards common goals. Teamwork among community members and collaboration with stakeholders like local government, NGOs, travel agencies, and tourism institutions will ensure the success of community-based tourism initiatives (Herath & Munasinghe, 2016). To ensure that tourism development helps the community, forming alliances and collaborations with local businesses, organizations, and leaders is necessary. The partnership agreement with tourism operators and their participation in planning and decision-making will promote tourism (Ashley & Roe, 1998). In Slovenia, the community of Solčava collaborated with a local NGO and developed an ecotourism initiative that involved local community members offering tours of the local area (UNWTO, 2021b). This involves creating effective policies, laws, and regulations that promote sustainable development, and ensuring that institutions are accountable and transparent in their decision-making processes. Thailand and Nepal have developed national policies and programmes to support community-based tourism.

Communities can invest in developing tourism infrastructure such as roads, public restrooms, and community centres to improve their tourism offerings. For example, the community of Omo Valley in Ethiopia, with the support of a non-governmental organization, built a visitor centre to welcome tourists and introduce them to local culture. In many tropical regions, local communities have formed cooperatives to manage tourism activities. These cooperatives are often responsible for developing and marketing community-based tourism products, such as homestays, cultural tours, and handicraft workshops. To support local community, in the Amazon rainforest, Brazil's Mamirauá Sustainable Development Reserve promotes community-based enterprises like handicraft production, sustainable fishing, guided forest walks, canoe trips, and wildlife watching (Ozorio & Janér, 2013). This has paved the way for income and employment opportunities for local people and the rainforest conservation.

Public–private partnerships (PPPs) are a popular form of collaboration in the tourism industry, where the public and private sectors come together to develop and manage tourism infrastructure and services. For example, in Costa Rica, the government has developed PPPs to manage national parks and protected areas, which includes tourism services such as lodges, guided tours, and transportation (Herrero Amo & De Stefano, 2019). Community–private partnerships (CPPs) are partnerships between local communities and private tourism operators to develop and manage tourism activities that benefit both parties. For example, in the Philippines, the community of El Nido has developed CPPs with private operators to promote sustainable tourism activities such as island hopping, snorkelling, and scuba diving (Asian Development Bank (ADB), 2021). Destination management organizations (DMOs) bring together stakeholders in the tourism industry to develop and promote tourism in a particular destination. Collaborations between different countries can promote regional tourism and economic development. For example, the Mekong Tourism Coordinating Office (MTCO) promotes tourism in the Mekong region, which includes Thailand, Vietnam, Cambodia, Laos, Myanmar, and China, by developing sustainable tourism initiatives and cross-border collaborations (Asian development Bank (ADB), 2008).

*A – **Advertising and promotions:*** Promotion must be seriously considered by the operators of the travel and tourism sector and by the government. Effective advertising and promotions are important to ensure the success of community-based tourism (Gansauer, 2021). Recognizing and promoting the unique cultural heritage of the community and preserving the cultural sites and traditions can be promoted by cultural tourism products and experiences for instance organizing cultural tours, festivals, and events. The only way to find competitive advantages in the tourism ecosystem is to continuously enhance the capability of market perception (Day, 1994)

The unique experiences, services, and local culture need to be highlighted in advertisements and promotional materials on social media. In Indonesia, the community of Tenganan in Bali successfully highlights their traditional culture and handicrafts through advertising and promotions (Nilasari et al., 2019). The destination appeal needs to be created to attract the tourists (Kline et al., 2020).

Communities can preserve their cultural heritage through the promotion of traditional crafts, music, and dance. This can be done through cultural tours and workshops, where visitors can learn about local traditions and crafts. For example, in Bali, Indonesia, the community of Ubud has developed cultural tourism initiatives, which include traditional music and dance performances, wood carving workshops, and visits to rice terraces and temples (Ernawati et al., 2018). The tropical regions can highlight their unique attractions and experiences, such as pristine beaches, diverse wildlife, and rich cultural heritage. The strategic positioning of the tourism matters (Crompton et al., 1992) as it creates distinctive tourism image (Echtner & Ritchie, 1993).

Destinations should create engaging content that showcases the unique features of the destination and use targeted advertising to reach specific audiences. Examples of successful tourism promotion strategies in tropical regions include the 'Amazing Thailand' campaign, which highlights the country's diverse attractions and unique cultural experiences, and the 'Incredible India' campaign, which showcases India's rich heritage and cultural diversity. Collaborating with travel agents, tour operators, and other industry stakeholders can help to promote a destination to potential visitors. Offering special packages can encourage tourists to choose a destination. Positive reviews and recommendations from past visitors can be powerful marketing tools. Destinations should strive to provide high-quality experiences that exceed visitor expectations.

*T – **Taking stock of available resources and effective utilization:*** Focusing on the available resources (local art, culture, traditions, artefacts, etc.) and showcasing them to meet the tourist's expectations can promote tourism in tropical regions. The essential components of a tourist destination can serve as a representation of the destination's distinctive brand and help create and maintain an emotional bond with visitors. As a result, the destination's brand can possess personality traits, radiate human touch, and revitalize; and the quality and culture of the destination can be effectively communicated to visitors (Ekinci & Hosany, 2006).

Cultural festivals are a great way to showcase local culture and traditions. In Bali, Indonesia, the annual Bali Arts Festival features performances of traditional music, dance, and theatre, as well as exhibitions of local crafts and art. In Fiji, the Bula Festival is a week-long event that celebrates Fijian culture and attracts tourists from around the world. Cultural tours are a great way to learn about local culture and heritage (Jureniene & Stonyte, 2016). For example, in the Caribbean, many tour companies offer tours of historic plantations, which provide visitors with a glimpse into the region's colonial history and the lives of the people who worked on these plantations. Handicraft workshops provide visitors with the opportunity to learn about traditional crafts and techniques. In Guatemala, visitors can participate in weaving workshops to learn about the traditional Mayan weaving techniques that have been passed down through generations. Many community-based tourism initiatives involve the preservation of cultural heritage sites. For instance, in Peru, the Inca Trail to Machu Picchu is a popular tourist attraction, but the trail is also a UNESCO World Heritage site, and efforts are being made to preserve the site for future generations. The functional and material consumption patterns of tourists are gradually shifting to symbolic and experiential patterns (Kumar, 2016).

I –Innovation: Innovation is crucial to the growth and sustainability of the tourism sector in tropical regions (Tsekouropoulos et al., 2022). Post-pandemic recovery offers a chance for innovation, including a shift to a community-based tourism framework. This involves promoting innovation and experimentation in community-based tourism initiatives to find new and more effective ways of promoting sustainable tourism. Innovation with a sustainability focuses on highlighting cutting-edge local products and services by exhibiting deeply ingrained historical connections and culture. Tourists will remember the innovativeness in curating immersive experiences in local culture, custom, people, and history. The secret to attract tourists is to incorporate innovations into services while considering the needs of tourists. For instance, the Habitas hotel company (Habitas, n.d.) built its own factory in Mexico using 3D printing technology. This factory can create modular hotel pieces, flat pack, ship, assemble on-site, and be operational in less than a year. Instead of grand lobbies and enormous buildings, each hotel is built around trees, rocks, and bodies of water, and hardly any foundation is ever laid. The outcome contributes to the growing appeal of remote, undeveloped destinations that provide access to vast open spaces. Since Tulum, Habitas hotels have made their debuts in far-flung regions all over the world. The most recent retreat was established in the Ashar Valley of Saudi Arabia and the surrounding countryside of San Miguel de Allende. There are plans to create additional retreats in 2023 in Mexico, Morocco, Costa Rica, Bhutan, and other places. Each year, 10 to 12 hotels are intended to start. This type of construction is not only more cost-effective than conventional techniques but also more environmentally friendly, which is allowing Habitas to quickly grow its chain of flat-pack hotels.

In tropical regions, technology-enabled tourism initiatives such as online booking platforms, virtual tours, and mobile apps are becoming popular. For instance, in Thailand, the government has developed a mobile app that provides tourists with information on local attractions, accommodation, and transportation. The innovation of a user-friendly map named 'USE-IT maps' is gaining popularity. With the help of these maps, a tourist can find niche local attractions of the local place. The innovative application of customer friendly chatbots for providing quick response is also gaining popularity (Adam et al., 2021). It is also useful for a service provider as it responds to inquiries of customers beyond office hours thus increasing customer engagement. Virtual reality and augmented reality are often used by destination promoters (Ozdemir, 2021). It provides the experiential aspect to prospective tourists. For instance, VR agency, Poppr, has extended catalogue with AR, thus bringing the tourist closer to the destination in mind and generating the need to visit the place physically. With the aid of augmented reality (AR), WELC Map enhances a standard paper tour map with in-depth multimedia, showcasing each location in detail. Blipparhas developed a digital city map application that includes guidance as a feature. Any trip or package can use gamification as a tool to add an immersive experience. Nexto provides destination-specific in-app quests, tests, and challenges that use augmented reality to tell new stories and provide a fresh experience. These innovations are changing the tourism ecosystem (UNWTO, 2018). The self-adaptive ability and strengthening connection and interaction with consumers is essential to gain competitive advantage (Felicity et al., 2018). Innovation is critical to the development and sustainability of the tourism sector in tropical regions. By developing innovative tourism practices that promote sustainability, cultural preservation, and economic development, the tourism sector can contribute to the long-term growth and prosperity of tropical regions. In Costa Rica, the eco-tourism industry has grown significantly in recent years, with many operators offering sustainable tourism activities such as hiking, bird watching, and canopy tours. Agro-tourism activities such as fruit picking, coffee and cocoa tours, and rice paddy tours are becoming popular in tropical regions. For example, in Bali, Indonesia, many farmers have developed agro-tourism activities such as rice paddy tours, coffee plantation tours, and fruit picking tours. In tropical regions, community-based tourism initiatives such as homestays, guided tours, and cultural exchange programmes are becoming popular. In the Amazon rainforest, many indigenous communities have developed community-based tourism initiatives that allow visitors to learn about their culture and way of life. By focusing on a niche, the tropical regions can be differentiated from others to attract tourists who are specifically interested in that particular experience. Specialized, personalized, and flexible features have turned out to be an essential part of tourism destinations' strategies among competition and development (Robinson & Novelli, 2005).

O – Opportunities: Tourists are looking for healing experiences to help them get through the difficult COVID-19 period of their lives (Kwon, 2021). Most tourists are giving more importance to events and locations that advance environmental viability and the local community culture immersion experiences. Tourists will be pushing the boundaries even further in the coming years to make a long-lasting positive impact to the places and people they visit. This could be a great opportunity for tropical areas to serve as learning and healing retreats maximizing the desired experiences. There is high possibility for the tropical areas to become preferred tourist destinations. Although the Caribbean, Mediterranean, and East Atlantic islands are more popular travel locations, the islands of the Mid- and West Indian Ocean and Polynesia appear to have the greatest natural tourist potential. By focusing on planned marketing and tourism development strategies these places could be developed as attractive tourist destination. The development in technology and social media can help in showcasing the destination through digital tour guides. The aesthetic appeal of the place will attract more tourists. Promoting lifelong learning opportunities for local community will make the travel more sustainable and yielding to better experience. Another opportunity which can be looked for is exploring the unexplored destinations. For example, Brunei has greatest potential for developing as a tourism destination as its Tropical Rainforests covers 81% of the country's landmass (Ahmad & Hanipah, 2018).

N – ***Need driven:*** Understanding the need of local community and tourist is necessary in promoting sustainable tourism. The following diagram depicts American Psychologist Abraham Maslow's need hierarchy theory analogy with local community and tourist's needs. The ultimate objective, according to Maslow, is self-actualization, or simply 'being yourself best,' once we have satisfied all of the other 'needs.'

From Figure 9.2, Maslow's hierarchy of needs is represented by a pyramid with five levels, where each level depicts a different category of needs and it is evident that the physiological needs are the most basic level of survival needs (food, water, shelter, etc.). In the local community, it translates to fulfilling basic needs, and in tourists, it is basic amenities required during travel and stay. Similarly, the safety needs are translated to financial stability for local community and safe travel for tourists. Love and belongingness needs are translated to sense of belongingness and building human connections

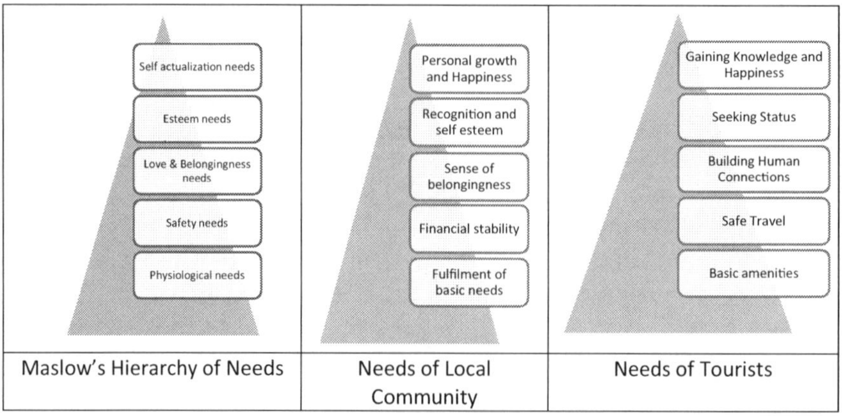

Figure 9.2 Understanding needs of local community and tourists through Maslow's hierarchy of needs

for local community and tourists, respectively. The next level is of esteemed needs which are represented as recognition and self-esteem among local community and seeking status in tourists. The fifth level is self-actualization needs which are translated as personal growth and happiness for local community and gaining knowledge and happiness in tourists. Tourist views 'me time' as an investment that allows them to reflect and pay attention to themselves. They no longer only think about travelling for pleasure but also make a difference in their own lives and the lives of others – for instance, ecotourism, volunteering while on vacation, taking classes to learn a new skill, visiting a local market, eating traditional food, taking culinary walking excursions, etc. Community-based tourism promotes the destination to tourists who are looking for immersive and authentic cultural experiences. The heightened offerings will suffice the needs of tourists as today's tourists are open to try to new experiences to gain much deeper understanding of the tourist place (Rasoolimanesh et al., 2021)

9.5 Conclusion

The main purpose of this study is to understand the role of CBT in promoting local community welfare and sustainable tourism. The tourism sector plays an important role in the economic, social, and cultural development. By promoting sustainable tourism practices and working collaboratively with local communities, the tourism sector can help to create long-term benefits for both visitors and local residents alike. However, the intensive tourism should not be advocated, as it has various adverse consequences like depletion of local natural resources, increase in generation of waste, soil erosion and pollution, and disruption of natural habitat (Andlib and Salcedo-Castro, 2021). In addition to adverse consequences on natural resources, the intensive tourism can lead to negative socio-economic impacts like increase in cost of living, high property rates, poverty, increase in crime, overcrowding, etc. These factors pose new challenges for the local community as evident by the issues faced by Orang Asli in Malaysia (Aziz et al., 2016). The Philippines has become a preferred tourist destination due to its beaches and rainforests; at the same time, it is facing problems of overcrowding and poverty issues due to its fast development (Felongco, 2018). Vietnam tourism industry has faced setback as it is struggling to be an ecotourism destination as forests are rapidly decreasing. It is essential for tourists to adopt more responsible approach towards travelling and tourism (Budeanu, 2005).

Community-based tourism can gain popularity as a niche sector by creating and modifying the tourism promotion plans to appeal to tourists by collaborating with local community to provide rich local experiences. Based on the latest trends, the destination places in tropical regions can be developed by offering unique and purposeful activities along with their local products and services. CBT initiatives in tropical regions can help to promote sustainable tourism development while also supporting local communities and preserving natural and cultural heritage (Dangi & Jamal, 2016). This chapter emphasizes on CBT to promote tourism in tropical regions. The objective of the study is to explore the role of CBT for sustainable tourism development. In order to achieve these objectives, a framework (*ADAPTATION*) is suggested as a solution to address underdevelopment problems and to suggest ways to accelerate sustainable tourism development in tropical regions. The proposed '*ADAPTATION*' framework highlights the positive effects of destination image through the promotion of in-depth local culture and traditional art, culture, food, and medicines, which enhances the tourist experience with local community thus contributing to the sustainable socio-economic development of tropical regions. The findings indicated that it is crucial to involve local community for sustainable tourism development. The '*ADAPTATION*' framework highlights that developing community-based tourism requires a collaborative effort between the community, stakeholders, and tourism industry. By using these strategies, communities can create tourism initiatives that benefit the local economy, preserve culture, and environment and provide unique experiences for visitors. This can also help to lessen prejudice, encourage tolerance, and raise public knowledge of problems like poverty, environmental degradation, and social inequality on a global scale. The participatory planning for community engagement in promoting tourism can help to ensure that tourism development initiatives are sustainable, responsible, and beneficial to the local community (Bello et al., 2018). CBT empowers the local community and the local community acts as a driving force in promoting tourism. It can inspire research ideas by identifying gaps or inconsistencies, thus helping the future researcher to go for further research. The examples cited in the study will act as guide for others so as to develop their understanding and implementation of CBT in meeting local community needs and promoting sustainable tourism.

References

Adam, M., Wessel, M., & Benlian, A. (2021). AI-based chatbots in customer service and their effects on user compliance. *Electronic Markets*, *31*(2), 427–445.

Ahmad, A., & Hanipah, A. (2018). *Island ecotourism in Brunei Darussalam: Its role in biodiversity conservation and environmental education*. Nova Science

Andlib, Z., & Salcedo-Castro, J. (2021). The impacts of tourism and governance on CO_2 emissions in selected south Asian countries. *ETIKONOMI*, *20*(2), 385–396. https://doi.org/10.15408/etk.v20i2.17449.

Aneksuk, B. (2013). *The concept and management of community-based cultural tourism in the kingdom of Cambodia: A case study of Banteay Chhmar Community, Banteay Meanchey Province* [Paper presentation]. The 3rd Regional Conference on Tourism, Langkwai, Malaysia.

Armstrong, R. (2012). *An analysis of the conditions for success of community-based tourism enterprises* (pp. 1–52). ICRT Occasional Paper (OP21).

Ashley, C., & Roe, D. (1998). *Enhancing community involvement in wildlife tourism: Issues and challenges*. IIED Wildlife and Development. ISBN:9781904035176

Asian Development Bank (ADB). (2008). *Tourism sector in the greater Mekong subregion.* https://www.oecd.org/countries/mongolia/42221951.pdf
Asian Development Bank (ADB). (2021). Philippines: Sustainable tourism development project El Nido. *Tourism Infrastructure and Economic Zone Authority.* https://www.adb.org/projects/53191-001/main
Aziz, T. A. T. A., Teh, L. K., Idris, M. H. M., Bannur, Z., Ashari, L. S., Ismail, A. I., Ahmad, A., Isa, K. M., Nor, F. M., Rahman, T. H. A., &Shaari, S. A. B. (2016). Increased risks of cardiovascular diseases and insulin resistance among the Orang Asli in Peninsular Malaysia. *BMC Public Health*, *16*(1), 1–13.
Baja Ecotours. (2023, July 25). *Baja whale watching – Baja ecotours.* www.bajaecotours.com/
Beeton, S. (2006). *Community development through Tourism.* Landlinks Press. ISBN 0 643 06962 3. https://doi.org/10.1071/9780643093881
Bello, F. G., Lovelock, B., & Carr, N. (2018). Enhancing community participation in tourism planning associated with protected areas in developing countries: Lessons from Malawi. *Tourism and Hospitality Research*, *18*(3), 309–320. www.jstor.org/stable/26478290
Benitez-Capistros, F., Camperio, G., Hugé, J., Dahdouh-Guebas, F., & Koedam, N. (2018). Emergent conservation conflicts in the Galapagos Islands: Human-giant tortoise interactions in the rural area of Santa Cruz Island. *PLoS One*, *13*(9), e0202268.
Briguglio, L., Archer, B., Jafari, J., & Wall, G. (1996). *Sustainable tourism in islands and small sates: Issues and policies.* Pinter.
Budeanu, A. (2005). Impacts and responsibilities for sustainable tourism: A tour operator's perspective. *Journal of Cleaner Production*, *13*(2), 89–97. https://doi.org/10.1016/j.jclepro.2003.12.024.
Carley, M., & Christie, I. (2017). *Managing sustainable development.* Routledge.
Cater, E. (1993). Ecotourism in the third world: Problems for sustainable tourism development. *Tourism Management*, *14*(2), 85–90. ISSN 0261–5177; https://doi.org/10.1016/0261-5177(93)90040-R; www.sciencedirect.com/science/article/pii/026151779390040R
Charles, A. (2021). *Communities, conservation, and livelihoods.* IUCN, Community Conservation Research Network.
Cohen, E. (1988). Traditions on the qualitative sociology of tourism. *Annals of Tourism Research*, *15*, 29–46.
Conlin, M. V., & Baum, T. (Eds.). (1995). *Island tourism: Management principles and practice.* Wiley.
Corlett, R. T. (2012). Climate change in the tropics: The end of the world as we know it? *Biological Conservation*, *151*(1), 22–25.
Crompton, J. L., Fakeye, P. C., & Lue, C. C. (1992). Positioning: The example of the lower Rio Grande Valley in the winter long stay destination market. *Journal of Travel Research*, *31*(2), 20–26. https://doi.org/10.1177/004728759203100204
Cullen, D. (2023, April 17). Sustainable travel in Thailand: A homestay at the Ban Rai Kong thing community. *World Footprints.* www.worldfootprints.com/sustainable-travel-in-thailand-a-homestay-at-the-ban-rai-kong-khing-community/
Dangi, T. B., & Jamal, T. (2016). An integrated approach to "sustainable community-based tourism". *Sustainability*, *8*(5), 475.
Day, G. S. (1994). The capabilities of market-driven organizations. *Journal of Marketing*, *58*(4), 37–52. https://doi. org/10.1177/002224299405800404

Echtner, C. M., & Ritchie, J. R. B. (1993). The measurement of destination image: An empirical assessment. *Journal of Travel Research*, *31*(4), 3–13. https://doi.org/10.1177/004728759303100402

Ekinci, Y., & Hosany, S. (2006). Destination personality: An application of brand personality to tourism destinations. *Journal of Travel Research*, 45(2), 127–139. https://doi.org/10.1177/0047287506291603

El Remanso Lodge. (2023). www.elremanso.com/

Ernawati, N. M., Sudarmini, N. M., & Sukmawati, N. M. R. (2018). Impacts of tourism in Ubud Bali Indonesia: A community-based tourism perspective. *Journal of Physics: Conference Series*, *953*(1), 012078. IOP Publishing.

Ertuna, B., & Kirbas, G. (2012). Local community involvement in rural tourism development: The case of Kastamonu, Turkey. *PASOS Revista de Turismo y Patrimonio Cultural*, *10*(2), 17–24.

Felicity, K., Arthur, K., & Denis, H. (2018). Managing innovation in the hospitality micro firm: A framework for sensing, seizing and reconfiguring dynamic capabilities. *Hospitality & Society*, *8*(2), 159–178. https://doi.org/10.1386/hosp.8.2.159_7

Felongco, G. P. (2018, November 7). Environmental degradation in tourist spots underscore earth day in the Philippines. *Philippines – Gulf News*. https://gulfnews.com/world/asia/philippines/environmental-degradation-in-tourist-spots-underscore-earth-day-in-the-philippines-1.2209486

Gansauer, F. (2021). *Marketing of community-based tourism: A case study of Central Asia*. Uppsalla Universitet.

Giampiccoli, A., & Saayman, M. (2018). Community-based tourism development model and community participation. *African Journal of Hospitality, Tourism and Leisure*, *7*(4), 1–27.

Ginsberg, M. (1961). *Sociology*. Oxford University Press.

Graburn, N. (Ed.). (1976). *Ethnic and tourist arts: Cultural expressions from the fourth world*. University of California Press. www.sciencedirect.com/science/article/pii/0160738383901135; https://doi.org/10.1016/j.tourman.2018.09.003)

Gupta, J., & Vegelin, C. (2016). Sustainable development goals and inclusive development. *International environmental agreements: Politics, Law and Economics*, *16*, 433–448.

Gutierrez, E., Lamoureux, K., Matus, S., & Sebunya, K. (2005). *Linking communities, tourism and conservation: A tourism assessment process*. Conservation International and The George Washington University.

Habitas. (n.d.). *Luxury for the soul*. www.ourhabitas.com/

Hardy, A., Beeton, R., & Pearson, L. (2002). Sustainable tourism: An overview of the concept and its position in relation to conceptualisations of tourism. *Journal of Sustainable Tourism*, *10*. https://doi.org/10.1080/09669580208667183

Herath, H., & Munasinghe, S. (2016). Networking and stakeholder participation in community-based tourism: A case study. In *Sustainable tourism in the global south: Communities, environments and management*. Cambridge Scholars Publishing.

Herrero Amo, M. D., & De Stefano, M. C. (2019). Public – private partnership as an innovative approach for sustainable tourism in Guanacaste, Costa Rica. *Worldwide Hospitality and Tourism Themes*, *11*(2), 130–139.

Hunt, C. V., Harvey, J. J., Miller, A., Johnson, V., & Phongsuwan, N. (2013). The Green Fins approach for monitoring and promoting environmentally sustainable scuba diving operations in South East Asia. *Ocean & Coastal Management*, *78*, 35–44.

Jureniene, V., & Stonyte, A. A. (2016), Recreational activities in cultural centres. *Transformations in Business & Economics*, *15*(37), 244–253.

Kline, C., Duffy, L., & Clark, D. (2020). Fostering tourism and entrepreneurship in fringe communities: Unpacking stakeholder perceptions towards entrepreneurial climate. *Tourism and Hospitality Research*, *20*(1), 3–17. http://libres.uncg.edu/ir/listing.aspx?id=24380

Koens, J. F., Dieperink, C., & Miranda, M. (2009). Ecotourism as a development strategy: Experiences from Costa Rica. *Environment, Development and Sustainability*, *11*, 1225–1237.

Kukreti, M. (2021). Natural resources and policies for community-based ecotourism: An Uttarakhand perspective. *The Holistic Approach to Environment*, *11*(4), 128–136.

Kumar, V. (2016). Examining the role of destination personality and self-congruity in predicting tourist behavior. *Tourism Management Perspectives*, *20*, 217–227. https://doi.org/10.1016/j.tmp.2016.09.006

Kwon, Y. S. (2021). *A case study on local cultural sensibility and healing tourism in Korea*. SCITEPRESS – Science and Technology Publications, Lda.

Leal, P. H., & Marques, A. C. (2022). The evolution of the environmental Kuznets curve hypothesis assessment: A literature review under a critical analysis perspective. *Heliyon*, *8*(11), 1–18.

Lee, T. H., & Jan, F. H. (2019). Can community-based tourism contribute to sustainable development? Evidence from residents' perceptions of the sustainability. *Tourism Management*, *70*, 368–380.

Li, C., & Li, G. (2021). Impact of China's water pollution on agricultural economic growth: An empirical analysis based on a dynamic spatial panel lag model. *Environmental Science and Pollution Research*, *28*, 6956–6965. https://doi.org/10.1007/s11356-020-11079-2

Lockhart, D., & Drakakis-Smith, D. W. (1997). *Island tourism: Trends and prospects*. Pinter.

López-Guzmán, T., Borges, O., & Cerezo, J. M. (2011). Community-based tourism and local socio-economic development: A case study in Cape Verde. *African Journal of Business Management*, *5*(5), 1608.

Maldonado-Erazo, C. P., del Río-Rama, M. D. L. C., Noboa-Viñan, P., & Álvarez-García, J. (2020). Community-based tourism in Ecuador: Community ventures of the provincial and cantonal networks. *Sustainability*, *12*(15), 6256.

Marites, R., & Glenne, B. L. D. (2023). Best practices in the implementation of livelihood training program for indigenous peoples. *International Journal of Research and Innovation in Social Science* (IJRISS), 7(2), 1–14.

Masud, M. M., Aldakhil, A. M., Nassani, A. A., & Azam, M. N. (2017). Community-based ecotourism management for sustainable development of marine protected areas in Malaysia. *Ocean & Coastal Management*, *136*, 104–112.

Menon, A. G. K. (1993). *Case study on the effects of tourism on culture and the environment, India: Jaisalmer, Khajuraho and Goa*. UNESCO Principal Regional Office for Asia and the Pacific.

Muganda, M., Sirima, A., & Ezra, P. M. (2013). The role of local communities in tourism development: Grassroots perspectives from Tanzania. *Journal of Human Ecology*, *41*(1), 53–66.

Murphy, P. (1985). *Tourism: A community approach (RLE tourism)* (1st ed.). CRC Press.

Nagarjuna, G. (2015). Local community involvement in tourism: A content analysis of websites of wildlife resorts. *Atna Journal of Tourism Studies*, *10*(1), 13–21.

Nemani, S. (2018). *FIJI museum strategic plan 2019 2028 new*. https://www.academia.edu/49455065/FIJI_MUSEUM_SRATEGIC_PLAN_2019_2028_NEW

Nilasari, P. F., Sitinjak, R. H. I., & Wardani, L. K. (2019). *Tenganan indigenous village as a cultural historical tourism destination*. [Doctoral dissertation, Petra Christian University].

Nurse, L. A., McLean, R. F., Agard, J., Briguglio, L. P., Duvat-Magnan, V., Pelesikoti, N., Tompkins, E., & Webb, A. (2014). Small islands. In V. R. Barros, C. B. Field, D. J. Dokken, M. D. Mastrandrea, K. J. Mach, T. E. Bilir, M. Chatterjee, K. L. Ebi, Y. O. Estrada, R. C. Genova, B. Girma, E. S. Kissel, A. N. Levy, S. MacCracken, P. R. Mastrandrea, & L. L. White (Eds.), *Climate change 2014: Impacts, adaptation, and vulnerability. Part B: Regional aspects. Contribution of working group II to the fifth assessment report of the intergovernmental panel on climate change* (pp. 1613–1654). Cambridge University Press.

Organisation for Economic Co-operation and Development (OECD). (2022, December 14). *Rebuilding tourism for the future: COVID-19 policy responses and recovery*. www.oecd.org/coronavirus/policy-responses/rebuilding-tourism-for-the-future-covid-19-policy-responses-and-recovery-bced9859/

Ozdemir, M. A. (2021). Virtual Reality (VR) and Augmented Reality (AR) Technologies for Accessibility and Marketing in the Tourism Industry. In C. Eusébio, L. Teixeira, & M. Carneiro (Eds.), *ICT Tools and Applications for Accessible Tourism* (pp. 277–301). IGI Global. https://doi.org/10.4018/978-1-7998-6428-8.ch013

Ozorio, R. Z., & Janér, A. (2013). Community-based ecotourism in the Mamirauá reserve: Evaluation of product quality and reflections regarding the economic and financial feasibility of the activity. *Scientific Magazine UAKARI*, *8*(2), 95–114.

Palau Pledge. (n.d.). *Palau pledge*. www.palaupledge.com/

Rasoolimanesh, S. M., Seyfi, S., Hall, C. M., & Hatamifar, P. (2021). Understanding memorable tourism experiences and behavioural intentions of heritage tourists. *Journal of Destination Marketing & Management*, *21*, 100621.

Robinson, M., & Novelli, M. (2005). Niche tourism: An introduction. In M. Novelli (Ed.), *Niche tourism: Contemporary issues, trends and cases* (pp. 1–11). Butterworth-Heinemann.

Roseland, M. (2012). *Toward sustainable communities: Solutions for citizens and their 632 governments*. New Society Publishers.

Ruiz-Ballesteros, E. (2011). Social-ecological resilience and community-based tourism: An approach from Agua Blanca, Ecuador. *Tourism Management*, *32*, 655–666.

Sarapiqui Conservation Learning Centre (SCLC). (2017). http://learningcentercostarica.org/

Scheyvens, R., & van der Watt, H. (2021). Tourism, empowerment and sustainable development: A new framework for analysis. *Sustainability*, *13*(22), 12606.

Schoch, M., & Lakner, C. (2020, December 16). The number of poor people continues to rise in sub-Saharan Africa, despite a slow decline in the poverty rate. *World Bank Blogs*. https://blogs.worldbank.org/opendata/number-poor-people-continues-rise-sub-saharan-africa-despite-slow-decline-poverty-rate#:~:text=This%20translates%20to%2040%25%20of,of%20poor%20continues%20to%20rise.

Sharma, R., & Kamble, Z. (2021). Shifting paradigms in human resource management while striving for service excellence in the tourism industry. In *Service Excellence in Tourism and Hospitality* (pp. 177–190). Springer.

Silva, N. M., Santos, N. C., & Martins, I. C. (2020). Dengue and Zika viruses: Epidemiological history, potential therapies, and promising vaccines. *Tropical Medicine and Infectious Disease*, *5*(4), 150.

Simpson, M. C. (2008). Community benefit tourism initiatives – a conceptual oxymoron? *Tourism Management*, *29*, 1–18. http://dx.doi.org/10.1016/j.tourman.2007.06.005

Spangenberg, J. H. (2007). The institutional dimension of sustainable development. *Sustainability Indicators: A Scientific Assessment*, *67*, 107.

Spangenberg, J. H., & Bonniot, O. (1998). *Sustainability indicators: A compass on the road towards sustainability* (No. 81). Wuppertal Papers.

Srinivasan, K., Muñoz, S., & Chensavasdijai, V. (2020, April 29). COVID-19 pandemic and the Caribbean: Navigating uncharted waters. *IMF Blog*. www.imf.org/en/Blogs/Articles/2020/04/29/covid-19-pandemic-and-the-caribbean-navigating-uncharted-waters

State of the Tropics. (2014). *State of the tropics 2014 report*. James Cook University.

Thananusak, T., & Suriyankietkaew, S. (2023). Unpacking key sustainability drivers for sustainable social enterprises: A community-based tourism perspective. *Sustainability*, *15*(4), 3401. http://dx.doi.org/10.3390/su15043401

Tolkach, D., & King, B. (2015). Strengthening community-based tourism in a new resource-based island nation: Why and how? *Tourism Management*, *48*, 386–398.

Tosun, C. (2000). Limits to community participation in the tourism development process in developing countries. *Tourism Management*, *21*(6), 613–633.

Toubes, D. R., Araújo Vila, N., & Fraiz Brea, J. A. (2021). Changes in consumption patterns and tourist promotion after the COVID-19 pandemic. *Journal of Theoretical and Applied Electronic Commerce Research*, *16*(5), 1332–1352.

Tsekouropoulos, G., Gkouna, O., Theocharis, D., & Gounas, A. (2022). Innovative sustainable tourism development and entrepreneurship through sports events. *Sustainability*, *14*(8), 4379.

Uddin, R. (2022, December 31). Community-based tourism: Connecting Thailand's experiences and reframing sustainable tourism in Bangladesh. *UNDP*. www.undp.org/bangladesh/blog/community-based-tourism-connecting-thailands-experiences-and-reframing-sustainable-tourism-bangladesh

United Nations World Summit. (2005). *World summit outcome*, 139 (U.N. Doc A/RES/60/1, 16th of September 2005). https://www.un.org/en/development/desa/population/migration/generalassembly/docs/globalcompact/A_RES_60_1.pdf

United Nations World Tourism Organization (UNWTO). (2018). *World tourism day 2018: Sustainability & digital transformation in tourism*. www.unwto.org/world-tourism-day-2018#:~:text=article%20on%20facebook-,World%20Tourism%20Day%202018%3A%20Sustainability%20%26%20digital%20transformation%20in%20tourism,and%20sustainable%2C%20responsible%20growth%20strategies.

United Nations World Tourism Organization (UNWTO). (2020, May). *UNWTO world tourism barometer* (Vol. 18, No. 2). https://www.e-unwto.org/toc/wtobarometereng/18/2

United Nations World Tourism Organization (UNWTO). (2021a). *Tourism highlights*. https://www.unwto.org/2021-a-year-in-review

United Nations World Tourism Organization (UNWTO). (2021b). *Best tourism villages*. www.unwto.org/tourism-villages/en/villages/solcava/

United Nations World Tourism Organization (UNWTO). (2022). *Women Empowerment and Tourism*. https://www.unwto.org/gender-and-tourism

Wei, F. (2014). *Compendium of best practices in sustainable tourism*. United Nations Department of Economic and Social Affairs Publication.

Wierucka, A. (2018). Living with strangers: Huaorani and tourism industry in the 21st Century. *Anthropological Notebooks*, *24*(1).

Woodley, S., Kay, J., & Francis, G. (1993). *Ecological integrity and the management of ecosystems*. St. Lucie Press.

World Population Review. (2023). *Tropical Countries 2023*. https://worldpopulationreview.com/country-rankings/tropical-countries

World Travel & Tourism Council (WTTC). (2021). *Global economic impact & trends 2020 and travel & tourism: Economic impact 2021 – global economic impact & trends 2021*. https://wttc.org/Portals/0/Documents/Reports/2021/Global%20Economic%20Impact%20and%20Trends%202021.pdf

World Wide Fund. (2021, May 17). *New study finds 94% of deforestation and habitat destruction in Brazil's Amazon and Cerrado could be illegal*. www.wwf.org.uk/press-release/illegal-deforestation-report-brazil

Wu, Z., Lai, I. K. W., & Tang, H. (2021). Evaluating the sustainability issues in tourism development: An adverse-impact and serious-level analysis. *Sage Open*, *11*(4), https://doi.org/21582440211050384

10 Killing the Economy

The Political Economy of Fuel Subsidy Regime and Oil Corruption in Nigeria

Usman Sambo and Babayo Sule

10.1 Introduction

Energy subsidies, or fossil fuel subsidies, have recently been the focus policy and consultation by critical interest groups. The payment of a substantial amount of money from government coffers to cover fuel costs by many countries around the world is based on the social contract of providing welfare, affordability, and accessibility to the poor and vulnerable (Price, 2022). However, this practice is detrimental to sustainable economic growth and development. Payment of subsidies increases fuel consumption, emission of carbon dioxide emissions, climate change, and waste (Saddiki & Chaouti, 2022). However, the complete removal of fuel subsidies will lead to an increase in the price of fuel and other consumer goods, which will exacerbate poverty among poor and disadvantaged populations (Couharde & Mouhoud, 2020). The issue of fuel subsidies poses difficult choices for key stakeholders and policymakers worldwide. Despite a crucial decision in December 2015 under the Paris Agreement and later by the International Energy Agency (IEA) on the need to completely eliminate all fuel subsidies, many countries continue to subsidise due to protests from labour unions, politicians, and the desire to win elections and avoid unnecessary unrest (Rentschler, 2018).

At the end of 2022, it is reported (World Economic Forum, 2023) that the world has paid fossil fuel subsidies of US$1 trillion. It is observed that the payments were made in the Global South or developing countries, but the Global North or developed countries have not been spared from this practise. For instance, in 2015 alone, the G-20 countries paid around US$450 billion to subsidise fuels in their respective countries (Rentschler, 2018). The arguments against fuel subsidies are the tendency to distort the price below the standard average, leading to economic inefficiency, and excessive release of high greenhouse gas emissions (Houeland, 2022a; Organisation for Economic Cooperation and Development, 2021). Moreover, the cost of fuel subsidies weighs on countries' finances, weakens economic growth potential, and leads to wasteful energy consumption and corruption (International Energy Agency, 1999; Sovacool, 2017; Organisation for Economic Cooperation and Development, 2018). Conversely, OECD (2021) observes that fuel subsidies

DOI: 10.4324/9781003349204-10

are justified by supporting important domestic policy objectives such as facilitating energy supply to rural areas, job creation, energy security, and poverty reduction.

Several studies (Nwosu, 1996; Balouga, 2012; Rentschler & Bazilian, 2016; Rentschler, 2018; Skovgaard & van Asselt, 2018; Egbezien, 2020; Houeland, 2022a; World Economic Forum, 2023) identified Nigeria as one of the high-cost fuel-subsidy states. Nigeria paid N15 trillion (US$34,443,168,000.00 billion) in fuel subsidies between 2009 and 2021 and is expected to spend about N6.7 trillion (US$15,384,615,040.00) in 2022 and the first two quarters of 2023 (Uduu, 2020; Ifeanyi, 2022; Tunji, 2022). This amount exceeds Nigeria's annual budget for three years, and the N6.7 trillion in fuel subsidies expected for 2022 and the first two quarters of 2023 is almost half of the 2022 annual budget. In the Nigerian case, the issue is not the amount paid, but about the circumstances of the entire fuel subsidy scheme. Nigeria is the tenth largest oil-producing country in the world, but the failure of functioning refineries forced the export of crude oil and importation of refined petroleum products. This led to a significant increase in the price of fuel, and to cushion the impact of skyrocketing prices, the Nigerian Government began paying subsidies (Houeland, 2022b).

The government has warned on several occasions that fuel subsidies in Nigeria cannot continue but must be discontinued for the good of the economy and its performance. Efforts to remove the subsidies often ended in violent protests that forced the suspension. The 2012 protests shook the government and almost resulted in lawlessness (Akanle et al., 2014). The government continues to argue that the fuel subsidy is unsustainable and cannot be sustained. But labour unions and citizens continue to resist, taking advantage of the government's failure to revive ailing refineries and the negligence of the policymakers to plan for the construction new refineries that will sustain domestic production and thus eliminate the additional costs of imported refined ones (Chikem, 2016). In essence, the Nigerian case is a paradox. This is because the issue of fuel subsidy should not have arisen if the refineries were functioning or new ones were built during the period in which the crisis arose. Fuel subsidies involved large-scale corruption, with allegations of diversion of products, dubious payments to marketers without delivery, and other fraud. This has led many stakeholders to claim that paying subsidies kills the economy, while the other side of the debate justifies that removing subsidies will make the lives of the poor and middle class miserable, unbearable, and wretched (Siddig et al., 2014). This chapter examines how fuel subsidies are destroying the Nigerian economy and the dilemma that subsidy removal will deepen the economic crises by causing unbearable hardships for poor Nigerians. This chapter suggests a plausible middle ground that has the potential for practical policy implications.

This chapter adopts a qualitative descriptive research design. Data was collected through documented sources. Existing works of literature are consulted critically and were rigorously analysed. Google Scholar search engine was used to consult numerous articles, and other sources were visited to review books and other materials. The data obtained were discussed and interpreted using logical empirical literature analysis. The works of literature are grouped into various themes and analysed on that perspective. This chapter is structured into six: introduction, explanation of fuel subsidy and sustainability from the global context, fuel history in Nigeria, its history and trajectories, impact of fuel subsidy on Nigeria's economy and infrastructure supply, analysis of whether fuel subsidy should continue in Nigeria or not, and conclusion.

10.2 Fuel Subsidy Reforms and Sustainability: The Global Context

Fuel subsidy reforms are increasingly attracting debates and policy initiatives in both the Global South and North. The vast resources devoted to subsidising energy are prompting global actors to call for radical reforms to address perceived waste and shifting public priorities in infrastructure provision. Removing fuel subsidies could free up funds in many countries to invest in access to clean water, sanitation, electricity, and other basic infrastructure (Jakob et al., 2015). A major reason why fuel subsidies are becoming a problem is their costs and impact on the budget deficit of most countries that grant them (Simon, 2012). However, the biggest obstacle is the impact on the welfare of the poor. Rentschler (2016) argues that uncompensated energy reforms will increase the incidence of poverty for many households. Using Nigeria as an example, Rentschler (2015, 2016) emphasises that the Nigerian government's approach to fuel subsidy reforms without a well-designed compensation model will increase poverty in the country by 3.4%. As important as fuel subsidy reform is, the policy of phasing it out is difficult due to the volatile challenges of the political economy (Rentschler & Bazilian, 2016). Nevertheless, it is believed (Sivaram & Harris, 2016) that maintaining fuel subsidies in the future is not feasible and that governments must demonstrate political acumen to ensure a gradual phase-out of subsidies.

The amount of money countries spend on fossil fuel subsidies is considered wasteful and an undertaking that is unsustainable given the current global economic shock. In 2014, for example, countries around the world spent US$500 billion on fuel subsidies (Rentschler, 2018). Fuel subsidy spending is not unique to developing countries or the Global South. The G-20 reportedly spent US$450 billion on fuel subsidies in 2014 (Rentschler, 2018), with more than US$350 billion spent in European countries (World Economic Forum, 2023). The G-20's spending is alarming because they created the Paris Climate Agreement to reduce fossil fuel consumption and promote the use of renewable energy. But they also subsidise recklessly. The International Monetary Fund (IMF) reported in 2018 that the estimated annual cost of fossil fuel subsidies is US$5.3 trillion, or 6.5% of global GDP (Rentschler, 2018). However, the World Economic Forum (2023) reports that total subsidy payments by countries around the world in 2022 were US$1 trillion. To make the situation even more precarious, commitment made by the world leaders are not being honoured, as natural gas and electricity subsidies tripled in 2022 and oil subsidies increased by 85% in the same year (World Economic Forum, 2023). The Russian invasion of Ukraine is seen is seen as the triggering factor for the increase in subsidies for global energy consumption, according to a report by the International Energy Agency (World Economic Forum, 2023).

Eastern European states are not letting up in their support of fuel subsidies. After Africa and some Asian states, this is the second most common region (OECD, 2021). The states of Armenia, Azerbaijan, Belarus, Georgia, the Republic of Moldova, and Ukraine are pioneers in subsidy support. Ukraine has the highest subsidy support in the region, spending US$5 billion in 2019. Fossil fuel subsidies in Ukraine reach 2.3% of GDP and exceed the budget deficit of 0.3% (OECD, 2021). These countries support the subsidies through budget transfers, which affects the deficit and the lack of infrastructure supply. Globally, fuel subsidies lead to an undervaluation of the value of fuel. In most cases, this is case in OECD countries. However, there are also countries outside the OECD that subsidise fuel below the market levels, including China, India, Indonesia, Iran, Kazakhstan, Russia, South Africa, and Venezuela (OECD, 2018). In these countries, the price of fuel is about 20% below the opportunity cost or landed price. This under-pricing results in significant economic losses in these countries, and it is estimated that removing energy subsidies in these countries will result in a 13% decrease primary consumption, a 1% increase in GDP, and a 16% decrease in CO_2 emissions, and removing subsidies in these countries will decrease global energy consumption by 3.5% while decreasing global CO_2 emissions by 4.6% (OECD, 2018). Between 1980 and 2010, 36% of global carbon emissions were caused by fossil fuel subsidies, according to Rentschler and Bazilian (2016), necessitating increased calls for fuel subsidy removal. In particular, countries in the Middle East and North Africa have high subsidies relative to the value of supply. In 2014, Saudi Arabia (78.9%), Iran (73.8%), Iraq (62.4%), Libya (80.2%), Algeria (56.7%), and Egypt (53.7%) had the highest subsidy rates in the world (Rentschler & Bazilian, 2016). The World Bank estimates that 48% of global fossil fuel subsidies are paid in the Middle East (Rentschler & Bazilian, 2016).

The elimination of fuel subsidies has repeatedly met with fierce opposition from labour unions, workers, and members of civil society, particularly in countries of the Global South. For all the expected benefits of fuel subsidy reforms, protests, violent ones, and opposition threatening regime abolition are obstacles to the reform and removal (Perry, 2020; Houeland, 2022a). Such popular protests in Russia, China, India, Trinidad and Tobago, Nigeria, Brazil, Yemen, Bolivia, Egypt, Nepal, Indonesia, Sudan, Jordan, Iran, Ghana, Cameroon, and Venezuela are perceived as policies against the interests of workers and the poor, even though subsidies have recognised climate impacts (Houeland, 2022b). Politics is a critical factor in the persistence of fuel subsidies around the world, despite the 2015 Paris Climate Agreement, and many political actors fear for their future political careers if they take decisive action against fuel subsidies, thereby allowing them to continue (Skovgaard & van Asselt, 2018). Price (2022) also notes that fuel unrest has the potential to cause conflicts, rebellion, political movements, and instability. Saddiki and Chaouti (2022) report that economic, social, environmental, political, and institutional factors drive fuel subsidy reforms, while impeding factors include lack of communication with the public, lack of credibility and trust in governments, weak macroeconomic conditions, impact on the welfare of the poor and households, exposure to powerful interest groups, and institutional capacity of governments. Victor (2009) and Simon (2012) add that political distributive interests are influential behind fuel subsidies and that, once introduced, they are difficult to remove.

Fossil fuel subsidies are redistributive policy tools that bridge the inequality gap and alleviate poverty among vulnerable households (Couharde & Mouhoud, 2020). Couharde and Mouhoud (2020), in contrast to most of the aforementioned studies, see fuel subsidy as a good policy framework for assisting the poor in developing countries. Dennis (2016) argues that the removal of fuel subsidies has welfare implications for poor households if the compensation is not replaced by equivalent or higher benefits to households after removal. Lockwood (2013, 2015) views energy subsidies as a political rent that can be more easily passed onto beneficiaries than other dividends of democracies. Their abolition will result in violent protests and political unrest. However, Gelb and Mukherjee (2019) prefer the option of political choice for digital technologies as a plausible alternative to the effects of fuel subsidies and environmental hazards. The introduction of electric vehicles, the use of renewable energy, and other technological and digital sources can replace fuel subsidies with fewer hiccups for the policymakers than the current policy approach (Gelb & Mukherjee, 2019). But Benes et al. (2016) suggest that the declining price of oil during COVID-19 should be utilised by world governments to reduce fuel subsidies with less risk of countering by citizens to be replaced with more efficient social policy.

The actors behind the global fossil fuel reforms are predominantly from the Global North, even though most of the targets of the reforms are in the Global South. This raises suspicions of neoliberal policies to that continue to disenfranchise the Global South, strangulate economic growth, and impede political freedom and sovereignty (Perry, 2020). It is evident that the IMF and World Bank are using their influence over debtor countries in the Global South by imposing their structural adjustment programmes and other neoliberal policies (Osunmuyiwa & Kalfagianni, 2017). For example, the main actors in this debate are the World Bank, IMF, the OECD, the G-20, and IEA (Houeland, 2022a). In order to achieve the international 1.5 °C targets agreed in the Paris Agreement, these actors believed that fuel subsidy reform is necessary. The foundation of fuel subsidy reform was laid at the G-20 meeting in London in 2009, where fuel subsidy reform was seen as one of the most important measures to mitigate climate change. However, the actual decision to phase out subsidies was made in 2015 in the Paris Agreement on Climate Change, which 197 countries ratified and in which countries committed to mobilise US$100 billion in 'climate finance' annually to promote renewable energy and low-carbon development (Rentschler, 2018, p. 18). The credibility dilemma caused by Article 4 of Paris Agreement and the need to be cautious in setting national climate plans make it necessary to design appropriate policies that are congruent with domestic programmes to avoid an external, incompatible approach that will trigger a backlash (Elliott et al., 2022).

Fuel subsidies are associated with democratic backwardness and the creation of rentier states (Fails, 2019). Fails (2019) argues that most states that discovered oil and immediately became rich in oil money had difficulty democratising because higher spending on these subsidies delayed the transition to democracy, as authoritarian leaders can have the support and approval of the governed, who found life less difficult because of over subsidy. Fails (2019) speculates on corruption and scandals related to oil subsidies. The ruling elites found it convenient to maintain budgets for fuel subsidies, a significant portion of which benefitted the elites and a few cabals, rather than the actual goals of poor households. The issue of fuel subsidies and reform is therefore a matter of debate. While all scholars analysed earlier agreed that they are detrimental to climate policy and global warming, the impact on poor households excites the sympathy of those who believed sustainability is possible, while the economic burden and financial impact caused the other side of the coin to think otherwise and to advocate a complete removal of subsidies. The Nigerian case, an area that is the subject of this study, may not be consistent with some of the observed cases as this study concludes that the paradoxical Nigerian subsidy dilemma is a move orchestrated by elites to reward political allies and enrich themselves. It is unnecessary, and spending should have been significantly reduced if local refineries were in operation. This is discussed in the next section.

10.3 Fuel Subsidy in Nigeria: History and Trajectories

The Nigerian government has discovered the provision of subsidies as a policy tool to cushion the impact of economic policies that may impose hardship on the poor. Nigeria's oil subsidies date back to the oil boom period of the 1970s. Since Nigeria had enough money to spend, it decided to subsidise everything, including pilgrimages and imported manufactured goods (Nwosu, 1996). The introduction of fuel prices in a society has many negative economic consequences. One is that the market cannot function. Second, such energy policies unnecessarily burden government finances (Balouga, 2012). However, the removal of petroleum subsidies in Nigeria also has consequences such as higher transportation costs, price increases of other goods, and finally macroeconomic impacts, especially on poor households who face an increase in the cost of basic goods and services (Egbezien, 2020). Poverty among poor households will increase if the fuel subsidy is removed without adequate social measures (Siddig et al., 2014; Rentschler, 2016).

Following the 1973/1974 oil price increase, the fuel subsidy in Nigeria increased to 83% in 1975. In 1978, the fuel subsidy was reduced to 2% following an oil price revision, but increased to 65.5% in 1980 due to an increase in the price of crude oil price to US$40 per barrel on the world market (Nwosu, 1996, p. 84). In 1982, the Shagari government increased the price of Premium Motor Spirit (PMS) from 15.3 kobo per litre to 20 kobo per litre, leaving a subsidy of N4.00 per litre for Nigerians paid by the government (Nwosu, 1996, p. 84). In 1986, the Babangida military government announced the withdrawal of oil subsidy by 80% and increased the price from 20 kobo per litre to 39 kobo but with price discrimination between private consumers and commercial vehicles (Nwosu, 1996, p. 84). In 2003, the Nigerian government declared that N12 was spent on subsidies for each litre of PMS. This amounted to a subsidy of N74 billion, which was equivalent to 1.42% of GDP (Balouga, 2012, p. 33).

The politics of fuel subsidy and its removal in Nigeria are a triangular relationship between the Nigerian Labour Congress (NLC), students, and masses on the one hand, the government on the other, and the international financial institutions and creditor nations on the other (Nwosu, 1996). The Federal Government as the main actor in the policy of fuel subsidy was faced with the dilemma of social choice between the abolition and provision of public welfare. Increased economic pressure and the oil shock forced borrowing from international financial institutions and creditor nations, which in turn put pressure on the Nigerian government to remove the subsidy, as noted by Houeland (2022b). Unions, students, civil society, and the public always resist, protest, and criticise the measures as unsustainable. In the last 12 years, the Nigerian Labour Congress (NLC), Trade Union Congress (TUC), Civil Liberty Organisation (CLO), National Association of Nigerian Students (NANS), Academic Staff Union of Universities (ASUU), and Occupy-Nigeria have protested every proposed subsidy cut (Akanle et al., 2014). The 2012 protest is the largest and most coordinated in the country's history. The explosion of the Internet and social media explosion enabled massive mobilisation inside and outside the country (Akanle et al., 2014; Titus, 2017). These protests of resistance remain the biggest obstacle to fuel subsidy removal in Nigeria and will continue to be the only weapon against removal in the future (Houeland, 2020, 2022b). Switching to renewable energy is the best method of removing subsidies, but the rentier nature of the Nigerian state hinders this option (Osunmuyiwa & Kalfagianni, 2017).

Oil production in Nigeria is anchored on government control and regulation of the oil sector. Several attempts to unburden and deregulate the government have failed. In addition to economic pressures on the Nigerian government, the corruption scandals have characterised the subsidy payment and allocation process. In 2011, for example, Nigeria spent N1.3 trillion on fuel subsidies, equivalent to 20% of the federal budget, in a country with a huge infrastructure gap (Balouga, 2012, p. 31). Balouga (2012) adds that fuel subsidy policies in Nigeria are supposed to benefit the poor, but the poor benefit a little from the spending because most of the subsidy payment go to the richest 10% and not to the majority of the poor. It is reported that only 7.1% of subsidies go to the poorest 10% of the population (Balouga, 2012, p. 31). The top 10% rich receive 47.6% of the total payments, while the top 20% received 67.5% of the total subsidies (Balouga, 2012, p. 31). There is no doubt that the rich households consume more fuel or energy than the households as a whole, but to justify the removal of subsidies for this reason will hit the poor harder and plunge them into more poverty, because the rich can afford any price while the poor will suffer from the rising prices of goods and services that may come from the increase in fuel prices (Akinwale et al., 2013). Some studies (Ayodele, 2014; Ezeoha & Uche, 2017) suggest that fuel subsidy removal is not about political choices, political economy of consequences, or macroeconomic impacts, but a matter of trust in government. More than 80% of Nigerians distrust the government and consider it corrupt. Many Nigerians could not believe the subsidy released by the government. Some believed that there were no subsidies but that the government was simply playing a political manipulation game with its psychology (Ayodele, 2014). Thus, in this environment of mutual distrust, it is practically impossible to initiate a policy.

The fuel subsidy system in Nigeria is associated with a massive corruption scandal (Beedell, 2017). Apart from the high heavy cost to the government, the process leads to rent-seeking in the Nigeria's oil sector, detour, smuggling, and black market where marketers receiving subsidies from government funds divert products and sell the, on the black markets instead of paying the official price at fuel stations (Beedell, 2017). Between 2011 and 2013, the Nigerian National Petroleum Corporation (NNPC) failed to account for an estimated US$6 billion in discretionary spending, including subsidy payments (Beedell, 2017). Beedell (2017) further reports that the government's compensation to marketers for fuel landed costs has led to inflation in the amount that has gone into the pockets of a few officials. Fuel marketers have raked in €13 billion in subsidy payments after bribing officials from the NPA, the PPPRA, the Department of Petroleum Resources (DPR), and the Nigerian Navy to falsify documents for fuel imports from fictitious cargo ships (Beedell, 2017, p. 52). This creates a haven for corruption and looting of public coffers by public officials is created. This is an act of sabotage on the Nigerian economy and leads to the destruction of the economy by the actions of a few selfish officials. Oil subsidies doubled the health budget in 2020, but a survey (McCullough et al., 2021) shows that many Nigerians oppose the removal of the subsidies because they do not trust that the Nigerian government to compensate them with an adequate social policy replacement after removal. The reason for this is respondents' perceived corruption of the policymakers (McCullough et al., 2021).

An amazing conundrum of the Nigerian oil sector and fuel subsidies is the issue of poorly performing refineries. Nigeria is the tenth largest oil producer and the sixth producer in the Organisation of Petroleum Exporters Countries (OPEC), and relies on the importation of refined petroleum products for 85% of its products (Chikem, 2016). There are several unanswered questions as to why refineries are not operating or are allowed to collapse, and why no effort have been made to build new refineries since 2010 until now. The scandals of involving allegations of corruption in subsidy payments led to numerous investigations beginning in 2010. These investigations include the NNPC fuel importation audit reports, the Nigeria Extractive Industries Transparency Initiative (NEITI) 1999–2011 reports, the KPMG Professional Services audit report of the NNPC that exposed fuel subsidy fraud, and the House of Representatives Ad-hoc Committee report with Resolution No. HR.1/2012 on fuel subsidy investigation (Chikem, 2016). The findings of the aforementioned reports show that, from 1999 to 2013, a period of only 14 years, Nigeria subsidised more than was subsidised in the previous 35 years, and the report also revealed a US$6.8 billion fuel subsidy fraud between 2009 and 2011 alone (Chikem, 2016). The most vexing dimension of subsidy fraud in Nigeria is not the scandals, but the impunity that accompanies the practise. Attempts are made to prevent investigations, and when the investigations are successful, close associates of those in power are indicated, but the reports are swept under the rug without decisive action being taken against the perpetrators.

10.4 Impact of Fuel Subsidy on Nigeria's Economy and Infrastructure Supply

The fuel subsidy has several serious implications for the Nigerian economy. The failure of refineries to refine crude oil contributes to the crisis. The arguments for subsidy are always based on the threshold of landed cost by marketers and the need for under-recovery to make the product affordable. Since the 1980s, Nigeria has not been able to build a new refinery or maintain the existing ones. In 2015, the country's four refineries had a combined production capacity of 445,000 barrels per day, while the daily quota allocated to Nigeria by OPEC is 2.5 million (Dawn Commission, 2016). This implies that Nigeria refines only 18% of and exports 82% of crude to countries where it is refined, and in return, the country imports the refined products (Dawn Commission, 2016). In the process, additional unnecessary costs are incurred driving up cost beyond what is affordable. This prompted the government to pay subsidies Nigeria is the second largest oil producer in Africa possessing 28% of total reserves. Thus, petroleum resources contribute immensely to the Nigerian economy, but overpayment of subsidies cripples the economy and minimises the benefits generated (Uduu, 2020).

In the last ten decade, Nigeria has spent over N10 trillion on fuel subsidies at the expense of infrastructure. The country, which is severely deprived of basic infrastructures such as electricity, roads, housing, potable water, health care, and education prioritises fuel, subsidies over these basic services.

Onyeiwu (2021) posts it that fuel subsidy is a bad economy because of its on infrastructure gaps in Nigeria. The N10 trillion spent by FG in 12 years from 2010 to 2022 is 200% more than education spending, 240% more than security spending, 250% more than infrastructure spending, and 290% more than health spending (Uduu, 2020). The money spent on subsidies, if properly channelled into other productive sectors of the economy, can spur stimulate growth and development. Nigeria can reinvest the subsidy amount into better and improved infrastructure in many sectors. For example, the subsidy money could have been used to build over 328,100 primary health-care centres nationwide at the cost of N30 million each (Uduu, 2020). This will improve healthcare delivery and extend life expectancy beyond the current average life expectancy of 54.5 years, as the N10 trillion in fuel subsidies can insure 190 million people, almost 85% of the population (Uduu, 2020).

In terms of job creation, the amount spent on subsidies would have enabled 2.5 million youths to be trained annually at N12,000 per month within the spending period. This will mitigate the 30% unemployment rate currently faced by the youth (Uduu, 2020). The same amount of subsidy could have relieved many homeless Nigerians by providing about 656,200 houses with mortgaged at an average cost of N15 million, generating revenue for the government (Uduu, 2020). Access to clean water will be improved by drilling 16,405,000 boreholes across the country with the same amount of subsidy within the period (Uduu, 2020). In addition, 27,342 megawatts (MW) of solar power will be injected into the national grid at a cost of N360 million per megawatt, improving electricity supply to households and manufacturing industries (Uduu, 2020). With the same amount, 1,968,000 Nigerians could be educated and received skilled tertiary education at a cost of N5 million per person (Uduu, 2020). In turn, in the education sector, about 984,300 quality classrooms could have been built at N10 million apiece, and about 21.8 million children could have been supported in education with the same amount (Uduu, 2020). In the area of road infrastructure, about 19,686 kilometres could have been built at N500 million each (Uduu, 2020). About 9,843,000 entrepreneurs could have received a loan of N1 million to start or expand their businesses (Uduu, 2020).

A major problem with fuel subsidies in Nigeria is the corruption scandal allegations that sabotaging the Nigerian economy. The House of Representatives report revealed that the national oil company, NNPC, is involved in opaque and shady deals that lack transparency when it comes to oil subsidies (Mark, 2012). The NNPC was accused in the report of being unaccountable and corrupt. In addition, the reported indicated 72 fuel importers, most of whom had close ties to high-ranking government officials. In one case, payments worth US$6.4 million were transferred 128 times from the government treasury to anonymous marketers in less than 24 hours (Mark, 2012). This indicates a high level of corrupt practices in the oil subsidy regime.

The oil subsidy bill is becoming an unsustainable burden on the Nigerian government and economy. In the first quarter of 2022, Nigeria is spending

N500 billion per month to cover subsidy costs, which means that the total amount will be N6 trillion by the end of 2022. This cost represents almost 50% of total fuel imports (Tunji, 2022). The World Bank warned Nigeria that some economically burdensome bills, including the foreign exchange crisis, fuel subsidies, and others, will wipe out Nigeria's perceived gains from the rising oil prices in the post-COVID-19 global oil market (Ifeanyi, 2022). Other loses identified by the World Bank report include the fiscal deficit, lower oil output of 1.5 million (the lowest in a decade due to oil bunkering and pipeline vandalisation and explosion), inflation, and rising debt profile accompanied by high debt servicing (Ifeanyi, 2022). The consequence of all these indicators is the weakening of the economy, which makes Nigeria's macroeconomic sector volatile, fluctuating, and vulnerable to shocks and recessions intermittently.

10.5 To Continue or Not? Oil Subsidy Dilemma and Alternative Choices

In order to establish a definitive position in this study, it is pertinent to reflect the various views on the need to maintain or eliminate fuel subsidies. Six different views were identified in this study. The first category (Lockwood, 2013; Lockwood, 2015; Dennis, 2016; Sovacool, 2017; Rentschler, 2018; Fails, 2019; Couharde & Mouhoud, 2020; Houeland, 2022a; Price, 2022) either strongly or partially emphasises that fuel subsidies must be maintained by world's governments out of compassion for poor households, who will bear the brunt of the increase in the price of goods and services if the price is increased or fuel subsidies are eliminated. The second category argues that fuel subsidies should be eliminated entirely. This category (International Energy Agency, 1999; Simon, 2012; Jakob et al., 2015; Sivaram & Harris, 2016; OECD, 2021; Saddiki & Chaouti, 2022) considered that fuel subsidies are unsustainable due to the impact on climate, the economic stress on government finances, and the desire to transfer welfare benefits to other sectors to avoid national budget deficits. The third category, specifically, in the Nigerian context, like the first category, supports the continuation of the fuel subsidy policies. The reasons cited by this group are the impact on poor households, the government's social contract, and the need to reduce poverty and bridge the inequality gap (Akinwale et al., 2013; Siddig et al., 2014; Rentschler, 2015; Chikem, 2016; Egbezien, 2020; Houeland, 2020, 2022b). The fourth category (Balouga, 2012; Mark, 2012; Beedell, 2017; Onyeiwu, 2021; Ifeanyi, 2022; Tunji, 2022) opposed the continuation of fuel subsidy in Nigeria because of its impact on the national budget, crippling of government finances, infrastructural deficit, and corruption scandal. The other category (Victor, 2009; Akanle et al., 2014; Ayodele, 2014; Ezeoha & Uche, 2017; Skovgaard & van Asselt, 2018; Perry, 2020; McCullough et al., 2021; Houeland, 2022a) is in favour of neither maintaining nor removing the fuel subsidy, but insists that protests and resistance movements by labour unions and organised civil societies will prevent the policy of subsidy removal. The last category (Benes et al., 2016; Gelb & Mukherjee, 2019; Elliott et al., 2022) prefers that governments develop alternative renewable energy strategies, take advantage of the window of opportunity of falling crude oil prices at the global level, and phase out subsidies once a sustainable alternative has been successfully provided.

Going by the aforementioned perspectives, it is indisputable that fuel subsidy funds can be much better and more resourceful if they are injected into other social security nets that will cushion the effects of subsidy removal. It will even enhance accountability, foster transparency, and eschew corrupt practices. This is, particularly, when the resources of government are inadequate and are insufficient to take care of the subsidies, tut the impact on macroeconomic conditions of the poor is another consideration that is always recognised. There are many reasons why this study is not convinced that fuel subsidy is evil in itself. It is the circumstances heralding the payments and transfers that are believed to have been worrisome to the Nigerian economy.

The arguments that fuel subsidies increase carbon emissions and global warming should not be a justification for the removal of subsidies in states like Nigeria. The whole of Africa contributes 2–3% of the total global emissions only, negligible and not softening, it does not imply that the continent is unaffected by the process of climate change. Nigeria is not contributing up to 1% of global warming despite gas flaring and bush burning. The justification to eliminate subsidies is applicable in states like the US and China. The two countries contribute 40% of the total global emissions. Countries like Nigeria should not be coerced into signing climate change agreements and fuel subsidy reform policies. Instead, they should be allowed to decide domestically and gradually depending on policy choices preferences as observed by Gelb and Mukherjee (2019). The scenario of a universal imposition of agreements and policies confirms the allegations of neoliberal arm-twisting of weak countries by World powers to surrender (Osunmuyiwa & Kalfagianni, 2017).

The second argument is revolving around the cost of fuel subsidy on the Nigerian economy, particularly, the percentage to GDP, impact on budget deficit, and infrastructure gap. All these can be ameliorated if local refineries are functioning appropriately. Costs of fuel subsidy in Nigeria are estimated in the context of the expenses of importation. But we have seen oil-producing states like Saudi Arabia, Russia, and Venezuela subsidising fuel. Thus, even if the local refineries commence operation again, or new ones are built like the impending Dangote refinery in Lagos, the government may still have to battle with subsidies. However, if the landing cost from importation is the accrued cost that is subsidised, local refining and distribution will immensely reduce the cost of fuel subsidies to affordable cost by the government thereby, saving Nigeria the trouble of fuel subsidy reform.

The other side of the argument which is found unconvincing by this study is the submission that only about 10% of the poor households benefits from fuel subsidies in Nigeria, while the top 20% enjoys about 67% of it. This statistical analysis cannot stand the test of reality. The majority poor are, of course, not buying fuel or possessing vehicles and other machines that used fuel but the multiplier effects affect all of them. For instance, once fuel price increases in Nigeria, transportation fare goes up and the consumer goods that are transported to nooks and crannies in the country rise up, in addition to increase in services and fees. Thus, the lower the price the lower the negative impact on poor households and vice versa irrespective of the beneficiaries. Simply put, the poor that benefits from fuel subsidy can't be 10% as reported by some aforementioned studies if the trickle-down effects is considered.

Alternatively, Nigeria is blessed with geographical features that can accommodate alternative energy sources. The country is susceptible to directional wind which can generate energy, a warming sun shines covering the entire periods of the seasons enabling for solar energy generation, and dams are still functional for generating energy and utilisation for g hydroelectric sources. Instead of an abrupt withdrawal of subsidy, Nigeria should exploit its options, while retaining subsidy temporarily. An aggressive approach to generating energy using alternative means identified earlier should be adopted. In addition, the use of alternative fuel-consuming machines should be encouraged. Electric cars and other machines should be utilised, but this requires a steady and regular power supply which is now unavailable but can be obtained with sound policies.

In an anticipated move but unexpected too-soon pronouncement, the sworn-in President of Nigeria, Ahmed Bola Tinubu, declared on 29 May 2023 during his inaugural speech that fuel subsidy is no longer in Nigeria. The departed government of former President Buhari announced during the presentation of 2023 budget that fuel subsidy is included for only January to May, and with effect from June, it will no longer hold. A day after President Tinubu announced that subsidy is removed, fuel queues re-appeared in Nigerian cities, and the cost of PMS rose from the range of N189–N198 instantly to N500–N600. By 31 May, 2023, the Nigerian masses are feeling the effects in the rising cost of transport. The prices of commodities and services are yet to be affected, because it is too close to call with just two days of the incident. The NLC, umbrella body of all labour unions in the country, issued a strong warning to the government to prepare for a showdown. On whether the labour union (NLC) could succeed this time in pressurising the government to reverse the policy reform, the projected effects on the poor, the promised cushioning effects palliatives by the government and how the economy will fair is too early to predict in this study but one certain development is, people have started suffering untold hardship and the government will face popular resistance while the unpopular policy reform may politically affect future chances of the ruling party in general elections.

10.6 Conclusion

This chapter concludes that fuel subsidy is a global policy issue attached to programme of climate change and global warming in addition to economic downsizing of governments for a rationale utilisation of the funds toward better social security policies. The issue is not limited or unique to the Nigerian state alone but the Nigerian perspective is peculiar. Nigeria is an oil-producing state that lacks functioning refineries leading to the exportation of crude oil and the importation of refined petroleum products. The process led to increased landing costs that the government is subsidising, but in the course of the payments, corruption scandals, fraud, and misplacement of priorities in infrastructural provision emerged. It is argued in the chapter that fuel subsidy payments by World governments are not a wise policy choice owing to their implications on the economies of the affected states but the fuel subsidy reforms that target at removal of the cost have their own sharp effects on, especially, the poor households. In Nigeria, the study concludes that subsidy should be gradually phased out but it should be retained at the moment to avoid the implications on poor households who will suffer more in the event of rising fuel costs due to soaring transport costs and services. However, the government is advised to expedite quick action in exploring plausible alternatives that will phase out the subsidy in a shorter period time.

President Bola Ahmed Tinubu in his inaugural speech on 29 May 2023 declared that subsidy has gone signalling that fuel subsidy is ended. Thus, the post-COVID-19 Nigeria will be interesting in this study. If the government plans to remove subsidy completely, there must be alternative strategies on ground to palliatives that will commensurate with the anticipated rising cost of transport, goods, and services. The best option is rapid diversification of the economy to widen the tax nets and income sources, to apply progressive taxation, and to ensure that food items and other basic needs are affordable to the people.

References

Akanle, O., Adebayo, K., & Adetayo, O. (2014). Fuel subsidy in Nigeria: Context of governance and social protest. *International Journal of Sociology and Social Policy*, *34*(2), 88–106.

Akinwale, Y. O., Olaopa, O. R., Ogundari, I., & Siyanbola, W. O. (2013). Political economy of phasing out fuel subsidy in Nigeria. *Energy and Power*, *3*(4), 37–43.

Ayodele, J. (2014). Trust in government and the politics of fuel subsidy removal in Lagos, Nigeria. *Inkayiso, Journal of Humanities and Social Sciences*, 6(1), 39–40.

Balouga, J. (2012). The political economy of oil subsidy in Nigeria. *International Association for Energy Economics: Second Quarter*, 2, 31–35.

Beedell, E. (2017, June 19). *Evaluating the impact of Nigeria's fuel subsidy regime*. University of Graduate School of Public and International Affairs.

Benes, K., Cheon, A., Urpelainen, J., & Yang, J. (2016). *Low oil prices: An opportunity for fuel subsidy reform*. International Growth Centre.

Chikem, F. C. (2016). The political economy of fuel importation probes and development of refineries in Nigeria. *Insight on Africa*, *8*(1), 18–39.

Couharde, C., & Mouhoud, S. (2020). Fossil fuel subsidies, income inequality, and poverty: Evidence from developing countries. *Journal of Economic Surveys*. https://doi.org/10.1111/joes.12384.

Dawn Commission. (2016, June 13). The history of oil subsidy in Nigeria. *Face book*. Retrieved May 17, 2023, from www.facebook.com/dawncommission/psts/thc-history-of-oil-subsidy-in-nigeriathe-history-of-the-fuel-subsidy-in-nigeria-/961255387330702/

Dennis, A. (2016). Household welfare implications of fossil fuel subsidy reforms in developing countries. *Energy Policy*, *96*(1), 597–606.

Egbezien, I. H. (2020). Petroleum subsidy withdrawal, fuel price hikes and the Nigerian economy. *International Journal of Energy Economics and Policy*. https://doi.org/10.32479/ijeep.8307.

Elliott, C., Bernstein, S., & Hoffman, M. (2022). Credibility dilemmas under the Paris agreement: Explaining fossil fuel subsidy reform reference s in INDCs. *International Environ Agreements*, *22*, 735–759.

Ezeoha, A. E., & Uche, C. U. (2017). State legitimacy and the unending crisis of petrol subsidy reforms in Nigeria. *Society and Natural Resources*. https://doi.org/10.1080/08941920.2017.1290180.

Fails, M. D. (2019). Fuel subsidies limit democratisation: Evidence from a global sample, 1990–2014. *International Studies Quarterly*, *63*, 354–363.

Gelb, A., & Mukherjee, A. (2019). *Fuel subsidy reform and green taxes: Can digital technologies improve state capacity and effectiveness?* Centre for Global Development.

Houeland, C. (2022a). Labour resistance against fossil fuel subsidies reform: Neoliberal discourses and African realities. In N. Rathzel, D. Stevis, & D. Uzzell (Eds.), *The Palgrave handbook of environmental labour studies* (pp. 493–517). Palgrave Macmillan.

Houeland, J. (2020). Contentious and institutional politics in a petro-state: Nigeria's 2012 fuel subsidy protests. *The Extractive Industries and Societies*. https://doi.org/10.1016/j.exis.2020.05.010

Houeland, J. (2022b). The social contract and industrial citizenship: Nigerian trade unions' role in the recurring fuel subsidy protests. *Africa*, *92*, 860–879.

Ifeanyi, U. J. (2022, April 26). World Bank says Forex crisis, fuel subsidy, others are offsetting Nigeria's gains from rising oil price. *Naira Metrics*. Retrieved May 17, 2023, from https://nairametrics.com/2022/06/20/world-bank-says-forex-crisis-fuel-subsidy-others-are-offsetting-nigerias-gains-from-rising-oil-prices/

International Energy Agency. (1999). *World energy outlook. Looking at energy subsidies: Getting the prices right*. IEA.

Jakob, M., Chen, C., Fuss, S., Marxen, A., & Edenhofer, O. (2015). Development incentives for fossil fuel subsidy reform. *Nature Climate Change*, *5*(1), 709–711.

Lockwood, M. (2013, February 28). *The political economy of fossil fuel subsidies in developing countries*. Climate change and development seminar series. University of Sussex.

Lockwood, M. (2015). Fossil fuel subsidy reform, rent management and political fragmentation in developing countries. *New Political Economy*, *20*(4), 475–490.

Mark, M. (2012, April 19). Nigeria fuel subsidy scheme hit by corruption. *The Guardian*. Retrieved May 17, 2023, from www.theguardian.com/world/2012/apr/19/nigeria-fuel-subsidy-scheme-corruption

McCullough, N., Moerenhout, T., & Yang, J. (2021). Fuel subsidy reform and the social contract in Nigeria: A micro-economic analysis. *Energy Policy*. https://doi.org/10.1016/j.enpol.2021.112336

Nwosu, N. I. (1996). The politics of oil subsidy in Nigeria. *Africa: Rivista trimestrale di studi e documentazione dell'Istituto italiano per l'Africae l'Oriente*, *51*(1), 80–94.

Onyeiwu, S. (2021, November 4). Fuel subsidies in Nigeria: They are bad for the economy, but the lifeblood of politicians. *The Conversation*. Retrieved May 17, 2023, from https://theconversation.com/fuel-subsidies-in-nigeria-theyre-bad-for-the-economy-but-the-lifeblood-of-politicians-170966

Organisation for Economic Cooperation and Development. (2018). *Inventory of energy subsidies in the EU's Easter partnership companies*. OECD.

Organisation for Economic Cooperation and Development. (2021). *Fossil-fuel subsidies in the EU Eastern partner countries: Estimates and recent policy development*. OECD.

Osunmuyiwa, O., & Kalfagianni, A. (2017). The oil climax: Can Nigeria's fuel subsidy reforms propel energy transition? *Energy Research & Social Sciences*. http://dx.doi.org/10.1016/j.erss.2017.03.003

Perry, K. K. (2020). For politics, people or the planet? The political economy of fossil fuel reform, energy dependence and climate policy in Haiti. *Energy Research & Social Sciences*. https://doi.org/10.1016/j.erss.2019.101397

Price, R. (2022). *Links between energy prices, Fuel subsidy reforms and instability: Help desk report*. Foreign, Commonwealth and Development Office.

Rentschler, J. (2015). *Incidence and impact: A disaggregated poverty analysis of fossil fuel subsidy reform*. The Oxford Institute for Energy Studies.

Rentschler, J. (2016). Incidence and impact: The regional variation of poverty effects due to fossil fuel subsidy reform. *Energy Policy*, *96*(1), 491–503.

Rentschler, J. (2018). *Fossil fuel subsidy reforms: A guide to economic and political complexity*. Routledge, Taylor & Francis.

Rentschler, J., & Bazilian, M. (2016). Reforming fossil fuel subsidies: Drivers, barriers and the state of progress. *Climate Policy*, *17*(7), 891–914.

Saddiki, A., & Chaouti, A. (2022). Drivers and barriers of fossil fuel subsidy reforms in developing countries: A review. *Journal of Economics Studies and Research*. https://doi.org/10.5171/2022.212515

Siddig, K., Aguiar, A., Grethe, H., Minor, P., & Wamsley, T. (2014). Impact of removing fuel import subsidies in Nigeria on poverty. *Energy Policy*, *69*, 165–178.

Simon, C. (2012). *A guide to the political economy of reforming energy subsidies* (IZA Policy Paper No. 52). Institute for the Study of Labour (IZA).

Sivaram, V., & Harris, J. M. (2016). *Sustaining fuel subsidy reform*. Council on Foreign Relations.

Skovgaard, J., & van Asselt, H. (2018). The politics of fossil fuel subsidies and their reform: Implications for climate change mitigation. *Climate Change*. https://doi.org/10.1002/wcc.581

Sovacool, B. K. (2017). Reviewing, reforming, and rethinking global energy subsidies: Towards a political economy research Agenda. *Ecological Economics*, *135*(1), 150–163.

Titus, O. S. (2017). From social media space to sound space: Protest songs during occupy Nigeria fuel subsidy removal. *Muziki, Journal of Music Research in Africa*, *14*(2), 109–122.

Tunji, S. (2022, June 6). Subsidy hits 45% of fuel import bill-NBS report. *Punch*. Retrieved May 17, 2022, from https://punchng.com/subsidy-hits-45-of-fuel-import-bill-in-q1-nbs-report/

Uduu, O. (2020, June 27). FG spent N10 trillion on fuel subsidy in 12 years expense of infrastructure. *Dataphyte*. Retrieved May 17, 2023, from www.dataphyte.com/latest-reports/economy/fg-spent-n10-trillion-on-fuel-subsidy-in-12-years-at-the-expense-of-infrastructure/

Victor, D. (2009). *The politics of fossil-fuel subsidies*. International Institute for Sustainable Development.

World Economic Forum. (2023). *Fossil-fuel consumption subsidies soared to record heights in 2022*. Retrieved May 17, 2023, from www.weforum.org/agenda/2023/02/fossil-fuel-consumption-subsidies-energy-2022/

11 Unveiling ASEAN's Logistics Infrastructure Investments and Their Intended Economic Impacts

Chun Meng Tang and Adrian Bradshaw

11.1 Introduction

Logistics, which includes functions such as warehousing, transportation, material handling, packaging, and inventory management (APICS, 2020), is critical to national and international connectivity, as well as national, industry, and business competitiveness (Goel et al., 2021; Tang & Abosedra, 2019). Logistics and its performance have a direct impact on a country's economic growth (Arshed et al., 2022) in areas such as international trade (Celebi, 2019), gross domestic product (GDP) (Sharipbekova & Raimbekov, 2018), and productivity (Tang & Abosedra, 2019).

The importance of logistics in today's global supply chains has been recognised by the Association of Southeast Asian Nations (ASEAN) countries in the Master Plan on ASEAN Connectivity 2025 (MPAC 2025), which includes "seamless logistics" as one of the five key strategies driving greater economic development and growth in member countries (ASEAN, 2016). The World Bank also publishes the Logistics Performance Index (LPI), which tracks a country's logistics performance in six aspects, that is, customs, infrastructure, international shipment, logistics competence, tracking and tracing, and timeliness (Arvis et al., 2023).

Logistics infrastructure is the foundation of logistics (Swamidass, 2000). Logistics performance necessitates an effective and efficient logistics infrastructure (Qi et al., 2020; Sharipbekova & Raimbekov, 2018), from planning to execution and control, to reduce total logistics costs while maintaining the desired service levels (APICS, 2020), such as reducing trade times and increasing supply chain reliability (Arvis et al., 2023).

Past studies on how logistics infrastructure contributes to economic development have primarily focused on transportation infrastructure and utilised GDP as a surrogate measure of economic development for statistical analysis (e.g. Ke et al., 2020; Nenavath, 2023; Wang et al., 2020). However, transportation infrastructure is only one kind of logistics infrastructure, and GDP is only one dimension of economic development. There are other kinds of logistics infrastructure (e.g. warehousing and distribution facilities, logistics information systems) (APICS, 2020; Bowersox et al., 2020), and GDP alone

DOI: 10.4324/9781003349204-11

does not provide a complete picture of logistics infrastructure contributions to economic development.

Based on the premise that ASEAN countries would have invested in logistics infrastructure projects to improve their overall logistics performance for better economic development, this study, therefore, aims to answer two research questions: (1) What kinds of logistics infrastructure projects have ASEAN countries initiated in recent years? and (2) What project impacts, particularly in terms of economic development, are these logistics infrastructure projects intended to deliver?

To answer both questions, this study conducted a qualitative content analysis of newspaper articles (in each country's leading English language newspaper) to identify regional or national logistics infrastructure projects initiated in recent years by ASEAN countries using search terms, such as "logistics," "supply chain," and "project."

The study's findings may be valuable towards identifying future investment opportunities in logistics infrastructure in ASEAN countries, which may aid the achievement of the United Nations' Sustainable Development Goal No. 8 of creating jobs, improving living standards, and sustaining economic growth (The United Nations, 2015). Furthermore, categorising the various dimensions of project impacts lays the groundwork for the further development of a performance framework and the relevant performance indicators for measuring the success of logistics infrastructure projects.

The remainder of this chapter provides an introduction to ASEAN and logistics infrastructure (Section 11.2), describes the research design and method (Section 11.3), presents the data analysis and results (Section 11.4), and concludes with a discussion of the study findings (Section 11.5).

11.2 Literature Review

11.2.1 The Association of Southeast Asian Nations (ASEAN)

The Association of Southeast Asian Nations (ASEAN), established in 1967, consists of ten member countries, that is, Brunei Darussalam, Cambodia, Indonesia, Lao PDR, Malaysia, Myanmar, the Philippines, Singapore, Thailand, and Viet Nam (ASEAN, n.d.). It was estimated that in 2022, ASEAN had a total population of 672.22 million people, which would increase to 700.83 million in 2027 (O'Neill, 2023a). With a total combined gross domestic product (GDP) estimated at US$3619.92 billion in 2022 and increasing to US$5199.17 billion in 2027 (O'Neill, 2023b), ASEAN is the third largest regional economy in Asia and the fifth largest economy in the world (Allurentis, 2022; World Economic Forum, 2022).

ASEAN's strategic location for trade and supply chains has made the region attractive for foreign direct investments (FDIs) and free trade agreements (FTAs), which are expected to accelerate the region's economic development (Shastry, 2021). FDI inflows to ASEAN increased by 53.47% from US$116.77 billion in 2012 to US$179.22 billion in 2021. In 2021, the top five industries that received the most FDI inflows were financial and insurance activities; manufacturing; wholesale and retail trade; real-estate activities; and information and communication. In 2021, intra-ASEAN trade in goods increased by 17.36% from US$605.64 billion to US$710.78 billion, whereas extra-ASEAN trade in goods increased by 40.24% from US$1874.95 billion to US$2,629.35 billion. In 2021, the top five trading partners in ASEAN trade in goods were China (US$669.20 billion), the US (US$364.46 billion), the EU-27 (US$268.82 billion), Japan (US$240.39 billion), and Korea (US$189.59 billion) (ASEAN, 2022).

ASEAN member countries have worked closely together to integrate the ASEAN region in order to stimulate economic development, increase competitiveness, and strengthen regional sustainability. For example, at the 12th ASEAN Summit, member countries decided to expedite the development of an ASEAN Community by 2015, comprised of three main pillars: the ASEAN Economic Community (AEC), the ASEAN Political-Security Community (APSC), and the ASEAN Socio-Cultural Community (ASSC) (ASEAN, 2007). Later, at the 27th ASEAN Summit, member countries reaffirmed their vision for the ASEAN Community 2025 (ASEAN, 2015).

To provide support to the development of the ASEAN Community, at the 17th ASEAN Summit, ASEAN adopted the Master Plan on ASEAN Connectivity 2010 (MPAC 2010) to improve connectivity among member countries and between ASEAN and the rest of the world through three main elements: physical connectivity, institutional connectivity, and people-to-people connectivity (ASEAN, 2011). MPAC 2010 was succeeded at the 28th ASEAN summit by the Master Plan on ASEAN Connectivity 2025 (MPAC 2025), with a vision of "achieving a seamlessly and comprehensively connected and integrated ASEAN that will promote competitiveness, inclusiveness, and a greater sense of community" (ASEAN, 2016, p. 7). To fulfil this vision, MPAC 2025 focuses on five strategic areas: sustainable infrastructure, digital innovation, seamless logistics, regulatory excellence, and people mobility (ASEAN, 2016).

Logistics infrastructure improvements, in particular, are critical to better connectivity, which helps boost trade volume, lower trade costs, improve trade efficiency, and foster regional and international competitiveness for greater economic development (Park, 2022; Shen, 2023). Drawn by the abundance of infrastructure investment opportunities, infrastructure development initiatives such as China's Belt and Road Initiative (BRI) and Japan's Expanded Partnership for Quality Infrastructure (EPQI) are motivated to provide financial funding for infrastructure projects in ASEAN (Valockova, 2021).

11.2.2 Logistics Infrastructure

To facilitate the movement of goods within or across countries, logistics infrastructure at the national, regional, and business levels plays a critical role (Swamidass, 2000). Logistics infrastructure serves several connectivity functions, including physical connectivity that allows goods and services to be moved between locations, personnel connectivity that supports the labour market and personal interactions, and information connectivity enabled by information and communication technology (Qi et al., 2020).

Some examples of logistics infrastructure include transportation networks (e.g. roads, railways, seaports, airports, terminals, depots), warehousing and distribution facilities that provide storage, inventory management, and order fulfilment services (e.g. warehouses, distribution centres, cross-docking facilities, fulfilment centres), logistics information systems (e.g. transportation management systems, warehouse management systems), and cross-border facilities (e.g. customs checkpoints, border crossings) (APICS, 2020; Bowersox et al., 2020).

Past studies have used proxies for logistics infrastructure in their research. Some examples of these proxies include land transport (e.g. density of railways and roads), air transport (e.g. number of flights), water transport (e.g. port cargo throughput, inland waterways length), the internet (e.g. number of internet users), and storage (e.g. number of warehouses) (Qi et al., 2020); the length of paved roads, the length of railways, the number of cargo trucks, the weight of cargo freight by air transport, the number of vessel arrivals and departures, and the cargo handling capacity in metric tonnes (Wang et al., 2021).

Past studies have provided evidence that logistics infrastructure contributes positively to economic growth in the form of surrogate measures such as the annual growth rate of real per capita GDP (Ke et al., 2020); GDP per capita income (Nenavath, 2023; Wang et al., 2020); the sum of exports and imports, the sum of exports, the sum of imports, national GDP, and GDP per capita (Wang et al., 2021).

Logistics infrastructure can aid regional and national economic development in a variety of ways, including aggregate demand (e.g. job opportunities during infrastructure construction and maintenance); spatial accessibility (e.g. human mobility and trade); spatial spillover effects (e.g. investments); and attractiveness to foreign direct investment (FDI) (Li et al., 2018). Particularly, because economic activities in various regions are spatially connected, the spatial spillover effects can lead to mutual economic growth at regional levels and promote regional economic development (Qi et al., 2020; Wang et al., 2020).

The link between logistics infrastructure and economic growth is thought to be bidirectional. Infrastructure contributes to economic growth (e.g. trade volumes), which necessitates improved infrastructure or infrastructure investments as growth increases (Bensassi et al., 2015; Cigu et al., 2019).

Given the significance of logistics infrastructure for long-term regional and national economic development, meticulous planning is required (Parola & Lam, 2018). Wang et al. (2021) propose that logistics infrastructure decisions can seek to improve maritime transport, develop an intermodal logistics network for domestic and international markets, and build inland logistics hubs. Maciulyte-Sniukiene and Butkus (2022), on the other hand, argue that countries should invest in infrastructure that provides not only economic but also social and environmental benefits.

11.3 Research Design and Method

This study followed an inductive approach to conduct a qualitative content analysis (QCA) of newspaper articles to identify project impacts and code these impacts into categories and subcategories (Mayring, 2014; Schreier, 2012). QCA is a systematic data analytic method for examining and summarising the meanings of textual or visual data such as interview transcripts, news articles, emails, and images. The method may involve counting and measuring occurrences or interpreting and understanding meaning contained in texts. The texts that are relevant to the research questions are aggregated into categories through a coding process to yield meaningful insights (Schreier, 2012). Hence, QCA is an appropriate method to achieve the aims of this study.

The scope of the research was limited to logistics-specific projects, that is, movement of goods from suppliers to manufacturers to customers in physical supply and distribution. Thus, projects such as e-commerce sites and power plants were deemed irrelevant. However, information-technology projects targeted at facilitating information sharing for logistics management were deemed relevant.

The initial search attempted to search each ASEAN country's leading English language newspaper for articles that contained both the search terms "logistics" or "supply chain" and "project" and were published between 2012 and 2022 to find news on regional or national logistics infrastructure projects. However, it appeared that only articles from the last few years prior to 2022 were available on the majority of the newspaper sites, except Bangkok Post and Phnom Penh Post (the earliest articles were from 2012). Furthermore, the search was limited to nine countries, excluding Myanmar, because the Myanmar Times was no longer accessible. Table 11.1 summarises the search and filter results.

In the first filter round, two reviewers independently screened out articles that were unrelated to logistics or supply chains. In cases of different opinions, the two reviewers met to reconcile the differences. In the second filter round, the reviewers further screened out the remaining articles based on three criteria: (1) those that only provided a summary of projects and reported project impacts in general with no reference to a specific project; (2) those that only reported on project progress without discussing project impacts; and (3) projects undertaken by companies to deliver an output, such as a warehouse and distribution centre, for their own private use.

In the case of some articles reporting on the same project that were relevant to the analysis, these articles were retained, and their article texts that

Table 11.1 Summary of the article search and filter results

Country	*Newspaper*	*Initial search*	*After the first filter round*	*After the second filter round*	*No. of projects*
Brunei	Borneo Bulletin	268	18	1	1
Cambodia	Phnom Penh Post	503	114	16	14
Indonesia	The Jakarta Post	115	24	14	10
Laos	Vientiane Times	173	92	27	8
Malaysia	The Star	563	80	15	9
Vietnam	Việt Nam News	516	119	13	9
The Philippines	Manila Bulletin	487	105	9	7
Singapore	The Straits Times	351	28	5	2
Thailand	Bangkok Post	579	132	12	11
Total		*3555*	*712*	*112*	*71*

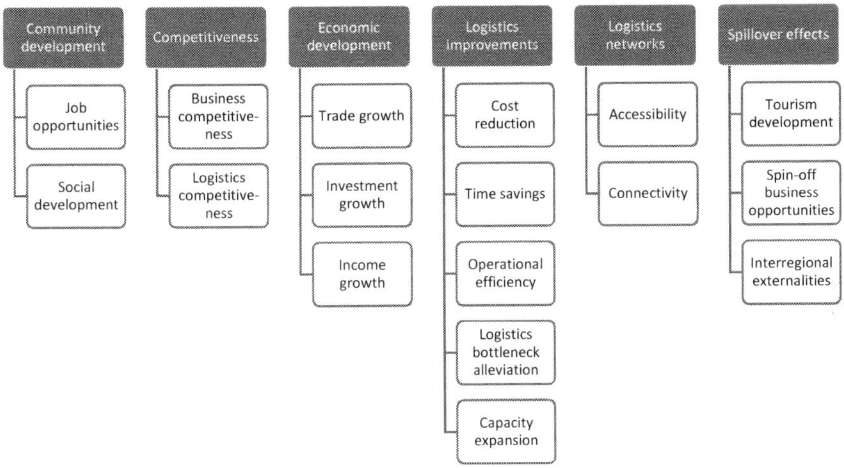

Figure 11.1 Coding frame

were relevant to project impacts were later consolidated for that specific project (excluding highly similar impacts). In total, 112 articles were retained, and these articles covered 71 projects (excluding duplicate projects). The 71 projects were the units of analysis in this study.

To begin the analysis, this study first built a two-level coding frame with six level-one categories and 17 level-two subcategories. The primary dimensions are the level-one categories, and the subdimensions are the level-two subcategories. The coding frame satisfied four methodological requirements: unidimensionality, mutual exclusiveness, exhaustiveness, and saturation (Schreier, 2012). Figure 11.1 depicts the coding frame.

Subsequently, the article texts that were relevant to project impacts were segmented into coding units. The coding units could be an incomplete sentence, a complete sentence, or multiple sentences. There were 313 coding units in total. The coding frame was then pilot-tested in two rounds, yielding a percentage agreement of 90%. As a result, intra-coder stability was satisfactory. In the main analysis, each coding unit was coded into one or more subcategories based on the criterion that a coding unit cannot be coded to more than one subcategory within the same category. In total, 313 coding units were coded 331 times, with each coding unit being coded an average of 1.06 times.

11.4 Data Analysis and Results

Table 11.2 summarises the kinds of logistics infrastructure projects initiated by ASEAN countries in recent years. These projects could be new construction or upgrading of existing structures. Among the 71 projects, logistics hubs (31%), which provide facilities such as warehouses, cross-docking, inland ports, distribution centres, and cold storage, were the most common. Other prominent project types included seaports (21.1%), roads (e.g. highways, ring roads) (18.3%), and railways (15.5%). Besides physical infrastructures, two of the projects were related to logistics information systems (e.g. data-sharing platforms, real-time container tracking systems).

Table 11.3 shows the frequency and percentage of the coding units that have been coded into subcategories. The top five subcategories in order of frequency are cost reduction (10.3%), income growth (9.4%), connectivity (7.6%), logistics competitiveness (7.3%), and operational efficiency (7.3%). The bottom five subcategories are spin-off business opportunities (4.8%), capacity expansion (3.6%), social development (3.3%), tourism development (2.7%), and interregional externalities (2.7%).

Table 11.2 Kinds of logistics infrastructure projects

	Frequency	*Percentage (%)*
Logistics hubs	22	31.0
Seaports	15	21.1
Roads	13	18.3
Railways	11	15.5
Inland waterways	4	5.6
Airports	2	2.8
Information systems	2	2.8
Bridges	1	1.4
Others	1	1.4
Total	*71*	*100.0%*

Table 11.3 Frequency and percentage of coding units coded into a subcategory

Subcategory	*Frequency*	*Percentage (%)*
Cost reduction	34	10.3
Income growth	31	9.4
Connectivity	25	7.6
Logistics competitiveness	24	7.3
Operational efficiency	24	7.3
Logistics bottleneck alleviation	22	6.6
Trade growth	21	6.3
Investment growth	21	6.3
Time savings	20	6.0
Job opportunities	18	5.4
Accessibility	18	5.4
Business competitiveness	16	4.8
Spin-off business opportunities	16	4.8
Capacity expansion	12	3.6
Social development	11	3.3
Tourism development	9	2.7
Interregional externalities	9	2.7
Total	*331*	*100.0%*

Table 11.4 shows the frequency and percentage of the coding units that have been coded into a subcategory within and across categories. Job opportunities (62.1%), logistics competition (60%), income growth (42.5%), cost reduction (30.4%), connectivity (58.1%), and spin-off business opportunities (47.1%) were the leading topics in the community development, competitiveness, economic development, logistics improvements, logistics networks, and spillover effects categories, respectively. Across categories, the logistics improvements category is the largest impact category (33.8%), followed by economic development (22.1%), logistics networks (13%), competitiveness (12.1%), spillover effects (10.3%), and community development (8.8%).

11.5 Discussion and Conclusions

Overall, the findings show that ASEAN countries initiated logistics infrastructure projects to build warehousing and distribution facilities (e.g. warehouses, cross-docking or transshipment facilities, distribution centres) and to create logistics information systems (e.g. data sharing platforms, real-time container tracking systems), in addition to transportation networks (e.g. seaports, roads, railways). These projects were initiated by governments, public–private partnerships, or private investors and were in line with the aims of MPAC 2025. Given the geographical diversities within ASEAN, the types of projects varied according to geography. For example, countries with long coastlines, such as Indonesia, developed more seaports, while a landlocked country, such as Loas, built inland or dry ports.

Table 11.4 Frequency and percentage within and across categories

Category	*Subcategory*	*Frequency*	*Within category percentage (%)*	*Across category percentage (%)*
Community development	Job opportunities	18	62.1	
	Social development	11	37.9	
	Subtotal	*29*	*100.0*	*8.8*
Competitiveness	Logistics competitiveness	24	60	
	Business competitiveness	16	40	
	Subtotal	*40*	*100*	*12.1*
Economic development	Income growth	31	42.5	
	Trade growth	21	28.8	
	Investment growth	21	28.8	
	Subtotal	*73*	*100.0*	*22.1*
Logistics improvements	Cost reduction	34	30.4	
	Operational efficiency	24	21.4	
	Logistics bottleneck alleviation	22	19.6	
	Time savings	20	17.9	
	Capacity expansion	12	10.7	
	Subtotal	*112*	*100.0*	*33.8*
Logistics networks	Connectivity	25	58.1	
	Accessibility	18	41.9	
	Subtotal	*43*	*100.0*	*13.0*
Spillover effects	Spin-off business opportunities	16	47.1	
	Tourism development	9	26.5	
	Interregional externalities	9	26.5	
	Subtotal	*34*	*100.0*	*10.3*

The largest impact category is logistics improvements, accounting for about one-third of the total coded units. Given that the majority of projects sought to improve logistics performance, it is not surprising that these projects targeted cost reduction (e.g. lower logistics costs, reduce shipping costs) (The Jakarta Post, 2016; Viet Nam News, 2021); operational efficiency (e.g. streamline operations, improve processing) (The Star, 2020; Viet Nam News, 2022a); logistics bottleneck alleviation (e.g. reduce congestion, ease burden of overcrowded ports) (Phanet, 2022b; The Jakarta Post, 2016); time savings (e.g. shorten shipping time; cut travel time) (Phanet, 2022b; Viet Nam News, 2021); and capacity expansion (e.g. enhance port capacity, improve transport capacity) (Pisei, 2021; Viet Nam News, 2022b). Cost reduction appears to have received greater emphasis in these projects. These projects are in synergy with MPAC 2025 with its focus on seamless logistics by addressing bottlenecks and lowering cross-border transportation costs (ASEAN, 2016).

The second largest impact category is economic development, accounting for over one-fifth of the total coded units. These projects aimed to boost regional and national income (e.g. GDP), trade (e.g. imports and exports), and investment (e.g. foreign direct investments) (Aulia, 2022; Baliga, 2015; Vientiane Times, 2022). These projects are in synergy with MPAC 2025 which recognises that promoting investment and trade requires enhanced logistics infrastructure (ASEAN, 2016). These findings are also consistent with past studies showing that logistics infrastructure contributes to regional and national economies in a variety of ways, including GDP per capita income (Nenavath, 2023), exports and imports (Wang et al., 2021), and foreign direct investment (Li et al., 2018).

The third largest impact category is logistics networks, accounting for slightly more than one-tenth of the total coded units. The project impacts in this category centred on connectivity (e.g. linking the intermodal transport system, and linking road and rail transport networks) (Bangprapa, 2021; Quismorio, 2022) and accessibility (e.g. improving access to major economic centres, providing more transportation options) (Abadilla, 2022; Reuy, 2022) enabled by logistics infrastructure. Connectivity refers to the quality and extent of transportation links between nodes in a logistics network, whereas accessibility refers to the ease of reaching or accessing a certain location (Mamun et al., 2013; Vulevic, 2016). Connectivity and accessibility are both critical variables in logistics performance (Deng et al., 2022). Connectivity is also the main tenet of MPAC 2025 which seeks to create an ASEAN network of people and infrastructure (ASEAN, 2016). The projects in this impact category lend well to this endeavour.

The fourth largest impact category is competitiveness, accounting for around one-tenth of the total coded units. These projects aided in improving a country's (and by extension the region's) logistics competitiveness (e.g. becoming a regional import-export hub, improving national logistics competitiveness) (Baliga, 2015; Gunawan, 2019) and business competitiveness (e.g. strengthening the industrial corridor, improving the country's trade competitiveness) (The Star, 2021b; Viet Nam News, 2022a). These findings support the idea that improving a country's position in international shipment will also increase supply chain resilience and hence business competitiveness (Arvis et al., 2023).

The fifth largest impact category is spillover effects, accounting for just under one-tenth of the total coded units. The spillover effects from these projects included spin-off business opportunities (e.g. creating opportunities to develop industrial parks, spurring other activities in the logistics market) (The Star, 2021a; Viet Nam News, 2019); tourism development (e.g. increasing tourist arrivals, increasing tourism attractiveness) (The Phnom Penh Post, 2021; Vientiane Times, 2022); and interregional externalities (e.g. developing the hinterland and rural parts, spurring development in adjacent areas) (Ling, 2020; Phanet, 2022a). The findings are consistent with past studies that have shown that spillover effects can result in mutual economic growth at the regional level (Qi et al., 2020; Wang et al., 2020).

The sixth largest impact category is community development, accounting for just under one-tenth of the total coded units. These projects promoted community development by creating job opportunities not just during the construction but also throughout the operation of logistics infrastructure (Ismail, 2021). Furthermore, the accompanying economic development from the projects served to improve a community's social well-being (The Star, 2022). These findings are similar to the impacts that have also been reported in past studies of logistics infrastructure (e.g. Bîzoi et al., 2015; Shi et al., 2020).

The findings also illustrate how ASEAN has collaborated on infrastructure projects (e.g. China-Laos Railway, Malaysian East Coast Rail Line) with infrastructure development initiatives such as China's Belt and Road Initiative (BRI) (Gong, 2019). As trade volume is expected to increase with FTAs such as the Regional Comprehensive Economic Partnership (RCEP) and the Comprehensive and Progressive Agreement for Trans-Pacific Partnership (CPTPP) (Shastry, 2021), ASEAN should continue to improve logistics infrastructure to eliminate inefficiencies in supply networks in order to overcome supply-chain vulnerability such as that seen during the COVID-19 pandemic (Jomthanachai, 2022).

In conclusion, this study has answered questions about the kinds of logistics infrastructure projects initiated by ASEAN countries in recent years and the impacts these projects were intended to deliver. The findings provide supply-chain professionals, investors, and policymakers with an overview of logistics infrastructure projects and may point to new investment opportunities. These findings can also help define the main performance metrics for the development of a logistics performance measurement framework, which can be a useful tool to provide a measure of progress for the MPAC 2025 initiative of seamless logistics.

This study does not intend to provide an exhaustive overview of all ASEAN logistics infrastructure projects that have been initiated. It simply provides a snapshot of regional and national projects that have received media attention. Future research could include a more in-depth analysis of similar projects in ASEAN countries.

References

Abadilla, E. V. (2022, December 14). DOTr rolling out 3 priority PPPs. *Manila Bulletin*. https://mb.com.ph/2022/12/14/dotr-rolling-out-3-priority-ppps/

Allurentis. (2022). *Investing in ASEAN 2023*. www.allurentis.com/_files/ugd/ff7369_4b1e54515fcf416fbc7237d0a78fbfe3.pdf?index=true

APICS. (2020). *APICS certified in logistics, transportation and distribution (CLTD) learning system (version 2.0)*. APICS.

Arshed, N., Hassan, M. S., Khan, M. U., & Uppal, A. A. (2022). Moderating effects of logistics infrastructure development and real sector productivity: A case of Pakistan. *Global Business Review*, *23*(3), 676–693. https://doi.org/10.1177/0972150919879307

Arvis, J. F., Ojala, L., Shepherd, B., Ulybina, D., & Wiederer, C. (2023). *Connecting to compete 2023: Trade logistics in an uncertain global economy – the logistics performance index and its indicators*. The World Bank.

ASEAN. (2007). *Cebu declaration on the acceleration of the establishment of an ASEAN community by 2015*. https://asean.org/cebu-declaration-on-the-acceleration-of-the-establishment-of-an-asean-community-by-2015/

ASEAN. (2011). *Master plan on ASEAN connectivity*. https://asean.org/book/master-plan-on-asean-connectivity/

ASEAN. (2015). *ASEAN 2025: Forging ahead together*. www.asean.org/wp-content/uploads/2015/12/ASEAN-2025-Forging-Ahead-Together-final.pdf

ASEAN. (2016). *Master plan on ASEAN connectivity 2025*. https://asean.org/wp-content/uploads/2018/01/47.-December-2017-MPAC2025-2nd-Reprint-.pdf

ASEAN. (2022). *ASEAN statistical yearbook 2022*. https://asean.org/book/asean-statistical-yearbook-2022/

ASEAN. (n.d.). *About us*. https://asean.org/about-us/

Aulia, A. (2022, June 22). Development of Patimban port as a well-planned project. *The Jakarta Post*. www.thejakartapost.com/paper/2022/06/21/development-of-patimban-port-as-a-well-planned-project.html

Baliga, A. (2015, July 2). New SEZ aims for logistics hub. *Phnom Penh Post*. www.phnompenhpost.com/business/new-sez-aims-logistics-hub

Bangprapa, M. (2021, May 4). Plans afoot for logistics hub. *Bangkok Post*. www.bangkokpost.com/business/2109799/plans-afoot-for-logistics-hub

Bensassi, S., Márquez-Ramos, L., Martínez-Zarzoso, I., & Suárez-Burguet, C. (2015). Relationship between logistics infrastructure and trade: Evidence from Spanish regional exports. *Transportation Research. Part A, Policy and Practice*, *72*, 47–61. https://doi.org/10.1016/j.tra.2014.11.007

Bîzoi, C., Popescu, A., Sipos, G., & Sipos, C. (2015). The transportation and logistics sector's performance and the social development – a comparison within the European Union. *Oeconomica*, *60*(1), 68–81.

Bowersox, D., Closs, D., & Cooper, M. B. (2020). *Supply chain logistics management* (5th ed.). McGraw-Hill.

Celebi, D. (2019). The role of logistics performance in promoting trade. *Maritime Economics & Logistics*, *21*(3), 307–323. https://doi.org/10.1057/s41278-017-0094-4

Cigu, E., Agheorghiesei, D. T., Gavriluță, A. F., & Toader, E. (2019). Transport infrastructure development, public performance and long-run economic growth: A case study for the EU-28 countries. *Sustainability*, *11*(1), 67. https://doi.org/10.3390/su11010067

Deng, P., Song, L., Xiao, R., & Huang, C. (2022). Evaluation of logistics and port connectivity in the Yangtze river economic belt of China. *Transport Policy*, *126*, 249–267. https://doi.org/10.1016/j.tranpol.2022.07.019

Goel, R. K., Saunoris, J. W., & Goel, S. S. (2021). Supply chain performance and economic growth: The impact of COVID-19 disruptions. *Journal of Policy Modeling*, *43*(2), 298–316. https://doi.org/10.1016/j.jpolmod.2021.01.003

Gong, X. (2019). The Belt & Road initiative and China's influence in Southeast Asia. *Pacific Review*, *32*(4), 635–665. https://doi.org/10.1080/09512748.2018.1513950

Gunawan, A. (2019, November 22). Dutch and Chinese operators to help expand Kuala Tanjung port. *The Jakarta Post*. www.thejakartapost.com/news/2019/11/22/dutch-and-chinese-operators-to-help-expand-kuala-tanjung-port.html.

Ismail, H. (2021, September 4). Enormous potential of east coast rail link project. *The Star*. www.thestar.com.my/opinion/letters/2021/09/04/enormous-potential-of-east-coast-rail-link-project

The Jakarta Post. (2016. May 2). Govt confirms Patimban megaport, plans another big one in Java's north coast. *The Jakarta Post*. www.thejakartapost.com/news/2016/05/02/govt-confirms-patimban-megaport-plans-another-big-one-in-javas-north-coast.html

Jomthanachai, S., Wong, W. P., Soh, K. L., & Lim, C. P. (2022). A global trade supply chain vulnerability in COVID-19 pandemic: An assessment metric of risk and resilience-based efficiency of CoDEA method. *Research in Transportation Economics*, *93*, 101166. https://doi.org/10.1016/j.retrec.2021.101166

Ke, X., Lin, J. Y., Fu, C., & Wang, Y. (2020). Transport infrastructure development and economic growth in China: Recent evidence from dynamic panel system-GMM analysis. *Sustainability*, *12*(14), 5618. https://doi.org/10.3390/su12145618

Li, K. X., Jin, M., Qi, G., Shi, W., & Ng, A. K. Y. (2018). Logistics as a driving force for development under the Belt and Road initiative – the Chinese model for developing countries. *Transport Reviews*, *38*(4), 457–478. https://doi.org/10.1080/01441647.2017.1365276

Ling, S. (2020, September 26). Awang Tengah: Coastal highway will spur economic growth. *The Star*. www.thestar.com.my/metro/metro-news/2020/09/26/awang-tengah-coastal-highway-will-spur-economic-growth

Maciulyte-Sniukiene, A., & Butkus, M. (2022). Does infrastructure development contribute to EU countries' economic growth? *Sustainability*, *14*(9), 5610. https://doi.org/10.3390/su14095610

Mamun, S. A., Lownes, N. E., Osleeb, J. P., & Bertolaccini, K. (2013). A method to define public transit opportunity space. *Journal of Transport Geography*, *28*, 144–154. https://doi.org/10.1016/j.jtrangeo.2012.12.007

Mayring, P. (2014). *Qualitative content analysis: Theoretical foundation, basic procedures and software solution*. Klagenfurt.

Nenavath, S. (2023). Does transportation infrastructure impact economic growth in India? *Journal of Facilities Management*, *21*(1), 1–15. https://doi.org/10.1108/JFM-03-2021-0032

O'Neill, A. (2023a, February 10). Total population of the ASEAN countries from 2017 to 2027. *Statista*. www.statista.com/statistics/796222/total-population-of-the-asean-countries/#:~:text=Total%20population%20of%20the%20ASEAN%20countries%20from%202017%20to%202027&text=In%202021%2C%20the%20total%20population,an%20estimated%20633.55%20million%20inhabitants

O'Neill, A. (2023b, February 10). *Gross domestic product (GDP) of the ASEAN countries from 2017 to 2027*. Statista. www.statista.com/statistics/796245/gdp-of-the-asean-countries/#:~:text=Gross%20domestic%20product%20of%20the%20ASEAN%20countries%20from%202017%20to%202027&text=In%202021%2B%2C%20the%20estimated%20total,increase%20from%20the%20previous%20years

Park, S. C. (2022). The roles and strategies of ASEAN in the Belt and Road initiative (BRI). *Cuadernos Europeos de Deusto*, *3*, 115–148. https://doi.org/10.18543/CED-03-2022PP115-148

Parola, F., & Lam, J. S. L. (2018). An empirical investigation of logistics infrastructure projects in emerging economies. *Maritime Economics & Logistics*, *20*(1), 48–71. https://doi.org/10.1057/s41278-016-0045-5

Phanet, H. (2022a, May 30). Capital's third ring road nearly 74% finished. *Phnom Penh Post*. www.phnompenhpost.com/business/capitals-third-ring-road-nearly-74-finished

Phanet, H. (2022b, July 26). Ministry mulling road linking S'ville port to new expressway. *Phnom Penh Post*. www.phnompenhpost.com/business/ministry-mulling-road-linking-sville-port-new-expressway

The Phnom Penh Post. (2021, December 15). ABA Bank invests $30 million in development of Techo International Airport. *Phnom Penh Post*. www.phnompenhpost.com/business/aba-bank-invests-30-million-development-techo-international-airport

Pisei, H. (2021, May 17). EDI system, upgrades in the pipeline for Kingdom's ports. *Phnom Penh Post*. www.phnompenhpost.com/business/edi-system-upgrades-pipeline-kingdoms-ports

Qi, G., Shi, W., Lin, K. C., Yuen, K. F., & Xiao, Y. (2020). Spatial spillover effects of logistics infrastructure on regional development: Evidence from China. *Transportation Research. Part A, Policy and Practice*, *135*, 96–114. https://doi.org/10.1016/j.tra.2020.02.022

Quismorio, E. (2022, July 17). Here's why it's crucial for Marcos admin to finish Bicol railway. *Manila Bulletin*. https://mb.com.ph/2022/07/16/heres-why-its-crucial-for-marcos-admin-to-finish-bicol-railway/

Reuy, R. (2022, April 23). Firm wraps up study of waterborne logistic hub in capital. *Phnom Penh Post*. www.phnompenhpost.com/business/firm-wraps-study-waterborne-logistic-hub-capital

Schreier, M. (2012). *Qualitative content analysis in practice*. SAGE.

Sharipbekova, K., & Raimbekov, Z. (2018). Influence of logistics efficiency on economic growth of the CIS countries. *European Research Studies*, *21*(2), 678–690. https://doi.org/10.35808/ersj/1032

Shastry, V. (2021). FDI in the ASEAN states: The engine that roared. *Asia Policy*, *28*(4), 37–48. https://doi.org/10.1353/asp.2021.0047

Shen, C. (2023). The impact of infrastructure development on China-ASEAN trade – evidence from ASEAN. *Sustainability*, *15*(4), 3277. https://doi.org/10.3390/su15043277

Shi, W., Lin, K. C., McLaughlin, H., Qi, G., & Jin, M. (2020). Spatial distribution of job opportunities in China: Evidence from the opening of the high-speed rail. *Transportation Research. Part A, Policy and Practice*, *133*, 138–147. https://doi.org/10.1016/j.tra.2020.01.006

The Star. (2020, February 29). Bolder, better innovation in logistics. *The Star*. www.thestar.com.my/business/business-news/2020/02/29/bolder-better-innovation-in-logistics

The Star. (2021a, January 19). Logos inks first Malaysia JV to develop integrated logistics hub. *The Star*. www.thestar.com.my/business/business-news/2021/01/19/logos-inks-first-malaysia-jv-to-develop-integrated-logistics-hub

The Star. (2021b, June 11). MRCB launches Ipoh Raya integrated park. *The Star*. www.thestar.com.my/business/business-news/2022/06/11/mrcb-launches-ipoh-raya-integrated-park

The Star. (2022, July 30). *One northern hub catalyses Bukit Kayu Hitam border trade*. www.thestar.com.my/business/business-news/2022/07/30/one-northern-hub-catalyses – bukit-kayu-hitam-border-trade

Swamidass, P. M. (2000). Logistics infrastructure. In P. M. Swamidass (Ed.), *Encyclopedia of production and manufacturing management* (pp. 369–370). Springer. https://doi.org/10.1007/1-4020-0612-8_522

Tang, C. F., & Abosedra, S. (2019). Logistics performance, exports, and growth: Evidence from Asian economies. *Research in Transportation Economics*, *78*, 100743. https://doi.org/10.1016/j.retrec.2019.100743

The United Nations. (2015). *Take action for the sustainable development goals*. www.un.org/sustainabledevelopment/sustainable-development-goals/

Valockova, B. (2021). ASEAN's limited centrality in connectivity: Managing infrastructure competition between China and Japan. *Asia Policy*, *16*(1), 129–153. https://doi.org/10.1353/asp.2021.0006

Vientiane Times. (2022, January 6). China-Laos railway service progressing. *Vientiane Times*. www.vientianetimes.org.la/Region_world/Reworld_China03.php

Viet Nam News. (2019, January 10). Trần Đề seaport in Sóc Trăng to be developed with private capital. *Viet Nam News*. https://vietnamnews.vn/economy/483573/tran-de-seaport-in-soc-trang-to-be-developed-with-private-capital.html

Viet Nam News. (2021, June 4). Chu Lai Port, a new gateway for exports in central region. *Viet Nam News*. https://vietnamnews.vn/economy/966107/chu-lai-port-a-new-gateway-for-exports-in-central-region.html

Viet Nam News. (2022a, February 18). IFC partners with Singapore's YCH and Vietnamese T&T to develop super port in Việt Nam. *Viet Nam News*. https://vietnamnews.vn/economy/1155597/ifc-partners-with-singapore-s-ych-and-vietnamese-t-t-to-develop-super-port-in-viet-nam.html

Viet Nam News. (2022b, December 25). Project to improve capacity of Mekong Delta waterways approved. *Viet Nam News*. https://vietnamnews.vn/society/1440988/project-to-improve-capacity-of-mekong-delta-waterways-approved.html

Vulevic, A. (2016). Accessibility concepts and indicators in transportation strategic planning issues: Theoretical framework and literature review. *Logistics & Sustainable Transport*, *7*(1), 58–67. https://doi.org/10.1515/jlst-2016-0006

Wang, C., Kim, Y. S., & Kim, C. Y. (2021). Causality between logistics infrastructure and economic development in China. *Transport Policy*, *100*, 49–58. https://doi.org/10.1016/j.tranpol.2020.10.005

Wang, C., Lim, M. K., Zhang, X., Zhao, L., & Lee, P. T. W. (2020). Railway and road infrastructure in the Belt and Road Initiative countries: Estimating the impact of transport infrastructure on economic growth. *Transportation Research. Part A, Policy and Practice*, *134*, 288–307. https://doi.org/10.1016/j.tra.2020.02.009

World Economic Forum. (2022). *ASEAN is poised for post-pandemic inclusive growth and prosperity – here's why*. www.weforum.org/agenda/2022/01/asean-is-poised-for-post-pandemic-inclusive-growth-and-prosperity-heres-why/

12 Vietnam's Export-Led Growth Model and Environment Performance

Thi Thuy Linh Truong, Pengji Wang, and Jacob Wood

12.1 Introduction

In 1986, the Vietnamese government implemented "Doi Moi", a policy to transition the Vietnamese economy from one that was agricultural to industrial (Anwar & Nguyen, 2011). The policy, followed by other related initiatives, has encouraged the involvement of multinational corporations (MNCs), which have given Vietnam access to innovative technology, raw materials, energy resources, and know-how from developed nations, which has contributed to greater production capacities and competitive advantages among Vietnam businesses. Such developments have allowed Vietnam to be more deeply embedded in global supply chains, which has provided further benefits to the country's export-oriented industries. As a result of this export-led growth model, Vietnam has achieved impressive growth. From 1985 to 2021, Vietnam achieved an annual gross domestic product (GDP) growth rate of 6.38%, with GDP per capita reaching roughly US$3,700 in 2021 (World Bank, 2023c).

Although the policies and the resulting flourishing export-oriented industries have substantially benefitted Vietnam's economic development, such an economic growth model also has some significant environmental consequences. According to World Bank (2022), economic growth has had various environmental effects, such as air pollution, water pollution, deforestation, and the negative impact on wildlife habitats which caused some US$10 billion in environmental degradation in 2020. Despite this impact, Vietnam recognizes the importance of balancing economic growth and environmental protection. As part of its green growth agenda, the country aims to reduce its emissions by 30% and halt deforestation by 2030 while also achieving net zero carbon emissions (CO_2 emissions) by 2050 (World Bank, 2023c).

Over the last two decades, studies have explored the relationship between international trade and environmental pollution in Vietnam, with some studies suggesting that trade and foreign investment can improve Vietnam's environmental performance (Tran, 2020; Luong, 2022), while others show the opposite, for example, Nguyen and Le (2020); Antweiler et al. (2001); and Anwar and Alexander (2016). With such mixed findings, this chapter aims

DOI: 10.4324/9781003349204-12

to provide more empirical evidence as to the impact of the export-led growth model on the environmental performance of Vietnam. Given the limited sample size due to limited time-series data, we employ the Bayesian linear regression on the data from 1995 to 2023 and find that the export-led growth model has had a significant impact on environmental performance such as CO_2 emissions and biodiversity. From our assessment of the results, a series of relevant policy recommendations are also provided that seek to better balance the aims of environmental sustainability and economic growth.

12.2 Literature Review

12.2.1 Vietnam's Export-Led Growth Policy

Since 1986, Vietnam has amended and revised its policy agenda (Table 1 in the Appendix) to expand its trade activities and promote foreign investments (Nguyen et al., 2022).

In addition to those domestic policies and measures to encourage trade and FDI, Vietnam has also actively engaged in various trade agreements, which have further contributed to the expansion of the Vietnamese economy and increased trade flows (Duong et al., 2019). Vietnam's trading activities further boom after joining the World Trade Organization (WTO) in 2007, which has contributed to the ease of trade and capital flows between Vietnam and its trading partners. In the past two decades, Vietnam has explored various Regional Trade Agreements (RTAs), including RTAs between ASEAN and China in 2005, Japan in 2008, India in 2010, Korea in 2010, and Free Trade Agreements (FTAs) in Chile, Australia, and New Zealand in 2010–2014 (Duong et al., 2019). Table 2 in the Appendix lists the trade agreement that Vietnam has been involved in.

The domestic policies, together with various trade agreements, allow Vietnam to capitalize on its comparative advantages through international trade. Particularly, trade agreements provide a range of benefits that can contribute to the economic development of a country (Wood, 2017), which is certainly true for Vietnam. For example, by reducing 90% of tariffs, Vietnam has become a more appealing investment destination (Vietnam Briefing, 2022). Its fast-growing FDIs have boosted the country's production through the growth of physical capital, the development of human capital, and the transfer of technology (Nguyen et al., 2022). For example, Samsung has made considerable greenfield and research and development investments in Vietnam since the opening of its first facility in Bac Ninh in 2008. This led Vietnam to become the second-largest cellphone exporter in the world, with US$35.5 billion in exports in 2019 (Kim et al., 2020). In fact, trade expansion has been promoted by a significant increase in FDI because the primary investors are also Vietnam's primary trading partners (Anwar & Nguyen, 2011). According to Vietnam Customs trade statistics (2023), FDI traders' trade-in-goods reached US$506.83 billion in 2022, a yearly increase of 9.3%.

Moreover, foreign trade also allows domestic industries to continue strengthening their own primary markets while also looking for new ones. Through considerable effort, Vietnam has been able to fast-track its international trade developments. According to the Ministry of Industry and Trade of the Socialist Republic of Vietnam (2022), Vietnam's ranking in terms of export has progressed from 50th in 2006 to 26th in 2018. Since 2021, Vietnam has been consistently ranked among the top 30 nations in terms of the value of its trade on a global scale.

However, the adoption of an export-led growth model can also lead to some undesirable environmental impacts for Vietnam, particularly when the environment is not safeguarded when introducing new domestic regulations and policies, or the establishment of FTAs (the key exceptions being the Comprehensive and Progressive Agreement for Trans-Pacific Partnership and EU-Vietnam Free Trade Agreement). The next sections provide an assessment of the literature so as to provide a broad understanding of the impact of Vietnam's export-led economic growth model on the environment.

12.2.2 General Literature on the Implication of Trade on the Environment

Research has reported a myriad of findings on the impact that trade has on the environment. On the one hand, some studies report that trade has a negative impact on the environment. For example, Sorroche-del-Rey et al. (2022), by analyzing the existing literature from 1994 to 2022, found that international trade could positively or negatively impact the natural environment; however, the relationship between international trade and environmental performance is mostly negative in developing countries. Moreover, Cole (2004) reported a negative relationship between air and water pollutants and the rising imports of environmentally hazardous products from emerging countries. Ozturk and Al-Mulali (2015) showed that trade openness (export as a ratio of GDP) increases CO_2 emissions. Munir and Ameer (2022) also showed in African and Asian emerging countries that economic growth through economic activities, such as trade, foreign investment, and industrialization, has resulted in higher energy usage (coal, fuel, or petrol) to CO_2 emissions. This finding has also been supported in numerous other empirical studies (see Wang, Zhao, et al., 2020; Wang, Wood, Geng, et al., 2020; Wang, Wood, Wang, et al., 2020; Sikder, Wang, Yeboah, et al., 2022; Sikder, Wang, Yao, et al., 2022)

On the other hand, other studies have reported the positive impact that trade has had on the environment; however, these benefits have been more clearly evident in a developed country context. For example, Antweiler et al. (2001) focused on 43 nations from 1971 to 1996 and found that trade openness is related to lower emissions; however, the environmental impacts of trade openness differ between OECD and developing nations because of the strength of environmental policy that is being implemented and adhered to.

Similarly, Yu et al. (2022) and Le and Le (2023) found that trade openness only benefits environmental efficiency in high-income nations due to their strict environmental laws. Furthermore, Managi et al. (2009) concluded only OECD nations can cut down the emission levels of pollutants in the short and long terms because developing nations have weak environmental regulations, which might open the door to the threat of environmental degradation occurring. However, these studies also suggest that developing countries can reduce the negative effects of trade on the environment by improving laws on environmental protection. Given these mixed findings, some scholars have tried to explore a non-linear relationship between trade and environmental impact. For instance, Munir and Ameer (2022) supported a U-shaped relationship between trade openness and environmental degradation in African and Asian emerging countries, suggesting that there might be some critical points at which the impact of trade on environmental performance may change.

Mixed findings are also found in regard to the impact that FDI may play. For example, Al-mulali and Tang (2013) claimed that FDI reduces pollution levels by bringing in advanced and environmentally friendly technologies from developed to less-developed economies. However, Wang (2012) and Cole and Elliott (2005) found that FDI has a positive effect on CO_2 emissions where pollution-intensive industries are more likely to move from developed to less-developed economies because developing countries can be said to provide a "pollution haven" if their environmental standards are below their efficiency levels or if they fail to enforce their standards in order to attract foreign investment (Neumayer, 2001).

12.2.3 Trade and Environment in Vietnam

As for the evidence related to Vietnam, the findings on the relationship between trade and the environment are also mixed. A large amount of research has provided evidence of the negative effect of trade on the environment in Vietnam due to its economic growth model and trade structure.

The literature suggests at least two mechanisms through which trade and FDI cause harm to biodiversity. First, the expansion of export-oriented agriculture and industrial activities leads to environmental degradation, which can then in turn destroy animal habitats. Feridun et al. (2006) pointed out that the impacts of trade expansion on natural resources are detrimental in that it leads to an over-exploitation of natural resources. Vietnam's forests have been cut down to make room for agriculture and other industries, leading to deforestation and soil erosion. Furthermore, the initial agricultural development was to increase the number of products, such as rice, coffee, and pepper, instead of efficiency and quality; thereby, pesticides or fertilizers were used to increase agricultural exporting activities and sales (Tang & Tan, 2015). Tinh et al. (2022) stated that expanding aquacultural and agricultural sectors accounted for 43.4% and 24.8% of the overall amount of environmental degradation, respectively. More than 50% of the nation's natural areas have suffered from different degrees of land degradation (erosion, nutrient loss in the soil, desertification, and drought), with the Mekong Delta, Central Highlands, and Northwest Region the hardest hit (Tien et al., 2020). The degradation of forests and land negatively affects biodiversity. In addition, illegal trade is also reported to be a threat to biodiversity. Some illegal trade activity was driven by the extraction of threatened wildlife in the Red List Index (RLI). Lenzen et al. (2012) found that a considerable number of species are in danger due to the international trade activities that are being conducted in Vietnam and other developing countries. Developed nations also see their native species under threat due to consumer and business demand for animal products, leather goods, or medicines. Cao and Wyatt (2013) pointed out that illegal wildlife trading inside and outside Vietnam is a widespread and dangerous activity contributing to biodiversity loss and species extinction. Meanwhile, Luong (2022) and Nguyen et al. (2019) also stated that the favorable transit borders of Vietnam act as an important gateway for illegal traders that carry many endangered species in and out of China, Korea, and Japan. Despite such issues, the Vietnamese government has done little to stop such illegal trading activities. As a result, the wildlife trade from Vietnam (also Cambodia, Laos, and Indonesia) to China, Korea, and Japan has grown to some 4,000 tons of illegal live wildlife being exported each year (Luong, 2022).

Another environmental impact of international trade is air pollution. Nguyen (2020) showed that Vietnam's trade significantly impacts CO_2 emissions in both the short and long run due to the inadequate management of transportation systems and the manufacturing industry, especially, the shortcomings in the management of emissions from vehicles used in Vietnam's manufacturing, import, and export activities. Tran (2020) and Nguyen (2022) also showed that in Vietnam and other export-driven countries in Asia, Latin America, and Africa, a 1% increase in trade openness is associated with a 0.2% increase in CO_2 emissions. Ho and Ho (2021) pointed out that the cause of environmental pollution is that Vietnam mainly imports highly energy-intensive and polluted machinery, steel products, raw materials, and automobiles.

However, some literature has identified a range of ways that trade positively impacts emissions in Vietnam. One way that international trade helps to mitigate the emission problem is through FDI. It is suggested that foreign investors have brought growing level of an environmental awareness, and green practices such as efficient ways in natural resource utilization and advanced environmental technologies. For instance, Tang and Tan (2015) and Ho and Ho (2021) reported that FDI has only a minor impact on CO_2 emissions but benefits the environment by transferring environmentally friendly technologies and production processes to Vietnam. Additionally, Nguyen and Le (2020) also found that exports decrease CO_2 emissions in the short and long terms in Vietnam.

Furthermore, exporters from Vietnam face greater pressure when dealing with environmentally sensitive customers, regulatory requirements, and public concern about the environment in developed nations, such as countries in the EU. Gadenne et al. (2009) also noted that legal provisions can help to raise broad environmental awareness, with firms willing to adapt their business operations and environmental projects. As a result, they are under increased pressure to shift their export strategy toward more ecologically friendly approaches, since doing so allows them to gain access to the global marketplace and capitalize on green-related chances to accomplish SDGs (FAO, 2012).

In addition, trade might encourage the government and businesses in Vietnam to reshape their policies and business practices so that they are more in sync with the need to develop in more environmentally sustainable ways. The Vietnamese government has begun doing several things in this space, with most being relatively unsuccessful. The first *Law on Environmental Protection* (LEP) was launched in 1993. However, the results were not satisfactory due to a lack of detailed guidelines to inform the enforcement (Clausen et al., 2011). The overlapping of State management functions in the context of the Environmental Impact Assessment (EIA) policy has also created several barriers against the successful implementation of these laws (Pham et al., 2020). Then, the LEP was further enhanced in 2005, 2014, and 2020. The 2020 LEP was implemented in January 2022 (Vietnam Patent No. Law 72/2020/QH14, 2020), with more detailed specifications on the identification of environmentally harmful activities, the definition of environmental responsibilities, assessments, classification, and implementation of the investment project that have implications on the environment. More specific details on the LEP regulations are provided in the Appendix (see Table 7). Although the environmental regulations and policies are far from perfect, the government is gradually moving towards achieving a more sustainable balance between economic growth and environmental sustainability. Such regulations and policies are expected to have a positive impact on firms' environmentally friendly practices. Nguyen and Adomako (2022) collected survey data from 332 top and mid-level managers of exporting enterprises in Vietnam and found that the pressures from stakeholders, such as governments and regulators, drive firms' environmental commitment.

With an array of findings clearly evident, it is imperative that more is done to understand whether the export-led growth model driven by export and FDI affects environmental performance in Vietnam in a non-linear way. Specifically, we are keen to investigate the following research questions (RQ):

(RQ1) Is there a non-linear relationship between total export and environmental performance in Vietnam?

(RQ2) Is there a non-linear relationship between export structure, in terms of contribution by foreign investors versus domestic players, and by industrial good export versus agricultural good export, and environmental performance in Vietnam?

(RQ3) Is there a non-linear relationship between FDI inflow and environment performance in Vietnam?

12.3 Methodology

The variables used to assess our research question were collected from various sources. Table A12.3 in the Appendix shows the indicators used for dependent variables, independent variables, and control variables, the year range, sample size, and data source. As shown in Table A12.3 in the Appendix, the sample size is small due to the limited availability of longitudinal data. Small datasets in longitudinal research can cause power issues and often suffers from biased parameter values. Bayesian estimation can be used to solve these issues. Because Bayesian statistics do not rely on large samples (i.e., the central limit theorem), smaller data sets can be analyzed while maintaining power (Van de Schoot & Miočević, 2020). As Lee and Song (2004) have shown, the Bayesian estimation requires a much smaller parameter-to-observation ratio, specially 1:3 for the models used in their study instead of 1:5. Based on this context, our study uses the Bayesian linear regression to test the statistical relationship between the concerned variables.

12.4 Results

12.4.1 Descriptive Statistics

In this section, we report environmental performance, trade, and FDI trends from across our observational window between 1985 and 2023.

12.4.1.1 CO_2 Emission

International trade, like any economic activity, generates greenhouse gas (GHG) emissions. Carbon emissions embedded in an exported or imported product or service include the direct GHG emissions from its final production, assembly, packaging, and shipping to the market (consumers), and the indirect GHG emissions generated by the production and transportation of the inputs used to produce the final product or service, including the GHG emissions from the generation of the electricity used during production. In this section, we focus on CO_2 emission. As can be seen in Figure 12.1, the total level of CO_2 emissions in Vietnam went up from 73,264 to 470,578 kt of CO_2 equivalent between 1990 and 2020. However, when looking into the CO_2 emissions' intensity of GDP (measured by CO_2/GDP) in Figure 12.2, a generally declining trend is visible.

12.4.1.2 Biodiversity

Biodiversity is measured by the Red List Index (RLI), which shows the changes in total extinction risk for species and is used to track their progress toward targets for decreasing biodiversity loss. It is measured on a scale of 0 to 1, with 1 indicating that all species are categorized as Least Concern on the IUCN Red List, and 0 indicating that all species in the nation or region are extinct. Looking into the RLI in Vietnam in Figure 12.3, we could see that the RLI

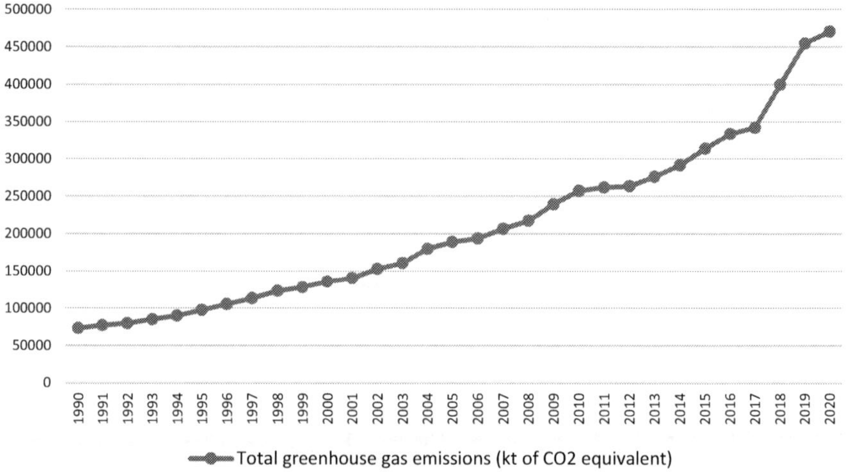

Figure 12.1 Total CO_2 emissions in Vietnam
Source: World Bank (2023b)

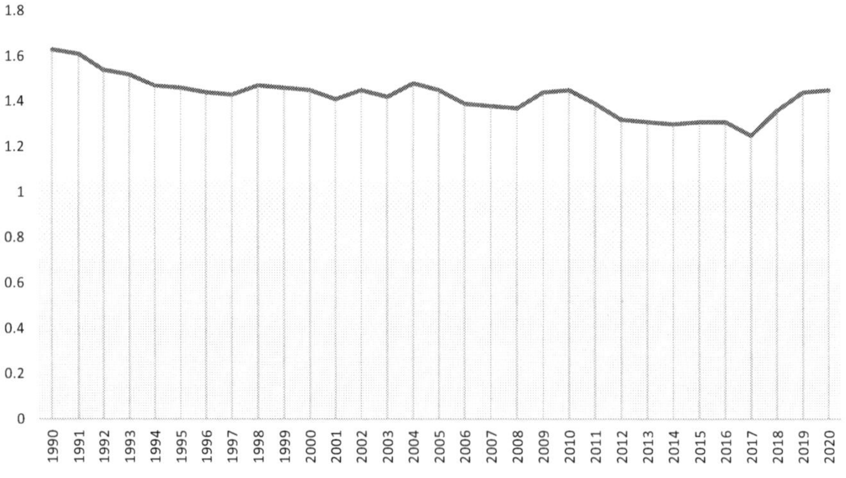

Figure 12.2 CO_2 emissions' intensity of GDP (measured by CO_2/GDP)
Source: World Bank

kept decreasing from 1993 to 2023 (from 0.81 to 0.72), indicating that more and more species in the country are going extinct (United Nations, 2022).

12.4.1.3 Export

As shown in Figure 12.4, the values of exports have increased significantly since 1995. Export's contribution to GDP has also continued to increase

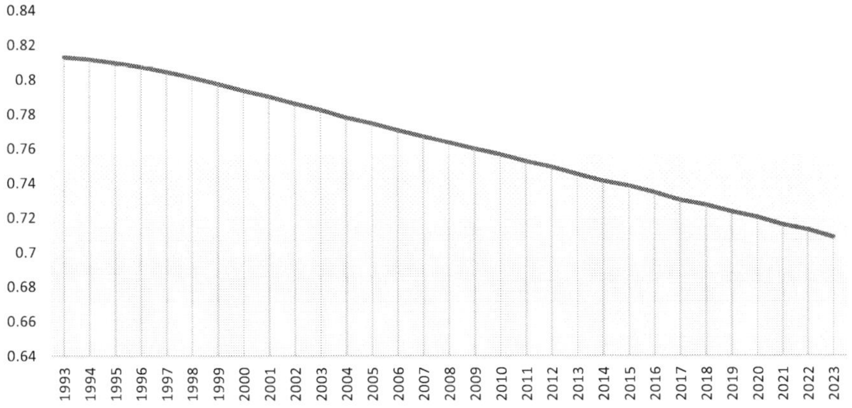

Figure 12.3 Vietnam Red List Index

Source: UN Statistics (United Nations, 2022)

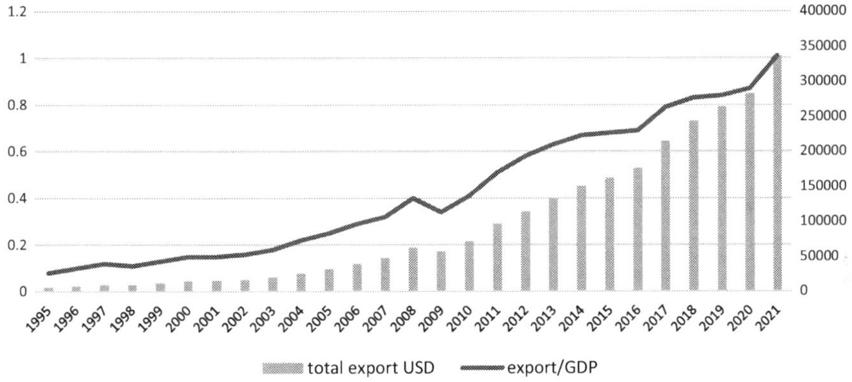

Figure 12.4 Total export value and export/GDP

Source: General Statistics Office of Vietnam

since 1995, suggesting that Vietnam is becoming more and more dependent on an export-led growth model. At the same time, the foreign-invested sectors are contributing an increasing percentage to exports (Figure 12.5). With regard to the export structure, industrial processing products have become increasingly dominant, while agricultural and forest products contribute to a smaller percentage of total export levels (Figure 12.6).

12.4.1.4 FDI

FDI is the total equity capital, earnings reinvestment, other long-run capital, and short-run capital as represented in the balance of payments to acquire

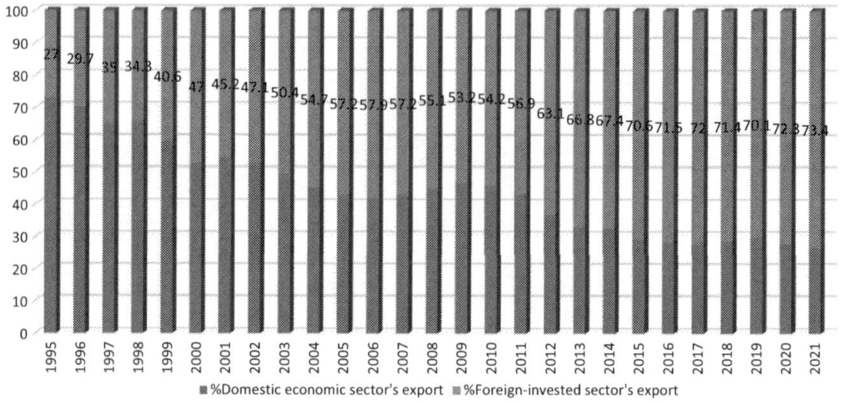

Figure 12.5 Percentage of domestic and foreign-invested economic sectors' export

a long-term management interest (10% or greater of voting stock) (World Bank, n.d.a.). Figure 12.7 shows that FDI inflow to GDP has expanded from 0% in 1985 to 4.3% in 2021.

12.4.2 Regression Analysis

Table A12.4 in the Appendix shows the descriptive and correlation matrix, based on Bayesian analysis of Pearson linear correlation. Considering the small sample size of the time series, we conducted the Bayesian linear regression. In view of the mixed findings of export and FDI on environment performance reported by the literature, we specified the following two models, testing the possible non-linear relationship between the export and FDI and environment performance indicators:

Environment indicators = total export + total export^2 + FDI inflows + FDI inflows^2 + control variable (GDP growth)

Environment indicators = %foreign-sector's export + %foreign-sector's export^2 + %industrial good export + %industrial good export ^{2} + control variable (GDP growth)

In models 1–6 reported in Table A12.5 in the Appendix, we tested the general impact of export and FDI inflow on environmental performance. In models 1, 3, and 5, we included the main effect of export and FDI inflow. In models 2, 4, and 6, we included the squared terms of export and FDI inflows. In models 7–12, reported in Table A12.6 in the Appendix, we tested the effect of types of export on the environmental performance indicators. Since the

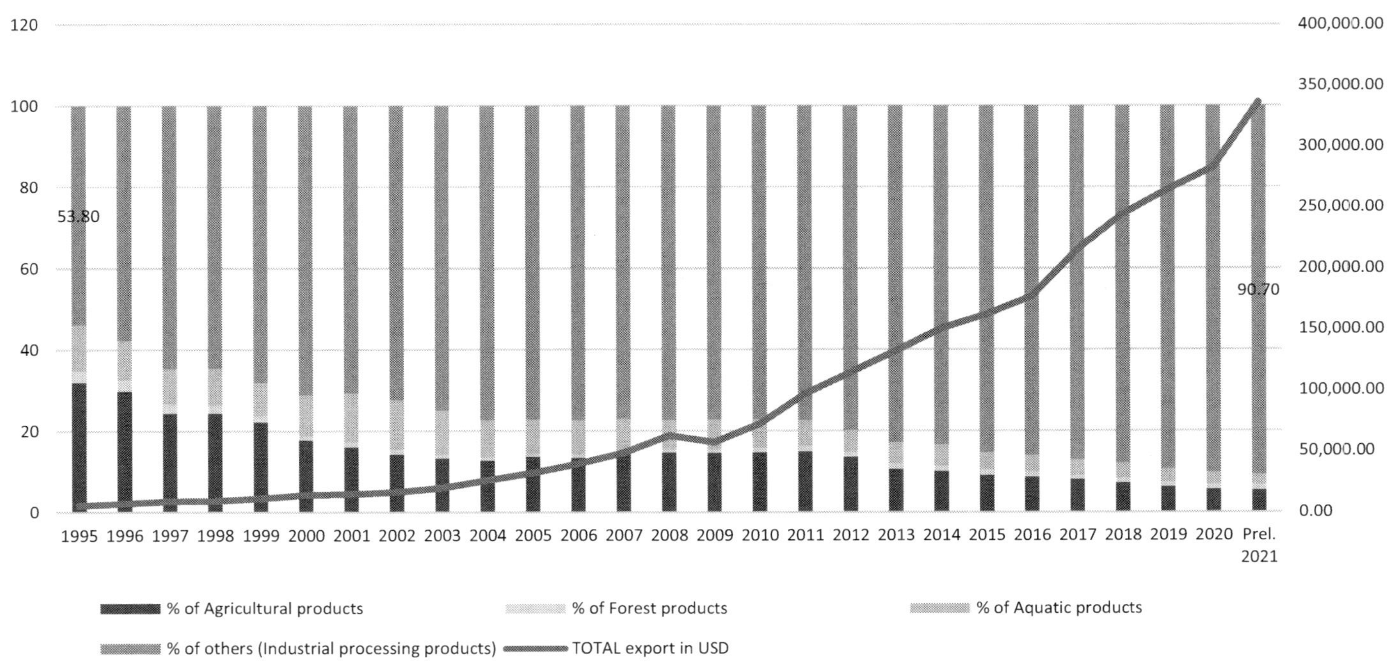

Figure 12.6 Vietnam's export structure

Source: General Statistics Office of Vietnam

Figure 12.7 Vietnam's FDI inflow to GDP

Source: World Bank (n.d.a.)

percentage of Foreign sectors' export and the percentage of Industrial goods export are highly correlated (as shown in Table A12.3 in the Appendix), we mean-centered the two variables to avoid multicollinearity in the regression (Iacobucci et al., 2016). In models 7, 9, and 11, we included the main effect of % foreign sectors' export and % industrial good export, while in models 8, 10, and 12, we further included the squared terms of the two variables.

12.4.2.1 CO_2 Emission Intensity

The results in model 2 show that Export is negatively related to CO_2 emission intensity, while Export^2 is positively related to CO_2 emission at a significant level. Such results suggest that exports have a U-shaped relationship with CO_2 emission intensity, with a turning point where export/GDP = –(–.584)/(2*.451) = 0.6475. That is, when export/GDP is lower than 0.6475, the greater the export level, the lower the level of CO_2 emissions; however, when export/GDP exceeds 0.6475, greater exports lead to a higher level of CO_2 emissions. Based on this turning point, since 2018, exports have started to contribute to more CO_2 emissions. On the other hand, FDI inflow is not significantly related to CO_2 emission in either model 1 or model 2.

In models 7 and 8, the % foreign sectors' export is negatively related to CO_2 emission, while the square term of % foreign sectors' export is positively related to CO_2 emission at a significant level, suggesting a U-shaped relationship between % foreign sectors' export and CO_2 emission. The turning point is 23*. That is, when the % foreign sectors' export is lower than 23%, the more the foreign sectors export, the lower the CO_2 emission levels; however, when the % foreign sectors export exceeds 23%, more foreign sectors' exports lead to a higher level of CO_2 emission. At the same time, the % of industrial goods exported is always positively related to CO_2 emission.

12.4.2.2 RLI

Results in models 3 and 4 show that Exports are negatively related to RLI at a significant level, while Export^2 is positively related to RLI at a significant level. Such results suggest that exports have a U-shaped relationship with RLI, with a turning point where export/GDP = – (–.164)/(2*.070) = 1.71. That is, when export/GDP is lower than 1.71, the more export, the lower RLI, indicating that more species in the nation are going extinct, but when export/GDP exceeds 1.71, higher export levels lead to greater RLI, that is, less species going extinct. Given the high turning point of export/GDP, export, from 1994 to 2021, has been contributing to more species being extinct.

On the other hand, FDI inflow is positively related to RLI at a significant level, suggesting that FDI inflow contributes to the extinction of species. In models 9 and 10, none of the concerned variables show a significant relationship with RLI, suggesting that the structure of export does not influence the extinction of species.

12.5 Discussion

Our results generally show that the export-led growth model driven by export and FDI has a non-linear impact on the environmental performance in Vietnam.

12.5.1 CO_2 Emission Intensity and Export-Led Growth Model

Regarding the contribution of foreign companies to CO_2 emission intensity in Vietnam context, prior studies gave mixed evidence (Nguyen, 2022; Tang & Tan, 2015; Ho & Ho, 2021). In our results, when exports represent a low proportion of GDP, greater export levels lead to fewer CO_2 emissions; however, when exports make up a substantial contribution to GDP, the higher export levels create more CO_2. Industrial good exports are always positively related to CO_2 emissions. In addition, our findings suggest that FDI inflow is not shown to significantly affect CO_2 emissions; yet foreign sectors' export at a lower level contributes to fewer CO_2 emissions, while at a higher level, more CO_2 emissions are created.

Considering that the foreign-sector is playing an increasingly important role in exporting (the foreign-sector's export levels have increased from 27% in 1995 to 73.4% in 2021, see Figure 12.5), and industrial good export has kept increasing substantially from 53.8% in 1995 to 90.7% in 2021 (as shown in Figure 12.6), such results suggest both the green practice effect (Ho & Ho, 2021; Tang & Tan, 2015) and pollution-haven hypothesis (Neumayer, 2001) may hold for the FDI's impact on CO_2 emission but at different stages. On the one hand, MNCs when investing in emerging economies, such as Vietnam, used energy sources that are friendly to the environment, which is supportive to the neo-liberal argument that FDI inflows are good for the environment and reduce pollution by transferring environmentally friendly technologies and manufacturing techniques from developed countries to Vietnam. The positive effect is salient when the export volume and production scale are relatively small (export/GDP < 23% before 2016). However, when MNCs substantially increase their production level to cope with increasing demand of export, it is likely that they will transfer more pollution-intensive value chain activities to domestic supply chain members. However, the majority of manufacturing firms in Vietnam are SMEs, young, private owned firms, and about half of all firms assigned environmental personnel and established EMS. Nonetheless, in general, the environmental performance of the larger part of firms did not satisfy government requirements and only a small percentage met ISO 14001 environment standards; this is particularly the case for those small firms without foreign ownership (Anh, 2015). Pham et al. (2016) also showed that foreign-invested firms only contributed to 9.34% of the air pollution in Vietnam, while the remaining was contributed by various domestic firms. Due to a lack of green facilities and technologies among domestic firms, such high levels of export demand might have resulted in increased non-renewable energy consumption and air pollution (Anwar & Alexander, 2016), with more of the investment going into industrial good production, which in turn uses more energy. Such findings align with those from both Nguyen (2022) that production for exports creates carbon emissions at a faster rate than production for domestic demand and Tran (2020) that industrial processing industries contribute to 80% of the total emissions in Vietnam. Such results could be further supported by the data about energy usage and renewable energy usage: energy consumption has generally increased from 1990 to 2021, while the percentage of renewable energy has declined during the same period of time, as shown in Figure 12.8.

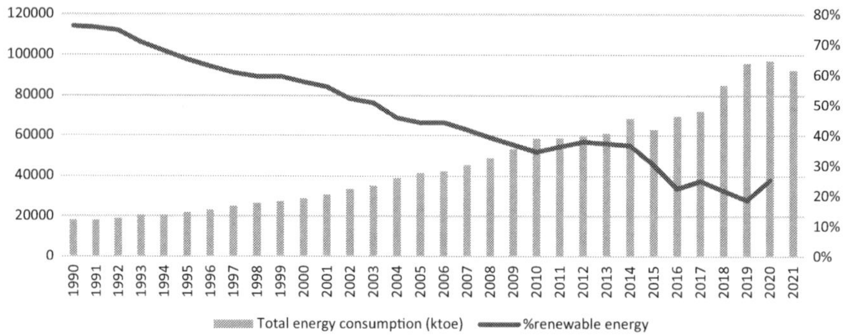

Figure 12.8 The total energy consumption and proportion of renewable energy consumption

Source: Ener Data (n.d.); International Trade Administration (2021); World Bank (2023a)

Note: Renewable energy in total final energy consumption is measured by the proportion of total energy consumption produced from renewable resources (United Nations, 2022). The target for a sustainable environment is boosting the percentage of renewable energy consumption in total energy significantly. As shown in the figure, renewable energy consumption has reduced significantly from 76.08% to 18.65% from 1990 to 2019.

12.5.2 Biodiversity

According to Pham and Tran (2022), Vietnam has 4,846 wild animals as of 2021, but these are mainly extinct or endangered due to wildlife trading and the degradation of the environment that these wild species inhabit. Luong (2022), and Cao and Wyatt (2013) found that leopards, snakes, wild boar, deer, crocodiles, turtles, etc., are all common species for illegal wildlife trade. Our results show that FDI contributes to biodiversity loss. Since 1994, research has shown that export as a percentage of GDP generally contributes to biodiversity loss, when the export/GDP ratio exceeded the threshold (the turning point of export/GDP = 1.71 indicated in Section 12.4). At the same time, the export structure does not have a significant impact on species extinction. We thus deduce that it is probably because FDI and export-oriented production activities, no matter the sector, are associated with the destruction of wildlife habitat. This aligns with the findings from the literature that FDI-driven and domestic production activities encouraged the allocation of land and the related natural resources for agricultural, aquacultural, and forestry purposes (Tinh et al., 2022) and the manufacturing industry (Nguyen et al., 2022), thus threatening the habitat of wild animals. Cao and Wyatt (2013) also agreed that exploiting natural resources causes a loss of habitat and food shortages for wildlife in Vietnam. The results can be also supported by looking into the land use policy and data in Vietnam, particularly those regarding protected land. As of 2020, 7.6% of the total land area in Vietnam is protected, which is well below the world average (14.75%) (World Bank, n.d.b). In addition, the protected areas in Vietnam tend to be small and isolated. Large tracts of deforested or agricultural land separate most protected areas from each other. Small areas of habitat tend to lose species faster than large areas (International Centre for Environmental Management et al., 2003). Many protected areas have lost those species which are vulnerable to human disturbance and hunting, or which require large range sizes for survival (e.g., tiger). The small size of most protected areas, and the fragmented nature of the protected area system as a whole, makes conservation more difficult and costly. Lastly, levels of conflicts between people and protected areas are poorly documented and understood in Vietnam. The revised regulations for special-use forests (SUFs) restrict all extractive and most non-extractive uses of protected areas (GoV, 2001). Low levels of enforcement have left few incentives for forest users to comply with official regulations.

12.6 Conclusion and Recommendations

Being one of the larger emerging economies in Southeast Asia, Vietnam has several competitive advantages, such as low-cost labor (Hai & Speelman, 2020) and favorable investment policies to transfer foreign production capacity to Vietnam, which has sped up the industrialization process, and the types of export and economic growth that have been achieved. Although there are conflicting opinions, it is hard to deny the importance of export and

FDI for Vietnamese economic growth (Nguyen et al., 2022; Phan, 2011). On the other hand, such an export-led economic growth model has some adverse impact on the environment. As shown in the Bayesian linear regression based on the data of Vietnam from 1995 to 2023, exports have a U-shaped relationship with CO_2 emission and generally contributes to biodiversity loss during our observational window. Industrial goods export is always positively related to CO_2 emissions. Foreign sectors' export shows a U-shaped relationship with CO_2. FDI inflow is shown not to significantly affect CO_2 but contributes to species extinction.

Given the aforementioned findings, there are several points that Vietnamese policymakers may need to take into consideration in order to draft effective environmental policies that combat global warming while stimulating economic growth at the same time. First, based on the findings that FDI itself does not significantly contribute to CO_2 emission intensity, but high levels of foreign sectors' export and industrial good export contribute to more CO_2 emission intensity, we attributed the results to the belief that MNCs may have adopted the clean production practice, while their domestic supply chain members have not. As a result, FDI inflows should be better positioned to improve and uphold higher environmental standards in Vietnam's economy. From a policy perspective, Vietnam should adopt green FDI policy to encourage both existing and new foreign investors to not only adopt green practice themselves but also help their domestic supply chain members to embrace clean and pollution-free production facilities, technologies, and practices. For example, holistic assessment criteria should be implemented to assess the green practice and environment performance of an MNC, including the MNC itself and its supply chain members. Subsidies and tax rebates could be offered to incentivize MNCs to step forward to transfer green technologies, knowledge, and facilities to their local counterparts.

Second, considering that FDI and export are generally positively related to the bio-diversity threat, mainly due to the expanded production capacities which threaten the wildlife habitat, it is important for the government to plan its land use carefully. Improved integration of conservation objectives into mainstream land-use planning and forest policy, while also strictly enforcing the policies and regulations, is critically important.

With the findings, we acknowledge some limitations. For several of our concerned variables, Vietnam did not start reporting the data until 1995. Due to the limited times series data, we could not account for other important factors in the regression analysis. The small sample size may also threaten the reliability, reproducibility, and validity of the results, although we tried to employ Bayesian Linear Regression which is less sensitive to small sample size. Hence the results should be interpreted with caution and the same model could be tested using a larger sample size in the future. In addition, we only examined two of the environment performance indicators, CO_2 emission, and bio-diversity loss. Other aspects of environment performance, for example, water stress and pollution and deforestation, were not included due to an insufficient number of data points. Future research could examine the relationship between export-led economic growth model and other environment performance indicators when more data are available.

References

Al-Mulali, U., & Tang, C. F. (2013). Investigating the validity of pollution haven hypothesis in the gulf cooperation council (GCC) countries. *Energy Policy*, *60*, 813–819.

Anh, P. Q. (2015). Internal determinants and effects of firm-level environmental performance: Empirical evidences from Vietnam. *Asian Social Science*, *11*(4), 190.

Antweiler, W., Copeland, B. R., & Taylor, M. S. (2001). Is free trade good for the environment? *American economic review*, *91*(4), 877–908.

Anwar, S., & Alexander, W. R. (2016). Pollution, energy use, GDP and trade: Estimating the long-run relationship for Vietnam. *Applied Economics*, *48*(53), 5221–5232. https://doi.org/10.1080/00036846.2016.1173182

Anwar, S., & Nguyen, L. P. (2011). Foreign direct investment and trade: The case of Vietnam. *Research in International Business and Finance*, *25*, 39–52. https://doi.org/10.1016/j.ribaf.2010.05.004

Cao, N., & Wyatt, T. (2013). A green criminological exploration of illegal wildlife trade in Vietnam. *Asian Criminology*, *8*, 129–142. https://doi.org/10.1007/s11417-012-9154-y

Clausen, A., Vu, H. H., & Pedrono, M. (2011). An evaluation of the environmental impact assessment system in Vietnam: The gap between theory and practice. *Environmental Impact Assessment Review*, *31*(2), 136–143. https://doi.org/10.1016/j.eiar.2010.04.008

Cole, M. A. (2004). Trade, the pollution haven hypothesis and the environmental Kuznets curve: Examining the linkages. *Ecological economics*, *48*(1), 71–81.

Cole, M. A., & Elliott, R. J. (2005). FDI and the capital intensity of "dirty" sectors: A missing piece of the pollution haven puzzle. *Review of Development Economics*, *9*(4), 530–548.

Duong, M., Holmes, M. J., Strutt, A., & Lim., S. (2019). Effects of trade agreements and foreign direct Investment on trade: Evidence from Vietnam. *International Journal of Economics and Financial Issues*, *9*(3), 116–126. www.econjournals.com/index.php/ijefi/article/view/7767

EnerData. (n.d.). www.enerdata.net/estore/energy-market/vietnam/#:~:text=Vietnam%20Related%20Research&text=Energy%20consumption%20per%20capita%20is,in%202021%20to%2092.5%20Mtoe.

Environmental Protection Tax Law, No. 57/2010/QH12 issued by Vietnamese National Assembly dated November 2010 (effective date as of January 1, 2012).

FAO. (2012). *The state of world fisheries and aquaculture*. Food and Agriculture Organization of the United Nations.

Feridun, M., Ayadi, F. S., & Balouga, J. (2006). Impact of trade liberalization on the environment in developing countries: The case of Nigeria. *Journal of Developing Societies*, *2*(1), 39–56. https://doi.org/10.1177/0169796X06062965

Gadenne, D. L., Kennedy, J., & McKeiver, C. (2009). An empirical study of environmental awareness and practices in SMEs. *Journal of Business Ethics*, *84*, 45–63.

GoV (Government of Vietnam). (2001). *Decision No. 08/QD-TTg on the management of Special-Use Forest, protection forest and production forest*. January 11, 2001. The Prime Minister of the Government.

Hai, A. T., & Speelman, S. (2020). Economic-environmental trade-offs in marine aquaculture: The case of lobster farming in Vietnam. *Aquaculture*, *516*, 734593. https://doi.org/10.1016/j.aquaculture.2019.734593

Ho, T. L., & Ho, T. T. (2021). Economic growth, energy consumption and environmental quality: Evidence from Vietnam. *International Energy Journal*, *21*, 213–224.

Iacobucci, D., Schneider, M. J., Popovich, D. L., & Bakamitsos, G. A. (2016). Mean centering helps alleviate "micro" but not "macro" multicollinearity. *Behavior Research Methods*, *48*, 1308–1317.

International Centre for Environmental Management; IUCN; WWF International; BirdLife International; UNDP; Mekong River Commission; National Parks and Wildlife Service; Tropical Forest Trust. (2003). *Lessons learned in Cambodia, Lao PDR, Thailand and Vietnam*. IUCN Publication. https://icem.com.au/documents/biodiversity/pad/vietnam_lessons.pdf

International Trade Administration. (2021). www.trade.gov/market-intelligence/vietnam-renewable-energy-options#:~:text=Vietnam's%20total%20power%20capacity%20was,Vietnam%20Power%20Group%20(EVN)

Kim, I. S., Liao, S., & Miyano, S. (2020). *Why trade and FDI should be studied together*. Forthcoming. http://web.mit.edu/insong/www/pdf/fditrade.pdf

Law on Environmental Protection (LEP), 1993 No. 29-L/CTN issued by Vietnamese National Assembly dated December 27, 1993.

Law on Environmental Protection, No. 52/2005/QH11 issued by Vietnamese National Assembly dated November 29, 2005.

Law on Environmental Protection, No. 55/2014/QH13 issued by Vietnamese National Assembly dated June 23, 2014 (effective date as of January 1, 2015)

Law on Environmental Protection, No. 72/2020/QH14 issued by Vietnamese National Assembly dated November 17, 2020.

Law on Foreign Investment, No. 4-HDNN8 issued by Vietnamese National Assembly dated December 29, 1987.

Law on Foreign Trade Management, No. 05/2017/QH14 issued by Vietnamese National Assembly dated June 12, 2017 (effective date as of January 1, 2018).

Law on Investment, Decree 31/2021/ND-CP ("Decree 31") providing guidance on the implementation of the Law on Investment 2020 ("Law on Investment") issued by Vietnamese government dated March 26, 2021.

Le, H. C., & Le, T. H. (2023). Effects of economic, social, and political globalization on environmental quality: International evidence. *Environment Development Sustainability*, *25*(5), 4269–4299. https://doi.org/10.1007/s10668-022-02243-4

Lee, S. Y., & Song, X. Y. (2004). Evaluation of the Bayesian and maximum likelihood approaches in analyzing structural equation models with small sample sizes. *Multivariate Behavioral Research*, *39*(4), 653–686.

Lenzen, M., Moran, D., Kanemoto, K., Foran, B., Lobefaro, L., & Geschke, A. (2012). International trade drives biodiversity threats in developing nations. *Nature*, *486*(7401), 109–112. https://doi.org/10.1038/nature11145

Luong, H. T. (2022). Understanding the illegal wildlife trade in Vietnam: A systematic literature review. *Laws*, *11*(4), 64. https://doi.org/10.3390/laws11040064

Managi, S., Hibiki, A., & Tsurum, T. (2009). Does trade openness improve environmental quality? *Journal of Environmental Economics and Management*, *58*, 346–363. https://doi.org/10.1016/j.jeem.2009.04.008

Ministry of Industry and Trade of the Socialist Republic of Vietnam. (2022, December 15). *Ngày 15/12/2022, xuất nhập khẩu hàng hóa của Việt Nam đạt mốc 700 tỷ USD*. Ministry of Industry and Trade of the Socialist Republic of Vietnam. https://moit.gov.vn/tin-tuc/thi-truong-nuoc-ngoai/ngay-15–12–2022-xuat-nhap-khau-hang-hoa-cua-viet-nam-dat-moc-700-ty-usd.html

Munir, K., & Ameer, A. (2022). Assessing nonlinear impact of urbanization, economic growth, technology, and trade on environment: Evidence from African and Asian emerging economies. *GeoJournal*, *87*, 2195–2208.

Neumayer, E. (2001). Pollution havens: An analysts of policy options for dealing with an elusive phenomenon. *The Journal of Environment & Development*, *10*(2), 147–177.

Nguyen, A. T., Anwar, S., Alexander, W. R., & Lu, S. H. (2022). Openness to trade, foreign direct investment, and economic growth in Vietnam. *Applied Economics*, *54*(29), 3373–3391. https://doi-org.elibrary.jcu.edu.au/10.1080/00036846.2021.2009112

Nguyen, N. P., & Adomako, S. (2022). International orientation and environmental performance in Vietnamese exporting small- and medium-sized enterprises. *Business Strategy and the Environment*, *31*(5), 2424–2436. https://doi.org/10.1002/bse.3035

Nguyen, P. T. (2022). Carbon emissions versus value-added in export-driven countries: Case of Vietnam. *Journal of Economic Structures*, *11*. https://doi.org/10.1186/s40008-022-00272-w

Nguyen, T. C., & Le, Q. H. (2020). Impact of globalization on CO_2 emissions in Vietnam: An autoregressive distributed lag approach. *Decision Science Letters*, *9*, 257–270. https://doi.org/10.5267/j.dsl.2019.10.001

Nguyen, V. S., Vu, N. H., Dinh, V. T., Thai, V. H., Nguyen, T. M., Thai, T. K., Huyen, V. T. K., & Nguyen, T. T. (2019). Vietnam, the big market and cross bridges of illegal wildlife trade in Asia: Causes and solutions. *AgBioForum*, *21*(3), 35–47.

Nguyen, V. T. (2020). The role of foreign direct investment and trade on environmental quality in Vietnam. *The Journal of Asian Finance, Economics, and Business*, 7(3), 289–294. https://doi.org/10.13106/jafeb.2020.vol7.no3.289

Ozturk, I., & Al-Mulali, U. (2015). Investigating the validity of the environmental Kuznets curve hypothesis in Cambodia. *Ecological Indicators*, *57*, 324–330.

Pham, M. T., Bui, N. K., & Puzirevsky, R. (2020). Legal framework for environmental impact assessment in Vietnam: The challenges between the regulations and practice. *E3S Web of Conferences*, *164*, 11008.

Pham, T. H., Bui, A. T., & Nguyen, T. C. (2016). *The impact of trade liberalization on industrial pollution: Empirical evidence from Vietnam*. EEPSEA Research Report, Economy and Environment Program for Southeast Asia (EEPSEA). https://EconPapers.repec.org/RePEc:eep:report:rr2016042.

Pham, T. T., & Tran, Y. L. (2022). Khó khăn và thuận lợi trong việc quản lí chuỗi giá trị sản phẩm động vật hoang dã tại Việt Nam. In A. T. Nguyen & T. T. Pham (Eds.), *Chuỗi giá trị và thương mại ngành hàng nông lâm sản Việt Nam: Trong bối cảnh hội nhập quốc tế và khủng hoảng sinh thái* (pp. 847–875). Nhà Xuất Bản Đại Học Quốc Gia.

Phan, T. C. (2011). Mô hình tăng trưởng kinh tế dựa vào xuất khẩu của Việt Nam. *Tạp chí Khoa học ĐHQGHN, Kinh tế và Kinh doanh*, *27*, 265–275.

Sikder, M., Wang, C., Yao, X., Xu, H., Wu, L., Kwame Yeboah, F., Wood, J., Zhao, Y., & Dou, X. (2022). The integrated impact of GDP growth, industrialization, energy use, and urbanization on CO_2 emissions in developing countries: Evidence from the panel ARDL approach. *Science of the Total Environment*. https://doi.org/10.1016/j.scitotenv.2022.155795

Sikder, M., Wang, C., Yeboah, F. K., & Wood, J. (2022). Driving factors of CO_2 emission reduction in the logistics industry: An assessment of the RCEP and SAARC economies. *Environment, Development, and Sustainability*. https://doi.org/10.1007/s10668-022-02840-3

Sorroche-del-Rey, Y., Piedra-Muñoz, L., & Galdeano-Gómez, E. (2022). Interrelationship between international trade and environmental performance: Theoretical approaches and indicators for sustainable development. *Business Strategy and the Environment*. https://doi.org/10.1002/bse.3270

Tang, C. F., & Tan, B. W. (2015). The impact of energy consumption, income, and foreign direct investment on carbon dioxide emissions in Vietnam. *Energy*, *79*, 447–454. https://doi.org/10.1016/j.energy.2014.11.033

Tien, N. H., Phu, P. P., Phuc, N. T., Duc, L. D., & Thuc, T. D. (2020). Sustainable development and environmental management in Vietnam. *International Journal of Research in Finance and Management*, *3*(1), 72–79.

Tinh, P. H., MacKenzie, R. A., Hung, T. D., Hanh, N. T., Hanh, N. H., Manh, D. Q., Ha, H. T., & Tuan, M. S. (2022). Distribution and drivers of Vietnam mangrove deforestation from 1995 to 2019. *Mitigation and Adaptation Strategies for Global Change*, *27*(4), 29. https://doi.org/10.1007/s11027-022-10005-w

Tran, N. V. (2020). The environmental effects of trade openness in developing countries: Conflict or cooperation? *Environmental Science and Pollution Research*, *27*, 19783–19797. https://doi-org.elibrary.jcu.edu.au/10.1007/s11356-020-08352-9

United Nations. (2022). *SDG indicators database*. https://unstats.un.org/sdgs/dataportal/countryprofiles/vnm#goal-15

Van de Schoot, R., & Miočević, M. (2020). *Small sample size solutions: A guide for applied researchers and practitioners*. Taylor & Francis.

Vietnam Briefing. (2022). *Vietnam's international free trade agreements*. www.vietnam-briefing.com/doing-business-guide/vietnam/why-vietnam/vietnam-s-international-free-trade-and-tax-agreements

Vietnam Customs. (2023, January 18). *Preliminary assessment of Vietnam international merchandise trade performance in full year 2022*. www.customs.gov.vn/index.jsp?pageId=4967&tkId=6085&group=undefined&category=Scheduled%20analysis#:~:text=In%202022%2C%20Vietnam's%20trade,to%20US%20dollars%20358.9%20billion

Wang, C., Wood, J., Geng, X., Wang, Y., Qiao, C., & Long, X. (2020). Transportation CO_2 emission decoupling: Empirical evidence from countries along the belt and road. *Journal of Cleaner Production*, *263*, 121450. https://doi.org/10.1016/j.jclepro.2020.121450.

Wang, C., Wood, J., Wang, Y., Geng, X., & Long, X. (2020). CO_2 emission in transportation sector across 51 countries along the Belt and Road from 2000 to 2014. *Journal of Cleaner Production*, *263*, 122000

Wang, C., Zhao, Y., Wang, Y., Wood, J., Kim, C-Y., & Li, Y. (2020). Transportation CO_2 emission decoupling: An assessment of the Eurasian logistics corridor. *Transportation Research Part D: Transport and Environment*, *86*, 102486.

Wang, K. M. (2012). Modelling the nonlinear relationship between CO_2 emissions from oil and economic growth. *Economic Modelling*, *29*(5), 1537–1547.

Wood, J. (2017). An industrial sector analysis of the factors effecting FTA negotiation outcomes. *Global Business Review*, *18*(4), 1–16.
World Bank. (2022, July 1). *Key highlights: Country climate and development report for Vietnam*. World Bank. www.worldbank.org/en/country/vietnam/brief/key-highlights-country-climate-and-development-report-for-vietnam
World Bank. (2023a). https://data.worldbank.org/indicator/EG.FEC.RNEW.ZS?locations=VN
World Bank. (2023b). *Total greenhouse gas emissions (kt of CO_2 equivalent) – Vietnam*. https://data.worldbank.org/indicator/EN.ATM.GHGT.KT.CE?locations=VN
World Bank. (2023c, April 14). *The World Bank in Vietnam*. World Bank. www.worldbank.org/en/country/vietnam/overview
World Bank. (n.d.a). *Foreign direct investment, net inflows (% of GDP) – Vietnam*. https://data.worldbank.org/indicator/BX.KLT.DINV.WD.GD.ZS?locations=VN
World Bank. (n.d.b). *Terrestrial protected areas (% of total land area) – Vietnam*. https://data.worldbank.org/indicator/ER.LND.PTLD.ZS?locations=VN
Yu, Y., Yamaguchi, K., & Kittner, N. (2022). How do imports and exports affect green productivity? New evidence from partially linear functional-coefficient models. *Journal of Environmental Management*, *308*, 114422. https://doi.org/10.1016/j.jenvman.2021.114422

Appendix

Table A12.1 The policies on trade and FDI

Policies	*Year*	*Main focus*
Law on Foreign Investment (No. 4-HDNN8)	1987	This regulation was taken by the Vietnamese government to increase exports and support domestic enterprises' innovation and productivity by increasing FDI inflows and transferring technology from foreign enterprises. There were three modes of foreign investment. First, only business-to-business (B2B) interaction in the oil exploration sector was permitted. Second, joint ventures which are only formed by state-owned firms were mostly used for infrastructure projects like seaports and airports. Lastly, only fully owned foreign enterprises were permitted in areas regarded as critical to Vietnam's industrial growth. However, foreign ownership can only be held for a maximum of 20 years.
Law on Foreign Investment	1991	Firms located in the export processing zones were given additional incentives to export and the maximum period of foreign ownership was expanded from 20 to 70 years. Export processing zones are industrial zones that specialize in manufacturing goods for export as well as offering services, including tax reductions or lower cost of land. These zones are also non-tariff zones, meaning that businesses benefit from export taxes when they export their goods and material. Vietnam has four export processing zones (three in Ho Chi Minh City, and one in Tay Ninh), where the firms are easily accessible to seaports and airports.

Policies	*Year*	*Main focus*
Law on Foreign Investment	1996	The government gives attention to foreign investment proposals in high-tech industries, such as machinery, pharmaceuticals, and electronics. Therefore, export performance conditions and the implementation of local content criteria led to greater linkages. For example, firms that export 30% of their output were awarded import charges only if they met 30% local content criteria.
World Trade Organization commitments	2007	The commitment concentrates on developing countries' trade, debt, and technology transfer through provisions in trade agreements between developed and developing countries. It also assists developing countries in effectively negotiating lower import barriers and increased market access.
Law on Foreign Trade Management (No. 05/2017/ QH14)	2017	FDI firms with export rights are permitted to export goods purchased in Vietnam, processed in Vietnam, and legally imported in Vietnam to another foreign country or non-tariff zone, while those with import rights are permitted to import goods from another foreign country or customs zone into Vietnam. Moreover, the goods are listed for export and import under license or specific conditions, FDI firms are required to have the license and meet the regulations.
Law on Investment (Decree 31/2021/ ND-CP)	2021	FDI firms need to apply for a business registration license for the rights to export and import. By this regulation, they can completely minimize any risks (taxation or legislation).

Table A12.2 Current trade agreements of Vietnam

Free trade agreement (FTA)	*Year*	*Signatories*
ASEAN Free Trade Area Agreement	1993	Vietnam, Malaysia, the Philippines, Singapore, Thailand, Laos, Myanmar, Cambodia, Indonesia, and Brunei.
ASEAN-China Comprehensive Economic Cooperation Agreement (ACFTA)	2005	China and ASEAN members.
ASEAN-South Korea Comprehensive Economic Cooperation Agreement (AKFTA)	2007	South Korea and ASEAN members.
ASEAN-Japan Comprehensive Economic Partnership (AJCEP)	2008	Japan and ASEAN members.
Japan-Vietnam Economic Partnership Agreement (VJEPA)	2009	Vietnam and Japan.
ASEAN-India Comprehensive Economic Cooperation Agreement (AIFTA)	2010	India and ASEAN members.
ASEAN-Australia and New Zealand Free Trade Agreement (AANZFTA)	2010	Australia, New Zealand, and ASEAN members.
Vietnam-Chile Free Trade Agreement (CVFTA)	2012	Chile and Vietnam.
South Korea-Vietnam Free Trade Agreement (VKFTA)	2015	Vietnam and South Korea
Eurasian Economic Union-Vietnam Free Trade Agreement (VEAEU)	2016	Vietnam, Belarus, Kazakhstan, Russian Federation, Armenia, and Kyrgyz Republic.
Comprehensive and Progressive Agreement for Trans-Pacific Partnership (CPTPP)	2019	Vietnam, Canada, Australia, Japan, Mexico, Singapore, New Zealand, Peru, and Malaysia.
ASEAN-Hong Kong, China Free Trade Agreement (AHKFTA)	2019	Hong Kong and ASEAN members.
EU-Vietnam Free Trade Agreement (EVFTA)	2020	Vietnam and 27 countries of the EU.
United Kingdom-Vietnam Free Trade Agreement (UKVFTA)	2021	Vietnam and the United Kingdom.
Regional Comprehensive Economic Partnership (RCEP)	2022	Australia, Japan, China, New Zealand, South Korea, and ASEAN members.
Vietnam-Israel Free Trade Agreement (VIFTA)	Under negotiation	Israel and Vietnam.

Table A12.3 Indicators, data source, and range

Indicator	*Year range*	*Sample size*	*Data source*
Dependent variables			
CO_2 emission/GDP	1990–2020	31	CO_2 emission: World Bank[1] GDP (constant 2015 US$): World Bank[2]
Red List Index	1993–2023	31	UN Statistics[3]
The percentage of renewable energy usage over total final energy usage.	2000–2019	20	World Bank[4]
Independent variables			
Total export value in USD	1995–2021	32	General Statistics Office of Vietnam[5]
%Foreign-invested sector's export	1995–2021	32	General Statistics Office of Vietnam[5]
% Processing industrial products	1995–2021	32	General Statistics Office of Vietnam[5]
The net inflow of FDI as a percentage of GDP	1985–2021	37	World Bank[6]
Control variable			
GDP growth	1985–2021	37	World Bank[7]

Note:

1. https://data.worldbank.org/indicator/EN.ATM.GHGT.KT.CE?locations=VN
2. https://data.worldbank.org/indicator/NY.GDP.MKTP.KD?locations=VN
3. https://unstats.un.org/sdgs/dataportal/countryprofiles/VNM#goal-15
4. https://data.worldbank.org/indicator/EG.FEC.RNEW.ZS?locations=VN
5. www.gso.gov.vn/en/px-web/?pxid=E0810&theme=Trade%2C%20Price%20and%20Tourist
6. https://data.worldbank.org/indicator/BX.KLT.DINV.WD.GD.ZS?locations=VN
7. https://data.worldbank.org/indicator/NY.GDP.MKTP.KD.ZG?locations=VN

Table A12.4 Descriptive and correlation matrix

	CO_2/GDP	*RLI*	*Export/GDP*	*FDI inflow/ GDP*	*% foreign-invested sector export*	*% Others (industrial goods) export*	*GDP growth*
	1						
	31						
RLI	0.665	1					
	(.004)						
Export/GDP	−0.631	−0.976	1				
	(.018)	(.000)					
FDI inflow/GDP	−0.003	0.458	−0.292	1			
	(7.190)	(.317)	(2.277)				
% foreign-invested sector export	−0.649	−0.959	0.908	−0.488	1		
	(.011)	(.000)	(.000)	(.248)			
% Others (industrial goods) export	−0.553	−0.954	0.897	−0.501	0.986	1	
	(.094)	(.000)	(.000)	(.000)	(.000)		
GDP growth	0.044	0.464	−0.470	0.557	−0.453	−0.523	1
	(6.995)	(.258)	(.326)	(.013)	(.413)	(.138)	
Mean	1.43	0.76	0.43	4.75	55.60	76.99	6.38
Minimum	1.25	0.71	0.08	−0.001	27.0	53.80	2.56
Maximum	1.63	0.81	1.01	11.939	73.4	90.70	9.54

Note: Pearson's correlation (Bayes factor).

The significance level of the coefficient is assessed based on Bayes factors (BF) representing how closely variables are related to support two hypotheses.

- Null hypothesis (H_0): There is no relationship between the two variables. $\rho = 0$. (i.e., trade/FDI and environmental performance)
- Alternative hypothesis (H_1): Two variables have a linear relationship. $\rho \neq 0$.

BF gives the likelihood of the data under the null hypothesis divided by the likelihood of the data under the alternative. Therefore, BF values greater than 1 signal more evidence in favor of the null while values less than 1 signal more evidence in favor of the alternative. BF equal to 1 signal with no evidence.

Table A12.5 Bayesian estimates of regression of environmental performance on export and FDI

	DV = CO_2 emission		*DV = RLI*	
	Model 1	*Model 2*	*Model 3*	*Model 4*
Export/GDP	***−0.162***	***−0.584***	***−0.096***	***−0.164***
	(−.248, −.076)	***(−.960, −.208)***	***(−.106, −.085)***	***(−.192, −.136)***
$(\text{Export/GDP})^2$		***0.451***		***0.070***
		(.052, .851)		***(.043, .098)***
FDI inflow/GDP		0.008	***0.001***	0.002
		(−.088, .104)	***(.000, .002)***	(−.007, .010)
$(\text{FDI inflow/GDP})^2$	6.019E−06	−0.001		$-6.42 * 10^{-5}$
	(−.012, .012)	(−.008, .007)		(−.001, .001)
GDP growth	−0.008	−0.010	0.000	0.001
	(−.025, .010)	(−.027, .007)	(−.002, .002)	(−.001, .002)
Constant	1.518	1.576	0.797	0.803
	(1.383, 1.653)	(1.243, 1.909)	(.781, .813)	
R	0.650	0.746	0.979	0.991
R-square	0.422	0.557	0.958	0.982
N	25	25	26	26

Note: Coefficient (95% credible interval).

Table A12.6 Bayesian estimates of regression of environmental performance on types of export

	DV = CO_2 emission		*DV = RLI*	
	Model 7	*Model 8*	*Model 9*	*Model 10*
%Foreign sectors' export	***–0.017***	***–0.018***	–0.002	–0.001
	(–0.024, –0.009)	***(–0.024–0.012)***	(–0.003, 4.630*10^{-5})	(–0.002, 0.000)
(%Foreign sectors' export)^2		***3.904*10^{-4}***		1.045E–05
		(–0.001, 0.000)		(–0.003, 4.630*10^{-5})
% Industrial goods export	***0.021***	***0.022***	–0.001	–0.002
	(0.009, 0.032)	***(0.013, 0.031)***	(–0.003, 0.002)	(–0.004, 0.000)
% Industrial goods export^2		***0.001***		-7.005*10–5
		(0.000, 0.001)		(0.000, 1.366*10^{-6})
GDP growth	0.002	–0.001	0.001	0.001
	(–0.012, 0.017)	(–0.013, 0.010)	(–0.002, 0.004)	(–0.001, 0.003)
Constant	1.385	1.420	0.758	0.761
	(1.286, 1.483)	(1.341, 1.498)	(0.739, 0.778)	(0.747, 0.776)
R	0.820	0.908	0.961	0.982
R-square	0.672	0.824	0.924	0.963
N	25	25	26	26

Note: Coefficient (95% credible interval).

Table A12.7 Vietnamese law on environmental protection

Policies	*Main focus*	*Measurement*
Law on Environmental Protection (1993)	*General provision*: The definition of environmental protection and various terms of degradation, pollution, and incidents in the environment. *Prevention against environmental degradation*: The government stipulates a list of environmental standards (biodiversity, natural resources, water resource, land use), decentralizes the promulgation, and inspects the implementation of those standards. *Provision for remedy of those issues*: All organizations and individuals are required to take action to tackle environmental degradation, pollution, and accidents in compliance with the environmental protection requirements of the government. The actions include saving human lives and property; eliminating the cause of the incident; stabilizing people's lives; production recovery; disease prevention; environmental sanitation; observing environmental change; reporting on damages; rebuild the ecosystem in damaged areas. *State management*: Ministry of Science, Technology, and Environment coordinate with other Ministries that are responsible for directly implementing environmental protection strategies and regulations. State management organizations develop approaches to prevent and overcome environmental degradation, pollution, and incidents. *International relations in environmental protection*: Signed international environmental commitments and agreements are implemented based on independence and mutual benefit principles. *Environment inspection and settlement of violation*: The inspection teams or inspectors have the right to settle violations for organizations or individuals who get involved in destructive activities that harm the environment.	The government carried out the EIA policy framework to evaluate the severity of environmental degradation and pollution in production and business activities. This allows for treating damages, which need to report to the local authorities and State management immediately on environmental protection. There were two kinds of EIA: – Full EIA for medium and large projects, examined at national and provincial levels. – Simplified EIA for small projects, examined at the district level. Project owners are required to submit environmental impact assessments (EIAs). They are responsible for sharing information with the community, government, and employees in manufacturing, commercial, and service enterprises about the environmental status, steps to prevent and mitigate negative environmental impacts, and efforts to reduce pollution and degradation.

(*Continued*)

Table A12.7 (Continued)

Policies	*Main focus*	*Measurement*
Law on Environmental Protection (2005)	This Law was revised based on Law on Environmental Protection (1993). The National Assembly passed the additional principles of environmental protection: – Environmental protection must be inseparably associated with economic and social development for the country's long-term growth. – National environmental protection must be related to regional and global environmental protection. – Environmental protection is a social concern, with the rights and duties of governments, organizations, and individuals. – Environmental protection operations must be carried out regularly, with prevention acting as the primary means of preventing pollution and degradation and enhancing environmental quality. – Environmental protection must be in line with the national laws, nature, culture, and level of socio-economic development in each period.	This Law improved the timeline of the EIA process in the project cycle by requiring EIAs to be written at the time of the project. This process included criteria to evaluate: – EIA must be performed at an appropriate stage of the project cycle. – Adequate capability exists to develop. – Projects are reviewed to identify the level of EIA necessary, and acceptable requirements for the scope and content of EIA documentation. – EIAs must tackle all stages of project environmental management, from pre-construction to operation. – EIA commitments and evaluation findings are compulsory and supervised.
Environmental Protection Tax Law (2012)	The Environmental Tax charges on a variety of environmentally hazardous activities and materials. This regulation assesses the manufacture and importation of certain items, notably petroleum products. This is computed as an absolute sum based on the quantity of goods. Meanwhile, energy is mostly taxed in the form of various fuels, with coal and refined fuels (gasoline, diesel, etc.) accounting for 99.5%. All tax revenues are used for environmental programs.	

Law on Environmental Protection (2014)	This Law was revised to the 2005 Law on Environmental Protection, with the following major updates: – Including more prohibited acts, such as the destruction of natural resources, releasing toxic chemicals and pollutants, or cover-up acts of the destruction of the environment. – Including stronger regulations on the contents, concepts, and responsibilities for implementing environmental protection planning. – Additional laws on the major parts of the assessment report on how the strategic environmental assessment should be carried out. – Removing specific provisions in the Law related to issues subject to EIA and allocating to the government detailing the list of projects. – Specific further regulations and orders for drafting environmental protection plans for exploiting and using natural resources.	Apart from EIA, this Law also implemented Strategic Environment Assessment (SEA) to evaluate the national, local, and provincial growth of economic, processing and exporting, high technology, and industrial zones that can significantly impact the environment. The Ministry of Natural Resources and Environment will verify the report on both SEA and EIA, decided by the National Assembly, Government, and Prime Minister.
The 2020 Law on Environmental Protection (Vietnam Patent No. Law 72/2020/QH14, 2020)	The Law has inherited and promoted positive factors in the implementation of legal provisions on environmental protection from the previous Laws. This Law prioritized regulations on environmental component protection. Furthermore, environmental management for each phase of the project begins with the discussion of investment strategy, project evaluation, project implementation, and finalization of the project. In particular, the Law has added a separate section (Section 4, Chapter II) to regulate the environmental preservation of natural heritage, which includes natural heritage rules and protection content. Moreover, to improve resources, capacity, and efficiency in environmental management, this Law has included provisions on environmental economic development, environmental industry policies, development of natural capital, circular economy, etc. in Articles 142 to 147. In addition, climate change adaptation and greenhouse gas emissions mitigation have also added to respond to international commitments and climate change in Articles 90 to 96.	The following additional information must be included in the EIA reports: – The location and current status of the implementation region. – The main production technique, technology, and materials. – Prediction of factors with environmental implications. – Measures to mitigate negative environmental consequences. Apart from SEA and EIA, the new Preliminary Environmental Impact Assessment (PEIA) was carried out during the pre-feasibility research on construction investment, the proposal for investment guidelines, and the request for approval to make the decision.

Evidence categories for the Bayes factor

Bayes factor (BF_{10})	*Level*
>100	Extreme evidence for H_0
30–100	Very strong evidence for H_0
10–30	Strong evidence for H_0
3–10	Moderate evidence for H_0
1–3	Anecdotal evidence for H_0
1	No evidence
1/3–1	Anecdotal evidence for H_1
1/10–1/3	**Moderate evidence for H_1**
1/30–1/10	**Strong evidence for H_1**
1/100–1/30	**Very strong evidence for H_1**
<1/100	**Extreme evidence for H_1**

Note

* Turning point is calculated as $-\dfrac{-.018}{2 \times 3.904 \times 10^{-4}} = 23$

13 Uncovering Interdependencies Between Crude Palm Oil Commodity and ASEAN-5 Equity Markets

A Time–Frequency Connectedness Analysis

Xiu Wei Yeap, Sook Rei Tan, and Hooi Hooi Lean

13.1 Introduction

Palm oil is a versatile product that has found widespread use in various applications, particularly as a vegetable oil. In recent years, there has been a significant surge in the utilization of palm oil for biofuel production. This increased demand for palm oil has led to a remarkable expansion in its production over the past few decades. Specifically, global palm oil production has surged by 35 times, from 2 million tons in 1970 to 71 million tons in 2018 (Ritchie & Roser, 2021).

Palm oil is derived from the oil palm, the world's leading oil crop that only grows in tropical regions. The major producers of palm oil are Malaysia and Indonesia, both situated in tropical Southeast Asia. As a number of studies have pointed out, the commodities and financial markets often exist spillover relationships (see, e.g., Babar et al., 2023; Garcia-Jorcano and Sanchis-Marco, 2022). As such, it is anticipated that the palm oil market will play an increasingly vital role in the Southeast Asian region's economic and financial conditions, given it is the primary region for palm oil production and consumption. However, research about the spillover effects of crude palm oil on the region's financial markets remains limited.

Against such a backdrop, this chapter aims to investigate the spillover of returns and volatilities between the crude palm oil commodity and equity markets in five of the Association of Southeast Asian Nations' (ASEAN-5) member countries, including Malaysia, Indonesia, the Philippines, Singapore, and Thailand. Following robust economic performance and a continued trend of economic integration within the ASEAN bloc, the equity markets in the region have experienced tremendous growth in market capitalization. As of 2017, the regional stock exchanges hosted a combination of over 3,400 listed companies with a total market capitalization of US$2.7 trillion (CEIC, n.d.). Therefore, it is essential to examine the impact of crude palm oil, one of the most significant commodities in the region, on the equity markets of these countries.

DOI: 10.4324/9781003349204-13

Using a time-varying parameter vector autoregression (TVP-VAR)-based frequency connectedness approach, our result findings reveal different patterns in how returns and volatilities are linked between the crude palm oil and equity markets of ASEAN-5 nations. In particular, return connectedness is primarily influenced by shock transmissions in the short run, with the equity markets being a net transmitter and the crude palm oil being a net receiver of return spillovers. Conversely, volatility connectedness is driven by shock transmissions in the long run, in which the crude palm oil is the net transmitter, and the equity markets are the net receivers of volatility spillovers.

This work presents two significant contributions. First, it is the first comprehensive study to explore the relationship between the equity markets of the ASEAN-5 countries and crude palm oil prices over an extended period. In contrast to traditional VAR-based approaches that are limited to analyzing the time domain, our method excels in tracking dynamic spillovers at different time–frequency bands. Leveraging the time–frequency domain grants us valuable insights into how the interconnectedness between these markets evolves across different frequency bands, offering a more comprehensive understanding of the intricate interactions between equity markets and commodity prices amid the COVID-19 crisis. Second, while this study is related to Lim et al.'s (2014) analysis of spillovers between commodities and ASEAN-5 countries using a static method, our research stands apart by focusing specifically on crude palm oil and extensively exploring the time-varying connectedness. By delving deeply into the dynamics of crude palm oil market interrelationships with equity markets, we provide a deeper understanding of the fluctuations and temporal variations in their connectedness, shedding light on the changing nature of their interactions.

The remainder of this chapter is organized as follows. Section 13.2 provides the literature review of spillover analysis of commodity and financial markets. Section 13.3 outlines the methodology of TVP-VAR-based frequency connectedness framework. Section 13.4 describes the data used in this study. Section 13.5 presents the empirical results. Finally, Section 13.6 concludes this chapter.

13.2 Literature Review

Our research closely aligns with existing literature on time-varying spillovers among diverse commodities. For example, Luo and Ji (2018) study the interconnections between crude oil prices in the US and agricultural commodity futures in China, while Fasanya and Akinbowale (2019) examine the links between crude oil and food prices in Nigeria. Notably, our findings reveal that return spillovers demonstrate a consistent trend without bursts, whereas volatility spillovers exhibit both trend and burst patterns over the study period. Guhathakurta et al. (2020) explore the connectedness and directional spillovers between oil and various agricultural commodities, emphasizing a robust volatility connectedness between oil prices and agricultural products. Similarly, Maitra et al. (2021) investigate the connectedness between oil and 21 commodity futures, including the palm oil market, uncovering substantial evidence of asymmetric volatility spillovers, where negative shocks dominate positive ones. Furthermore, Akyildirim et al. (2022) delve into the connectedness among different agricultural commodities, documenting the influence of COVID-19-induced uncertainty on agricultural commodity returns. Additionally, Chandrarin et al. (2022) employ innovative approaches, using frequency connectedness analysis, to measure volatility spillovers among exchange rates, consumer price index, crude palm oil price, and coal price in Indonesia, providing valuable insights into the complex relationships between these indicators and commodity prices.

Our research builds upon several relevant studies and makes a substantial contribution to the understanding of the interconnections between equity and commodity markets. For example, Lin et al. (2021) investigate the risk spillovers between Chinese, American, and European equity markets and the global crude oil market. Similarly, Mensi, Shafiullah, et al. (2021) explore the volatility spillovers between strategic commodities futures markets and equity markets in both advanced and emerging economies. Meanwhile, Mensi, Vo, et al. (2021) analyze the time–frequency relationship between major rare-earth-element markets and the stock indexes of their exporting and importing nations. Notably, Billah et al. (2023) focus on agribusiness and find that the degree of inverse shocks determines the connectedness of returns, with larger impacts of anticipated shocks on the left and right tails compared to estimated shocks on the average. Moreover, Mensi et al. (2022) and Cagli et al. (2023) study frequency volatility spillovers among crude oil, gold, and ten sector indices, as well as volatility spillovers for ten agribusiness equity prices and different types of agricultural commodities in the US context, using innovative approaches. Furthermore, Wen et al. (2021) examine the connectedness among rare earth elements, non-ferrous metals, energy, chemicals, grains, oil, soft goods, and equity markets, revealing a significant dependency between equity and commodity markets. Chang and Fang (2022) support Wen et al.'s (2021) findings by showing a positive linkage between the equity market and the commodity market, analyzing various types of commodity and equity connectedness. Adopting a time–frequency approach, Qi et al. (2022) study the time-varying association between renewable energy equity markets and energy commodity markets in China. On the other hand, Rehman et al. (2023) use the quantile connectedness method to investigate the connectedness of equity and commodity markets in the Chinese context, revealing spillovers that vary across different quantiles. Additionally, Bossman and Agyei (2022) analyze the connectedness among various classes of commodities and African equity markets, noting that commodity and equity markets can produce safe returns, but high commodity price volatility and financialization suggest that the behavior of commodity returns may vary.

Although other academics have identified a link between commodities prices and equity market volatility, many studies tend to concentrate on the US and Chinese markets. The ASEAN market has received very little research attention. The relationship between the ASEAN-5 stock markets and commodities, including rice, rubber, gold, palm oil, and gasoline, is examined by Lim et al. (2014). The goal of this study is to build on the work of Lim et al. (2014) by examining the relationship between the ASEAN-5 stock markets and crude palm oil. The choice of crude palm oil is made since Malaysia and Indonesia, two ASEAN nations, account for more than half of the palm oil's output.[1] Besides that, Yeap and Lean (2022) also state that crude palm oil serves as significant contributor to the gross national income (GNI) of Malaysia. In addition, Lim et al. (2014) also find that palm oil prices significantly affect the stock market returns of Indonesia and Malaysia.

Our work differs from Lim et al.'s (2014) in several aspects. First, we aim to examine the connectedness in different frequencies, an aspect that was neglected in their study. Mensi, Shafiullah, et al. (2021) have found evidence indicating that spillovers are more prominent in the short term compared to the long term across crude oil, gold, and stock markets. Similarly, Mensi, Vo, et al. (2021) show that short-run contagion dominates long-run contagion between rare-earth elements and equity markets. Additionally, Mensi et al. (2022) demonstrate that the responsiveness of stocks to commodity price shocks may vary across different frequencies. These findings underscore the importance of examining connectedness in various frequency bands. Second, while Lim et al. (2014) employed a static method to investigate spillovers, we recognize the limitations of this approach in capturing the time-varying fluctuations of real markets. Hence, our study employs a time-varying approach that can account for extreme events such as the global financial crisis (GFC) and the COVID-19 pandemic. By incorporating the time-varying dimension, our research aims to fill this gap and provide a more comprehensive understanding of the connectedness between crude palm oil and ASEAN-5 equity markets over different time frames, thus offering valuable insights for investors and policymakers.

13.3 Methodology

By merging the work of Baruník and Křehlík (2018) and Antonakakis et al. (2020), this research employs the TVP-VAR-based frequency connectedness approach presented by Chatziantoniou et al. (2021) to examine the interconnectivity between the crude palm oil and stock markets. We employ a TVP-VAR model with a *p*-order lag, which is similar to the strategy utilized in the works of Chatziantoniou et al. (2021), Antonakakis et al. (2020), and Cui and Maghyereh (2023):

$$x_t = \Phi_{1t}x_{t-1} + \Phi_{2t}x_{t-2} + \ldots + \Phi_{pt}x_{t-p} + \xi_t \qquad \xi_t \sim N(0, \Sigma_t) \qquad (1)$$

where x_t and ξ_t are $N \times 1$ dimensional vectors. By incorporating time-varying coefficients denoted by ϕ_{it}, we allow for changes in the relationship between variables over time, providing a more realistic depiction of the time-varying nexus between the crude palm oil and equity markets. Additionally, we account for the time-varying nature of the data by using the variance-covariance matrix Σ_t, which captures changes in volatility and correlations among the variables.

To estimate the generalized forecast error variance decomposition (GFEVD), it is necessary to convert the TVP-VAR model into a TVP vector moving average (TVP-VMA) representation according to the Wold representation theorem. The forecast error variance of the endogenous variables is quantified by the GFEVD by accounting for the contributions of each shock. It has the following representation:

$$\psi_{ij,t}(H) = \frac{\sum_{h=0}^{H-1}\left(e_i^{'}A_{ht}\Sigma_t e_j\right)^2}{\left(e_j^{'}\Sigma_t e_j\right)\sum_{h=0}^{H-1}\left(e_i^{'}A_{ht}\Sigma_t A_{ht}^{'} e_i\right)} \tag{2}$$

$$\tilde{\psi}_{ij,t}(H) = \frac{\psi_{ij,t}(H)}{\sum_{j=1}^{K}\psi_{ij,t}(H)}$$

where e_i is a $K \times 1$ zero selection vector with a value of 1 in its i-th position. The term $\psi_{ij,t}(H)$ denotes the proportional reduction of the H-step forecast error variance of variable i resulting from conditioning on the future shocks of variable j. Diebold and Yilmaz (2012, 2014) suggest that the normalization method, the connectedness table represented as $\tilde{\psi}_{ij,t}(H)$, is transformed into a range of [0,1], making it more readily interpretable.

The generalized spillover table is used to compute summary measures of spillover effects. These measures include the total directional connectedness from other variables to variable i, which quantifies the network's influence on variable i. It helps understand the collective impact of other variables on variable i. Additionally, the total directional connectedness to other variables resulting from a shock in variable i indicates variable i's impact on the entire network. It measures how much variable i contributes to the time-dependence dynamics and volatilities of other variables. These metrics can be expressed as:

$$S_{i\leftarrow\bullet,t}^{From} = \sum_{j=1,j\neq i}^{K}\tilde{\psi}_{ij,t}(H) \tag{3}$$

$$S_{\bullet\leftarrow i,t}^{To} = \sum_{j=1,j\neq i}^{K}\tilde{\psi}_{ji,t}(H) \tag{4}$$

The net total directional connectedness of variable i is an important fundamental statistic in the connectedness method in addition to the metrics described earlier. This metric is employed to assess whether variable i exerts more influence on the network compared to being influenced by it, or vice versa. It can be calculated using the formula:

$$S_{i,t}^{Net} = S_{\bullet\leftarrow i,t}^{\text{To}} - S_{i\leftarrow\bullet,t}^{From} \tag{5}$$

For portfolio and risk managers, the total connectedness index (TCI) is a crucial tool for determining the degree of network interconnectivity or market risk. The total directional connectedness *FROM* (or *TO*) other variables is averaged to create the TCI. It may be described using the following equation:

$$TCI_t = \frac{1}{K}\sum_{i=1}^{K} S_{i\leftarrow\bullet,t}^{From} = \frac{1}{K}\sum_{i=1}^{K} S_{\bullet\leftarrow i,t}^{\text{To}} \tag{6}$$

The equations previously discussed form the core of the TVP-VAR-based connectedness method and provide the basis for our connectedness metrics in the time domain. The frequency response function is introduced first before moving on to the connectedness metrics in the frequency domain:

$$\psi\left(e^{-i\omega}\right) = \sum_{h=0}^{\infty} e^{-i\omega h}\psi_h, i = \sqrt{-1} \tag{7}$$

Following that, the Fourier transformation of the TVP-VMA model may be used to describe the spectral density of x_t at the frequency as follows:

$$S_x(\omega) = \sum_{h=-\infty}^{\infty} E\left(x_t x_{t-h}'\right)e^{-i\omega h} = \psi\left(e^{-i\omega h}\right)\Sigma_t \psi'\left(e^{+i\omega h}\right) \tag{8}$$

By combining the spectral density and the GFEVD, the frequency GFEVD and normalized frequency GFEVD are presented as follows:

$$\psi_{ij,t}(\omega) = \frac{(£_t)_{jj}^{-1} \left| \sum_{h=0}^{\infty}\left(\ddot{}\left(e^{-i\omega h}\right)£_t\right)_{ij,t} \right|^2}{\sum_{h=0}^{\infty}\left(\ddot{}\left(e^{-i\omega h}\right)£_t \ddot{}\left(e^{i\omega h}\right)\right)_{ii}} \tag{9}$$

$$\tilde{\psi}_{ij,t}(\omega) = \frac{\psi_{ij,t}(\omega)}{\sum_{k=1}^{N}\psi_{ij,t}(\omega)}$$

where $\tilde{\psi}_{ij,t}$ represents the proportion of market i's spectrum that can be attributed to the shock originating from market j at the specific frequency ω. To assess the connectedness at different frequency bands, we integrate across all frequencies within a particular range, denoted as $d = (a,b)$, where a and b lie in the interval $(-\pi, \pi)$, with $a<b$. This integration enables us

to measure the level of connectedness at various frequency bands using the following approach:

$$\tilde{\psi}_{ij,t}(d) = \int_a^b \tilde{\psi}_{ij,t}(\omega)d\omega \tag{10}$$

The frequency connectedness measurements are now presented as follows:

$$S_{i\leftarrow\bullet,t}^{From}(d) = \sum_{j=1,j\neq i}^{K} \tilde{\psi}_{ij,t}(d) \tag{11}$$

$$S_{\bullet\leftarrow i,t}^{To}(d) = \sum_{j=1,j\neq i}^{K} \tilde{\psi}_{ji,t}(d) \tag{12}$$

$$S_{i,t}^{Net}(d) = S_{\bullet\leftarrow i,t}^{To}(d) - S_{i\leftarrow\bullet,t}^{From}(d) \tag{13}$$

$$TCI_t(d) = \frac{1}{K}\sum_{i=1}^{K} S_{i\leftarrow\bullet,t}^{From}(d) = \frac{1}{K}\sum_{i=1}^{K} S_{\bullet\leftarrow i,t}^{To}(d) \tag{14}$$

13.4 Data Description

For the purpose of this study, the crude palm oil commodities' market is represented by the daily settlement prices of crude palm oil traded on the Malaysia Derivatives Exchange (MDEX). The information was extracted from the website of Bursa Malaysia Derivatives. In addition, five ASEAN nations – Malaysia, Indonesia, the Philippines, Singapore, and Thailand – had their equities markets chosen for examination. The different stock markets of each nation are represented by the stock indexes of the Kuala Lumpur Stock Exchange (KLSE), Indonesia Stock Exchange (IDX), Philippine Stock Exchange, Singapore Exchange (SGX), and The Stock Exchange of Thailand (SET).

This study covers a sample period ranging from 1 June 2007 to 31 May 2023, consisting of a total of 4,094 observations. This time frame encompasses significant events such as the GFC in 2008 and the impact of the COVID-19 pandemic on equity markets. It also includes the effects of structural changes that occurred in 2012, resulting from supply and demand factors, as well as the shortage of supply caused by the COVID-19 pandemic in the palm oil market. To mitigate the unit root problem, all the data in this study were transformed into log returns.

Figures 13.1 and 13.2 present the price and return plots for crude palm oil alongside the equity markets of the five ASEAN nations. Figure 13.1 illustrates that the GFC caused a decline in crude palm oil prices between 2008 and 2012. Moreover, during the COVID-19 epidemic, crude palm oil prices experienced a significant surge followed by a sharp decline due to overpricing. The equity markets of the ASEAN nations also exhibited notable falls

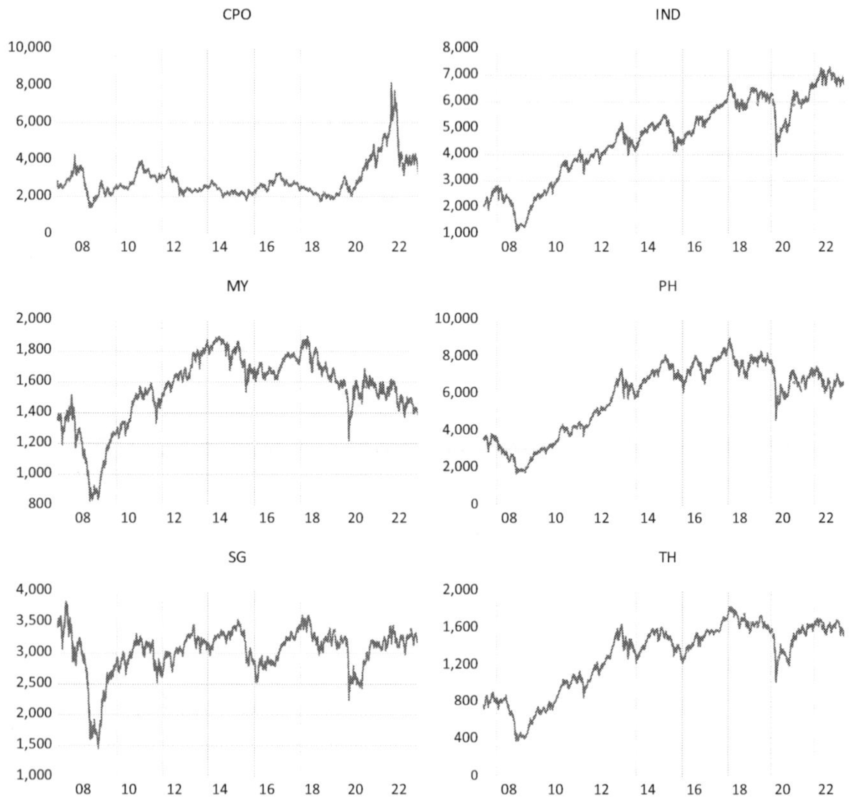

Figure 13.1 Price plot for the crude palm oil and equity markets

during both the COVID-19 outbreak and the GFC, as evident in Figure 13.1. Additionally, Figure 13.2 demonstrates that both the crude palm oil market and the equity markets showed higher return volatility during these significant events, reflecting increased market uncertainty and fluctuations. These observations emphasize the interconnectedness between the crude palm oil market and the ASEAN-5 equity markets, wherein global events influence both markets, leading to comparable price and volatility patterns during major crises.

Table 13.1 presents an overview of the descriptive statistics for the daily returns of crude palm oil and the equity markets in the five ASEAN countries. Indonesia stands out among the ASEAN countries with the highest average return, while Malaysia exhibits the lowest average return in equity markets. Furthermore, the crude palm oil market demonstrates greater volatility

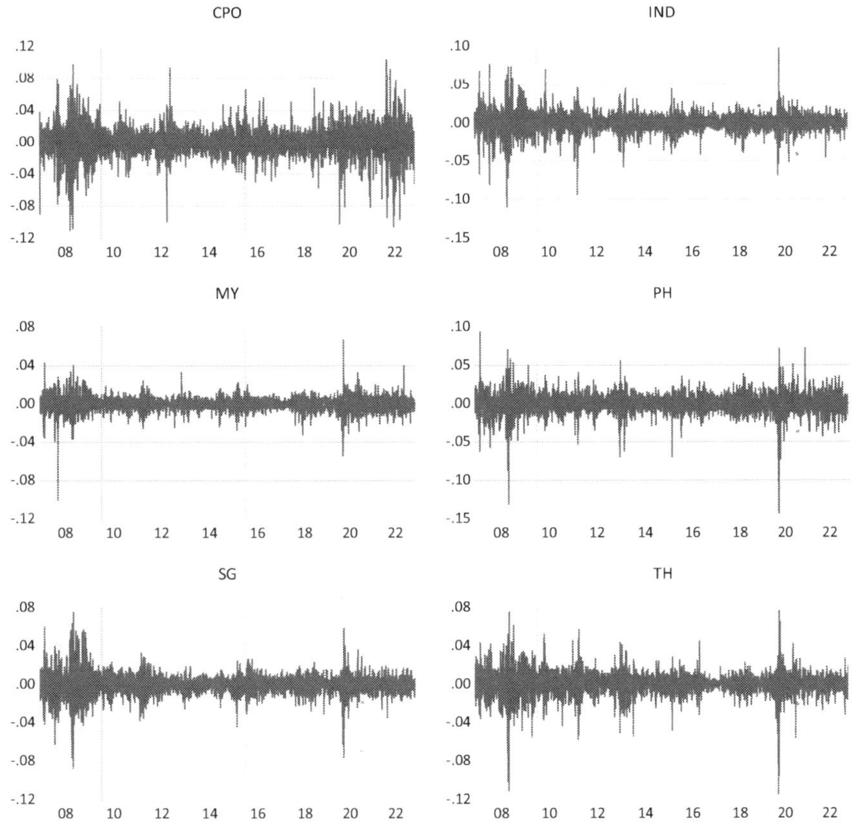

Figure 13.2 Return plot for the crude palm oil and equity markets

compared to the equity markets. Both the palm oil and equity markets show negative skewness, indicating a higher occurrence of extreme negative returns compared to extreme positive returns. Moreover, both markets display kurtosis values exceeding three, which suggests a leptokurtic distribution characterized by heavier tails and a lower, broader central peak. The normality test conducted using the Jarque and Bera (1987) method reveals that they are different from the normal distribution, yielding statistically significant results. Additionally, the Ljung-Box test shows the existence of autocorrelation in the series and the ARCH test confirms the presence of heteroskedasticity in the error terms for all the series. The presence of autocorrelation and heteroskedasticity supports the utilization of the TVP-VAR framework to model the time-varying variance–covariance structure (Li et al., 2023). Furthermore, the ADF unit root tests verify that all variables are stationary, thereby preventing any spurious regression outcomes.

Table 13.1 Descriptive statistics

	CPO	*Indonesia*	*Malaysia*	*The Philippines*	*Thailand*	*Singapore*
Mean	4.38×10^{-5}	$2.83E \times 10^{-4}$	4.81×10^{-6}	1.47×10^{-4}	1.74×10^{-4}	-2.37×10^{-5}
SD	0.0182	0.0124	0.0074	0.0128	0.0115	0.0106
Skewness	−0.2566	−0.5655	−0.7599	−0.9493	−0.9603	−0.2466
Kurtosis	7.6448	12.5862	16.6884	14.9464	15.5081	11.1013
Jarque-Bera	3723***	15886***	32341***	24948***	27304***	11232***
Ljung – Box	24.3138***	26.8368***	48.1890***	11.0027*	42.3041***	19.0193***
ARCH	498***	508***	292***	520***	569***	1044***
ADF	−14.3892***	−15.7408***	−16.1508***	−15.7874***	−14.7021***	−15.9090***

Note: ***, **, * denotes the significance at the 1%, 5% and 10% level, respectively.

13.5 Empirical Result

13.5.1 Connectedness Between Crude Palm Oil and ASEAN-5 Stock Returns

Table 13.2 displays the results of the static return connectedness analysis conducted for crude palm oil and ASEAN-5 equity. Each square in the connectedness table contains four numerical values: overall connectedness, short-run connectedness (one to five days), medium-run connectedness (5–22 days), and long-run connectedness (22-Inf days). The overall connectedness value is further divided into short-run, medium-run, and long-run connectedness, representing the connectedness within specific frequency ranges. This breakdown allows us to examine the varying degrees of connectedness across different time periods. Moreover, the diagonal elements of the connectedness table indicate the connectedness resulting from the shocks originating within each asset itself. They represent the impact that each asset's own shocks have on its returns. Conversely, the off-diagonal elements capture the connectedness arising from the interactions between assets within the network. These off-diagonal elements reveal the extent to which other assets influence the returns of a specific asset or vice versa.

From Table 13.2, the analysis reveals that the total connectedness index between crude palm oil and ASEAN-5 equity is 39.20%. This connectedness can be further broken down into specific time periods, with 29.74% attributed to short-run factors, 6.93% to medium-run factors, and only 2.54% to long-run factors. These findings indicate that the return connectedness is primarily driven by shock transmissions in the short run, with relatively less influence from medium and long-run factors. The finding is similar to Mensi et al. (2022) that short-run contagion dominates the long-run contagion. Besides that, from the diagonal elements of the table, we observe that 80.85% of the connectedness in crude palm oil can be attributed to its own shocks, while the remaining 19.15% originates from the equity markets. This suggests that the majority of return connectedness in crude palm oil is caused by its own shocks, indicating a higher level of self-influence. In contrast, the return connectedness resulting from idiosyncratic shocks in each ASEAN-5 equity market is as follows: Indonesia (56.29%), Malaysia (54.95%), the Philippines (59.31%), Thailand (58.92%), and Singapore (54.47%). This indicates that the equity markets in the ASEAN-5 countries are more responsive to shocks originating from other markets within the system, as compared to the crude palm oil market that is less susceptible to other markets' shocks.

When considering the total connectedness transmitted "TO" others, it is observed that the ASEAN-5 equity markets contribute a relatively higher level of return connectedness to the overall system compared to the crude palm oil market. A similar pattern is observed for the connectedness received "FROM" others. In addition, with the exception of the Philippines, all equity

Table 13.2 Return connectedness

	CPO	*Indonesia*	*Malaysia*	*The Philippines*	*Thailand*	*Singapore*	*FROM*
CPO	80.85(63.87)	3.6(2.75)	4.12(3.24)	2.96(2.29)	4.35(3.41)	4.13(3.35)	19.15(15.03)
	[12.47]{4.52}	[0.62]{0.23}	[0.64]{0.24}	[0.49]{0.18}	[0.69]{0.25}	[0.57]{0.21}	[3.02]{1.10}
Indonesia	2.51(1.93)	56.29(45.09)	11.14(8.77)	8.92(7)	9.03(6.8)	12.11(9.36)	43.71(33.87)
	[0.43]{0.16}	[8.23]{2.96}	[1.74]{0.63}	[1.41]{0.51}	[1.63]{0.59}	[2.02]{0.73}	[7.22]{2.62}
Malaysia	2.93(2.26)	11.5(8.46)	54.95(43.31)	9.11(6.85)	8.97(6.45)	12.54(9.06)	45.05(33.08)
	[0.49]{0.18}	[2.22]{0.82}	[8.54]{3.09}	[1.66]{0.61}	[1.84]{0.68}	[2.54]{0.94}	[8.75]{3.23}
The Philippines	2.42(1.83)	10.8(7.68)	10.25(7.54)	59.31(47.07)	7.85(5.33)	9.37(6.34)	40.69(28.74)
	[0.43]{0.16}	[2.28]{0.84}	[1.98]{0.73}	[8.99]{3.25}	[1.83]{0.68}	[2.2]{0.82}	[8.72]{3.23}
Thailand	3.04(2.41)	9.42(7.2)	8.99(7.12)	6.36(4.87)	58.92(46.77)	13.27(10.27)	41.08(31.88)
	[0.46]{0.17}	[1.62]{0.6}	[1.37]{0.5}	[1.09]{0.4}	[8.92]{3.24}	[2.2]{0.81}	[6.73]{2.47}
Singapore	2.77(2.28)	11.62(9.22)	11.8(9.45)	6.94(5.35)	12.4(9.54)	54.47(43.57)	45.53(35.83)
	[0.36]{0.13}	[1.77]{0.64}	[1.73]{0.62}	[1.17]{0.42}	[2.1]{0.76}	[8.01]{2.89}	[7.13]{2.57}
TO	13.67(10.72)	46.95(35.32)	46.3(36.12)	34.29(26.35)	42.59(31.53)	51.42(38.38)	235.22(178.42)
	[2.16]{0.79}	[8.51]{3.13}	[7.46]{2.71}	[5.82]{2.12}	[8.09]{2.97}	[9.53]{3.51}	[41.57]{15.22}
Inc.Own	94.52(74.59)	103.23(80.4)	101.25(79.44)	93.6(73.42)	101.51(78.3)	105.89(81.95)	TCI
	[14.63]{5.3}	[16.74]{6.09}	[16.01]{5.8}	[14.81]{5.37}	[17]{6.21}	[17.55]{6.39}	
NET	-5.48(-4.31)	3.23(1.45)	1.25(3.05)	-6.4(-2.39)	1.51(-0.35)	5.89(2.55)	39.2(29.74)
	[-0.86]{-0.32}	[1.28]{0.5}	[-1.29]{-0.52}	[-2.9]{-1.11}	[1.35]{0.5}	[2.41]{0.93}	[6.93]{2.54}

Note: In the connectedness table, numerical results were obtained using Chatziantoniou et al. (2021) innovative time-varying parameter frequency connectedness approach. The approach employs a TVP-VAR model with an optimized lag length determined by AIC, BIC, and SC criteria. A 100-step-ahead forecast error variance decomposition is used. Values in the upper-left square are time-domain connectedness results from the traditional DY connectedness approach. Values in (), [], and {} denote short-run, medium-run, and long-run frequency connectedness results, respectively. "FROM" column shows total connectedness received by market i, "TO" row displays total connectedness transmitted by market i. The "NET" row shows net connectedness, and "TCI" at the bottom right measures overall spillover effects within the system.

markets act as net transmitters, while the crude palm oil market acts as a net receiver (as indicated by a negative net connectedness value of –5.48%). The reason for the higher "TO" and "FROM" metrics in the ASEAN-5 equity markets is likely due to the high interdependency within the equity market itself. This suggests that the equity markets have a stronger influence on the overall connectedness within the system, compared to the crude palm oil market. To further examine the connectedness between crude palm oil and the equity markets, we can focus on the values in the first row and column of the connectedness table. It is observed that the transmission of shocks from crude palm oil to the equity markets (13.67%) is less significant compared to the transmission of shocks from the equity markets to the crude palm oil market (19.15%). This implies that the equity markets may have a greater influence on the crude palm oil market in terms of return connectedness, rather than the other way around.

Table 13.2 presents the static connectedness analysis and does not account for the time-varying nature of the connectedness over time. To address this limitation, we conduct an in-depth analysis of the time-varying evolution trajectories of connectedness based on TVP-VAR approach, aiming to highlight the significant effects of major political and economic events on the overall connectedness. Figure 13.3 displays the results for the time-varying total connectedness of returns. The thin solid line represents the entire interconnectivity

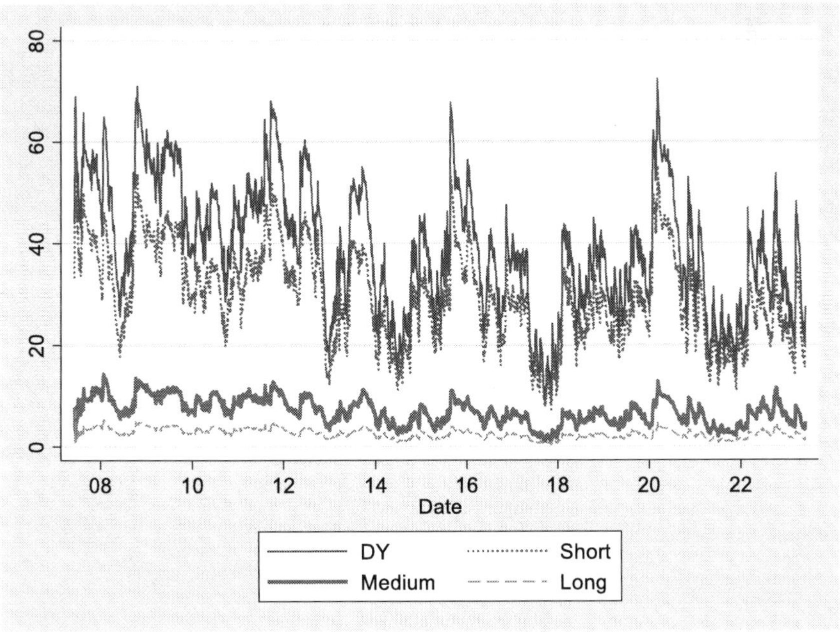

Figure 13.3 Time-varying total connectedness: return

in the time domain, calculated using the approach developed by Diebold and Yilmaz (2012, 2014). Additionally, the dashed line, thick solid line, and dotted line illustrate the short-run, medium-run, and long-run ranges of the TVP-VAR-based frequency connectedness results, respectively.

As depicted in Figure 13.3, the time-varying total return connectedness indices exhibit time-varying patterns and are significantly influenced by major events. These results align with recent findings by Niu and Hu (2021) and Rehman et al. (2023), highlighting that the magnitude and direction of spillovers between stocks and commodities change over time. Throughout the sample period, the total return connectedness varies approximately between 10% and 70%, illustrating a wide range of interconnectedness levels. The time-varying total return connectedness indices display significant volatility over time, consistent with the findings from Table 13.2. Additionally, in line with the results in Table 13.2, the analysis reveals that connectedness is primarily driven by the short-run shock, indicating no evidence of long-run cointegration between the crude palm oil and equity markets based on the return connectedness analysis.

The analysis of the time-varying total return connectedness indices reveals noteworthy peaks, with the first one occurring after the GFC at approximately 70%. Another significant peak is observed in 2012, which aligns with structural changes in the crude palm oil market driven by supply and demand factors, as discussed by Ab Rahman et al. (2013). During this period, there was a substantial decline in crude palm oil prices, impacting major producers like Malaysia and Indonesia, and leading to increased connectedness in other ASEAN countries. The third peak in the time-varying total return connectedness indices occurs in late 2015, resulting from the turbulence in the Chinese stock market. The significant decline in equity markets in response to the Chinese stock market turmoil contributed to heightened connectedness in the ASEAN-5 stock markets. The final peak coincides with the COVID-19 pandemic, which brought widespread lockdown measures impacting both equity and crude palm oil markets. Stock markets experienced volatility and declines due to pandemic-related uncertainties, while government restrictions on foreign labor created labor shortages affecting the crude palm oil market. These shared events led to increased connectedness between the equity and crude palm oil markets.

One limitation of the time-varying total return connectedness indices presented in Figure 13.3 is that they do not explicitly identify which market within the system dominates the transmission of shocks in the time domain and across the frequency bands. Additionally, while these indices capture the interconnectedness among the ASEAN-5 equity markets, our specific focus is on understanding the connectedness between the crude palm oil market and the equity market. To address this, we analyze the TO connectedness and FROM connectedness of the crude palm oil in Figures 13.4 and 13.5, respectively. These figures exhibit similar patterns, with peaks corresponding to significant events such as the GFC in 2008, the crude palm oil shock in 2012, the Chinese stock

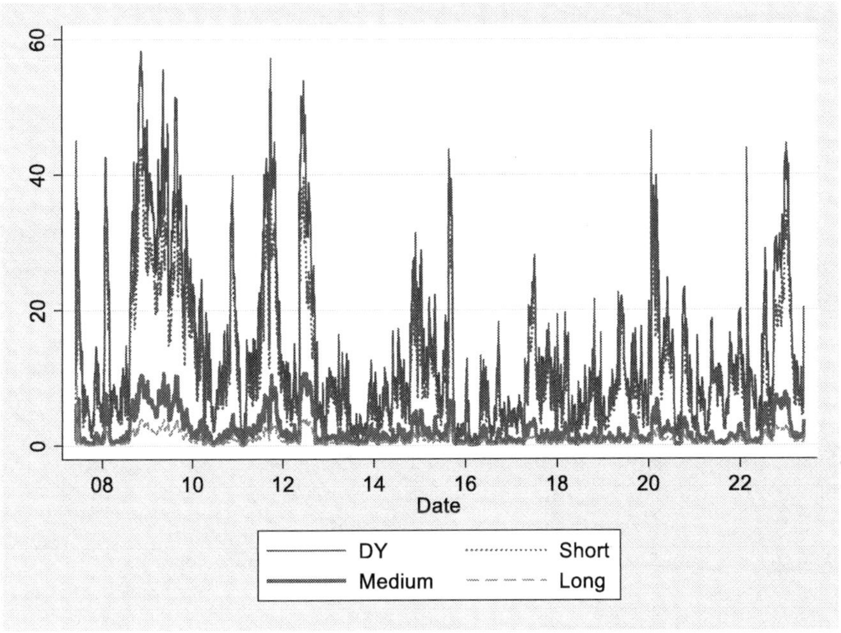

Figure 13.4 Time-varying TO connectedness: return (crude palm oil market)

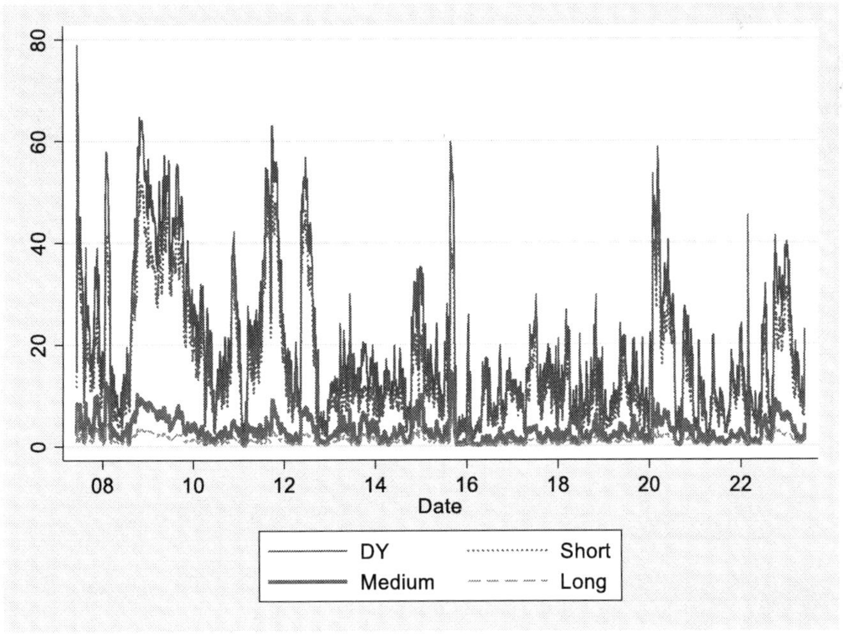

Figure 13.5 Time-varying FROM connectedness: return (crude palm oil market)

market crash in 2015, and the COVID-19 pandemic in 2020. Notably, we observe that the TO connectedness metric is lower than the FROM connectedness metric, indicating that the equity markets may exert a greater influence on the crude palm oil market compared to the reverse. This finding is consistent with the results presented in Table 13.2, which highlight the higher degree of influence from the equity markets on the crude palm oil market.

To further validate the conclusion regarding the greater influence of equity markets on the crude palm oil market, we analyze the time-varying net connectedness of the crude palm oil market. This analysis allows us to determine whether the crude palm oil market functions as a net transmitter or net recipient of connectedness within the system. By studying the time-varying net connectedness, we can gain insights into the directional flow of influence and ascertain whether the crude palm oil market is predominantly influenced by other markets or if it exerts more influence on them. As illustrated in Figure 13.6, the time-varying net return connectedness results exhibit typical characteristics of being time-varying and event-dependent. We can confirm that for the majority of the sample period, the crude palm oil market acts as a net recipient in the system. This suggests that the crude palm oil market is predominantly influenced by the ASEAN-5 equity markets in terms of return spillover transmission. This finding is consistent with previous studies by Zhang et al. (2020), Wu (2021), and Qi et al. (2022), which indicate that commodities can be easily impacted by other financial assets.

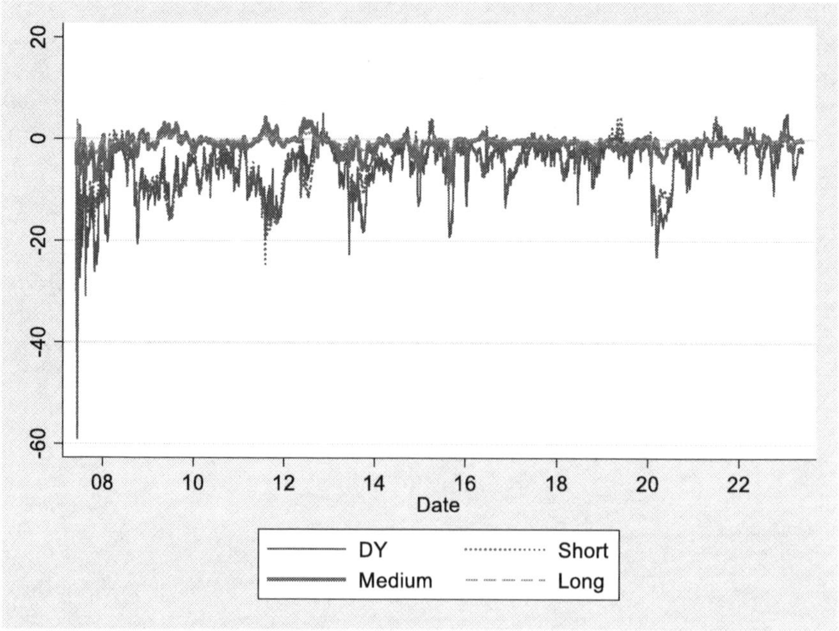

Figure 13.6 Time-varying NET connectedness: return (crude palm oil market)

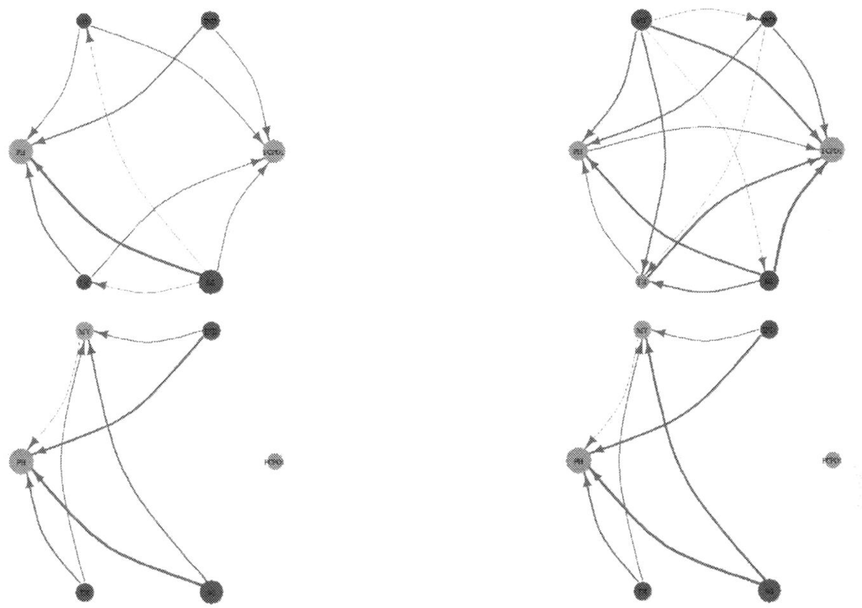

Figure 13.7 Directional net-pairwise connectedness network: return

Figure 13.7 presents a connectedness network that provides evidence of the directional net-pairwise connectedness from the crude palm oil market to individual equity markets. The visual representation in the network supports the conclusion that, in terms of overall connectedness, all the equity markets, except for the Philippines, have a significant impact on the crude palm oil market. This finding aligns with previous research by Maitra and Dawar (2019), Hernandez et al. (2021), and Cagli et al. (2023), confirming the existence of connectedness between commodity and stock markets. Notably, during the short term, all the equity markets exert a discernible influence on the crude palm oil market, corroborating the findings of Lin et al. (2021) on the presence of spillovers from the equity market to the commodity market in the short run. However, as we transition to the medium and long term, the connection between the crude palm oil market and the equity markets becomes insignificant. These observations shed light on the time-varying and time-dependent nature of the interconnections between these markets.

13.5.2 Connectedness Between Crude Palm Oil and ASEAN-5 Stock Volatilities

The investigation of volatility connectedness between crude palm oil and ASEAN-5 equities yields significant findings, as shown in Table 13.3. The overall connectedness index for volatility is found to be 58.89%, which is

Table 13.3 Volatility connectedness

	CPO	*Indonesia*	*Malaysia*	*The Philippines*	*Thailand*	*Singapore*	*FROM*
CPO	73.51(2.52)	5.4(0.26)	4.53(0.25)	4.27(0.22)	6.61(0.36)	5.68(0.3)	26.49(1.39)
	[5.97]{65.01}	[0.42]{4.72}	[0.42]{3.86}	[0.39]{3.66}	[0.58]{5.66}	[0.5]{4.88}	[2.32]{22.78}
Indonesia	22.8(0.75)	34.19(12.96)	8.62(2.66)	7.57(1.92)	15.68(4.04)	11.14(2.72)	65.81(12.1)
	[0.97]{21.08}	[6.25]{14.99}	[1.32]{4.63}	[1.29]{4.36}	[1.98]{9.66}	[1.72]{6.7}	[7.28]{46.44}
Malaysia	23.08(1.11)	9.2(2.69)	34.61(17)	7.39(2.47)	14.23(4.39)	11.49(3.76)	65.39(14.42)
	[0.92]{21.05}	[1.51]{5}	[6.67]{10.94}	[1.14]{3.78}	[1.48]{8.36}	[1.64]{6.08}	[6.69]{44.28}
The Philippines	23.32(0.71)	9.96(2.22)	7.59(2.23)	37.98(15.32)	11.54(2.88)	9.61(2.9)	62.02(10.95)
	[0.85]{21.75}	[1.84]{5.9}	[1.4]{3.96}	[9.25]{13.41}	[1.65]{7}	[1.53]{5.18}	[7.27]{43.8}
Thailand	22.04(0.95)	12.16(3.7)	10.24(3.66)	7.81(2.46)	36.08(13.52)	11.66(3.05)	63.92(13.83)
	[0.89]{20.21}	[1.93]{6.52}	[1.49]{5.08}	[1.23]{4.12}	[5.19]{17.37}	[1.54]{7.07}	[7.08]{43.01}
Singapore	24.9(1.16)	11.38(2.94)	9.82(2.81)	8.46(2.62)	15.14(3.25)	30.3(12.85)	69.7(12.79)
	[0.96]{22.78}	[1.64]{6.8}	[1.57]{5.44}	[1.28]{4.55}	[1.68]{10.21}	[5.05]{12.4}	[7.13]{49.78}
TO	116.15(4.68)	48.1(11.82)	40.8(11.62)	35.5(9.69)	63.21(14.93)	49.57(12.73)	353.33(65.48)
	[4.59]{106.87}	[7.34]{28.94}	[6.21]{22.98}	[5.34]{20.48}	[7.37]{40.9}	[6.92]{29.92}	[37.77]{250.08}
Inc.Own	189.65(7.2)	82.29(24.77)	75.41(28.62)	73.49(25.01)	99.29(28.46)	79.88(25.58)	TCI
	[10.56]{171.89}	[13.58]{43.93}	[12.88]{33.92}	[14.59]{33.89}	[12.56]{58.27}	[11.98]{42.32}	
NET	89.65(3.29)	−17.71(−0.28)	−24.59(−2.81)	−26.51(−1.25)	−0.71(1.1)	−20.12(−0.05)	58.89(10.91)
	[2.27]{84.09}	[0.06] {−17.49}	[−0.48]{−21.3}	[−1.94]{−23.32}	[0.29]{−2.11}	[−0.21]{−19.86}	[6.29]{41.68}

Note: See Table 13.2 notes.

lower than the return connectedness previously observed, indicating a higher level of interconnection in terms of the transmission of volatility. Further analysis of the volatility connectedness reveals that a substantial percentage of 41.68% is attributed to long-run causes, while the remaining 10.91% and 6.29% are attributed to short-run and medium-run factors, respectively. This underscores the importance of considering long-term temporal variations and interactions when assessing the level of volatility connectedness between different commodity and equity markets.

The volatility connectedness of crude palm oil is largely attributed to shock originating from itself (73.51%). As compared to the case of return connectedness, crude palm oil has a higher attributed shock to the equity market (26.49% vs. 19.15%). On the other hand, the volatility connectedness resulting from idiosyncratic shocks in each ASEAN-5 equity market is less than half of the total volatility connectedness. The specific values are as follows: Indonesia (34.19%), Malaysia (34.61%), the Philippines (37.98%), Thailand (36.08%), and Singapore (30.30%). These results align with the previous findings, indicating that the equity markets in the ASEAN-5 countries are more responsive to shocks originating from other markets within the system, compared to the crude palm oil market. This finding is consistent with the observations of Kang and Yoon (2019) and Rehman et al. (2023), who report that the equity market acts as the net recipient of spillover in the context of China.

When examining the total connectedness transmitted "TO" others, it is observed that the crude palm oil market contributes a relatively higher level of volatility connectedness to the overall system, contrasting the result found in return connectedness. However, a similar pattern to the finding of return connectedness is observed for the connectedness received "FROM" others, indicating that the ASEAN-5 equity markets receive a relatively higher level of volatility connectedness from other markets compared to the crude palm oil market, which receives less from other markets. In contrast to return connectedness, the crude palm oil market is found to be a net transmitter of volatility connectedness (as indicated by a positive net connectedness value of 89.65%), while the ASEAN-5 equity markets act as net receivers of volatility connectedness. Additionally, focusing on the values in the first row and column of Table 13.3, it is evident that the transmission of shocks from the crude palm oil market to the equity markets (116.15%) is more significant compared to the transmission of shocks from the equity markets to the crude palm oil market (26.49%). This suggests that the crude palm oil market may exert a greater influence on the equity market in terms of volatility connectedness, rather than the other way around.

Figure 13.8 depicts the time-varying total connectedness results for volatility, showcasing distinct patterns compared to the time-varying total return connectedness results in Figure 13.3. In contrast to return connectedness, which primarily stems from short-run influences, volatility connectedness

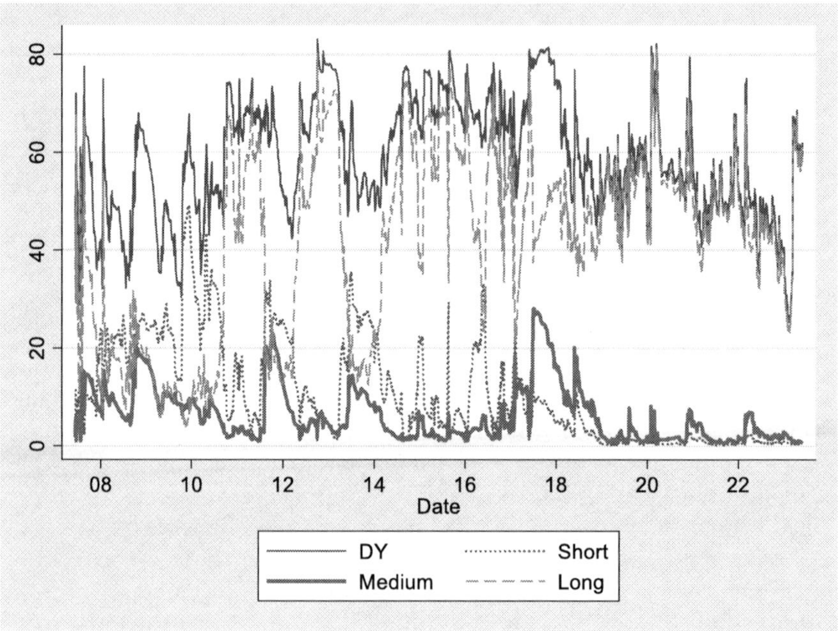

Figure 13.8 Time-varying total connectedness: volatility

is driven by both short- and long-run factors. This suggests that analyzing volatility can provide valuable insights to investors seeking to make decisions regarding asset diversification between crude palm oil and equity markets, in both directions. Notably, both short- and long-run connectedness exhibit greater fluctuations compared to the return connectedness analysis. The total volatility connectedness ranges from approximately 25% to 80%, indicating a wide spectrum of interconnectedness levels throughout the sample period.

Based on Figure 13.8, the short-run volatility connectedness reaches its peak between the years 2009 and 2010, reaching approximately 50%. This period corresponds to a time when both the crude palm oil and equity markets were experiencing significant growth and positive performance. However, after the occurrence of the COVID-19 pandemic, the short-run volatility connectedness becomes less significant. One possible reason for this is the increased uncertainty and unpredictability of future market conditions, leading to a greater emphasis on long-run volatility connectedness. Similar to the return connectedness analysis, the total volatility connectedness exhibits peaks in 2012 and during the COVID-19 pandemic. These peaks are primarily driven by the long-run volatility connectedness component. These observations suggest that long-run factors have a more substantial influence on the overall volatility connectedness between the crude palm oil and equity markets during these significant events.

In the volatility analysis, we examine the TO connectedness and FROM connectedness of the crude palm oil market, as depicted in Figures 13.9 and 13.10, respectively. In contrast to the return connectedness analysis, these figures reveal a different trend, indicating that the shocks originating from the crude palm oil market to the equity market and vice versa are influenced by different events or factors. Notably, we observe that, for certain periods, the TO connectedness metric is higher than the FROM connectedness metric. This suggests that the crude palm oil market may exert a greater influence on the equity market compared to the reverse direction of influence.

Figure 13.11 presents the time-varying net volatility connectedness, shedding light on the directional flow of shock transmission between the crude palm oil market and the equity market. From 2011 to 2017, we observe that the crude palm oil market predominantly acts as a net transmitter of shocks to the equity market, with some exceptions during certain periods. This is supported by the finding in Lin et al. (2021) the presence of spillovers from commodity market to equity markets in the long run. One factor contributing to this trend is the structural changes that occurred in the crude palm oil market in 2012, which resulted in a reduced impact on the equity market. Moreover, during the COVID-19 pandemic, the equity market exerted a stronger influence on the crude palm oil market compared to being influenced by it. Furthermore, we find that both the transmission and receipt of shocks by the crude palm oil market are primarily driven by long-run connectedness,

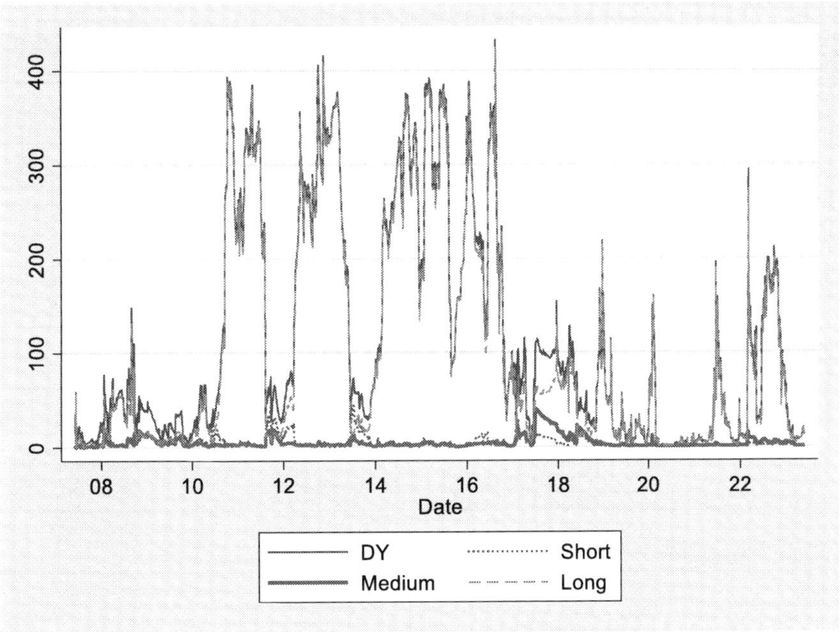

Figure 13.9 Time-varying TO connectedness: volatility (crude palm oil market)

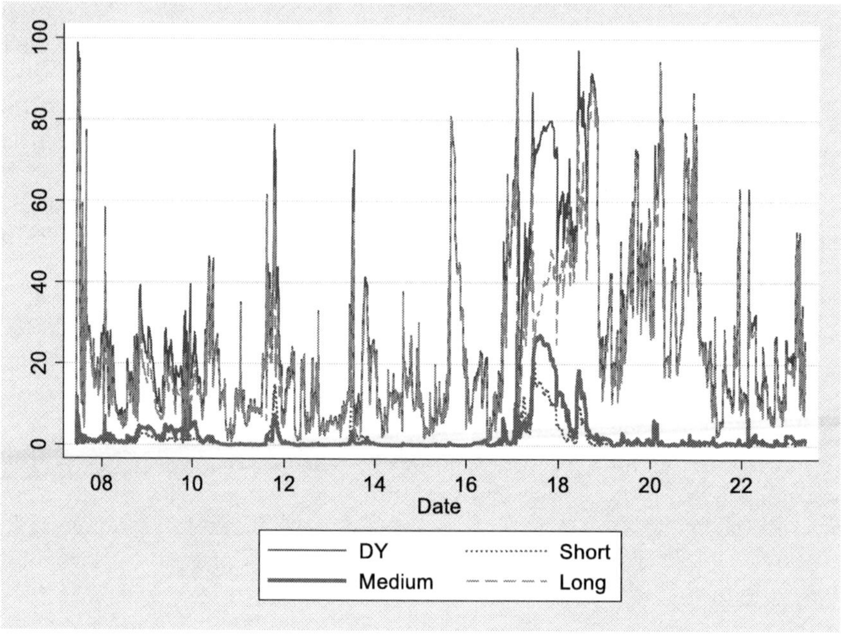

Figure 13.10 Time-varying FROM connectedness: volatility (crude palm oil market)

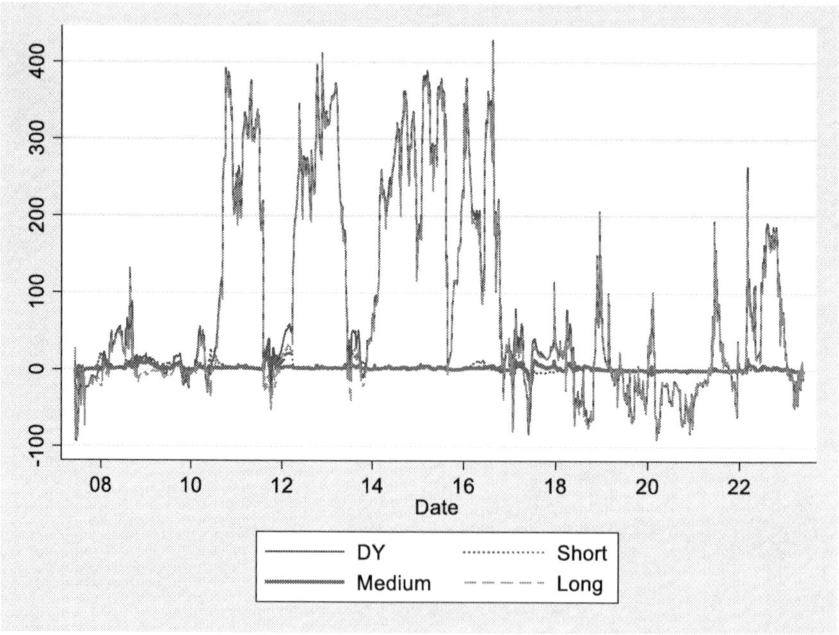

Figure 13.11 Time-varying NET connectedness: volatility (crude palm oil market)

as depicted in Figures 13.9–13.11. This indicates that the interconnectedness between the crude palm oil market and the equity market in terms of volatility is more pronounced in the long run.

Figure 13.12 showcases the directional net-pairwise connectedness network plot for volatility analysis. Notably, this analysis reveals contrasting results compared to the return connectedness analysis. In the volatility analysis, we observe that the crude palm oil market significantly affects the ASEAN-5 equity markets across all frequency domains (short-, medium-, and long-run). In terms of overall connectedness, there is no apparent interaction among the equity markets, with the influence primarily stemming from long-run connectedness. However, in the medium- and short-run connectedness, we observe the presence of interactions among the equity markets.

13.6 Conclusion

This study has provided valuable insights into the dynamics of return and volatility connectedness among the ASEAN-5 equity markets and the crude palm oil market. The findings indicate that short-run factors predominantly influence return connectedness, with the ASEAN-5 equity markets playing a significant role as both contributors and receivers of shock transmission. In terms of net return connectedness, equity markets of all studied ASEAN nations except for the Philippines are the net transmitters, while the crude

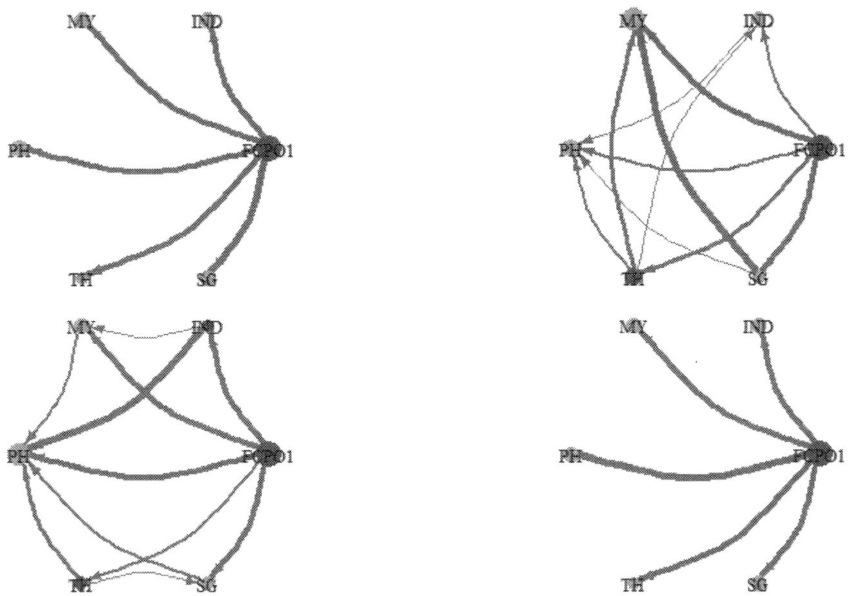

Figure 13.12 Directional net-pairwise connectedness network: volatility

palm oil market is the net receiver. On the other hand, volatility connectedness is primarily influenced by long-run factors, with the crude palm oil market acting as the net transmitter of shocks, while the ASEAN-5 equity markets serve as net receivers.

These time- and frequency-dependent characteristics highlight the importance of understanding the interplay between markets. It becomes crucial for investors to consider different factors – whether short-run, medium-run, or long-run – based on their specific investment goals and strategies, as the drivers behind return connectedness and volatility connectedness are distinct. This underscores the need for diversified approaches to risk management and investment decision-making, considering the different channels through which shock transmission propagates in these markets. Overall, this study contributes valuable knowledge for market participants and policymakers in navigating interconnected financial landscapes.

In future research, a promising direction would be to apply the methodology proposed in this chapter and to extend it to investigate higher-order connectedness, such as skewness and kurtosis, as explored by Cui and Maghyereh (2023) and Bouri (2023), where they have reported the existence of higher-order connectedness. This approach would provide a more comprehensive understanding of the volatility dynamics and risk transmission mechanisms between crude palm oil and ASEAN-5 equity markets, considering not only the mean and variance but also the asymmetry and fat-tailed characteristics of their interconnectedness. Furthermore, another valuable avenue for future investigation would involve exploring the lead–lag connectedness between crude palm oil and the ASEAN-5 stock markets across different frequency bands. By examining the timing and directionality of shock transmissions, this analysis would shed light on the causal relationships and dependencies between these markets. Understanding how the lead–lag relationships vary across different frequency ranges would enhance our insights into the dynamic interactions and interdependencies between crude palm oil and the ASEAN-5 equity markets under various market conditions.

Note

1 Source: Oil Seeds: World Markets and Trade, Global Oil Seeds Report, US Department of Agriculture, January 2023.

References

Ab Rahman, A. K., Abdullah, R., Balu, N., & Shariff, F. M. (2013). The impact of La Niña and El Niño events on crude palm oil prices: An econometric analysis. *Oil Palm Industry Economic Journal*, *13*, 38–51.

Akyildirim, E., Cepni, O., Pham, L., & Uddin, G. S. (2022). How connected is the agricultural commodity market to the news-based investor sentiment? *Energy Economics*, *113*, 106174.

Antonakakis, N., Chatziantoniou, I., & Gabauer, D. (2020). Refined measures of time varying connectedness based on time-varying parameter vector autoregressions. *Journal of Risk and Financial Management*, *13*(4), 84.

Babar, M., Ahmad, H., & Yousaf, I. (2023). Returns and volatility spillover between agricultural commodities and emerging stock markets: New evidence from COVID-19 and Russian-Ukrainian war. *International Journal of Emerging Markets*. https://doi.org/10.1108/IJOEM-02-2022-0226

Baruník, J., & Křehlík, T. (2018). Measuring the frequency time varyings of financial connectedness and systemic risk. *Journal of Financial Econometrics*, *16*(2), 271–296.

Billah, M., Balli, F., & Hoxha, I. (2023). Extreme connectedness of agri-commodities with stock markets and its determinants. *Global Finance Journal*, *56*, 100824.

Bossman, A., & Agyei, S. K. (2022). Interdependence structure of global commodity classes and African equity markets: A vector wavelet coherence analysis. *Resources Policy*, *79*, 103039.

Bouri, E. (2023). Spillovers in the joint system of conditional higher-order moments: US evidence from green energy, brown energy, and technology stocks. *Renewable Energy*, *210*, 507–523.

Cagli, E. C., Mandaci, P. E., & Taskin, D. (2023). The volatility connectedness between agricultural commodity and agri businesses: Evidence from time-varying extended joint approach. *Finance Research Letters*, *52*, 103555.

CEIC. (n.d.). *ASEAN stock markets*. Retrieved June 1, 2023, from https://info.ceicdata.com/our-insights-articles-asean-stock-markets

Chandrarin, G., Sohag, K., Cahyaningsih, D. S., Yuniawan, D., & Herdhayinta, H. (2022). The response of exchange rate to coal price, palm oil price, and inflation in Indonesia: Tail dependence analysis. *Resources Policy*, *77*, 102750.

Chang, C. L., & Fang, M. (2022). The connectedness between natural resource commodities and stock market indices: Evidence from the Chinese economy. *Resources Policy*, *78*, 102841.

Chatziantoniou, I., Gabauer, D., & Gupta, R. (2021). *Integration and risk transmission in the market for crude oil: A time-varying parameter frequency connectedness approach* (Working Paper Series). University of Pretoria Department of Economics.

Cui, J., & Maghyereh, A. (2023). Time-frequency dependence and connectedness among global oil markets: Fresh evidence from higher-order moment perspective. *Journal of Commodity Markets*, *30*, 100323.

Diebold, F. X., & Yilmaz, K. (2012). Better to give than to receive: Predictive directional measurement of volatility spillovers. *International Journal of forecasting*, *28*(1), 57–66.

Diebold, F. X., & Yılmaz, K. (2014). On the network topology of variance decompositions: Measuring the connectedness of financial firms. *Journal of econometrics*, *182*(1), 119–134.

Fasanya, I., & Akinbowale, S. (2019). Modelling the return and volatility spillovers of crude oil and food prices in Nigeria. *Energy*, *169*, 186–205.

Garcia-Jorcano, L., & Sanchis-Marco, L. (2022). Spillover effects between commodity and stock markets: A SDSES approach. *Resources Policy*, *79*, 102926.

Guhathakurta, K., Dash, S. R., & Maitra, D. (2020). Period specific volatility spillover based connectedness between oil and other commodity prices and their portfolio implications. *Energy Economics*, *85*, 104566.

Hernandez, J. A., Kang, S. H., & Yoon, S. M. (2021). Spillovers and portfolio optimization of agricultural commodity and global equity markets. *Applied Economics*, *53*(12), 1326–1341.

Jarque, C. M., & Bera, A. K. (1987). A test for normality of observations and regression residuals. *International Statistical Review/Revue Internationale de Statistique*, 163–172.

Kang, S. H., & Yoon, S. M. (2019). Financial crises and time varying spillovers among Chinese stock and commodity futures markets. *Physica A: Statistical Mechanics and its Applications*, *531*, 121776.

Li, R., Li, S., Yuan, D., Chen, H., & Xiang, S. (2023). Spillover effect of economic policy uncertainty on the stock market in the post-epidemic era. *The North American Journal of Economics and Finance*, *64*, 101846.

Lim, K. P., Goh, K. L., & Chong, C. S. (2014). The effects of global commodity prices on ASEAN-5 Stock Markets. *Rangsit Journal of Social Sciences and Humanities*, *8*(2), 96–108.

Lin, L., Zhou, Z., Jiang, Y., & Ou, Y. (2021). Risk spillovers and hedge strategies between global crude oil markets and stock markets: Do regime switching processes combining long memory and asymmetry matter? *The North American Journal of Economics and Finance*, *57*, 101398.

Luo, J., & Ji, Q. (2018). High-frequency volatility connectedness between the US crude oil market and China's agricultural commodity markets. *Energy Economics*, *76*, 424–438.

Maitra, D., & Dawar, V. (2019). Return and volatility spillover among commodity futures, stock market and exchange rate: Evidence from India. *Global Business Review*, *20*(1), 214–237.

Maitra, D., Guhathakurta, K., & Kang, S. H. (2021). The good, the bad and the ugly relation between oil and commodities: An analysis of asymmetric volatility connectedness and portfolio implications. *Energy Economics*, *94*, 105061.

Mensi, W., Al Rababa'a, A. R., Alomari, M., Vo, X. V., & Kang, S. H. (2022). Time varying frequency volatility spillovers and connectedness between strategic commodity and stock markets: US-based sectoral analysis. *Resources Policy*, *79*, 102976.

Mensi, W., Shafiullah, M., Vo, X. V., & Kang, S. H. (2021). Volatility spillovers between strategic commodity futures and stock markets and portfolio implications: Evidence from developed and emerging economies. *Resources Policy*, *71*, 102002.

Mensi, W., Vo, X. V., & Kang, S. H. (2021). Time and frequency connectedness and network across the precious metal and stock markets: Evidence from top precious metal importers and exporters. *Resources Policy*, *72*, 102054.

Niu, H., & Hu, Z. (2021). Information transmission and entropy-based network between Chinese stock market and commodity futures market. *Resources Policy*, *74*, 102294.

Qi, H., Ma, L., Peng, P., Chen, H., & Li, K. (2022). Time varying connectedness between clean energy stock markets and energy commodity markets during times of COVID-19: Empirical evidence from China. *Resources Policy*, *79*, 103094.

Rehman, M. U., Vo, X. V., Ko, H. U., Ahmad, N., & Kang, S. H. (2023). Quantile connectedness between Chinese stock and commodity futures markets. *Research in International Business and Finance*, *64*, 101810.

Ritchie, H., & Roser, M. (2021, February 9). Forests and deforestation. *Our World in Data*. https://ourworldindata.org/palm-oil#citation

Wen, F., Cao, J., Liu, Z., & Wang, X. (2021). Time varying volatility spillovers and investment strategies between the Chinese stock market and commodity markets. *International Review of Financial Analysis*, *76*, 101772.

Wu, B. B. (2021). The time varyings of oil on China's commodity sectors: What can we learn from a quantile perspective? *Journal of Commodity Markets*, *23*, 100158.

Yeap, X. W., & Lean, H. H. (2022). Trading activities and the volatility of return on Malaysian crude palm oil futures. *Journal of Risk and Financial Management*, *15*(1), 34.

Zhang, H., Cai, G., & Yang, D. (2020). The impact of oil price shocks on clean energy stocks: Fresh evidence from multi-scale perspective. *Energy*, *196*, 117099.

14 Green Finance, Carbon Emission, and Economic Development in the Selected ASEAN Countries

Changtai Li and Bing Gong

14.1 Introduction

The ASEAN economies stand as the vanguards of rapid economic advancement within the Asian continent. This dynamic region comprises a conglomerate of nations, including Brunei, Burma, Cambodia, Indonesia, Laos, Malaysia, Myanmar, the Philippines, Singapore, Thailand, and Vietnam. Collectively, these nations command an impressive 8.58% share of global population growth, reflecting their substantial demographic impact. Beyond their demographic influence, the ASEAN bloc has wielded economic prowess, accounting for 7% of the global Gross Domestic Product (GDP) and an impressive 9% of global GDP growth over the preceding decade (2012–2022). If envisaged as a singular economic entity, it would ascend to the coveted position of the world's fifth-largest economy. This notable stature unequivocally underscores its profound significance on the international stage, portraying a force that commands attention and respect. Even amid the formidable challenges posed by the pandemic crisis, the ASEAN region has demonstrated commendable resilience. Notably, it has not only weathered the storm but also managed to augment its economic output, surpassing the levels observed prior to the onset of the COVID-19 pandemic. This remarkable feat serves as a testament to the region's robust economic framework, adaptive capabilities, and steadfast commitment to progress, all of which contribute to its enduring influence on the global economic landscape.

While the ASEAN region showcases immense potential for economic development, it simultaneously grapples with the distinction of being one of the world's most susceptible areas to the adversities of climate change. This vulnerability is compounded by the presence of some of the most greenhouse gas (GHG)-intensive economies globally. Thus, the region confronts a dual-faceted challenge concerning climate change. On one facet, it must adapt to the repercussions of climate change, primarily instigated by established GHG emitters, encompassing advanced economies and significant emerging economies. On the other facet, it must recalibrate its developmental strategies to curtail its own contributions to the global warming phenomenon (Prakash, 2018). Within this context, the concept of green finance has gained

DOI: 10.4324/9781003349204-14

substantial traction, assuming a pivotal role in both academic discourse and policy-oriented research. Green finance, broadly defined as the allocation and utilization of financial resources to support environmentally protective endeavors while ensuring equitable returns for investors or lenders, has surged in significance (Berensmann & Lindenberg, 2019; Ozili, 2021). The surge of interest in this domain stems from its potential to act as a catalytic instrument for engendering green transitions on a global scale, a notion that extends its relevance to regions such as Southeast Asia. This transition, in essence, holds the promise of harmonizing sustainable economic progress with the reduction of GHG emissions. Evidently, scholarly and pragmatic contemplations on this topic are already underway. Discourses by Zhou et al. (2020) and Afzal et al. (2022) reflect this burgeoning dialogue, further underscoring the significance of green finance as a prospective avenue for steering the ASEAN region and the broader global community towards a trajectory that reconciles environmental preservation with continued socioeconomic advancement.

As succinctly outlined in the literature review conducted by Ozili (2022), recent years have borne witness to the emergence of seven prominent research trajectories within the domain of green finance. These directions encompass an array of critical perspectives, including (1) the identification and articulation of challenges intrinsic to green finance; (2) the evolutionary journey of green finance; (3) the active engagement of the private sector in the realm of green finance; (4) the influential role undertaken by central banks in advancing green finance initiatives; (5) the symbiotic role played by green finance in realizing the United Nations' sustainable development goals; (6) the discernible contributions of private sector involvement in green finance; and (7) the intricate interplay between green finance and a spectrum of alternative financial instruments. Furthermore, as the landscape of green finance advances in tandem with the maturation of corresponding market dynamics and policy frameworks, empirical investigations have surged. In particular, regions such as China and Europe have yielded enriched market data pertaining to green finance instruments, thereby fostering a fertile ground for quantitative exploration.

Noteworthy instances of such research endeavors include the work of Li et al. (2021), who harnessed comprehensive data spanning 2001–2019 across China's provinces to scrutinize the intricate influence mechanisms underpinning the relationship between green finance and the evolution of a low-carbon economy. The findings conclusively underscored the significant role of green finance in nurturing China's transition toward a low-carbon economic paradigm. Parallelly, the exploration by Lin et al. (2023), utilizing a similar dataset albeit with nuanced temporal parameters, yielded empirical validation of the transformative potential of green finance. The study compellingly showcased how the development of green finance catalytically diminishes the proportion of coal thermal power generation within China, thereby steering the power generation sector toward a trajectory characterized by low-carbon practices. Within the context of China, Zhou et al. (2020) embarked on a journey to discern the ramifications of green finance on the dual dimensions of economic development and environmental quality. Their robust model illuminated a positive nexus between green finance and economic betterment, further unveiling the varied impact on environmental quality, contingent upon distinct levels of economic advancement. Conversely, Afzal et al. (2022) harnessed an expansive dataset encompassing 40 European countries over a span spanning 1990–2019. Their empirical exploration sought to unravel the intricate correlation between (green) financial development and the ominous specter of environmental degradation, exemplified by CO_2 emissions. Their research yielded a compelling revelation of a negative relationship between financial development and environmental deterioration, thereby highlighting the pivotal role assumed by potent institutional frameworks and judicious green finance policies in ameliorating environmental degradation.

Recent years have borne witness to a burgeoning body of research delving into the pivotal role of green finance within the context of Southeast Asia. Notably, an escalating volume of studies has concentrated on empirically scrutinizing the intricate interplay between green finance and its impact on both energy efficiency and the reduction of carbon emissions across the region. Quang and Thao (2022) embarked on a comprehensive exploration, employing a two-stage generalized method of moments (GMM) system model, which unfolded over a quarterly timeframe spanning 2017–2020. Their meticulous analysis shed light on the catalytic effect of green finance in propelling energy efficiency within the ASEAN framework. Remarkably, their findings unveiled a notable trend: for every 1% increase in the volume of green bonds issued within the ASEAN economies, there ensued a corresponding reduction of 0.42% in energy intensity. Turning to a distinct facet, Sadiq et al. (2023) embarked on an investigation that delved into the intricate relationships binding green finance, eco-innovation, creativity, and their combined impact on the broader ambit of sustainable development across ASEAN nations. Their study illuminated a salient thread: these variables collectively exhibit positive associations with the overarching goals of sustainable development, proxied by the discernible reduction in CO_2 emissions. Similarly, Jahanger et al. (2023) traversed similar terrain, focusing on the intertwining realms of green finance, clean energy, and their collective influence on CO_2 emissions, particularly in the long-term trajectory. Their empirical analysis uncovered a noteworthy revelation: substantial, positive shocks emanating from green finance and clean energy exerted a commendable, suppressive influence on CO_2 emissions within an extended temporal context. Expanding the investigative horizon, Kamran et al. (2020) ventured into an examination of a distinct nexus: the ramifications of climate change on the stability of banking systems within select ASEAN nations. Their intricate estimates generated a compelling insight: the specter of climate change held a notably adverse impact on the stability of banks in the chosen ASEAN countries, a trend that was effectively counterbalanced by the ameliorative effects of green finance and renewable energy initiatives. This discernible moderation effect, engendered by green finance and renewable energy interventions, not only curtailed the deleterious influence of climate change but also exerted a constructive, bolstering impact on the stability of the banking sector.

In general, the exploration of green finance's role within the ASEAN context remains in its nascent and burgeoning phases. Existing research predominantly pivot around the empirical examination of the effects of green finance on the broader spectrum of environmental sustainability. However, the avenue for further investigation extends beyond this horizon, beckoning researchers to unravel green finance's multifaceted impact across various dimensions within the region. This study endeavors to bridge a noticeable gap within the scientific literature, thereby illuminating the path forward. At its core, this study embarks on a mission to address pivotal questions that have hitherto remained unanswered. The overarching aim is to illuminate the nexus between green finance and the sustainable economic development of a select group of ASEAN countries. It further endeavors to probe whether green finance serves as a catalytic instrument in the realm of green technology innovation and carbon emission reduction within the ASEAN economies. Furthermore, an underlying strand of investigation seeks to determine to what extent the evidence derived from this study effectively addresses existing gaps in prevailing policy frameworks.

14.2 Status and Development of Green Finance of the Selected ASEAN Countries

14.2.1 Regional Development

Since the first PHP 10.7 billion (US$226 million) green bond issued by the Philippines' AP Renewables in February 2016, the ASEAN green finance market has grown rapidly with participants with different background entering the market, and more prolific financial products being offered. According to *ASEAN Sustainable Finance State of the Market 2022* published by Climate Bond Initiative (CBI), the cumulative green debt volume issued in ASEAN-6 countries[1] between 2016 and 2022 reached US$51.2 billion, generated over 200-fold growth since debut of the market in 2016 (CBI, 2022). Tailwind of green finance also stimulated strong growth of social and sustainable (S&S) finance in the region, helping ASEAN formulate more comprehensive financial markets to achieve sustainable goals. For instance, the cumulative S&S bonds issued by Thailand, the Philippines and Malaysia, the region's top three S&S bonds issuers, reached US$19.9 billion (CBI, 2022), growing from virtually none in 2017. Meanwhile, despite impressive growth and expansion in recent years, ASEAN sustainable finance markets are still very small and experienced uneven development. In 2021, total share of sustainable debt markets in the region's five developing countries, Malaysia, Thailand,

Indonesia, the Philippines, and Vietnam, only accounted for 2.5% of their total debts (World Bank, 2022). This means ASEAN still has much untapped potential to achieve strong growth in the sphere.

Green debt dominates the ASEAN green finance markets, with green bond and green loan being the major financial instrument categories, while green Sukuk occupying a significant portion of green bond issuance. According to data published and summarized by CBI,[2] green debt issuance by ASEAN-6 countries grew more than threefold between 2018 and 2022 (from US$4.1 billion to US$12.8 billion), with cumulative green debt volume in the region reaching US$51.2 billion at the end of 2022 (Figure 14.1). In 2020, green bond and green loan, respectively, composited 54% and 43% of all green financial instruments in ASEAN-6 countries. The most popular instruments issued in the region in the year were: plain green loans (25% of all instruments), senior unsecured green bonds (25% of all instruments) and green Sukuk (19% of all instruments) (CBI, 2020). In 2022, green loans remained to be very popular green financial instruments in ASEAN, suggesting banks' prominent role in driving green transition of the region (CBI, 2022). On the other side, green Sukuk instruments were only issued in Indonesia and Malaysia over the past years.

Apart from issuance volume, ASEAN green debt market also saw a growing number of issuers with more diversified background over the past years. Per data from CBI, the number of green debt issuers grew more than threefold from 2018 to 2021 (15 issuers to 48 issuers). Despite the number of issuers declined to 24 in 2022 due to tightening of global financial conditions, cumulative number of issuers still increased from 39 in 2019 to 117 in 2022, showing significant growth. Besides, background of the issuers became more diversified and their issuance volume increased significantly over the past years. For instance, in 2018, financial corporates, sovereigns, and nonfinancial corporates represented almost all green debt issuance volume in

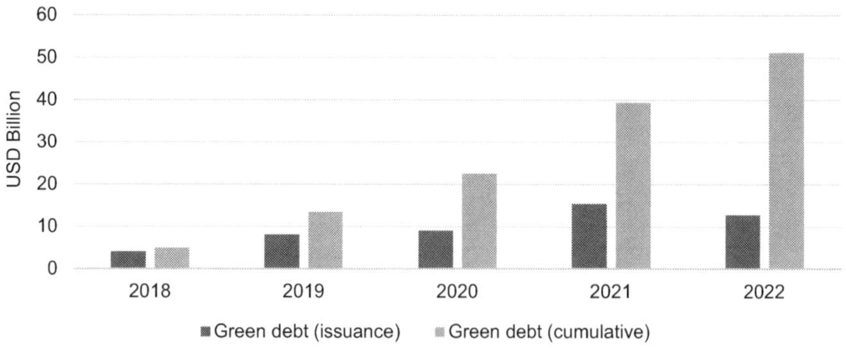

Figure 14.1 ASEAN-6 countries green debt volume

Source: CBI, calculated by the authors

the year; while in 2021, non-financial corporates, financial corporates, government-backed entities and sovereigns were major groups of issuers (CBI, 2021). Additionally, despite the total number of green debt issuers in the region shrunk almost by half in 2022 versus 2021, the total issuance volume decreased only by 25%, suggesting the average volume per issuer was significantly higher in 2022 than in 2021 (CBI, 2022).

Destinations of funds raised through green finance in ASEAN remained largely unchanged over the past years, with buildings and energy sectors consistently absorbing over 65% of all raised funds (Figure 14.2). In 2022, buildings and energy accounted for almost 80% of overall green finance fund allocations in the region. Meanwhile, major currency underlying ASEAN green bonds shifted from hard currencies outside the region (e.g., USD) to local currencies within the region, suggesting change of issuer and investor compositions. For instance, in 2018, 54% of ASEAN green debt volume was issued in foreign currencies (49% in USD and 5% in GBP), while the figure dropped to only 20% in 2022 (17% in USD) (CBI, 2018, 2022). Local currencies in each of the ASEAN-6 countries became more preferred in green debt issuance.

In summary, ASEAN green finance markets have grown rapidly and achieved fast development since 2016. Green debt denominated the markets, and green bond and green loan realized balanced development and importance in the region. Number of green debt issuers achieved fast growth from 2018 to 2021. Although the number experienced slight retreat in 2022 due to global financial tightening, the average volume per issuer/issuance kept growing from 2018 to 2022. In the meantime, the region's green finance markets became more mature over the years, with issuers' background more diversified, and local currencies' share larger. Yet ASEAN's green finance markets are still quite small, and destinations of the raised funds overly concentrated in building and energy sectors. This signals that the region's markets still have much potential for further development.

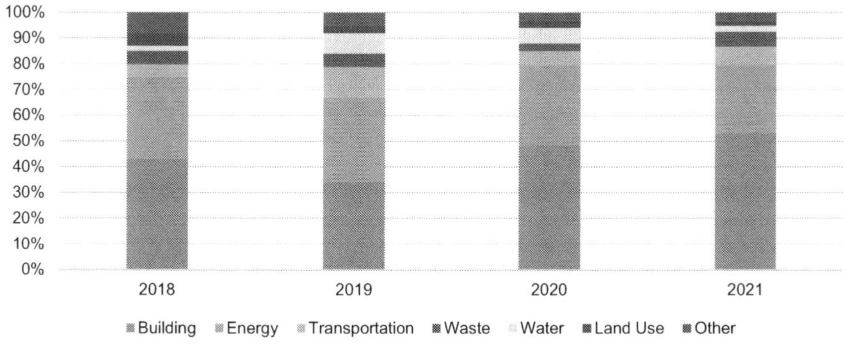

Figure 14.2 ASEAN-6 countries green finance fund destinations

Source: CBI, calculated by the authors

14.2.2 Country Development

Despite all of the selected countries' (Singapore, Malaysia, Thailand, Indonesia, and Vietnam) green finance markets achieved rapid growth other the past years, their green finance development showed structural differences, and development in the green finance markets of the respective countries is uneven.

Singapore is ASEAN's green finance hub and champion in green lending. It has developed the largest and broadest green and sustainable markets in the region. The country's green debt market volume increased drastically from US$1.76 billion issuance in 2018 to US$12 billion issuance in 2021 (CBI, 2018, 2021). By 2022, the country's 127 issuers had raised cumulatively US$81 billion from green, social, and sustainable (GSS) debt markets (CBI, 2022). Buildings sector is consistently the largest destination for funds raised in green finance over the years, absorbing nearly 70% of all funds in 2021 and 2022, according to CBI data. Due to financing preference of the sector, green loan is the most popular green finance instrument of the country, with green bond's share slightly lower.

Malaysia has developed a broad market for GSS financial instruments, and the overall market size grew from less than US$0.5 billion in 2021 to over US$2 billion in 2021 (CBI, 2022). However, the country's issuers appeared to prefer financial instruments in the broader "sustainability" category instead of the "green" category. For instance, in 2021, 51% of green, social, and sustainable financial instruments of the country were under sustainability label, while only 29% instruments were green debts; in 2022, the country did not issue any green debt (CBI, 2021, 2022). Noticeably, all green debts issued in Malaysia since 2015 were under green Sukuk category. And the country established the Green Sustainable and Responsible Investment (SRI) Sukuk Grant Scheme in 2018, an incentive structure to support green bond issuance.

Similar to Malaysia, sustainable finance is the largest market of Thailand's GSS finance markets, with green finance lagging behind. Different from other selected ASEAN countries, Thailand's green finance market development has been relatively steady since 2019. The market's issuance volume only increased slightly from 2019 to 2021, and decreased slightly in 2022 due to global tightening financial conditions, and green finance issuance volume had never passed US$1 billion over the years. According to CBI data, green bonds are the most popular green finance instrument in Thailand, while the share of green loans is much lower.

In terms of cumulative volume, Indonesia's green finance market is the second largest among the selected five ASEAN countries as of 2022. Green Sukuk dominates Indonesia's green finance market, with green loans far lagging behind. The country only had one green bond issuance in the past five years, which was in 2018. Different from other selected countries in the region, Indonesia's green finance issuance volume is dominated by sovereign transactions, which are in the form of green Sukuk. Cumulatively, the Republic of Indonesia issued US$5.49 billion green Sukuk from 2018 to 2022 (CBI, 2022). Despite the signals sent by Indonesia's government (through issuing green finance instruments), and despite various supportive policies released by the country's financial authorities, it appears that private corporates only had limited interests in participating in the market.

Finally, Vietnam has a smaller green finance market than that of Singapore and Indonesia, and its cumulative market volume is similar to those of Malaysia and Thailand. However, different from Malaysia and Thailand, green finance instruments dominate the GSS finance markets of Vietnam, and the country's green finance market enjoyed fast growth between 2019 and 2022. Green loan dominates Vietnam's green finance market. Vietnam's green finance market grew markedly in 2021, in which the issuance volume exceeded US$1 billion, almost three times of the volume in 2020. Despite the issuance volume dropped in 2022 due to global financial tightening, it is around two times of the volume in 2020.

14.2.3 Green Finance Policy Development

Development of green finance policy and regulatory frameworks correlates development of green finance activities, as the frameworks could help establish fundamental financial infrastructure and clear rules in the sphere, which would in turn promote green finance activities in particular and sustainable finance activities in general.

ASEAN countries have made significant achievement in developing green and sustainable finance policy initiatives and frameworks in the past, in both regional and country levels. These policies are helpful in fostering market environment and generating growth of GSS finance markets across the region. Yet the region's policy development is still lagging behind the global frontier markets such as EU and China. Additionally, policy development exhibited uneven trend in the five selected countries of ASEAN, with Singapore in the leading position, Malaysia and Indonesia slightly lagging behind, Thailand lagged further, and Vietnam still in the planning and preparation stage in many fields (World Bank, 2022).

14.2.3.1 Development of Regional-Level Green Finance Policies

At the regional level, progresses have been made in developing standards and taxonomies, and most central banks and supervisors have started to examine climate-related financial risks and preparing to introduce green central banking policies (Volz, 2021).

Among them, ASEAN has made significant progress in developing regulations and policies in the region's capital markets. In 2017, the ASEAN Capital Market Forum (ACMF) issued the ASEAN Green Bonds Standards as an effort to cultivate the market and facilitate investment into green activities (ACMF, 2018). In 2018, ACMF also issued ASEAN Social Bonds Standards and ASEAN Sustainability Bonds Standards. Subsequently in 2020, the forum published the ACMF Roadmap for ASEAN Sustainable Capital Markets; in 2021, it published the ASEAN SDG Bond Toolkit; and in 2022, ACMF further issued the ASEAN Sustainable and Responsible Fund Standards (ASEAN SPFS). These policies and regulatory guidelines helped pave the foundation for promoting the issuance of GSS-related bonds in ASEAN and helped guide further development of the region's capital market in these spheres (Ariyapruchya & Volz, 2022).

Apart from capital market policy development, ASEAN had dedicated to developing the region's common green and sustainable finance taxonomy to serve as a common building block that enables an orderly transition and fosters sustainable finance adoption by ASEAN Member States (ASEAN Taxonomy Board, 2023). In March 2021, four ASEAN finance sectoral bodies, ACMF, ASEAN Insurance Regulator's Meeting (AIRM), ASEAN Senior Level Committee on Financial Regulation (SLC) and ASEAN Working Committee on Capital Market Development (WC-CMD), jointly established the ASEAN Taxonomy Board (ATB) to develop a science-based and inclusive sustainable finance taxonomy for the region. ATB published the first version of the taxonomy for public consultation in November 2021, which contains a principles-based framework designed to allow each member state's flexible adaption (ASEAN Taxonomy Board, 2021; Ariyapruchya & Volz, 2022). In June 2023, ATB published the second version of the taxonomy for public feedback.

In green central banking sphere, ASEAN central banks began to realize the importance of analyzing and managing climate and environment-related risks. In 2020, central banks and monetary authorities in the region published a collaborative report on the roles of ASEAN central banks in managing climate and environment-related risks, in which they analyzed potential threat of climate change to the region's economy and their responsibility in addressing sustainability-related issues (Anwar et al., 2020).

Finally, the region's central banks also engaged in developing an ASEAN Green Map to ensure a high-level perspective of actions and coordinated alignment across financial markets in the region (AFMGM, 2022).

14.2.3.2 Development of Country-Level Green Finance Policies

Green finance policies in different spheres have also been developed in each of the five selected ASEAN countries. Yet these countries' policies exhibited uneven progress and trend.

Singapore, with the region's largest and broadest green finance market, has also developed the region's most comprehensive green finance policy framework. The country's policies expanded in all different spheres of green and/or sustainable finance, covering action plans (Singapore Green Finance Action

Plan), taxonomy (consultation papers published by Green Finance Industry Taskforce), information disclosure (Sustainability Reporting Guide released by Singapore Exchange), risk management (Guidelines on Environmental Risk Management for Banks/Issuers/Asset Managers released by Monetary Authority of Singapore [MAS]), and carbon price (Carbon Pricing Act of Singapore).

A distinct characteristics of Singapore's green finance policies is MAS's focus on setting up incentive policy schemes that stimulate development and expansion of the country's green finance markets. For instance, in as early as 2017, MAS introduced a Green Bond Grant Scheme and later expanded it to the world's first Sustainable Bond Grant Scheme, to encourage issuance of green financial products by compensating issuers' assessment and assurance service fees. In 2019, as part of MAS's Green Finance Action Plan, the authority set up a US$2 billion scheme that allocates funds to asset managers demonstrating commitment to green investment (BritCham & ICAEW, 2021).

Slightly lagging behind Singapore, Indonesia and Malaysia have also developed relatively comprehensive green finance policies covering various spheres. Indonesia is an earlier mover in developing green and sustainable finance policies. In as early as 2015, the country's financial regulator, Financial Services Authority of Indonesia (OJK) published its first Roadmap for Sustainable Finance in Indonesia (2015–2019). In information disclosure sphere, OJK in 2017 issued the Regulation of Financial Service Authority on Application of Sustainable Finance to Financial Services Institution, Issuer and Publicly Listed Company, in which it mandated all financial and publicly listed companies to publish sustainability reports by 2025 (OJK, 2017). In taxonomy sphere, OJK released the first edition of Indonesia's Green Taxonomy in 2022, a principle-based green taxonomy similar to the ASEAN taxonomy (World Bank and Institute of Finance and Sustainability, 2022). Additionally, similar to Singapore, Indonesia has put focus on developing green finance incentive schemes. For instance, OJK launched incentives to increase electric vehicle financing in 2020 (Ariyapruchya & Volz, 2022). And in 2021, Indonesia Law No. 7 introduced a carbon tax scheme on carbon emissions with negative impacts on the environment.

Malaysia has been active in introducing initiatives in multiple green finance policy dimensions. In 2019, the country's central bank, Bank Negara Malaysia (BNM) and its Securities Commission co-established the Joint Committee on Climate Change (JC3), which issued Sustainable and Responsible Investment Roadmap for the country. In 2020, BNM started pilot implementation of a Climate Change and Principles-Based Taxonomy, and the formal taxonomy was published in 2021 (BNM, 2021). In 2022, JC3 released a TCFD application guide which outlines key recommendations on adaptation of TCFD information disclosure recommendations by the country's financial industry (JC3, 2022). In 2022, BNM launched a Low Carbon Transition Facility as an incentive scheme to support SMEs in adopting sustainable and low carbon practices. Additionally, Malaysia is a pioneer in integrating green and sustainable finance in to Islamic finance. In 2015 and 2017, the country, respectively, launched the first sustainable Sukuk and the first green Sukuk of the world (Ariyapruchya & Volz, 2022).

Thailand's green finance policy development is relatively lagged behind those of Indonesia and Malaysia, and the country's policy scope is narrower than the other ones. In information disclosure sphere, the Stock Exchange of Thailand (SET) published mandatory ESG disclosure requirements for listed companies, which included social and environmental impact. But regarding green finance disclosure frameworks, Thai financial regulators have not revealed any plans endorsing TCFD recommendations (World Bank and Institute of Finance and Sustainability, 2022). In taxonomy sphere, Bank of Thailand (BOT) and Thailand's Securities and Exchange Commission (SEC) just published the draft of first phase of Thai green finance taxonomy for public consultation in June 2023, which primarily focuses on economic activities relating to the energy and transportation sectors (BOT and SEC, 2023).

Vietnam has the weakest green finance policy framework among the five selected ASEAN countries, and many green finance policies of the country are still under planning or developing stage. The country's existing policies mainly concentrate in information disclosure sphere. In as early as 2013, Vietnam's State Securities Commission (SSC) issued the Sustainability Reporting Handbook for Vietnamese Companies, encouraging companies to start sustainability disclosures on "report or explain basis". In 2016, SSC and the International Finance Corporation (IFC) published the Environment and Social Disclosure Guide, which was developed based on GRI standards (World Bank and Institute of Finance and Sustainability, 2022). In 2020, Vietnam's Ministry of Finance issued circular providing guidelines on disclosure of information on the securities market, putting mandatory ESG reporting requirements on pubic and listed companies.

14.3 CO_2 Emissions and Economic Development of the Selected ASEAN Countries

14.3.1 CO_2 Emissions

Based on calculation of the data from the Emissions Database for Global Atmospheric Research (EDGAR) published by European Commission, total CO_2 emissions from the selected ASEAN-5 countries increased by over 250% during the 30-year period between 1992 and 2021, from 424 million tons to over 1,503 million tons. The region's emissions peaked in 2019 at 1,585 million tons and then gradually decreased in the following years. Emissions in 2021 rebounded slightly from those in 2020, but still below the pre-pandemic level. Power industry is the largest emitter in the region, both in absolute volume and in ratio. Emissions from the sector grew from 100.53 million tons (23.7% of total emissions) in 1992 to 590 million tons in 2021, accounting for nearly 40% total emissions in the region. Noticeably, emissions from the buildings sector, which absorbed large volume of green finance funds in the past years, were in steady decline trend after 2004. In 2021, the sector's total emissions were 57 million tons, only around 75% of its emissions in 2004.

At the country level, all of the selected countries exhibited the similar CO_2 emission trend as the regional aggregate. Yet the growth rate and rankings (by volume) of their emissions exhibited uneven pattern. Among them, Singapore's emissions only grew by 70% during the 30-year period, from 34 million tons to 58 million tons, while Vietnam's emissions grew strongly by 1380%, from 22 million tons to 321 million tons. Indonesia has consistently been the region's largest CO_2 emitter, and it contributed over 40% emissions of the region during the 30-year period. In 2021, Vietnam is the second largest CO_2 emitter in the region, while it was the smallest one back to 1992.

Power sector accounted for the largest share of CO_2 emissions in all of the five countries in 2021: 39% in Singapore, 45% in Malaysia, 33% in Thailand, 35% in Indonesia, and 48% in Vietnam, suggesting they still have much potential to reduce emissions through power transition to renewable energies. Transportation sector also accounted for large share in total emissions of Malaysia and Thailand, while the sector's emission contribution in other three countries are relatively moderate.

The five countries exhibited different patterns on CO_2 emissions per capita level. Singapore's emissions per capita peaked in 1994 (at 12.3 tons per capita) and then gradually declined by over 20% to 9.7 tons per capita in 2021. Despite that, Singapore still has the highest emissions per capita in the region, around 4.5 times larger than the figure in Indonesia, which has the lowest emissions per capita (2.2 tons) in 2021. Malaysia, Thailand, Indonesia, and Vietnam's emissions per capita all peaked in 2019 and became flattened in 2020 and 2021 (Figure 14.3).

14.3.2 Economic Development

Overall economic development of the selected five ASEAN countries, measured by GDP, has the similar pattern as their CO_2 emissions in the 30-year period from 1992 to 2021. In fact, the correlation coefficients of the region's aggregate CO_2 emissions during the period and aggregate GDP, at current and constant prices, are respectively 0.962 and 0.987, suggesting the region's economy relies much on carbon-emitting industries.

In current prices, based on data released by the World Bank,[3] the five countries' aggregate GDP increased by 758% between 1992 and 2021, from US$361 billion to US$3,096 billion; and in constant prices,[4] the aggregate GDP increased by 286%, from US$698 billion to 2,697 billion. Large difference between current and constant-price GDPs is partly due to relatively high inflation of some of the countries during the period. Indonesia is the region's largest economy and represented over 40% of the region's economic output in 2021, both in current and constant dollar terms. GDPs of the other four selected countries are at similar sizes in 2021. On average, the region

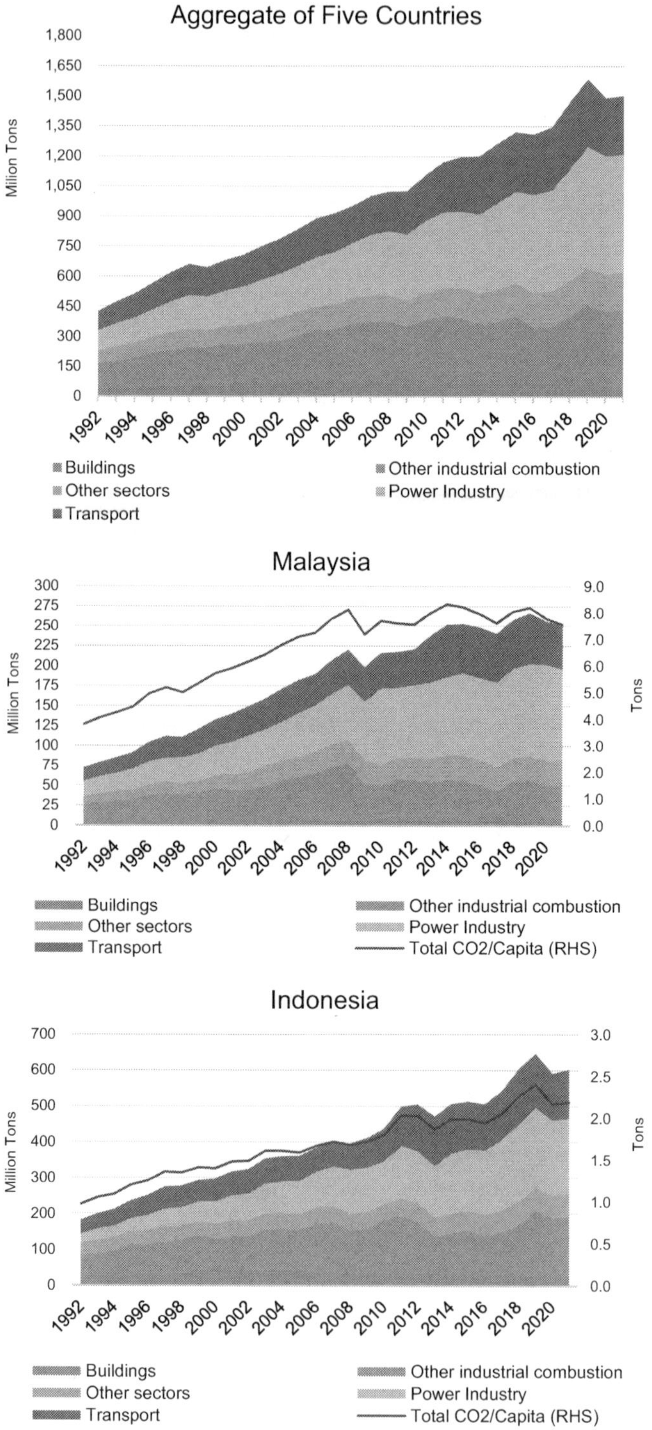

Figure 14.3 CO_2 emissions of the selected ASEAN countries

Source: EDGAR, calculated by the authors

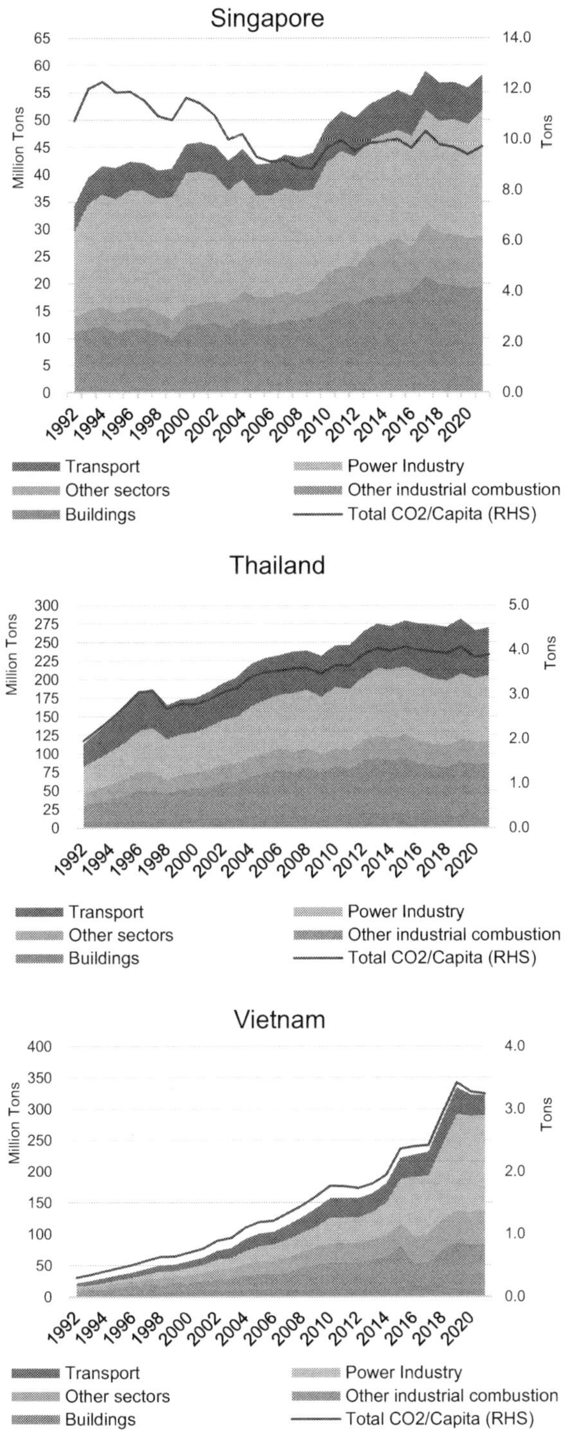

Figure 14.3 (Continued)

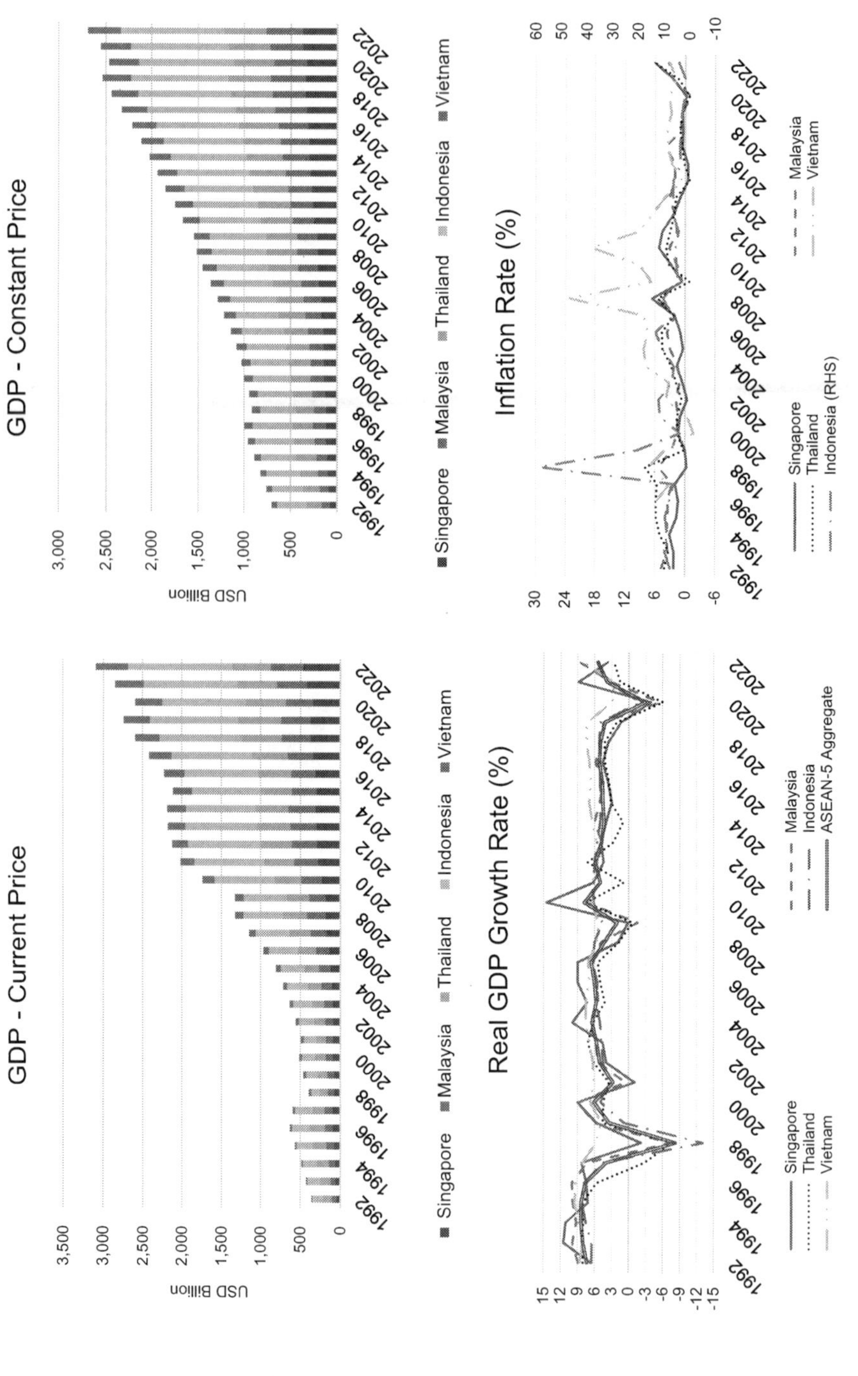

Figure 14.4 Economic growth of the selected ASEAN countries

Source: World Bank, calculated by the authors

achieved 4.75% real annual GDP growth rate during the 30-year period, with significant growth contraction/slowdown during financial and economic crises in 1998, 2009 and 2020. The five countries have similar GDP growth patterns over the past 30 years, while fluctuation of Singapore's growth rate is significantly larger than the other ones (Figure 14.4).

The selected countries' economies have uneven reliance on trade. Among them, Singapore's reliance is the strongest, as its annual trade volume (sum of exports and imports of goods and services) is on average about 3.5 times of its GDP during the 30-year period from 1992 to 2021. Indonesia has the least reliance on trade, and its annual trade volume is on average only around 53% of its GDP. Trade openness of Vietnam has significantly strengthened since the global financial crisis, increasing from 135% of GDP in 2009 to 187% of GDP in 2021. On the other side, Malaysia's trade openness largely declined after 2000, and Thailand's trade openness held steady after 2000.

Consequently, current account balance's share of GDP of the selected countries generally exhibited the similar pattern as their trade openness, with Singapore's ratio being the highest. However, the ratio of Vietnam is relatively low and fluctuated a lot around 0 after 2000, suggesting relatively weak current account of the country (Figure 14.5).

14.4 The Impact of Green Financing on Economic Growth, Carbon Emission, and Green Innovation

The primary purpose of green financing is to amplify the utilization of renewable energy sources, attract foreign direct investment, and foster the adoption of innovative technologies that facilitate the transition towards a sustainable, eco-friendly economy. Green finance plays a pivotal role in steering this economic transformation and has the potential to emerge as a key catalyst for driving economic expansion. Consequently, this study delves into the impact of green finance on economic growth, carbon emissions reduction, and the promotion of green innovation within a carefully selected group of ASEAN countries.

The global economy, in conjunction with a diverse array of industrial sectors and institutions, is progressively uniting in support of green finance, recognizing its paramount advantage in confronting the formidable challenges posed by climate change. Notably, ASEAN nations stand aligned with this emerging trend; in fact, they display a heightened sensitivity to this paradigm, placing a robust emphasis on both the generation and effective utilization of sustainable energy resources. The significance of green financing in fostering sustainable economic growth and curbing carbon emissions has been well documented in prior scholarly studies. Noteworthy contributions to this domain are evident in the works of He et al. (2019), Chen and Chen (2021), Zhang et al. (2021), Zakari and Khan (2022), Ngo et al. (2022), and Mngumi et al. (2022). However, it is prudent to underscore the regrettable omission of the ASEAN region from the purview of these academic investigations.

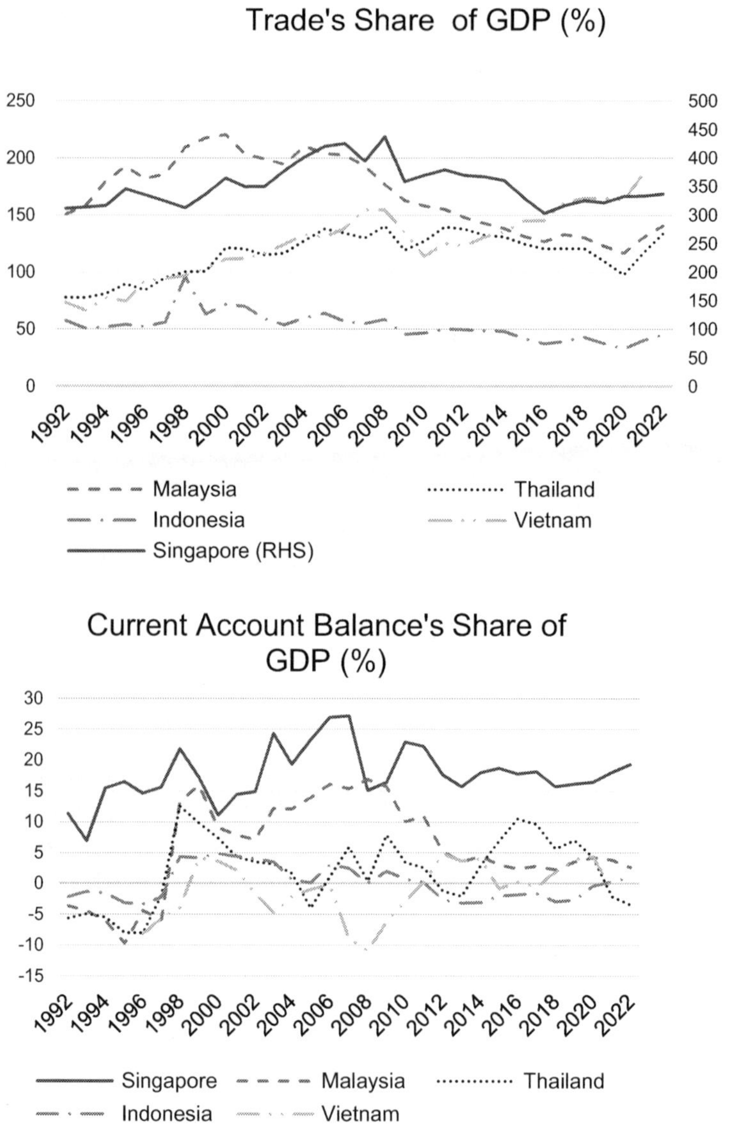

Figure 14.5 Trade openness and current account balance of the selected ASEAN countries

Source: World Bank, calculated by the authors

Furthermore, antecedent literature has predominantly centered on the exploration of green financing through proxies such as "green credit, green bonds, green insurance." While this conceptual approach has yielded valuable insights, it inadvertently sidesteps a pivotal aspect – climate development finance – distinguished by an array of financial instruments ranging from grants and debt instruments to equity shares and debt relief. These instruments have been extended to invigorate a spectrum of sectors within the ASEAN economic landscape, encompassing energy, transportation, industry, mining, construction, and environmental protection. Their overarching objective is to channel resources with precision, igniting a momentum for green initiatives that span from sustainable forest utilization and national resource management to environmental rehabilitation, industry detoxification, the cultivation of a cleaner environment, advancement in energy education, and the undertaking of meticulous policy and system analyses. Notably, these endeavors also encompass ambitious projects aimed at sea level and climate monitoring, the establishment of biomass plants, and groundbreaking forays into environmental research.

This section delves into the realm of environmental sustainability within the ASEAN nations, centering its focus on the pivotal sphere of green finance, particularly in the context of climate development financing. Given the predominant industrialization and substantial population within the ASEAN nations, the adverse ramifications of carbon emissions reverberate significantly across human activities and imperil the trajectory of sustainable economic growth. This pressing scenario underscores the imperative to chart out strategies aimed at curtailing environmental detriments stemming from various activities. The primary goal is to catalyze an acceleration of both sustainable economic progress and environmental well-being across the ASEAN member states. Moreover, the outcomes of this empirical study bear the potential to guide ASEAN industries towards a "green" trajectory, fostering technological advancements and unlocking novel avenues within the financial sector, such as the development of eco-friendly products and services. These developments, in turn, can facilitate access to emerging markets and, most crucially, serve as a buffer against environmental shocks.

This section aims to provide a robust understanding of the intricate interplay between these key factors and their impact on the specified dimensions, ultimately shedding light on the dynamics of economic growth, carbon emissions, and the advancement of green technology innovation within the context of the chosen ASEAN nations. Through these concerted efforts, the study endeavors to guide the ASEAN nations towards a harmonious synthesis of environmental preservation and economic advancement.

14.4.1 Data

The primary objective of this investigation is to evaluate the impact of green financing, foreign direct investment, urbanization, and CO_2 productivity on the economic growth, carbon emissions, and green technology innovation within a selection of ASEAN countries. To achieve this goal, we draw upon data extracted from the OECD database for green finance, CO_2 productivity, and green technology innovation, while sourcing the remaining variables from the "World Bank Development Indicators (WDI)" spanning the period from 2000 to 2020. Given the constraints imposed by data availability, our

Table 14.1 Variables with measurements

Variable	*Measurement*	*Source*
Green Finance	Climate-related development finance – commitment – current USD thousand	OECD
Economic Growth	GDP per capita	WDI
Carbon emission	CO_2 emissions (metric tons per capita)	WDI
Green Technology Innovation	Number of patents on Climate change mitigation	OECD
Foreign Direct Investment	Foreign direct investment, net inflows (% of GDP)	WDI
Urbanization	Urban population (% of the total population)	WDI
CO_2 Productivity	GDP per unit of energy-related CO_2 emissions	OECD

research focuses exclusively on Malaysia, Indonesia, Thailand, Vietnam, and the Philippines as the sample ASEAN countries. The comprehensive overview of the study variables is succinctly presented in Table 14.1.

To better present the data, we summarize the data in Table 14.2. The stationary of the data was tested to avoid a spurious regression. The commonly used panel unit root test methods including the Levin-Lin-Chu (LLC) test, the Im-Pesaran-Shin (IPS) test Phillips-Perron (PP)-Fisher test, and the augmented Dickey Fuller (ADF)-Fisher test. Given the specific characteristics of our panel data, which does not conform to a strictly balanced structure, we opted for the augmented Dickey Fuller (ADF)-Fisher test to thoroughly examine the presence of unit roots across the variables. The outcomes of these tests collectively affirm the stationarity of all variables under consideration, fortifying the foundation of our subsequent analytical steps.

14.4.2 The Impact of Green Finance on Economic Development

We propose a model that examines the influence of green finance on economic development. In this model, the focal independent variable is climate development financing, while the dependent variable is per capita GDP. Additionally, we incorporate several crucial control variables, namely foreign direct investment, urbanization, CO_2 emissions, CO_2 productivity, and innovation in green technology. The structure of the model is represented as follows in Equation (1):

$$\begin{aligned} \ln GDPper_{i,t} &= \beta_0 + \beta_1 \ln GreenFinance_{i,t} + \beta_2 FDI_{i,t} + \beta_3 urban_{i,t} \\ &+ \beta_4 CO_2em_{i,t} + \beta_5 CO_2pro_{i,t} + \beta_6 greentech_{i,t} + \gamma_i + \varepsilon_{i,t} \qquad (1) \end{aligned}$$

where $GDPper_{i,t}$ denotes the per capita GDP of country i in the tth year, $GreenFinance_{i,t}$ denotes climate development financing of country i in the tth year, $urban_{i,t}$ denotes the ratio of urbanization of country i in the tth year, $FDI_{i,t}$ denotes foreign direct investment net inflows at percentage of GDP of

Table 14.2 Descriptive statistics

Variable name	*Obs*	*Mean*	*SD*	*Min*	*Median*	*Max*	*Unit root*
Carbon Emission	101	2.92	2.219	0.64	1.94	7.93	NO
GDP growth	105	4153.25	2673.27	990.57	3250.57	11414.58	NO
FDI	105	2.70	1.85	−2.76	2.66	9.66	NO
Urbanization	105	47.82	13.72	24.37	46.05	77.16	NO
Green Finance	105	551318.36	8.60e + 05	468.67	130445.7	3897156	NO
Green Technology Innovation	99	10.40	10.09	.2	6.67	47.75	NO
CO_2 Productivity	105	4.82	1.283	2.88	4.64	7.72	NO

country i in the tth year, $CO_2em_{i,t}$ denotes total CO_2 emissions of country i in the tth year $CO_2pro_{i,t}$ denotes the GDP per unit of energy-related CO_2 emissions of country i in the tth year, and $greentech_{i,t}$ denotes green technology innovation of country i in the tth year.

The outcomes of the panel regression analysis are presented in Table 14.3, delineating both the results without fixed effects in the initial three columns, and subsequently, the outcomes incorporating the fixed effects in the latter three columns. Notably, the pivotal variable, Green Finance, consistently exhibits a positive and statistically significant coefficient across all six regressions. This compelling evidence underscores the affirmative and substantial influence of green finance development on economic development. Consequently, these findings substantiate the rationale that an escalation in the level of green finance is conducive to a concurrent rise in per capita GDP for the chosen ASEAN nations. As a corollary, it becomes imperative for the governmental authorities and economists within the ASEAN economies to formulate and implement strategies and policies aimed at attracting investments in green capital. Such initiatives are instrumental in propelling these economies towards a sustainable and environmentally amicable trajectory. Further analysis reveals a positive coefficient for CO_2 emissions, implying a direct correlation between economic growth and carbon dioxide emissions. In a similar vein, the positive coefficient for CO_2 productivity signifies that enhancements in carbon dioxide efficiency can potentially foster economic growth. However, it is notable that the influence of green technology innovation on economic growth lacks statistical significance in the current study.

14.4.3 The Impact of Green Finance on Carbon Emission

Carbon emissions stand as a paramount global apprehension, with a particularly pronounced resonance within the ASEAN region. Given the alarming depletion of natural resources and the consequential adverse climatic

Table 14.3 Results of green finance and economic development models

	(1)	(2)	(3)	(4)	(5)	(6)
Green finance	0.109*** (7.83)	0.071*** (5.67)	0.067*** (5.72)	0.120*** (9.58)	0.074*** (5.75)	0.065*** (6.49)
FDI		0.025* (1.82)	−0.042*** (−2.77)		0.024* (1.73)	0.015 (1.41)
urban		0.032*** (6.82)	−0.016*** (−3.85)		0.031*** (6.21)	−0.018** (−2.54)
CO_2emi			0.493*** (12.47)			0.428*** (7.87)
CO_2pro			0.191*** (5.19)			0.230*** (7.56)
Greentech			−0.008** (−2.28)			−0.003 (−1.20)
cons	6.884*** (31.59)	5.723*** (19.48)	5.941*** (25.48)	6.761*** (46.70)	5.749*** (28.47)	5.854*** (29.16)
Fixed Effect	No	No	No	Yes	Yes	Yes
N	105	105	99	105	105	99

Source: Authors' estimation

Note: *, **, and *** depict 1%, 5%, and 10% levels of significance

ramifications stemming from fossil fuel consumption, a meticulous analysis of pioneering determinants such as green finance, urbanization, and green technology innovation. This sub-section extends to exploring the potential of these factors in facilitating economies to realize their ambitious zero-carbon objectives. Central to this endeavor is an examination of the influence wielded by green finance, urbanization, CO_2 productivity, and green technology innovation on the intricate web of carbon emissions.

We propose a similar model as in Section 14.4.1 to examine the impact of green finance on carbon emission, in which the explanatory variable is the green finance development index, the explained variables are total carbon dioxide emission of the selected ASEAN countries, and the control variables are GDP growth, foreign direct investment, urbanization, CO_2 productivity, and green technology innovation. The structure of the model is represented as follows in Equation (2):

$$CO_2em_{i,t} = \beta_0 + \beta_1 lnGreenFinance_{i,t} + \beta_2 lnGDPper_{i,t} + \beta_3 FDI_{i,t} + \beta_4 urban_{i,t} + \beta_5 CO_2pro_{i,t} + \beta_6 greentech_{i,t} + \gamma_i + \varepsilon_{i,t} \quad (2)$$

The outcomes of the panel regressions are meticulously outlined in Table 14.4. Notably, the coefficient attributed to green finance emerges as both statistically significant and negative, offering a nuanced insight into its potential to influence carbon emissions. Intriguingly, the findings derived from the fixed effect model underscore a dual facet: the augmentation of

Table 14.4 Results of green finance and carbon emission models

	(1)	(2)	(3)	(4)	(5)	(6)
Green finance	-0.083*** (-2.59)	-0.234*** (-8.71)	-0.117*** (-6.40)	-0.054 (-1.65)	-0.085*** (-3.63)	-0.070*** (-4.18)
GDP growth	1.667*** (9.01)	1.951*** (12.97)	1.276*** (12.47)	1.476*** (7.70)	0.679*** (4.24)	0.965*** (7.87)
FDI		0.229*** (6.39)	0.101*** (4.32)		0.022 (0.94)	-0.002 (-0.12)
urban		0.051*** (6.99)	0.050*** (10.66)		0.092*** (9.70)	0.075*** (10.06)
CO_2pro			-0.519*** (-12.87)			-0.375*** (-8.74)
Greentech			0.028*** (5.22)			0.013*** (3.62)
cons	-9.658*** (-7.14)	-13.306*** (-12.55)	-6.555*** (-8.02)	-8.451*** (-6.36)	-6.054*** (-6.18)	-6.000*** (-8.03)
Fixed Effect	No	No	No	Yes	Yes	Yes
N	101	101	99	101	101	99

Source: Authors' estimation

Note: *, **, and *** depict 1%, 5%, and 10% levels of significance

green finance exerts a positive impact, while its diminution engenders a negative impetus on the reduction of carbon emissions within the focal nations. This empirical underpinning harmoniously resonates with earlier research by Zakari and Khan (2022), Chen and Chen (2021), and Gao et al. (2022), thereby reinforcing the salient role of green finance.

In light of these compelling results, this study unequivocally advocates for the imperative development of a robust green financial infrastructure within the ASEAN economies. This strategic endeavor encompasses the establishment of mechanisms for garnering and disseminating green funds as pivotal financial capital, intended to fortify the edifice of a green industry framework. This approach, in turn, promises to ameliorate the cost burden associated with procuring green investment resources, thereby catalyzing the expansion of the green sector. By extension, this concerted effort aims to curtail the prevalence of high-polluting industries and, consequently, reduce the quantum of carbon emissions. Moreover, an enhanced emphasis on green financial instruments, including green bonds, green loans, green credits, and climate mitigation tools, is essential for mitigating carbon emissions and fostering a trajectory of sustainable green economic growth. Concurrently, the converse correlation embodied by the negative coefficient of CO_2 productivity underscores its potential to abet carbon emission reduction.

Furthermore, in response to the pressing challenge of environmental degradation, ASEAN nations have embarked on robust green recovery initiatives, typified by the ASEAN Catalytic Finance Facility (ACGF). This forward-looking enterprise, boasting a substantial budget of US$4 billion, is poised to galvanize and propel green investments across pivotal sectors encompassing clean energy, transportation, sanitation, and agriculture. Innovative financial instruments such as climate credits, climate bonds, and environmental investments serve as the bedrock of this initiative, envisaging a remarkable reduction of 119 million tons of carbon emissions within pollutant sectors.

14.4.4 The Impact of Green Finance on Green Innovation

Green finance assumes the role of a catalytic force, furnishing essential funds and capital to propel the research, development, and application of cutting-edge environmentally conscious technologies. To elucidate the impact of green finance on the progression of green technology innovation, we present a model where the driving variable is the green finance development index. The variables under scrutiny encompass the green technology innovation within the chosen ASEAN nations, accompanied by pertinent control factors such as GDP growth, foreign direct investment, urbanization, CO_2 emissions, and CO_2 productivity. The structure of the model is represented as follows in Equation (3):

$$\begin{aligned} \text{greentech}_{i,t} = {} & \beta_0 + \beta_1 \text{lnGreenFinance}_{i,t} + \beta_2 \text{lnGDPper}_{i,t} + \beta_3 \text{FDI}_{i,t} \\ & + \beta_4 \text{urban}_{i,t} + \beta_5 \text{CO}_2\text{pro}_{i,t} + \beta_6 \text{CO}_2\text{em}_{i,t} + \gamma_i + \varepsilon_{i,t} \end{aligned} \tag{3}$$

The results of regressions are shown in Table 14.5. Extensive literature and empirical evidence have been brought to bear on the nuanced relationship between green finance and green technology innovation. While the notion of green finance as a potential catalyst for innovative ecological solutions holds theoretical promise, the practical impact appears to be nuanced and contingent. Notably, when accounting for fixed effects and a comprehensive array of control variables, the influence of green finance on green technology innovation does not exhibit a significant magnitude. This observation aligns with findings from studies such as those conducted by Huang et al. (2022) and Wang et al. (2022), which underscore the complex interplay of factors influencing the actualization of green technology innovation through financial mechanisms.

However, intriguing patterns emerge when considering specific contextual elements. CO_2 emissions and CO_2 productivity, for instance, emerge as compelling factors that wield a positive impact on the interplay between green finance and innovation in environmentally sound technologies. These findings mirror the trends highlighted in research by Xie and Jamaani (2022) and Ali et al. (2022), elucidating the dynamic relationship between carbon-related factors and the advancement of sustainable technology solutions.

Table 14.5 Results of green finance and green innovation models

	(1)	*(2)*	*(3)*	*(4)*	*(5)*	*(6)*
Green finance	-0.454	-0.126	0.778**	1.203***	-0.554	0.251
	(-1.06)	(-0.40)	(2.10)	(2.76)	(-1.10)	(0.48)
GDP growth		4.753***	-6.421**		4.471	-5.407
		(2.75)	(-2.28)		(1.30)	(-1.20)
FDI		1.215***	0.182		0.302	0.254
		(2.96)	(0.41)		(0.62)	(0.55)
urban		0.356***	-0.148		0.911***	0.017
		(4.25)	(-1.22)		(4.48)	(0.05)
CO_2emi			8.267***			10.215***
			(5.22)			(3.62)
CO_2pro			4.720***			3.241**
			(4.46)			(1.99)
cons	15.549***	-47.132***	13.190	-3.270	-63.941***	4.205
	(3.07)	(-3.82)	(0.72)	(-0.65)	(-3.02)	(0.15)
Fixed Effect	No	No	No	Yes	Yes	Yes
N	99	99	99	99	99	99

Source: Authors' estimation

Note: *, **, and *** depict 1%, 5%, and 10% levels of significance

14.5 Conclusion

The primary objective of this chapter was to assess the status of green finance and carbon emissions and to investigate the influence of green financing on economic development, carbon emissions, and the advancement of green technology innovation within ASEAN member countries. The escalating carbon emissions accompanying Southeast Asia's economic growth have imposed a significant burden on the region's environment and ecosystems. The mobilization of financial resources for environmentally sustainable projects in ASEAN countries is imperative not only for addressing climate change but also for meeting the rapidly growing energy demands. Despite existing barriers to attracting investments in energy efficiency and renewable energy, the realm of green development finance offers a distinct and promising avenue for mobilizing funds towards energy-efficient and eco-friendly initiatives. This strategic approach holds the potential to not only alleviate carbon emissions but also foster the overall economic development of ASEAN nations. Utilizing environmental and macroeconomic data from the ASEAN region, our analysis reveals a favorable economic trajectory within the region, albeit accompanied by a stark surge in CO_2 emissions. In pursuit of a substantive restoration of environmental viability and concurrently fostering sustainable economic growth, a strategic redirection of financial resources to reshape the incentive structure for resource allocation becomes imperative. Consequently, the prominence of green finance has emerged as a pivotal catalyst, essential for realizing the goal of sustainable development through a substantial reduction in carbon emissions.

This study employs panel regression models to examine the impact of green finance on economic development, carbon emission levels, and green technology innovation across ASEAN economies during the period from 2000 to 2020. The ensuing findings shed light on several key aspects. Notably, green finance demonstrates a positive influence on both economic development and the reduction of carbon emissions within ASEAN nations. However, the relationship between green finance and green technology innovation remains inconclusive. Furthermore, our analysis reveals that sustained economic growth and urbanization contribute to an enhancement of environmental quality over the long term. Leveraging these insights, the study formulates a set of informed suggestions and recommendations tailored to the specific ASEAN economies under investigation.

The primary policy implication underscored by this study is the imperative adoption of robust economic policies within the context of the green economy. As gleaned from the foregoing analysis, it becomes evident that green finance exerts a demonstrably positive impact in curbing CO_2 emissions. Hence, the establishment of a steadfast and enduring green finance strategy emerges as a critical necessity. By harnessing the potential of extensive green funding, the advancement of energy conservation initiatives can be duly ensured. In tandem with this, the formulation of a comprehensive industry-wide framework for the green finance policy of ASEAN countries becomes an indispensable requisite.

Moreover, the manifold virtues of green financing extend beyond emission reduction, encompassing the augmentation of economic growth, attraction of foreign direct investment, and facilitation of innovative technologies conducive to the transition toward a greener economy. This holistic approach contributes to the overarching goal of enhancing environmental quality through the abatement of carbon emissions. This ethos resonates both globally and within numerous industrial sectors and institutions, as the salience of green finance in countering climate change remains paramount. Notably, ASEAN nations align themselves with this worldwide trajectory, underscoring their proactive commitment to the concept. This commitment is further evidenced by the meticulous creation and judicious utilization of energy resources as a core facet of their green finance endeavors.

Notes

1 Singapore, Malaysia, Thailand, Indonesia, Philippines, Vietnam. ASEAN in this subsection refers to the aggregate of these six countries.
2 Databases include Green Bond Database (CBDB), Social and Sustainability Bond Database, SLB and Transition Bond Database, Unlabelled Climate-Aligned Database.
3 The data used in this subsection is from World Bank Open Data.
4 World Bank uses 2015 constant prices in the calculation.

References

ACMF. (2018). *ASEAN Green Bond Standards*. ASEAN Capital Markets Forum.

AFMGM. (2022, April 8). *Joint statement of the 8th ASEAN finance ministers' and Central Bank Governors'* [Paper presentation]. Meeting (AFMGM), 8th ASEAN Finance Ministers' and Central Bank Governors' meeting.

Afzal, A., Rasoulinezhad, E., & Malik, Z. (2022). Green finance and sustainable development in Europe. *Economic Research-Ekonomska Istraživanja*, *35*(1), 5150–5163.

Ali, N., Phoungthong, K., Techato, K., Ali, W., Abbas, S., Dhanraj, J. A., & Khan, A. (2022). FDI, Green innovation and environmental quality nexus: New insights from BRICS economies. *Sustainability*, *14*(4), 2181.

Anwar, R. S., Mohamed, M., Hamzan, S. M., Malek, N. S. A., Zain, M. H. M., Jaafar, M. H., Sani, S., Brazil-De Vera, R. M., Desquitado, M. C. T., Praneeprachachon, V., & Wong, D. (2020). *Report on the roles of ASEAN central banks in managing climate and environment-related risks*. ASEAN Central Banks and Monetary Authorities.

Ariyapruchya, S., & Volz, U. (2022). *Sustainable finance in Southeast Asia, chapter 19, scaling up sustainable finance and investment in the global south*. CEPR Press.

ASEAN Taxonomy Board. (2021). *ASEAN taxonomy for sustainable finance* (version 1). ASEAN Taxonomy Board.

ASEAN Taxonomy Board. (2023, June). *ASEAN taxonomy for sustainable Finance* (version 2). ASEAN Taxonomy Board.

Berensmann, K., & Lindenberg, N. (2019). Green finance: Across the universe. In Sabri Boubaker and Duc Khuong Nguyen (Eds.), *Corporate social responsibility, ethics and sustainable prosperity* (pp. 305–332). World Scientific.

BNM. (2021, April). *Climate change and principle-based taxonomy*. Bank Negara Malaysia.

BOT and SEC. (2023, June 30). *Joint press release publication of Thailand taxonomy phase I*. Bank of Thailand, Securities and Exchange Commission.

BritCham and ICAEW. (2021, November). *Green finance ASEAN & UK perspectives*. British Chamber of Commerce Singapore.

CBI. (2018). *ASEAN green finance: State of the market 2018*. Climate Bond Initiative. January 2019.

CBI. (2020). *ASEAN sustainable finance: State of the market 2020*. Climate Bond Initiative. April 2021.

CBI. (2021). *ASEAN sustainable finance: State of the market 2021*. Climate Bond Initiative. June 2022.

CBI. (2022). *ASEAN sustainable finance: State of the market 2022*. Climate Bond Initiative. May 2023.

Chen, X., & Chen, Z. (2021). Can green finance development reduce carbon emissions? Empirical evidence from 30 Chinese provinces. *Sustainability*, *13*, 12137.

Gao, B., Ozturk, I., & Ullah, S. (2022). A new framework to the green economy: Asymmetric role of public-private partnership investment on environment in selected Asian economies. *Economic Research-Ekonomska Istraživanja*, 1–12. https://doi.org/10.1080/1331677X.2022.2094441

He, L., Zhang, L., Zhong, Z., Wang, D., & Wang, F. (2019). Green credit, renewable energy investment and green economy development: Empirical analysis based on 150 listed companies of China. *Journal of Cleaner Production*, *208*, 363–372.

Huang, Y., Chen, C., Lei, L., & Zhang, Y. (2022). Impacts of green finance on green innovation: A spatial and nonlinear perspective. *Journal of Cleaner Production*, *365*, 132548.

Jahanger, A., Lorente, D. B., Hulio, M. A., & Samour, A. (2023, April). Going away or going green in ASEAN countries: Testing the impact of green financing and energy on environmental sustainability. *Energy & Environment*. https://doi.org/10.1177/0958305X231171346.

JC3. (2022, June). *Task force on climate-related financial disclosures (TCFD) application guide for Malaysian financial institutions*. Joint Committee on Climate Change.

Kamran, H. W., Haseeb, M., Nguyen, V. C., & Nguyen, T. T. (2020). Climate change and bank stability: The moderating role of green finance and reviewable energy consumption in ASEAN. *Talent Development & Excellence*, 12(2).

Li, W. Q., Fan, J. J., & Zhao, J. W. (2021). *Has green finance facilitated China's low-carbon economic transition?* Preprint posted on Research Square. https://doi.org/10.21203/rs.3.rs-1102808/v1

Lin, Z. Q., Liao, X. C., & Jia, H. R. (2023). Could green finance facilitate low-carbon transformation of power generation? Some evidence from China. *International Journal of Climate Change Strategies and Management*, *15*(2), 141–158.

Mngumi, F., Shaorong, S., Shair, F., & Waqas, M. (2022). Does green finance mitigate the effects of climate variability: Role of renewable energy investment and infrastructure. *Environmental Science and Pollution Research*, *29*, 59287–59299.

Ngo, Q. T., Tran, H. A., & Tran, H. T. T. (2022). The impact of green finance and COVID-19 on economic development: Capital formation and educational expenditure of ASEAN economies. *China Finance Review International*, *12*, 261–279.

OJK. (2017). *Application of sustainable finance to financial services institution, issuer and publicly listed companies: Regulation of financial services authority No. 51/POJK.03/2017*. Sustainable Banking and Finance Network.

Ozili, P. K. (2021). Digital finance, green finance and social finance: Is there a link? *Financial Internet Quarterly*, *17*(1), 1–7.

Ozili, P. K. (2022). Green finance research around the world: A review of literature. *International Journal of Green Economics*, *16*(1), 56–75.

Prakash, A. (2018). Boiling point. *Finance & Development*, *55*(3).

Quang, P. T., & Thao, D. P. (2022). Analyzing the green financing and energy efficiency relationship in ASEAN. *The Journal of Risk Finance*, *23*(4).

Sadiq, M., Le-Dinh, T., Tran, T. K., Chein, F. S., Phan, T. T. H., & Huy, P. Q. (2023). The role of green finance, eco-innovation, and creativity in the sustainable development goals of ASEAN countries. *Economic Research Ekonomska Istraživanja*, *36*(2), 2175010.

Volz, U. (2021, June). *Governing sustainable finance*. Asian Bond Monitor.

Wang, Q.-J., Wang, H.-J., & Chang, C.-P. (2022). Environmental performance, green finance and green innovation: What's the long-run relationships among variables? *Energy Economics*, 110, 106004.

World Bank and Institute of Finance and Sustainability. (2022, November). *Unleashing sustainable finance in Southeast Asia*. World Bank.

Xie, P., & Jamaani, F. (2022). Does green innovation, energy productivity and environmental taxes limit carbon emissions in developed economies: Implications for sustainable development. *Structural Change and Economic Dynamics*, *63*, 66–78.

Zakari, A., & Khan, I. (2022). The introduction of green finance: A curse or a benefit to environmental sustainability? *Energy Research Letters*, 3. https://elibrary.ru/item.asp?id =44182305.20

Zhang, D., Mohsin, M., Rasheed, A. K., Chang, Y., & Taghizadeh-Hesary, F. (2021). Public spending and green economic growth in BRI region: Mediating role of green finance. *Energy Policy*, *153*, 112256.

Zhou, X. G., Tang, X. M., & ZHANG, R. (2020). Impact of green finance on economic development and environmental quality: A study based on provincial panel data from China. *Environmental Science and Pollution Research*, *27*, 19915–19932.

Index

Note: Page numbers in *italics* indicate figures, and page numbers in **bold** indicate tables in the text

Made in the USA
Monee, IL
12 November 2026

86db3c08-116b-47ec-a301-9ebf34e4a5ddR01